THE BOLD EXPERIMENT

The Bold Experiment

JFK'S PEACE CORPS

Gerard T. Rice

University of Notre Dame Press
Notre Dame, Indiana 46556

Photos courtesy of Peace Corps except "JFK
at Cow Palace" (Wide World Photos) and
"JFK at University of Michigan" (The University of Michigan Information Services).

Library of Congress
Cataloging in Publication Data

Rice, Gerard T.
    The bold experiment.

    Bibliography: p.
    Includes index.
    1. Peace Corps (U.S.)—History. I. Title.
HC60.5.R49 1985   361.2'6'06073   85-40605
ISBN 0-268-00675-X

To Anne and John Rice,
My Mother and Father

Contents

Preface

Well, they may ask you what you have done in the
sixties for your country, and you will be able to say,
"I served in the Peace Corps."
          —John F. Kennedy, June 14, 1962

In 1961 John F. Kennedy took two risky and conflicting initiatives in the Third World. One was to send five hundred additional military advisers into South Vietnam; by 1963 there
would be seventeen thousand such advisers.[1] The other was to
send five hundred young Americans to teach in the schools and
work in the fields of eight developing countries. These were
Peace Corps Volunteers. By 1963 there would be seven thousand of them in forty-four countries.

Looking back almost twenty-five years later, the United
States dwelled on Vietnam, reflecting on the fifty-eight thousand
Americans who had died there and on the many other wounds
that the war had opened.[2] Few people noted that over the same
twenty-five year period, more than 100,000 Americans had served
overseas with the Peace Corps; at least ten thousand more were
scheduled to serve in 1985–86.[3]

Vietnam scarred the American psyche, leaving memories
of pain and defeat. But Kennedy's other initiative inspired, and
continues to inspire, hope and understanding among Americans
and the rest of the world. In that sense, the Peace Corps was
his most affirmative and enduring legacy.

This book focuses on the first few years of what, in 1961,
was viewed as a bold experiment. The story should be seen,
however, in the context of an institution that has since become

an integral part of American society and culture. The Peace Corps has also become one of the few federal agencies that receives almost unqualified bipartisan support on Capitol Hill.

In the first half of the 1960s, under the direction of Sargent Shriver, the Peace Corps grew by leaps and bounds. Nineteen sixty-six was the high point in terms of numbers, with over fifteen thousand Volunteers working overseas. By the 1980s this had leveled off to about five thousand per year. An opinion poll taken by the Overseas Development Council in the 1970s showed that 88 percent of those surveyed viewed the Peace Corps as the single "most effective" American organization helping people in the Third World.[4]

The agency has not been without its problems. In the later 1960s, the Vietnam experience led many young Americans to question all aspects of their government's role overseas, including Peace Corps service. Also, the CIA revelations of the 1970s tended to foster a skepticism in the developing countries toward the much-vaunted "idealism" of the United States. Some Third World nations refused the offer of Peace Corps participation in their development; others, convinced that American assistance was rooted in self-interest, asked the Peace Corps to leave their shores.[5]

The policies of the Nixon administration also had their impact. In 1971 Nixon placed the Peace Corps in a large, new bureaucratic unit called ACTION (an agency combining the government's domestic and overseas voluntary organizations). Many remembered his original distaste for Kennedy's idea in 1961 and claimed he was trying to stifle the Peace Corps by taking away its hard-won independence. Certainly the Peace Corps lacked real leadership in the 1970s, as seven different directors of the agency came and went in almost as many years.[6] In 1981, under Loret Miller Ruppe, the Peace Corps once again found a steady hand at the helm; the Peace Corps also regained its independent status out of ACTION.

The one constant throughout the Peace Corps' history has been the work of the Volunteers. Once overseas, they are virtually immune to political vagaries and leadership changes in Washington. In a steady stream, they have traveled to Africa, Asia, and Latin America to build their bridges of economic development and friendship. They have then returned to their home communities to tell of their experiences. Through them, countless links have been forged between the United States and the Third World.

This is the tale of how the Peace Corps idea was adopted by John Kennedy, and of how the institution was established by Sargent Shriver, Harris Wofford, Warren Wiggins, William Josephson, Bill Moyers, and many other dedicated men and women.[7] Together, they had the vision and the political courage to set in motion what Associate Justice William O. Douglas described as "the best thing we Americans have done overseas since the beginning."[8]

This is also the story of the first Volunteers, "Kennedy's Kids," as they were called. The years 1961–63, however, were only the beginning of the Peace Corps' odyssey. It continues today.

Acknowledgments

This book was begun in Scotland, where I wrote my doctoral dissertation on the Peace Corps. At the University of Glasgow, my tutor, Professor William R. Brock, provided me not only with guidance in scholarly ways, but also with friendship. At a critical juncture, the British Kennedy Memorial Trust, chaired by the late Lord Harlech, awarded me a scholarship to Harvard University and thus allowed me much-needed time to study in America. At Harvard, it was my pleasure to work under Professor Frank Freidel.

I spent a year working at the John F. Kennedy Memorial Library in Boston, which holds the official record of the Peace Corps as a government agency, 1961–63. This consists of internal memoranda, the Peace Corps' weekly reports to the President, and minutes of the Director's staff meetings. The personal and organizational papers of two former Peace Corps staff members, William Josephson and Gerald Bush, are also lodged at the Library; I found both of inestimable value. In addition, the Library holds transcripts of numerous oral history interviews of which I made extensive use. The entire staff at the JFK Library, but particularly William Johnson and Debbie Greene, unstintingly encouraged my research.

I also spent months in the Peace Corps Library and archives in Washington, D.C. where I was given access to previously classified documents relating to the agency's origins, policies and performance. I relied especially on the evaluation reports of Peace Corps country programs. Written by the agency's own "evaluators," these are detailed, candid reports on every aspect of the Peace Corps as it functioned overseas. I am indebted to the Peace Corps for declassifying about sixty of these reports on my behalf.

Joseph Manno, Genoa Million, Rita Warpeha, and Vicki Fries overcame all obstacles to get me the materials I needed. Thanks also to Anne Alvarez who helped me acquire the photographs which appear in this book.

I owe an enormous debt to the many Peace Corps staff and Volunteers whom I have interviewed over the years. These interviews allowed me a fresh and vital perspective on JFK's Peace Corps. Among those who offered special insight were: Sargent Shriver, Harris Wofford, William Josephson, Warren Wiggins, Charles Peters, William Kelly, Douglas Kiker, Frank Mankiewicz, Don Romine, David Gelman, Thomas Quimby, Nancy and Richard Graham, William Warner, Robert Gale, Rogers Finch, William Hutchison, Paul Tsongas, Roger Landrum, Loret Miller Ruppe, Ruth Saxe, Harriet Lancaster, and Richard Celeste. I also had the privilege of discussing the Peace Corps with Dean Rusk, McGeorge Bundy, Averell Harriman, John Kenneth Galbraith, Arthur M. Schlesinger, Jr., Theodore Sorensen, David Powers, Ralph Dungan, Lawrence O'Brien, Frederick Dutton, J. William Fulbright, Archibald Cox, and James Reston.

In writing the book, Richard Mahoney, Jack Hamilton, George Dorsey, and Bruce Ross-Larson coaxed me to the finishing line. The Notre Dame team of James Langford, Ann Rice, Beth Preuss, and Joseph Wilder, my editor, made sure that I crossed it.

My friend and fellow Scot, Thomas A. Casey provided me with an abundant supply of good counsel and good humor; in addition, he gave me shelter in a time of need. I also want to acknowledge the special roles played by Douglas Gustafson, Joseph Russo, and by Chris Casey whose friendship sustained me. Among others who have provided intellectual and spiritual companionship are: Brian and Geraldine Robertson, David McMillan, John McGinley, Olga Caceres, Donna Giuseppe, Jane and Kevin Hughes, Simon Goldhill, Anthony Marrinan, Gerard Hall, Dorothy Clarke, Marie Kerwan, Margaret Connor, and the teacher who started me down this road, Catherine Convery.

My family in Scotland—especially Elizabeth and John McCormick, Anne Marie Rice, and Nan and Pat Hughes—were with me in spirit throughout my adventure in America. My mother,

Anne Rice, was and remains a unique source of inspiration; my father, John Rice, is a source of strength.

Without my dear Eilish Maura, this bold experiment would never have been begun. She typed, read, and edited every word of every draft. I owe this book to her. At least a footnote, however, belongs to Johnathan Anthony who came along just in time to provide a magical finishing touch.

Gerard Rice
July 1985

1

Peace Corps Precedents

"I recall feeling myself a very instrumental part of what
I thought would be the beginnings of an historical
precedent on a significant scale. The Peace Corps de-
noted an idea and a movement . . . the organization
was incidental . . . the idea is the crux. It emerged long
before the Peace Corps . . . The American Peace Corps
was only the form that carried forth this idea at this
stage of history."

— A Peace Corps Volunteer

MISSIONARIES OF AMERICANISM

From the discovery of the New World, Franciscan friars
demonstrated the effectiveness of the grassroots, people-to-
people approach which came to distinguish the Peace Corps. By
working with native Americans, teaching them useful skills, and
imparting improved medical techniques, the missionary fathers
fulfilled their religious beliefs while making friends and meeting
human needs. Sixteenth-century American Indians praised and
admired the friars who went about "poorly dressed and bare-
footed like us; they eat what we eat, they settle down among
us, and their intercourse with us is gentle."[1]

New England missionaries continued in the same vein. In
1648, John Eliot proposed that the poverty-stricken Indians of
Massachusetts should be taught "letters, Trades and Labors, as
building, fishing, Flax and Hemp dressing, planting orchards
etc." in order to settle and pacify them.[2] Beginning in 1809, Christian evangelists from the United States traveled overseas not only

1

to preach the Gospel, but to build schools, teach trades, and educate doctors and nurses. John Franklin Goucher, for example, a Methodist minister from Pennsylvania, supported 120 vernacular primary schools in India and founded technical colleges in China and Japan. By the turn of the century, he had raised a quarter of a million dollars for these projects.[3]

Religious organizations have continued this tradition in modern times: Catholic Relief Services, the World Council of Churches, the American Jewish Joint Distribution Committee, the National Lutheran Council, the Church World Service, and many others. As President Kennedy set up the Peace Corps in 1961, there were over thirty-three thousand American missionaries abroad under the auspices of some four hundred religious bodies. One of the Peace Corps' first overseas administrators suggested that Volunteers only carried out "in greater numbers and without religious connotations much of the same work which church and church-inspired groups have done for many years." Indeed, long before he proposed the Peace Corps, Kennedy had expressed his admiration for the Mormon Church's requirement of full-time voluntary service (often overseas) by its young members.[4]

Peace Corps Volunteers could not escape the connection with their religious forebears. Some congressmen deemed the Peace Corps a preemption of the church's role overseas and objected to this federalization of the missionary movement. Others only wished Volunteers would display a little of the fervor so characteristic of religious groups. "The missionary is dedicated to the spreading of the philosophy of religion," said Frank Moss, Democratic senator from Utah. "The Peace Corps man must be dedicated, among other things, to spreading a philosophy of government." Senator Stephen Young of Ohio demanded that Volunteers should show "the zeal of hardy missionaries . . . by example, they will win friends for America and our way of life."[5]

The First Amendment, with its requirement for the complete separation of church and state, meant that Volunteers were forbidden to preach or proselytize in any manner whatsoever. Nevertheless, Congress and the public wished upon them the missionary zeal of their holy ancestors, even if it were to be spent propounding "Americanism" rather than a religious faith.

PRIVATE EFFORTS

The philanthropic impulse in the American past was by no means confined to the religious milieu. In 1961 the *New York Times* observed that the Peace Corps spirit could be traced back to the days when "the great procession of covered wagons rolled across our continent."[6] Once a frontiersman had built his own barn, he moved into the next field and helped a neighbor. On meeting the very first group of Volunteers—road surveyors bound for Tanzania—Kennedy was reminded of the frontier ethos. "I'm particularly glad that you are going there to help open up the back land," he told them.[7] Sargent Shriver agreed that the Peace Corps was "a milestone on the way to a new era of American pioneering."[8]

Certainly, the notion of the "doer" rather than the "adviser" appealed to Yankee traditions of industriousness and self-reliance. The biblical maxim "from those to whom much is given, much is required" was also deeply imbedded in the Protestant heritage and private philanthrophy for public purposes has always been encouraged as part of the American tradition. In the nineteenth century, for example, Dr. Samuel Gridley Howe of Massachusetts went overseas to impart knowledge of up-to-date medical methods and Western agricultural improvements to peoples of the Near East.[9] On the domestic front, Andrew Carnegie, Jane Addams, Frances Perkins, Herbert Lehman, and Henry Morgenthau, Jr., were obvious personifications of American altruism. This tradition of *noblesse oblige* was not lost on John Kennedy when he assumed leadership of the richest and most powerful country in the world. He often reminded his contemporaries that "Western Europe and the United States really are islands of prosperity in a sea of poverty. South of us live hundreds of millions of people on the edge of starvation, and I think it is essential that we demonstrate . . . our concern for their welfare."[10]

In the twentieth century, private voluntary assistance organizations proliferated, and they were to prove highly significant for the Peace Corps. They not only contributed useful advice and experience but also individuals who were to play important roles in the development of the new agency. Harris Wofford, one of the major architects of the Peace Corps, helped set up the International Development Placement Association, which, in the early 1950s, sent a small number of college graduates to teach or do community development work in the Third World. Albert Sims, first chief of the Peace Corps' Division of University Relations, spent eight years at the International Institute of Education in charge of its overseas exchange programs. Senator Jacob Javits of New York, one of the leading Republicans to endorse the Peace Corps in 1961, had been involved in a private effort to send young Americans to help the poor peoples of Latin America just after World War II. Democrat John Brademas also had embarked on a "Peace Corps-type" venture among the Aztecs during his college days. One of the cosponsors of the Peace Corps bill in the Senate, Claiborne Pell of Rhode Island, had served as a vice-president of the International Rescue Committee; this private body had backed MEDICO, the overseas medical aid mission which numbered among its members Dr. Tom Dooley. Harlan Cleveland, an assistant secretary of state for International Organizations in the Kennedy administration, who lent his experience to the Peace Corps during its formative period, had also been a member of one of the best-known American private voluntary organizations operating overseas: the Experiment in International Living.

Launched in 1932 by Dr. Donald B. Watt, the Experiment encouraged cross-cultural exchange through the placement of young Americans with families overseas. Some of the "Experimenters" proved to be major influences on the evolution of the Peace Corps. Henry S. Reuss, the Democratic congressman from Wisconsin who introduced the first Peace Corps legislation in 1960, was married to a former Experimenter. Gordon Boyce, an early Peace Corps administrator, was a former president of the Experiment in International Living. Another Experimenter who had led groups to Europe in the late 1930s contributed more to the development of the Peace Corps than any single individual: Sargent Shriver, the first Director and principal driving force behind the new organization.[11]

Numerous other private bodies had given a lead in the kind of task the Peace Corps was to undertake. In 1960 the Quaker-sponsored American Friends Service Committee expressed its

aim of world peace and understanding by extending its previously American-based camps to India and Africa. Through
these voluntary assignments, young Americans shared in community services with the local peoples of the Third World. The
International Farm Youth Exchange also sent young people to
developing countries to help improve agricultural techniques.
Operation Crossroads Africa, established in 1957 by Harlem
minister James H. Robinson, was one of the most effective pro-
moters of understanding between Americans and Africans. The
Operation's volunteers paid half their own costs for a summer's
work-and-study tour of an African country; the other half came
from donations. Addressing a group of Crossroaders in 1962,
Kennedy said that "This group and this effort really were the
progenitors of the Peace Corps."[12]

The American Red Cross, the Cooperative for American
Relief Everywhere (CARE), the National 4-H Club Foundation,
Project Hope, Volunteers for International Development, and
the African-American Institute were among numerous other
voluntary and nonprofit private agencies engaged in assistance
programs in the Third World. Many universities and colleges
also had their own voluntary aid schemes. These ranged from
brief periods of service during vacations to junior years abroad
and years of work overseas at the graduate level. Harvard, Yale,
Columbia, the Massachusetts Institute of Technology (MIT), and
the University of California were among the most prominent
educational institutions involved in these endeavors. At the same
time, the well-endowed private institutions like the Ford Foun
dation, the Carnegie Corporation, and the Rockefeller Foundation, established large Third World development programs; their
trained administrators and field workers, however, were well
paid.

In the postwar era, it was the volunteer working in the
villages and jungles of the Third World who became something
of a folk hero. The achievements of Tom Dooley, who brought
advanced medical techniques to the peoples of Southeast Asia,
were particularly well publicized. In Kennedy's first official announcement of the Peace Corps, he remarked on how struck he
had been by Dooley's "selfless example."[13]

Dooley, however, was not the most accurate precursor of

the Peace Corps. A private group called International Voluntary Services (IVS) was a closer prototype. Founded by Christian leaders from various countries in 1953, IVS contracted with both governments and private agencies. Like the Peace Corps, it was nondenominational; also like the Peace Corps, it worked at grassroots levels. Its volunteers were college graduates on two-year contracts who were paid only subsistence wages and were trained in a specific skill. Between 1953 and 1961, IVS sent nearly two hundred young Americans overseas to work in Third World communities. Peace Corps Volunteers were identical in almost every respect, the major difference being that they were organized and supported directly by the federal government.[14]

An early argument in favor of the Peace Corps was that several developed countries had enjoyed considerable success with their voluntary assistance programs. Some were partially financed by their governments. In this category were Australia's Volunteer Graduate Association, West Germany's Council for Development Aid, and Holland's Bureau for International Technical Assistance. Of particular note was Britain's Voluntary Service Overseas (VSO). Financed by a small grant from Parliament as well as by private contributions, it began sending young British men and women, between the ages of eighteen and twenty-four, overseas in 1958. They were given a brief training and were required to serve for two years. Although a very limited operation (there were only eighty-five workers overseas in 1960), VSO's principles and conditions of service, and its success, made it one of the Peace Corps' more timely precedents.[15]

The steady public participation in private voluntary assistance efforts in America was another important factor in persuading the U.S. government to institute the Peace Corps. Between 1940 and 1960 Americans gave over $3 billion to private assistance organizations.[16] The generally excellent record of these bodies in utilizing these resources helped advocates of the Peace Corps to put even more pressure on Washington to make the idea official policy and to back that policy with Treasury funds. Sargent Shriver even went as far as to say that "it was the success of these private efforts which led to the development of the Peace Corps."[17]

THE GOVERNMENT STEPS IN

Until 1961, the federal government had not, by and large, considered voluntary assistance programs to be its responsibility. For example, after the Spanish War of 1898, President William McKinley called upon Americans to volunteer to help "uplift, civilize and Christianize" the people of the Philippines; but the hundreds of "Thomasites" (named after the ship in which they sailed, the U.S.S. Thomas) who went to live and work in the *barrios*, received no government financing. Indeed, the first significant suggestion for a government-sponsored "peace army" limited its scope to working within the continental United States.

In 1904, during an address to the Universal Peace Conference in Boston, the philosopher William James proposed that the government should conscript young men to work among those living in poverty in America. James argued that this would not only ameliorate the conditions of the poor, but would provide an outlet for the baser, aggressive instincts which, he believed, were an intrinsic part of man's nature. He extended his argument in 1911 in an essay entitled "The Moral Equivalent of War." "The war against war," he wrote, "is going to be no holiday excursion or camping party." For the greater good of society, James argued that "Our gilded youths" should be packed off "to coal and iron mines, to freight trains, to fishing fleets in December, to dishwashing, clothes-washing, and window-washing, to road-building and tunnel-making, to foundries and stoke-holes, and to the frames of skyscrapers . . . according to their choice, to get the childishness knocked out of them, and to come back into society with healthier sympathies and soberer ideas."[18] Not surprisingly, James's plan was completely ignored by Washington. Conscription was repugnant to the American public and this rendered the plan politically unfeasible.

During the Depression, Franklin D. Roosevelt's work programs for young Americans bore a certain resemblance to the Peace Corps. While the Civilian Conservation Corps (CCC) had a somewhat militaristic style, with its members wearing uniforms and living in large camps, its underlying philosophy of young Americans in service to the nation was inherent in the Peace Corps. The CCC was limited to projects in American public parks and was aimed primarily at the unemployed; but as Arthur Schlesinger, Jr., later pointed out, in its origins at least, the Peace Corps was "undoubtedly suggested by Roosevelt's CCC."[19]

FDR's National Youth Administration (NYA), although again limited to the domestic scene, came even closer to the ideals of the Peace Corps. Over two million students and nearly three million jobless youths took on a wide range of activities: building schools and hospitals, teaching illiterate adults, exterminating vermin, and digging roads. In January 1961 an *Editorial Research Report* investigating the Peace Corps proposal noted that NYA youths served at a time when "economic conditions in some parts of the United States differed little from those in underdeveloped countries today."[20] An interesting footnote to the NYA was that one of its young administrators in Texas went on to play a vital role in the establishment of the Peace Corps: he was Lyndon B. Johnson.

After the Second World War, the United States—now clearly the world's leading economic power—found itself obliged to focus on the question of international assistance. The U.S. government played a key role in the founding of the United Nations family of agencies which included a major development institution, the World Bank. In addition, America initiated a series of its own bilateral aid programs. At first, the focus of virtually all of these efforts was the rehabilitation of postwar Europe. It soon became apparent to U.S. policymakers, however, that the Third World was also an area of concern.

In the new and dangerous nuclear age, America had become locked in a global struggle with the Soviet Union and foreign policy strategists feared that the developing countries, in their dire need, would fall prey to communism. In this atmosphere the idea of capital and technical assistance took on strategic connotations. As well as an expression of traditional American idealism, it also became an instrument of an avidly anti-Communist foreign policy. John Kennedy was not alone, at this time, in his interpretation of economic aid as "a method by which the United States maintains a position of influence and control around the world and sustains a good many countries which would definitely collapse, or pass into the Communist bloc."[21]

Idealism and self-interest were entwined in most postwar

American foreign policy initiatives. The billions of dollars doled out to Europe and the Third World under the Marshall Plan and the Point Four program evinced a generosity hitherto unknown in history, but the predominant rationale was the "containment" of communism. Point Four, President Truman's aid program for the developing countries, began as a bold attempt at "shirt-sleeve diplomacy" and its great appeal lay in its grassroots approach. In many cases, however, the intended benefits did not trickle down to the lower echelons of society. As the anti-Communist struggle intensified in the 1950s, American economic assistance concentrated more on governments than people.[22]

Critics attacked the International Cooperation Administration (ICA was Eisenhower's foreign aid agency) and its policy of massive capital investment accompanied by a few expert advisers. As the decade wore on, opinion grew in favor of a government-backed assistance program which would focus on the micro rather than the macro level. Congressman Reuss was in the vanguard of a number of groups and individuals who declared the bankruptcy of American aid policies. "Our grandiose Eisenhower-age economic type aid projects weren't really working," he recalled. "For example, in Cambodia I was struck that our principal and very expensive, some $30 million aid project was something designed to curry favour with Prince Sihanouk—an enormous superhighway from Phnom Penh." Reuss pointed out that this had no impact at all on the average Cambodian, who would never use the highway. He added that great military projects like this were the mark of decadence: "This is what the Roman Empire built in its last days . . . the Roman Empire built these vast highways . . . and then, to their embarrassment, the barbarians came down those highways and sacked Rome."[23]

In 1950 a group of World Federalists advanced the idea of a voluntary "peace force" to work in the developing countries. In the same year, the Public Affairs Institute published a pamphlet proposing American "work centers" in the Third World. The United Automobile Workers (UAW), led by Walter Reuther, put forward a blueprint for young American engineers, teachers, doctors, nurses, and agricultural specialists to use their energies and talents "to assist and train the people of underdeveloped countries."[24]

After visiting several Asian countries in the 1950s, Sargent Shriver also submitted an adventurous people-to-people scheme to President Eisenhower—a plan for sending three-man political action teams to Asia, Africa, and Latin America. "These teams were to consist of vigorous and imaginative young labor leaders, businessmen and politicians," Shriver later explained. "They would offer their services at a grassroots level and work directly with the people, contributing to the growth of the economies, to the democratic organization of the societies and the peaceful outcome of the social revolutions underway."[25] The Eisenhower administration disregarded Shriver's suggestion.

FOUNDING FATHERS

Significant political interest in the idea of an overseas people-to-people program was only aroused when two members of the U.S. Congress, Henry Reuss and Hubert H. Humphrey, proposed the idea in the late 1950s. Reuss's advocacy went back to 1957 when, as a member of the Joint Economic Committee, he had traveled to Southeast Asia to evaluate how American tax dollars were being spent. As already noted, he had not been impressed by the capital-intensive projects then in operation. On his travels, however, he had chanced upon a UNESCO team consisting of a few young teachers from America and other countries. Reuss was struck by the effect this group was having as it made its way through the jungle setting up small schools in local villages. For the next three years, he spoke about the possibility of establishing a "Point Four Youth Corps" at student conferences and wrote articles in several magazines. Finally, in January 1960, he introduced the first Peace Corps-type legislation. H.R. 9638 sought a study of "the advisability and practicability of the establishment of a Point Four Youth Corps."[26]

Hubert Humphrey, the senator from Minnesota, was one of the most respected figures in the Democratic party and a member of the influential Senate Foreign Relations Committee. In the late 1950s he too had suggested the enlistment of talented young men and women in an overseas operation for education, health care, vocational training, and community development. "I envisioned a program of national service in an international endeavor," he later wrote. "This was not to be a substitute for Selective Service, for the military. It was to be another dimension of American aid to the less fortunate—not in the form of massive economic aid but, rather, personal aid in the form of training and education."[27]

While it was warmly received on college campuses, Humphrey's scheme did not inspire much enthusiasm in the State Department or the Senate. "Some traditional diplomats quaked at the thought of thousands of young Americans scattered across the world," he noted, "and many senators, including liberal ones, thought it a silly and unworkable idea."[28] Nevertheless, he had his staff investigate the prospect of an overseas youth program. After months of research, they concluded there was a ground swell of popular support for the idea and he strongly advocated it during his unsuccessful campaign for the Democratic presidential nomination in the spring of 1960. In June of that year Humphrey introduced in the Senate S. 3675, a bill to send "young men to assist the peoples of the underdeveloped areas of the world to combat poverty, disease, illiteracy and hunger." His bill was the first to use the specific name "Peace Corps."[29]

Humphrey, a shrewd parliamentarian, realized that it was too late in the session for his proposal to have any hope of passing into legislation, but that had not been his main objective. "I wanted the bill to be printed and appropriately referred," he said, "so that it could be the subject of discussion and intensive study in the coming months."[30] In this respect he was successful, for his bill focused the congressional and the public eye on the Peace Corps idea at a critical moment—just before the presidential election of 1960.

Reuss's bill actually had more legislative success than Humphrey's. In August 1960 the House Foreign Affairs Committee added a rider to the Mutual Security Act which authorized $10,000 for a study of a Point Four Youth Corps. In a lengthy discussion, the committee criticized the Eisenhower administration for having failed to take "vigorous action in this direction." The committee concluded that should the study support the proposal, Congress would expect the executive branch to make a "serious and constructive effort to put the program into effective operation."[31]

As 1960 progressed, a number of other public figures expressed their strong support for the Peace Corps idea: General James Gavin, the celebrated army commander and author; Chester Bowles, former governor of Connecticut and ambassador to India; William O. Douglas, associate justice of the Supreme Court; columnist James Reston of the New York Times; Heinz Rollman, a businessman and Republican congressional candidate from North Carolina;* Milton J. Shapp. a prominent figure in Philadelphia corporate and political circles; and professors Walt W. Rostow of MIT and Robert R. Bowie of Harvard. Senator Jacob Javits also urged Republican presidential candidate Richard M. Nixon to adopt the idea, but Nixon refused.[32]

While these various figures might claim some part in the eventual founding of the Peace Corps, none was able to give it the political impetus needed to transform the idea into reality. Certainly the efforts of Humphrey and Reuss were significant and these two men deserve to be considered among the Peace Corps' founding fathers. Reuss conceded, however, that "if it had been left to us, the Peace Corps idea would still be cluttering up the legislative corridors."[33] It only became an issue of national political importance during the presidential campaign of 1960. The man who made it such was the forty-three-year-old junior senator from Massachusetts and the Democratic presidential nominee, John Fitzgerald Kennedy.

*Rollman had put forward his views on a so-called "peace army" as early as 1954 in his book World Construction (New York: Greenberg Press).

2

The Meeting of Idea and Fate

The truth is that the Peace Corps owes much of its success to its birth in a political campaign . . . Because of
the response of the American people President Kennedy decided to establish the Peace Corps as one of
his first major acts. This is an example of what Martin
Buber calls "the meeting of idea and fate in a creative
hour." It is the way ideas are born in American politics.
—Sargent Shriver,
first Director of the Peace Corps

SOMETHING NEW IN THE WIND

November 2, 1960, was yet another strenuous day in
Kennedy's campaign for the presidency. With the election less
than a week away he had taken to working a twenty-hour-a-day
schedule. He began his day in Los Angeles before moving on
to San Diego, San Jose, Oakland, and finally, San Francisco,
where he was to deliver a speech at the Cow Palace auditorium.
In addition to the by now standard exhortation to "get this country moving again," the main theme of Kennedy's speeches that
day had been peace and the means of securing it.[1]

The huge rally at the Cow Palace was the most important
event of the day and an enormous crowd of between thirty and
forty thousand people crammed the hall on the mild fall evening.[2] Only top aides had prior knowledge of the content of Kennedy's speech and they knew that he had employed some of
his best writers—Theodore Sorensen, Richard Goodwin, and
Archibald Cox—for its composition under his own specific direction.[3] They sensed something new in the wind.

13

The audience greeted Kennedy with tumultuous applause and it was several minutes before he could begin his speech entitled "Staffing a Foreign Policy for Peace."[4] "One week from tonight," he said, "the next President of the United States will be turning to the arduous tasks that lie ahead—selecting a Cabinet and preparing a program for peace." He was strongly critical of Eisenhower and his foreign policy efforts. "In this nuclear age," he warned, "peace is much too serious a matter to be entrusted to either generals or summit conferences. We need a stronger America—militarily, economically, scientifically, and educationally. We need a stronger free world, a stronger attack on world poverty, a stronger U.N., a stronger U.S. foreign policy— and, above all, a stronger foreign policy staff that is dedicated to peace."

Pinpointing weaknesses in vital areas of U.S. foreign policy machinery, Kennedy assailed the Foreign Service for its "ill-chosen, ill-equipped, and ill-briefed" ambassadors. He was particularly critical of the failure of American diplomats to learn the languages of the countries to which they were assigned: 70 percent of all new Foreign Service officers had no foreign language skills whatsoever; only three of the forty-four Americans in the embassy in Belgrade spoke Yugoslavian; not a single American in New Delhi could speak Indian dialects; only two of the nine ambassadors in the Middle East spoke Arabic. Kennedy also pointed out that there were only twenty-six black officers in the entire Foreign Service corps, less than 1 percent.

He warned that the United States would have to pay the price for its neglect of the newly independent countries of the Third World. "These are nations that vote in the U.N.," Kennedy noted. "They can affect our security." Placing America's grave deficiency in the Cold War context, he said that diplomats skilled in languages, teachers, doctors, technicians, and experts in many fields were pouring out of Moscow to advance the cause of communism in the Third World. "We have to do better," he said.

Kennedy pointed to the paucity of American technicians at work with the peoples of developing countries "outside the normal diplomatic channels." Again, he made an unfavorable comparison with the Lenin Institute, which was sending out hundreds of young people willing to serve at grassroots levels in the emerging nations. He noted that Asia had more Soviet than American technicians and that a similar trend was becoming apparent in Africa. Stressing the impact that skilled Americans might have in the Third World, "building goodwill, building the peace," he proposed a new government organization to accomplish this task, a Peace Corps:

> There is not enough money in all America to relieve the misery of the underdeveloped world in a giant and endless soup kitchen. But there is enough know-how and enough knowledgeable people to help those nations help themselves. I therefore propose that our inadequate efforts in this area be supplemented by a Peace Corps of talented young men willing and able to serve their country in this fashion for three years as an alternative to peacetime selective service — well-qualified through rigorous standards; well-trained in the language, skills, and customs they will need to know.[5]

Kennedy said that although Peace Corps service might be considered an alternative to the military draft, no conscription would be involved; this was to be a "volunteer" corps open to young Americans from "every race and walk of life." He was convinced that America was full of young people eager to serve the cause of peace. "I have met them on campaigns across the country," he said. Having highlighted the idealism inherent in the proposal, Kennedy returned to its Cold War advantages, claiming that "Our young men and women, dedicated to freedom, are fully capable of overcoming the efforts of Mr. Khrushchev's missionaries who are dedicated to undermining that freedom."

The next day's New York Times gave Kennedy's speech a front-page headline: "Kennedy Favors U.S. 'Peace Corps' to Work Abroad."[6] Nationwide, the media followed suit with reports extolling the virtues of the concept. Picking up on this positive response, Kennedy twice focused the public eye on the idea during the last few days of the campaign. In Chicago on November 4, he recommended "letting young Americans serve the cause of freedom as servants of peace . . . as the Communists work for their system." Again, on election eve, he referred to "a Peace Corps of young men and women who will be willing to spend two or three years of their lives as teachers and nurses, working in different countries . . . spreading the cause of freedom."[7]

AN ELECTION ISSUE

Kennedy's Republican opponent in the race for the presidency, Richard M. Nixon, was immediately critical of the idea. He took particularly strong exception to the prospect of the Peace Corps as a substitute for "a tour of duty in the uniformed service." He said it substantiated his charge that Kennedy was inexperienced and reckless in foreign affairs. In Nixon's view, the Peace Corps was another example of Kennedy's "fast and flashy technique of proposing a program that looks good on the surface—but which is inherently dangerous."[8] Kennedy responded with the suggestion that rather than an "alternative" to the selective service, Peace Corps duty would actually "supplement" it.[9] But many Republicans remained convinced that Kennedy was providing an "escape hatch for those who did not want to serve in the armed forces."[10] Ironically, however, the idea was so popularly received in the last week of the campaign that Nixon was forced into making a counterproposal. Two days before the election, he promised that, if elected, one of his first acts would be to "increase the effectiveness of our recruiting programs for service abroad, provide more accurate training facilities for those going abroad, and provide improved incentives for making a career out of such service."[11]

On November 8, in the closest-run presidential election of the twentieth century, Kennedy's popular vote margin of victory over Nixon was less than 120,000 out of a then record 69 million votes cast.[12] In the bitter aftermath of the election, Nixon and other critics accused Kennedy of using the Peace Corps as a gimmick to win votes at a crucial moment in the campaign. Certainly, with a week to go until voting day, the Kennedy campaign team had been aware of the political benefits to be gleaned from the introduction of a distinctive new proposal. An exciting idea like the Peace Corps, which received broad media coverage, could well have had a significant effect in persuading young people, independents, and even some liberal Republicans to vote for Kennedy.

In terms of major issues, many Americans could find little to choose between Kennedy and Nixon. Soviet premier Nikita Khrushchev compared them to Tweedledum and Tweedledee; Arthur Schlesinger, the Harvard historian and one of Kennedy's advisers, had deemed it necessary to publish a slim volume outlining the specific differences between the two: *Kennedy or Nixon: Does It Make Any Difference?* he asked in the book's title.[13] In opinion polls taken in late October, the two candidates were neck-and-neck.

In the penultimate week of the campaign, Nixon had introduced his biggest asset: President Eisenhower. Until then, Eisenhower had appeared unenthusiastic about Nixon's candidacy. When the President finally began actively campaigning on his behalf, it was a blow to the Kennedy camp. On the evening of the Cow Palace address, Kennedy confided his concern to an old wartime friend, Paul B. Fay. "Last week Nixon hit the panic button and started Ike speaking," Kennedy said, "and with every word he utters I can feel the votes leaving me."[14] In that last week of the campaign, Kennedy badly needed a new, attractive proposal.

In bringing the Peace Corps concept to national prominence exactly one week before the election, Kennedy was displaying a penchant for the opportunistic. His political advisers acknowledged that in the vital run-in to the election, it was the sort of issue everyone was looking for. Kennedy supporter James Gavin, who was to become U.S. ambassador to France in 1961, admitted that the closeness of the election race was on his mind when he wrote a memorandum to the candidate on October 28 urging him to make a formal pledge to a "Peace Corps" program (Gavin had given a speech on the idea a few weeks earlier).[15] However, political considerations notwithstanding, Kennedy's adoption of the idea was not just a vote-catching gimmick. As Pierre Salinger, Kennedy's press secretary, later noted, the speech at the Cow Palace was the culmination of an idea which had been "gradually building" in the candidate's mind throughout 1960.[16]

AN IDEA GRADUALLY BUILDING

Kennedy's first direct association with the Peace Corps concept came on February 21, 1960. While appearing on a college television show in New York, he was asked for his view on a bill calling for a study of a "Point Four Youth Corps" which Congressman Henry Reuss had introduced in the House. Kennedy was obliged to answer that he had no specific knowledge of the legislative proposal, but that he definitely favored more opportunities for young Americans to work in the developing countries.[17] Annoyed at having been caught off guard by the question, Kennedy later ordered one of his young staff members, Richard Goodwin, to research the idea.

After some brainstorming within the campaign team, Goodwin wrote to Professor Archibald Cox of Harvard Law School, who was acting as a channel of communication between Kennedy and his academic "brain trust" at Harvard. Goodwin asked Cox to "discuss the idea with some of the Cambridge group, get some reactions, and, if they think the idea is a good one, some specific questions as to how to proceed." Cox was told that Kennedy was thinking along the lines of having "several thousand college graduates" work at minimum pay for the government in technical and scientific jobs in the Third World. Kennedy was as yet unsure of the details of how to finance, train, and select these students, but "the whole idea would be to appeal to the imagination and interest of college graduates, give them an opportunity to make a real contribution to world peace and to receive valuable training and responsibility." It was also noted that the idea might have "propaganda advantages."[18]

In April and May, running in the Democratic primaries against Hubert Humphrey in Wisconsin and West Virginia, Kennedy was again confronted by the Peace Corps idea. A Wisconsin newpaper poll showed a very favorable response when Humphrey offered a Peace Corps-type program as one of his campaign pledges. Humphrey lost in both states but, as he wrote in his memoir, he was determined that Kennedy should adopt as many of his proposals as possible.[19] In June, Humphrey introduced in the Senate his bill for a "Peace Corps" and, during the summer, he transferred all his research materials and information on the proposal to Kennedy's office. The speech to come at the Cow Palace, with its proposals for draft exemption and three-year overseas service stints, owed a great deal to Humphrey's ideas.

When Kennedy accepted his party's nomination in July, he stood on a Democratic platform which stated that the United States had to change its image in the Third World by giving more technical and less military aid.[20] The manifesto also maintained that U.S. officials overseas would have to improve their language skills and cultural sensitivity. At the same time, the research unit of the Democratic party began compiling a report on the idea of an overseas youth corps.[21]

In early September, Kennedy asked both Congressman Reuss and Professor Samuel Hayes of the University of Michigan (who had extensive experience in international economic programs) to prepare position papers on a national youth service program. By the end of the month, they had submitted to him some particulars on how to put it together.[22] At this stage, however, Kennedy remained wary of a commitment to the idea in the form of an outright proposal. After all, it might prove a liability and leave him open to the charge of political naiveté.

The warm response given to a speech by Lyndon B. Johnson on September 22, helped nudge Kennedy toward a full endorsement of the concept. At the University of Nebraska, Kennedy's running mate called for "a Volunteers for Peace and Humanity program sponsored by our government . . . that would shatter the forces of communism."[23] Bill Moyers, Johnson's campaign manager, later observed that while it was not a well-prepared or detailed speech, it got a great reception. That night Johnson called Kennedy and told him that a voluntary "Peace and Humanity program" could be a great political asset.[24]

Remaining cautious, however, Kennedy chose a minor and safe platform for his first public exposition of the idea. On October 5, he was scheduled to send out a written "Message to the Nation's New Voters" arranged by the Young Democrats. Inspired by Humphrey, this organization had already done some work on a "Youth Corps." Two men prominent in the Young Democrats, Richard Murphy and Charles Manatt, seized the opportunity to insert the concept into a draft of the message. Thus

Kennedy promised that if elected he would "explore thoroughly the possibility of utilizing the services of the very best of our trained and qualified young people to give from three to five years of their lives to the cause of world peace by forming themselves into a Youth Peace Corps, going to the places that really need them and doing the sort of jobs that need to be done."[25]

Kennedy's office received some mail on the message and the delighted Young Democrats sent copies of it to college newspapers and Students-For-Kennedy groups. It received little national attention, however. During the famous television debates with Nixon in October, Kennedy discussed the Third World, the Communist threat, and the need for new foreign policy initiatives; there was no mention of a "Youth Peace Corps." In fact, his next reference to it came almost entirely by accident.

INCIDENT AT ANN ARBOR

At about 2 A.M. on October 14, Kennedy flew into Michigan from New York, where he had just completed his third debate with Nixon. Although exhausted, Kennedy had agreed to say a few brief words to students at the University of Michigan waiting to greet him. Since there was no prepared text or press release, he was expected to offer them the usual campaign clichés and Democratic slogans. On arrival at Ann Arbor, however, Kennedy found to his astonishment that some ten thousand students had waited up to see him. They chanted his name as he climbed the steps of the student union building.[26]

Somewhat startled by this reception, Kennedy launched into an extemporaneous address. He threw out challenges to the students: How many would be prepared to give years of their lives working in Asia, Africa and Latin America? How many would serve as teachers, doctors, and engineers? He spoke of the need for them to make a personal contribution, of the greater effort to be made and of the value of sacrifice. "On your willingness," he said, "not merely to serve one or two years in the service, but on your willingness to contribute part of your life to this country, I think will depend the answer whether we as a free society can compete." The audience was wildly responsive to his exhortations and, as the tired and hoarse candidate made his way to bed, he told an aide that he felt he had "hit a winning number."[27]

"No one is sure why Kennedy raised the question in the middle of the night at the University of Michigan," wrote Sargent Shriver in later years.[28] Possibly Kennedy thought of the Peace Corps at Michigan because someone reminded him that Professor Samuel Hayes taught at the University's International Studies Department. Hayes, in the report which he had submitted to Kennedy in September, had argued a case for American volunteers working in the Third World. This may have suggested a line of approach to the candidate at Ann Arbor. Other staff members felt that Kennedy's remarks were a counterattack to a criticism that Nixon had made during the debate earlier in the evening. Noting that the United States had become involved in foreign wars under Wilson, FDR, and Truman, Nixon had described the Democrats as the "war party." Harris Wofford, a member of the Kennedy campaign team, later wrote: "Stung by Nixon's words, Kennedy may have remembered the idea of a Peace Corps and spoken as he did in order to counteract the image of a Democratic war party."[29]

Whatever the reason, the enthusiasm he encountered at Ann Arbor made a deep impression on Kennedy. Inspired by his speech, several students there formed an organization called Americans Committed to World Responsibility; this group held seminars to discuss the Peace Corps idea and organized a petition requesting the establishment of an overseas program. By early November, about a thousand Michigan students had signed it. Kennedy was to mention these students during the Cow Palace address as evidence that there was a pool of talented and idealistic young Americans willing to serve in the developing countries. Moreover, three days before the election he arranged a meeting with this group where they presented him with their petition.[30]

Kennedy did not actually mention a "Peace Corps" or "volunteer" at Michigan, but his remarks clearly embodied the spirit of the idea. For him, Ann Arbor was a turning point. His speech there, however, attracted not the slightest national attention. Since the late-night address had been unscheduled, the press completely missed out on it. Journalist Russell Baker, covering the campaign in Michigan for the *New York Times* reported "nothing that was new."[31] What was new was that Kennedy had finally been persuaded to make a specific proposal of a Peace Corps before the campaign ended.

A few days after his speech at Ann Arbor, Kennedy promised that a Democratic administration would step up the effort to "educate the future leaders of Africa and Asia and Latin America. The youth of these areas are desperately in need of the training which will enable them to man the governments and run the economies of the developing nations."[32] Again, on October 29, he told an audience in Pennsylvania: "We need young men and women who will spend some of their years in Latin America, Africa, and Asia in the service of freedom."[33] His speech in San Francisco on November 2 built upon this momentum. But more than anything else, the Cow Palace address was an amplification of the responsive chord which Kennedy had struck, almost inadvertently, at the University of Michigan.

STREAMS OF INTEREST

Theodore C. Sorensen, special counsel to President Kennedy, claimed that the Peace Corps was the only new idea to emerge from the 1960 campaign.[34] Other politicians, including Richard Nixon, had the chance to adopt the concept, but only Kennedy did so.* One major reason was that it was consonant with several of his personal and political sympathies. Sorensen said that the Peace Corps was a "lake" into which a number of Kennedy's "streams of interest" flowed.[35]

One stream was Kennedy's empathy with the salient political and economic aspirations of the world's poor and oppressed peoples. As a young man, he had traveled extensively

*A memorandum circulated the Kennedy campaign headquarters in the fall of 1960 claiming that Nixon was about to propose a program for sending young American college graduates to the Third World to "teach the native peoples basic skills to assist them in fighting poverty, disease, illiteracy, and hunger." Nixon never did advocate such a plan, but the rumor that he intended to do so may have spurred Kennedy to quick and decisive action.

in Europe, Asia, and Latin America and had been shocked by the enfeebled state of many countries. This sympathy was reinforced by the memory of his paternal ancestors' experience in colonial Ireland. "I grew up in a community where the people were barely a generation away from colonial rule," he once wrote to Prime Minister Nehru of India. "I can claim the company of many historians in saying that the colonialism to which my immediate ancestors were subject was more sterile, oppressive and even more cruel than that of India. The legacy of Clive was on the whole more tolerable than that of Cromwell."[36]

Kennedy, a chairman of the Senate Subcommittee on African Affairs and a member of the Subcommittee on Latin American Affairs, was sometimes an outspoken advocate of Third World causes. "Call it nationalism, call it anti-colonialism, call it what you will," he warned his colleagues in the Senate, "the word is out and spreading like wildfire in nearly a thousand languages and dialects—that it is no longer necessary to remain forever in bondage."[37]

Travels across Asia in 1951 persuaded Kennedy that nationalism was the most vital political emotion in the Third World. Throughout that decade, he spoke out against the "imperialist" policies of both the Soviet Union and the Western powers. He was against American support of the colonial French presence in Southeast Asia, and, in one of the most controversial speeches of the 1950s, he advocated independence for Algeria. "The single most important test of American foreign policy today is how we meet the challenge of imperialism," he said in 1957. "On this test more than any other, this nation shall be critically judged by the uncommitted millions in Asia and Africa."[38]

Under Eisenhower, U.S. foreign policy was rigid in its monocular view of the world as an East-West Cold War, with Europe the major area of strategic concern. Little consideration was given to the development problems of the emerging nations of Asia, Africa, and Latin America, whose main concern was to initiate a North-South dialogue which might eventually lead to the restructuring of the international economic order. To the leaders of most developing countries, North represented white European colonialism; South stood for black Third World freedom. Kennedy sensed that the peoples of the Third World were "more interested in development than they are in doctrine. They are more interested in achieving a decent standard of living than in following the standards of either East or West."[39]

He voted against the bill to stop Point Four aid to the Third World; he was involved in the Friends of Vietnam movement; he personally helped finance African students' journeys to the United States; and he proposed the establishment of a multilateral African Educational Development Fund which would finance the sending of Western technicians to Africa and provide scholarships to Africans for study in the West.[40] President Ibrahim Abboud of Sudan noted that throughout Kennedy's years in Congress, he "consistently displayed an interest in the emerging nations, not only in his adherence to principle, but in his specific contributions."[41] Kennedy believed that the barriers of ignorance and poverty between the rich nations and the poor would have to be broken down before mutual respect and political understanding could be established. In the spring of 1959, he told Harris Wofford that he wanted to run for president in order to initiate a "new relationship" between the United States and the developing nations.[42] The Peace Corps was consonant with that philosophy.

A second stream running into Kennedy's proposal of a Peace Corps was his desire to reinvigorate U.S. foreign assistance programs. In his years in Congress, Kennedy persistently criticized America's failure to make the basic distinction between the type of aid needed for Western Europe, where an expanding industrial process was already underway, and that needed in the Third World, where technical and educational assistance was as important as capital. To Kennedy, U.S. aid seemed excessively oriented toward short-term military and political considerations rather than long-term social and economic objectives. "Our present foreign aid programs have neglected the great visionary partnership principles of the Marshall Plan and Point Four," he said in 1960, "they have been subordinated to narrow, expedient and temporary ends. Money has been poured into military assistance programs, and in many cases has been wasted, at the expense of vitally necessary economic development. The next President will have to devise an entirely revamped foreign aid program."[43]

Kennedy was one of a small group of senators who petitioned Eisenhower to reassess the relative importance of technical assistance as opposed to military aid. In his view, the main arm of U.S. aid, the International Cooperation Administration, was ineffective both in transferring resources and in transmitting an attractive U.S. image to the world. The Foreign Service, elite and out of touch with grassroots opinion in the countries which it served, was too much preoccupied with tennis and cocktails. In his speech at the Cow Palace, Kennedy stressed that "Men who lack compassion . . . were sent abroad to represent us in countries which were marked by disease and poverty and illiteracy and ignorance, and they did not identify us with those causes and the fight against them."

Rather than bureaucrats, dollars and guns, Kennedy felt that technical instruction and education programs should be in the vanguard of American assistance. He pointed out that there was an acute shortage of technical, managerial, and skilled labor in the developing countries. "Our aid now should be concentrated not on large-scale monuments to American engineering but on the village and the farm," he said.[44] Kennedy actively encouraged all kinds of cultural and technical exchanges in the hope that the poorer peoples might be given the means to help themselves. At the same time, he hoped to break down the extremely narrow focus of the vast majority of American aid programs in the 1950s. "For we have not always recognized," he said in 1958, "that the ideal contact is between peoples rather than governments. Governments come and go while lasting personal friendships and impressions remain."[45] With such ideas in mind, Kennedy gradually advanced toward the essence of the Peace Corps concept: a direct "people-to-people" foreign assistance initiative.

A third stream merging with the others was Kennedy's belief that America had a global mission. With his strong sense of history, he believed that it was the United States' duty to share its democratic virtues with other peoples, especially the poverty-stricken masses of the Third World. "The mantle of leadership has been placed upon our shoulders not by a nation nor by our own government or citizens but by destiny and circumstance," he said, "by the sheer fact of our physical and economic strength . . . and by what Washington termed 'the sacred fire of liberty.' "[46]

Kennedy appreciated that the burden of providing the world

with moral and physical leadership would involve tremendous sacrifice on America's part, but this only made the prospect more attractive to him. The major theme of his campaign was the need for courage, dedication, and hard work in meeting the challenge of his proposed New Frontier. Kennedy felt that there was a great fund of idealism in America waiting to be harnessed and discharged for a noble cause. The Peace Corps was his way of "demonstrating the reality of this idealism to the world."[47]

As Schlesinger has noted, however, Kennedy was also "a son of the Cold War," his sense of mission and idealism inextricably mixed with a determined anti-communism.[48] Certainly, Kennedy's interpretation of the struggle with the Soviets was more refined than that of John Foster Dulles, Eisenhower's secretary of state. Kennedy rejected Dulles's contention that the "neutralism" of independent nations could not be tolerated and that every conflict was a "moral crusade requiring the unconditional surrender of the enemy."[49] Nevertheless, he shared the view that "The great danger is the Communist system itself and its relentless determination to destroy us . . . We and the Communists are locked in a deadly embrace all around the world."[50] Anti-Communist rhetoric permeated Kennedy's campaign speeches, especially the argument that the Soviets were making advances in the Third World while American power and prestige declined.

This Cold War mentality was conducive to a foreign policy initiative which might contribute to the battle for the hearts and minds of the developing countries. Thus, when he proposed the Peace Corps, Kennedy placed it in a context where America's "ambassadors of peace" would be competing in the Third World against "Castro-type or Communist exploitation."[51]

1960: THE PUBLIC MOOD

Nineteen sixty found many Americans ill-at-ease with their country's performance and anxious to accept Kennedy's challenge to "get moving again." Throughout that year there was continuous debate as to whether the nation had lost its sense of purpose and was on the decline. For the first time, a President's

Commission on National Goals was established; among its findings were that the United States needed to extend its links with other countries, that more Americans should "live and work abroad" and that the country as a whole should commit itself to more "sustained effort and sacrifice." A report by the Senate Foreign Relations Committee stressed the necessity to "exhibit not only our material prosperity but also our dynamism, creativity, and desire for peace." Journalist Walter Lippmann criticized the lethargy of America in his book *The National Purpose*.[52] Many other intellectuals, theologians, and politicians seemed to agree with President Nathan M. Pusey of Harvard that the United States was "wandering along with no more thought . . . than the desire for diversion, personal comfort, and safety."[53]

In the spring of 1959, Schlesinger wrote Kennedy a memorandum entitled "The Shape of National Politics to Come."[54] His theory was that "there is an inherent cyclical rhythm in our national affairs." Drawing on historical examples, he advised Kennedy that periods of quietude in American politics were invariably followed by periods of action and liveliness. Schlesinger concluded that the period of passivity and acquiescence under Eisenhower was about to come to an end and that a politician of "intelligence and creativity" would be required to lead America's "national renaissance." Naturally, this theory appealed to Kennedy as he led the attack in 1960 on the affluent, purposeless society with his enunciation of a New Frontier which represented "not what I intend to offer the American people but what I intend to ask of them."[55]

Kennedy decried the 1950s as "the years the locusts have eaten."[56] In foreign affairs particularly, he criticized Eisenhower for having allowed the country to vegetate. In Kennedy's view, no significant new policies had been undertaken toward the emerging nations, despite some forty countries having gained independence since 1945. In the minds of many Third World leaders, the CIA had come to represent U.S. policy overseas, with its destabilization of governments deemed unfavorable to American objectives. The CIA aided and abetted the overthrow of the "pro-Communist" governments in Iran in 1953 and Guatemala in 1954, and tried to do so in Indonesia in 1958. It also helped install "pro-Western" governments in Egypt in 1954 and in Laos in 1959. By 1960, the CIA had already begun to plan the assassination of Fidel Castro.[57] "Covert action was over-used as an instrument of foreign policy," Roger Hilsman, Kennedy's director of Intelligence and Research later wrote, "and the reputation of America suffered more and more."[58]

In the late 1950s, one foreign policy panic followed another: the Soviets launched Sputnik; Castro defeated Batista in Cuba; Eisenhower was forced to cancel a tour of Japan for fear of protesters; Richard Nixon's car was mobbed in Caracas; an alarming number of newly independent countries voted against America in the UN; and Kennedy claimed that the Soviet Union had a "missile gap" advantage over the United States. The Russian capture of an American U-2 spy plane in 1960 was the capstone on what seemed like an unending procession of fiascoes.

Kennedy sprinkled his campaign speeches with statistics which charted America's apparent decline. He also noted the low number of student exchanges with Africa and Latin America, the many developing countries without a U.S. embassy, and the absurd imbalance in the distribution of U.S. foreign aid. Yugoslavia, for example, received more money than the whole of Africa.[59] As the campaign neared its conclusion, the Kennedy camp leaked some confidential U.S. Information Agency polls to the press; they indicated that American standing in Third World eyes was at an all-time low.[60]

THE UGLY AMERICAN

This sense of decline was evident in several self-critical but best-selling books of the time, such as *The Affluent Society, The Lonely Crowd, The End of Ideology,* and *Foreign Aid: Our Tragic Experiment.* In the postwar period, few books have had more impact on a nation's consciousness than did Eugene Burdick and William Lederer's *The Ugly American.* Although fictional, it exposed the "blundering hypocrisy of some of our top-level diplomats," and the "opportunism, incompetence and cynical deceit that have become imbedded in the fabric of our foreign relations."[61] The villains of the piece were the professional American diplomats who, more often than not, confined their work overseas to moving from air-conditioned offices to government-bought limousines, expatriate clubs, and cocktail parties. They rarely learned the native language, mixed with local peoples, or identified the real political and economic goals of the country that they purported to "serve."

The book's hero, Homer Atkins, was a skilled technician committed to helping at a grassroots level by building water pumps, digging roads, and building bridges. He was called the "ugly American" only because of his grotesque physical appearance. He lived and worked with the local peoples and, by the end of the story, was beloved and admired by them. The bitter message was that America's diplomats were, by and large, neither competent nor effective; and the implication was that the more the United States relied on them, the more its influence would wane. Atkins held the professionals in utter disdain. When an official asked him how the United States might improve the quality of its overseas representatives, he answered: "Tell 'em to get off their asses and out into the boondocks." In a factual epilogue, Burdick and Lederer summarized their major criticism of American foreign aid programs and pointed the way toward a new approach:

> Whatever the reasons, our overseas services attract far too few of our brightest and best qualified college graduates . . . What we need is a small force of well-trained, well-chosen, hardworking and dedicated professionals. They must be willing to risk their comforts and—in some lands—their health. They must go equipped to apply a positive policy promulgated by a clear-thinking government. They must speak the language of the land of their assignment and they must be more expert in its problems than are the natives.[62]

The Ugly American had a shock effect on the American public. First published in July 1958, it was a Book-of-the-Month Club selection in October; by November it had gone through twenty printings. It was so influential that in later paperback editions its blurb claimed that "President Kennedy's Peace Corps is the answer to the problem raised in this book." At the Cow Palace, Kennedy referred to The Ugly American and conceded that he had "shuddered" upon reading it.[63]

A NEW GENERATION

In 1960, America had just come out of a decade considered by many to have been stale and uninspiring. The youth of the nation had felt the most stultified. The baby boom following World War II had led to the growth of a population 50 percent of which was under 25-years old in 1960. Unlike their parents, who had suffered the deprivations caused by Depression and war, these children had grown up surrounded by material prosperity. For the first time, a college education was within the grasp of the majority of young people. In the 1950s adults had been engrossed in the pursuit of a decent standard of living; their children, well-provided for and increasingly well-educated, did not need to aspire to the same goals. *The Harvard Crimson* said it clearly: "This is the first generation of students which is not going to school for purely economic reasons."[64]

Unprecedented material wealth freed the new generation to heed their consciences and pursue their ideals. Tom Hayden, who was part of the early morning crowd which had greeted Kennedy at Ann Arbor and who was to become the doyen of radical student politics in the 1960s, argued that status and money were not "goals to be striven for."[65] In their own way, these young people were contributing to the debate on national purpose. The question they asked was: What is America's power and affluence for? Kennedy's proposal of a Peace Corps attempted to provide at least one answer.

Strickly speaking, John Kennedy was not of this younger generation. He had fought in the Second World War with their fathers. Nonetheless, he was the youngest President the country had ever had and the youth of America seemed especially attracted to his athletic and exciting image. The Peace Corps came to epitomize the idealism and hope which they invested in him. Kennedy asked them if they were prepared to travel to distant lands and work under straitened conditions to help impoverished peoples. Their answer was resoundingly affirmative.

This spirit of generosity and participation had been sorely missed under Eisenhower. As one of the Peace Corps' first young administrators put it: "The 1950s made ancient mariners of us all—becalmed, waiting and a little parched in the throat. Then we picked up momentum on the winds of change that Kennedy brought in—the New Frontier, the fresh faces in government, the vigorous, hopeful speeches, the Peace Corps."[66]

3

Launching the Peace Corps

Kennedy has started what is surely one of the most
remarkable projects ever undertaken by any nation.
—*New York Times*, March 2, 1961

HIGH HOPES

"The notion of a Youth Corps has excited the imagination
of university people and students all over the land," wrote Walt
Rostow of MIT, one of Kennedy's advisers, a few days after the
election. Urging the President-elect to build upon the already
acquired momentum behind the idea, Rostow said that it would
be worth consulting with the religious and private organizations
already experienced in overseas development.[1] Kennedy replied
that Rostow should confer with Max Millikan, a friend and colleague at MIT and a long-standing economic adviser to Kennedy
on Third World problems. "Have Max take on the responsibility of working up a Peace Corps idea into something I could implement," wrote Kennedy. He emphasized, however, that he
wanted to avoid appearing precipitant. He was worried that naive
young Americans might become embroiled in some debacle
overseas and that the blame would be charged to their President's
inexperience in foreign affairs. Kennedy wanted some assurance
that Volunteers would be responsible and useful to the countries in which they served.[2]

On November 20, the *Washington Post* advised Kennedy to
make the Peace Corps more than yet another campaign promise
broken immediately after the election. The *Post's* editors hoped

that on assuming the presidency, Kennedy would regard the Peace Corps as a serious scheme for using talent in a manner likely to benefit both the Foreign Service of the United States and the welfare of the emerging nations.[3] In a letter to the *New York Times*, Eugene Burdick, coauthor of *The Ugly American*, forcefully endorsed the idea.[4] Meanwhile, mail on the subject continued to flood Kennedy's offices in Boston and Washington as well as the Democratic National Committee headquarters and the White House. Most of it came from young people volunteering their services, but other letters contained blueprints on how the Peace Corps should be organized. Before the end of the year, Kennedy had received more than twenty-five thousand letters on the Peace Corps—more than on any other topic.[5]

Without official sanction from Washington, various meetings and conferences on the Peace Corps started to take place all over the country, especially on college campuses. In November, Princeton University sponsored "The Conference to Discuss the Challenge to American Youth from the World's Emerging Nations." Representatives from educational, business, and political groups resolved that "Thousands of America's youth are ready to answer the New Frontier's demands in the name of peace."[6] On December 18 the *New York Times* reported Peace Corps conferences taking place in every major state from New York to California.[7]

A further sign of the voracious public appetite for information on the proposal was the avalanche of reports and position papers which cascaded into Kennedy's offices. Universities, foundations, private voluntary services, and religious organizations sent in hundreds of suggestions. Harvard, Notre Dame, Yale, Berkeley, the National Student Association, the UAW, the Industrial Union Development, the American Friends Service Committee, and the Institute of International Education were among the countless number of bodies which put forward their viewpoints.[8] Some were a little overenthusiastic. American labor unions, represented by the AFL-CIO's "executive council on the Peace Corps," saw few problems in mobilizing the "energies and skills of American workers in the gigantic task of assisting the new nations to spark their industrial development." Others were more cautious. International Voluntary Services warned against "too large an initial program" and envisaged only five hundred volunteers in the field by 1963.[9]

Kennedy had given little indication of which view he favored. His last reference to the Peace Corps had been on election eve. Since then he had been engrossed in the great "talent hunt" for the new members of his administration. He appointed Chester Bowles (soon to be named under-secretary of state) as the general caretaker of the material coming in on the Peace Corps, but laid down no firm guidelines. The unprompted popular response to the idea had put Kennedy under considerable pressure to make a statement of renewed commitment. The difficulty was that as yet he had very little detailed knowledge to impart. He simply had not had the time or the opportunity to weigh the various options.

By the New Year, Millikan of MIT had acted on Kennedy's instructions to Rostow and had prepared a lengthy memorandum entitled "An International Youth Service." Millikan conceded that "we simply do not know a great deal about how to make a program of this kind work" and his recommendations were extremely tentative. All the same, he was definitely in favor of a "youth service" and his memorandum at least gave Kennedy a framework on which to base a public statement.[10]

On January 9, 1961, Kennedy issued Millikan's paper verbatim, under the letterhead of the President-elect. The statement recognized the mounting flow of incontestable evidence that there were "large and growing numbers of Americans in their 20s deeply motivated to place their energies and talents at the service of constructive world causes and prepared to devote two or three years of their lives to such services irrespective of their long-term career objectives." An International Youth Service Agency was proposed "on a limited pilot basis." No selective service exemption would be granted to participants, rigorous training and selection standards would be applied, and terms of service would last two years. The statement also stressed that the program would be a part of the overall U.S. foreign assistance effort, that it would be "experimental" in nature and that there would be no more than "several hundred young people in the first year or two."[11]

This tentative statement was successful on several fronts. It silenced critics by appearing cautious and by responding to the draft-evasion charge, and it satisfied supporters by giving substance to their hopes. A Gallup poll confirmed that these hopes had not subsided: 71 percent of Americans were in favor of a Peace Corps, with only 18 percent against. One week before the presidential inauguration, the *New York Times* described the Peace Corps as "something that is in the spirit of this democratic country, a forward-looking thing, and it is heartening that so many of our young people are responding with vigor and eagerness to it."[12]

On January 20, Kennedy made his famous inaugural address in which he exhorted Americans to "ask not what your country can do for you—ask what you can do for your country." While there was no specific mention of a Peace Corps, Kennedy pledged to the peoples in the huts and villages of the developing countries "our best efforts to help them help themselves, for whatever period is required—not because the Communists may be doing it, not because we seek their votes, but because it is right. If a free society cannot help the many who are poor, it cannot save the few who are rich."[13] The day after the inauguration, Kennedy telephoned his brother-in-law, Robert Sargent Shriver, and asked him to form a presidential Task Force "to report how the Peace Corps could be organized and then to organize it."[14]

THE TASK FORCE

During the transition Shriver, a Yale-educated lawyer whose professional background was in business, had supervised Kennedy's talent hunt. This had been an unmitigated success with Shriver personally finding and persuading some of the most able men in the country, including McGeorge Bundy, Robert McNamara, and Dean Rusk, to come to Washington. Describing Shriver and his determined persuasiveness in bringing the so-called "best and brightest" to Washington, journalist David Halberstam called him "a big-game hunter."[15]

Exhausted after the hectic campaign and transition, Shriver claimed he had no idea why Kennedy chose him to coordinate the planning of the Peace Corps. Kennedy surely would have been impressed by his brother-in-law's work on civil rights, agriculture, education, and other issues during the campaign as well as by his personnel selections for the administration. In addition, Shriver's experience in running a major business concern, Joseph P. Kennedy's Merchandise Mart in Chicago (at that time, the largest privately owned office building in the world), as well as his public service in education would have made him an attractive choice. Between 1956 and 1960 Shriver had been president of the Chicago Board of Education and a member of various school, university, and citizen boards. Nor would Kennedy have failed to notice that, as president of the Catholic Interracial Council of Chicago, Shriver had won a reputation as a strong proponent of civil rights. Besides, Kennedy was probably aware that in the 1930s, Shriver had been a leader of Experiment in International Living groups and, in the 1950s, had actually submitted an overseas service plan to the Eisenhower administration. In terms of dedication to the ideals of public service and interest in a Peace Corps-type project, Shriver's credentials were excellent. At the political level, Kennedy had taken note of Shriver's work for him during his Senate campaign in 1958 as well as in the race for the presidency. Within the Kennedy entourage, Shriver—forty-four in 1960—had gained a reputation as an "ideas man" who was bright, lively, and effective.[16]

On January 21, Shriver took his first step toward organizing the Peace Corps when he telephoned Harris Wofford, a brilliant law professor from Notre Dame who had acted as Kennedy's adviser on civil rights during the campaign. While working together on the election and talent hunt, Shriver and Wofford had become firm friends. Wofford, thirty-four in 1961, had long cherished the idea of government-sponsored voluntary service overseas. In the late 1940s, as a member of the Student World Federalists, he had proposed a "peace force" of volunteers to serve overseas in community development projects. In the 1950s, he had consulted with Justice William O. Douglas and with Walter and Victor Reuther of the UAW on the idea of a large-scale American volunteer service in the developing countries. Wofford had also been involved in establishing a small, privately sponsored overseas agency for students in the 1950s (the International Development Placement Association) and had gained broad experience of the Third World. He was only too glad, if a little startled, to be asked to help create what he called "this strange new animal, the Peace Corps."[17]

Initially, the Task Force consisted solely of Shriver and Wofford, sitting in a suite they had rented at the Mayflower Hotel in Washington. Most of their time was spent making calls to personal friends they thought might be helpful. Among these were Gordon Boyce, president of the Experiment in International Living; Albert Sims of the Institute of International Education; Adam Yarmolinsky, a foundation executive; Father Theodore Hesburgh, president of the University of Notre Dame; George Carter, a campaign worker on civil rights issues and former member of the American Society for African Culture; Louis Martin, a newspaper editor who had worked for the Democratic National Committee; and Franklin Williams, an organizer of the campaign for black voter registration and a knowledgeable student of African affairs.[18]

One name soon led to another. During the last week of January and the first week of February, scores of people from academic, government, business, and religious circles passed through the lobby of the makeshift Peace Corps headquarters in the Mayflower Hotel. It was an informal setup, more like a group of friends gathering together to discuss a pet subject than an official committee establishing a government organization. Shriver had no long-term, premeditated vision of what the Peace Corps might be. "My style," he confessed, "was to get bright, informative, creative people and then pick their brains."[19]

Besides people, Shriver was inundated by hundreds of reports all in favor of the Peace Corps, but all offering different and often conflicting advice on its execution. From government circles, the International Cooperation Administration (ICA) presented a study called *The National Peace Corps*. This report suggested that Volunteers should be paid an annual salary of about $3,000 and that the new organization should be incorporated into the overall U.S. foreign assistance effort. From academia, Professor Hayes of the University of Michigan submitted an extensive report on the potential of an International Youth Service, which recommended close cooperation with the United Nations and proposed that Volunteers should work at home as well as abroad. The $10,000 appropriated by Congress to the Colorado State University Research Foundation under the Reuss bill for a study of the Peace Corps idea produced a preliminary paper on *A Youth Corps for Service Abroad*. This advised a Volunteer age limit somewhere between twenty and thirty and recommended that the new agency should delegate the control of its country programs to other, more experienced bodies.[20]

There was even a plan from overseas. Alec Dickson, chief of Britain's Voluntary Service Overseas, prescribed that the Peace Corps should ensure above all else that its programs would respond to the requested needs of the developing countries. He pointed out that "One or two organizations in the United States have made a strategic error in starting with the recruitment of volunteers and the collection of money—only to find that there are no projects overseas."[21] Shriver, attempting to distill this cornucopia of material, discovered that the only point of unanimity among all the reports was that the Peace Corps should begin cautiously and on a small scale.

Meanwhile, the public debate continued. The correspondence columns of the *New York Times* showed that some Americans felt the new organization should not be part of the federal government, as this would cause it to be labeled "imperialist" by some Third World countries. Others argued that selection should not be limited to young people. Congressman Reuss took issue with the generally cautious approach which the administration seemed to be taking. He said that Kennedy's election was sufficient enough mandate to establish the Peace Corps and he claimed there was no reason why Volunteer numbers should not eventually reach the tens of thousands and undertake "almost everything under the sun."[22] Conversely, former President Eisenhower ridiculed the Peace Corps as a "juvenile experiment." Others, making an analogy with Henry Ford's Peace Ship, predicted that the idealistic Peace Corps would soon founder on the rocks of realism.[23]

The *New York Times*, however, took a strong stand in favor of the Peace Corps. With half the world starving, two-thirds of the world illiterate, and a life expectancy of thirty-six years in the Third World compared to seventy in the United States, journalist

Gertrude Samuels argued that the Peace Corps would provide a necessary outlet for "the individual American to do something positive and affirmative for peace."[24] On January 30, President Kennedy kept the public spotlight on the issue by reminding the country of the ongoing "formation of a National Peace Corps" in his first State of the Union address.[25]

Shriver had scheduled the first official meeting of his Task Force for February 6. As that date approached, he and Wofford consulted with an increasing number of experienced people: James Grant, Charles Nelson, Glen McClelland from ICA, Irving Lewis from the Bureau of the Budget, Gilbert White from Chicago University, Carroll Wilson from MIT, Eugene Rostow from Yale, Richard Neustadt from Columbia, Harlan Cleveland from Syracuse, James Russell from the National Education Association, James Scott from the National Student Association, Victor Reuther from the UAW, and scores of other prominent academic and business leaders. Humphrey and Reuss also visited the Mayflower Hotel, and Richard Goodwin, assistant special counsel to the President, acted as a channel of communication between the Task Force and the White House.[26]

Despite the multifarious recommendations, opinions, and reports, Shriver's group had made relatively little headway in defining the new program in terms of specific size, costs, organization, and objectives. When Kennedy requested a report by the end of February, Shriver had to concede that, as yet, he had not even settled on an official name for the new agency. "I needed help badly," Shriver recalled in later years. Although it was less than two weeks since the President had assigned him the task, "Kennedy wanted to know what was taking us so long . . . I replied weakly that no one had ever tried to put a Peace Corps together before."[27]

THE TOWERING TASK

Unknown to Shriver, at the same time as he was busily manning the Task Force, two officials in the Far Eastern division of ICA were working on a Peace Corps plan of their own. Warren W. Wiggins was the deputy director of Far Eastern operations in ICA. Although still in his thirties in 1960, Wiggins had already helped administer the Marshall Plan in Western Europe, served as U.S. economic adviser to the Philippines and acted as director of the American aid program in Bolivia.[28] He was totally dissatisfied with the manner in which American overseas programs were run. He referred to the luxurious "golden ghettoes" in which U.S. officials lived in Third World countries despite the poverty and disease which surrounded them. "Reflecting on my own service abroad," said Wiggins, "I think we were too much encumbered by peripheral service organizations, recreation associations, clubs, American-oriented theater groups, even exclusively American churches. I have sometimes had the feeling that the management of the official American community becomes an all-devouring juggernaut."[29]

Wiggins's foil was the Far Eastern regional counsel for ICA, William Josephson. Just turned twenty-six in 1961, Josephson had already earned a reputation as one of the brightest and most hard-driving lawyers in ICA. Both Wiggins and Josephson were attracted by the spirit and vision of Kennedy's campaign and were desperate to participate in the new administration. During the transition period they worked on various position papers: on Vietnam, Laos, the reorganization of foreign aid, and the Peace Corps. Josephson later remarked that at first he had thought the Peace Corps "a silly idea." Both he and Wiggins began with the notion that the program would be limited to sending young Americans overseas to teach English. As they drafted and redrafted their report, however, their vision broadened.[30]

They called their paper *The Towering Task*, taking the title from the phrase Kennedy had used in his State of the Union address: "The problems . . . are towering and unprecedented—and the response must be towering and unprecedented as well."[31] Wiggins and Josephson were not under the auspices of the official ICA working party on the Peace Corps, although they did submit to it a copy of their plan. They also sent a copy to Wofford and another to Goodwin at the White House. They used these different routes because, as Wiggins put it, they "wanted to make sure that Shriver would get it."[32] A copy did eventually fall into Shriver's hands and he read it late at night on Sunday, February 5. He thought it brilliant and immediately sent a telegram to Wiggins inviting him to attend the Task Force meeting the next morning. The so-called "midnight ride of Warren Wiggins" became one of the legends in Peace Corps annals.[33]

Shriver began the February 6 meeting by introducing Wiggins and Josephson and by distributing copies of *The Towering Task*. He advised the other members of the Task Force to read it carefully before commenting. It was a pregnant moment. From this point on, Wiggins and Josephson became the engine room of the Peace Corps. Shriver described Wiggins as "the figure most responsible" for the planning and organization that brought the Peace Corps into being.[34] *The Towering Task* had been written with the modest hope that it might "stimulate thought."[35] In fact, it provided a philosophy for the Peace Corps throughout the Kennedy era.

Wiggins fundamentally disagreed with most of the academic and other institutional approaches which counseled caution and a slow beginning. Instead, he advocated initiating the Peace Corps with "several thousand Americans participating in the first 12 to 18 months." Whereas almost all other reports had projected Volunteer numbers in terms of hundreds, Wiggins threw out figures of thirty-, fifty-, and even a hundred thousand.[36] This was precisely why Shriver had been so smitten by *The Towering Task*. It appealed to his own instinct that the Peace Corps ought to be bold, large, fast-moving, and created with the objective of becoming a truly significant force in the world arena.

The argument for bigness did not appear rash because Wiggins provided a persuasive rationale. He argued that "a small, cautious Peace Corps may be worse than no Peace Corps at all. It may not receive the attention and talent it will require even for preventing trouble." Moreover, Wiggins claimed that "a slow, cautious start may maximize the chance of failure."[37] *The Towering Task* reinforced Shriver's belief that not only could a sizeable Peace Corps be effective, but that it might well be the only hope of success.

Within the Task Force, various groups and individuals fought for the issues and opinions that they wished to see expressed in the final report to Kennedy. Gordon Boyce differed with Wiggins over the degree of direct administration of projects which the Peace Corps should have. Boyce, along with many academics and representatives from private organizations, argued that the Peace Corps should make grants to universities and private agencies and then leave the administration of country programs to them. Wiggins felt this would lead to a "Peace Corps Foundation" operating rather like the National Science Foundation—appropriating funds but having no effective control; he was insistent that the Peace Corps should play the central role in every aspect of its programs. Another area of disagreement within the Task Force was between "maximalists" (foreign assistance professionals like Wiggins and Josephson) who wanted a large program and "minimalists" (academics like Carroll Wilson and Eugene Rostow) who believed that smallness would be the best policy. Shriver harnessed the factions and focused discussion by continually emphasizing the simple but essential questions: "Were there people who wanted to volunteer? Was there a demand for them overseas? Could they serve effectively overseas?"[38]

He entrusted to Josephson the handling of the various legal and technical problems involved in setting up a new government agency. At this stage, speed was the primary consideration. There was not enough time for the detailed research and writing which the preparation of congressional legislation would entail. Josephson told Shriver that the Peace Corps was not yet ready to talk convincingly to the various congressional committees about "specific numbers or specific members in specific places by specific dates through specific means." He argued that if the Peace Corps waited the six months it would take to get a bill through Congress, it would miss the potential recruits from the colleges and universities in the summer of 1961 and would possibly not be in operation before the winter of 1962. A presidential Executive Order was the only viable means of giving the Peace Corps the headstart it needed.[39]

Josephson discovered that ample authority for the President to provide immediate "contingent" funding for the Peace Corps existed in Section 400 of the Mutual Security Act of 1954.[40] He also put forward the view that an Executive Order made sense vis-à-vis future congressional strategy. If the Peace Corps could put Volunteers in the field and prove itself a success before Congress actually had to consider its legal permanence, its chance of survival would be measurably increased. There was the risk

of alienating Congress by presenting it with a virtual *fait accompli;*
but Josephson argued that the Peace Corps would be in a much
less precarious position if it were a living body instead of just
an idea. The recommendation for an Executive Order was one
of the many judgments made by the Task Force in the critical
period when the report to Kennedy was being drafted.[41]

Another was the decision to adopt the name "Peace Corps"
as the official title for the new organization. Kennedy had used
the phrase "Peace Corps" in the Cow Palace address, but several
State Department officials complained that the word "peace" had
come to be associated with Soviet propaganda and that "corps"
carried undesirable military connotations. Dozens of alternative
titles were suggested, including the previously used International
Youth Service, Point Four Youth Corps, and Youth for Peace.
After much discussion, Shriver settled on the original. "What
we wanted," he said, "was a name which the public at large could
grasp emotionally as well as intellectually." He felt the term
"Peace Corps" had this quality. Moreover, he did not believe
that "peace" should be allowed to become the exclusive property of the Soviets. Besides, "Peace Corps" maintained the spirit
of Kennedy's original statement.[42]

THE REPORT TO THE PRESIDENT

Twice in February Kennedy telephoned Shriver to ask about
progress on the Peace Corps. While addressing a Youth Fitness
Conference on February 21, the President publicly expressed his
hope that the Peace Corps idea would soon be realized.[43] This
pressure from the White House was felt by the Task Force. As
it stepped up its pace, Shriver was forced "to make some drastic demands on people," he recalled.[44] Josephson described the
chaotic scene as the finishing touches were put to the Report:
"The final draft of the Report was done with Charles Nelson
sitting in one room writing basic copy, me sitting in another
room rewriting it, Wofford sitting in yet another room doing the
final rewrite, and Wiggins running back and forth between the
three rooms delivering pieces of paper along the chain."[45] The
last link in the chain, of course, was Shriver who read every

word with care before giving his approval. The last-minute rush was successful. On the morning of Friday, February 24, Shriver was able to deliver to Kennedy what was, in effect, the Peace Corps' Magna Carta: "The Report to the President on the Peace Corps."[46]

Shriver began the Report with a confident first sentence: "Having studied at your request the problems of establishing a Peace Corps, I recommend its *immediate* establishment."[47] This sense of urgency became one of the striking characteristics of the Peace Corps in the Kennedy era. However, while satisfied that "we have sufficient answers to justify your going ahead," Shriver added a note of caution. "Since the Peace Corps is a new experiment in international cooperation," he wrote, "many of the questions considered below will only be finally answered in action by trial and error. Our tentative conclusions are therefore submitted as working hypotheses."[48]

The Report argued that the shortage of time justified the recommendation for an Executive Order and the request for $12 million from the contingency fund of the Mutual Security Act. "If the world situation were moving at a snail's pace, the Peace Corps timidly conceived and administered could keep in step," the Report said.[49] It advised that the new organization should be situated within the Department of State so that it could utilize the experience of professional diplomats. Shriver was adamant, however, that the Peace Corps should not become a mere subdivision of ICA. He did not want it encumbered by ICA's political and bureaucratic disabilities. "This new wine should not be poured into the old ICA bottle," he wrote. The Peace Corps should be a "small, new, alive agency operating as one component in our whole overseas operation."

Shriver asked in the Report for "great flexibility to experiment with different methods of operation." While the Peace Corps would be related to other parts of the U.S. foreign aid effort, he was emphatic that it should not become overly formal and inflexible. This was the first sign of Shriver's intense hatred of red tape and traditional bureaucratic methods: "No one . . . wants to see a large centralized new bureaucracy grow up . . . This must be a cooperative venture of the whole American people—not the program of some alphabetical agency in Washington." Trying to be a "different" type of government agency was to become one of the Peace Corps' most distinguishing features.

To promote broad-based participation and to avoid self-perpetuation, the Report said the Peace Corps would function simultaneously by five different methods. First, some operations would be conducted through grants to private voluntary agencies already engaged in grassroots assistance programs: IVS, Operation Crossroads Africa, the 4-H Club, and many others. Second, the Peace Corps would work through contractual arrangements with colleges, universities, and other educational institutions willing and able to participate in overseas projects. A third alternative was for the Peace Corps to develop its programs in conjunction with the other government aid agencies like ICA; the Report claimed that these established organizations could use Volunteers as "personnel at the working level who can help translate high-level advice into action on the line." Fourth, the Peace Corps could function through the UN and other international technical assistance and development institutions. Last, the Report suggested that the Peace Corps might directly administer some of its own programs—from recruiting Volunteers to planning projects and implementing them in host countries. It was implied, however, that the Peace Corps would directly administer programs only under extenuating circum stances when "complexity or novelty or urgency" demanded they could not be efficiently managed by the other four channels. This proved to be the Report's least accurate projection.

The essence of the Peace Corps was "the placement of Americans in actual operational work in newly developing areas of the world," noted the Report. Accordingly, it went into great detail concerning the role of the Volunteer. It predicted that in most cases, Peace Corps service would be considered a ground for temporary deferment from military service and that few returned Volunteers would be drafted. It was recognized, however, that "the Corps must never be seen, in this country or abroad, as . . . a haven for draft dodgers." Thus it was recommended that there should be no automatic draft exemption for Volunteers.

Since no one could really be sure of who would volunteer,

the Report decided against any narrow, disqualifying regulations. Although Shriver imagined that most Volunteers would be young college graduates, there was to be no rigid age limit for either young or old. Any able-bodied American citizen over eighteen could join the Peace Corps. An academic qualification in the form of a college degree or otherwise would not be compulsory. The Report also emphasized that the Peace Corps would be open to both men and women.

From one to three years was the length of service recommended, and the Report urged that the Peace Corps should seek to form the "broadest possible national base." Following Foreign Service procedure, applicants were to take both a written test and an oral interview. The development of appropriate training programs was also deemed an "urgent priority." The Peace Corps would utilize college and university facilities and instructors wherever feasible and the emphasis would be on language instruction and preparation for a specific job overseas; training time could vary from six weeks to six months. Volunteers in the field would be paid the minimum to provide a "decent standard of living," live in circumstances akin to those of their host country counterparts, and avoid all "conspicuous consumption." A modest allowance would be given to them on leaving the Peace Corps.

Drawing upon evidence in the study undertaken by Colorado State University, the Report asserted that "the need for trained Peace Corpsmen is felt in every country in Latin America, Africa, and Asia" and it noted the lack of skilled personnel in teaching, public health, rural development, industrial projects, and government administration. In its first year, the Peace Corps would probably concentrate on teaching projects where the need was obvious and where it would be possible to recruit and train academically qualified people relatively quickly.

The Report predicted that the Peace Corps would contribute to a "more intelligent American participation in the world," to the social and economic development of "critical" countries and regions, and to the promotion of international cooperation and "goodwill toward this country." In a significant statement of intent, it urged Kennedy to take steps "to dispel the notion that the Peace Corps is merely an attempt to export surplus American spiritual or political zeal, and to show that the Peace Corps is not advanced as an arm of the Cold War but as a contribution to the world community." Shriver was determined that the Peace Corps should avoid being labeled an instrument of American cultural imperialism or a tool of U.S. foreign policy strategists. Accordingly, the Report highlighted the reciprocal educational advantages of the cross-cultural experience: "The Peace Corps can contribute to the education of America," it said. Indeed, the Report claimed that the Peace Corps carried the potential to add a new dimension to America's view of the world; that dimension would not consist of subterfuge and intelligence estimates but rather of "a better understanding and more responsibility toward the world."[50]

Shriver's "Report to the President" was in the spirit of *The Towering Task*. It proposed programs of a significant size and urged the federal government to provide bold and forceful leadership. It promised Kennedy that if he launched the Peace Corps "within the next two weeks in a determined way," there could be as many as two thousand Volunteers in the field by the end of the year. The Report also cautioned that no matter how well conceived and efficiently run, there would probably be failures. A resilient optimism, however, was the dominant theme. "The potential is very great," Shriver told Kennedy. "If you decide to go ahead, we can be in business Monday morning."[51]

NOW OR NEVER

The White House's initial reaction to the Task Force's findings was less than enthusiastic. Theodore Sorensen, the President's special counsel, told Shriver that the Report was very different from what he had envisaged.[52] Kennedy's staff had been thinking of a small, low-cost addendum to the overall foreign assistance program. Instead, Shriver proffered the vision of a large, independent new government agency which could be in the field within a few months. There was also the problem of the Executive Order. Although Kennedy was still in his honeymoon period with Congress, he was not overeager to expend his presidential prerogative unless absolutely necessary.

The last week of February was taken up with frequent consultation between the Task Force members and their White House counterparts. Shriver's group argued that momentum should not be lost; an organization had to be built, rooms full of mail answered, and Volunteers recruited. All this had to be begun immediately if Volunteers were to be in action before 1962. On the other hand, the President's staff were understandably nervous that a hastily assembled program for young people to work abroad would prove a political liability. Not the least of their worries was the proposal for an Executive Order. Congressmen would not take kindly to such an early invasion of their legislative rights.

Wiggins and Josephson, in particular, engaged in industrious research and argument on behalf of the Peace Corps. Josephson found relevant precedent for an Executive Order of the desired type going back to FDR's establishment of the Emergency Conservation Corps in 1933. He also argued that it made good political sense to present the Peace Corps as a "special case."[53] In this way, congressmen might not regard it as a trespass against their privilege. Wiggins also felt strongly that if Kennedy did not set up the Peace Corps at the beginning of his administration by swift executive action, then there was a possibility the program might never see the light of day. Presidential history had shown that opportunities to be both creative and idealistic did not come around often, and usually not in the second and third years of an administration. As March approached, Shriver and his Task Force felt it was now or never for the Peace Corps.

Lawrence O'Brien, special assistant to the President for congressional relations, recalled being "extremely impressed" by the Peace Corps' young advocates.[54] He agreed that the Executive Order would be an effective tactic. Shriver himself persuaded Kennedy that this was a special case. Thus, the Peace Corps became the only program of the Kennedy administration allowed the distinctive status of an "emergency agency."[55]

On March 1, a week after he had received Shriver's Report— and only three weeks after the first Task Force meeting—Kennedy signed Executive Order 10924. This gave the Peace Corps the power to move into action as a new program of assistance "for men and women of the United States . . . to nations and areas of the world." While underlining his personal support for the agency, Kennedy noted that the Peace Corps was established on a "temporary pilot basis" with only five hundred or so Volunteers going into the field by the end of the year.[56] To some extent, he remained cautious.

In a follow-up special message to Congress, Kennedy requested legislation. Mentioning the work done on the proposal by Humphrey and Reuss, he spoke of the beneficial impact which the Peace Corps would have on America's relationship with the Third World. "Our own freedom and the future of freedom around the world," he said, "depends, in a very real sense, on the underdeveloped countries' ability to build growing and independent nations where men can live in dignity, liberated from the bonds of hunger, ignorance and poverty." Kennedy also commented on the sacrifice and dedication of the Americans who would serve overseas in "the villages, the mountains, the towns, and the factories of dozens of struggling nations." Developing a line of argument included in the Report, he noted that the benefits of the Peace Corps would not be limited to the countries in which it served. "Our own young men and women," he said, "will return better able to assume the responsibilities of American citizenship and with greater understanding of our global responsibilities."[57]

Kennedy's dramatic stroke of the pen within the first hundred days of his administration was a considerable political risk. With the Executive Order, he made a political pledge to the Peace Corps and endorsed its general direction consonant with the Report's recommendations. He also focused public attention on the new agency. The *New York Times* and most of the other major dailies devoted lead articles to the Peace Corps' establishment.[58] If the popular reaction to the Executive Order was an accurate indicator, then Shriver had been correct in his Report to Kennedy that the Peace Corps was the type of initiative for which "people here and abroad have long been waiting."[59]

The period between November 1960 and March 1961 had been vital for the Peace Corps. In that short time, an idea had developed from political embryo to birth. The major administrators in the Peace Corps' early history had also taken the stage: Shriver, Wofford, Wiggins, and Josephson. In addition, *The*

Towering Task and "The Report to the President" had supplied the new agency with a basic philosophy and mode of operation. As Shriver and the others surveyed the scene in March 1961, they knew that many difficulties had still to be faced. The details of how the Peace Corps was to function—and even of who was to be its leader—had still to be decided. Yet, they took satisfaction in the knowledge that the single biggest problem had already been overcome: the Peace Corps had been launched.

4

A Special Identity

Your decision to preserve the special identity of the
Peace Corps by making it a semi-autonomous agency
in the State Department seems important and right.
—Harris Wofford, organizer and associate
director of the Peace Corps (memorandum to
President Kennedy, May 25, 1961)

THE FIRST DIRECTOR

In his "Report to the President" of February 1961, Sargent
Shriver specifically suggested the names of several well-qualified
academics to be leaders of the Peace Corps. Among these were
Eugene Rostow of Yale, Carroll Wilson of MIT, Gilbert White
of the University of Chicago, and Clark Kerr of UCLA. All had
had experience with small overseas service programs involving
the training or placement of American students in the Third
World.[1] Kennedy, however, rejected all of Shriver's nominees.
He wanted the Peace Corps to be an adventurous foreign policy
initiative and he did not feel that a "bookish" type of leader would
be consonant with that ethos.[2] He pressed Shriver to accept the
position.

Kennedy knew that Shriver was young enough (forty-four)
to endow the Peace Corps with the vital image which he hoped
it might project. He was also bright, handsome and, in the ter-
minology of the New Frontier, "vigorous." Moreover, he was
a respected figure in the world of education, business, and civil
liberties, and his family ties to Kennedy would give the Peace

Corps a much-needed visibility; the appointment of his brother-in-law as Director would also indicate the President's personal interest in the undertaking. These factors, as well as Shriver's sterling work as head of the Task Force, made him an appealing choice. Shriver, however, was reluctant to accept the offer. Abraham Ribicoff, secretary of Health, Education and Welfare, had already proposed to Kennedy that Shriver should be appointed as his undersecretary; but Shriver, sensitive to the charge of nepotism, had advised the President against this.[3]

Since the Peace Corps had been established as an executive agency, the appointment of its Director did not require Senate confirmation, and Kennedy's aides proposed that none should be sought. This gave Shriver most cause for concern. As he explained to Kennedy:

> It would be a serious mistake, in my judgment, to appoint me as Director of the Peace Corps, which is now a full-fledged agency, and then make me the only agency head in the government *not* approved by the Senate. This is not good for the agency, the people in it, or for me. When I do have to face Congress in May, June or July, they'll be tougher then—and they will have no responsibility for having O.K.'d me now.[4]

Shriver suggested that the President should select "another person to head the Peace Corps which is now well-organized, well-manned, and aimed in the right direction." But Kennedy wanted Shriver. He agreed that Senate confirmation should be sought.

On March 4, the appointment of Sargent Shriver as first Director of the Peace Corps was announced, subject to Senate confirmation. Warren Wiggins was made Director *ad interim*. On May 21, Shriver made a successful appearance before the Senate Foreign Relations Committee and his appointment was confirmed. The committee hearing was a formality; but looking toward the imminent Peace Corps legislation, Shriver had sensed the importance of paying attention to political etiquette. His deference helped allay fears that had been raised by the Executive Order. More importantly, it was to pay dividends when the Peace Corps went to Capitol Hill later in the year. As for the nepotism charge, it never became an issue.

THE SEARCH FOR STAFF

In his "Work Plan for March, 1961," Shriver outlined his main objectives for the Peace Corps' first month.[5] His "Fourteen Points" (as his plan was nicknamed by his staff) formed a comprehensive summary of necessary tasks to be performed, from the development of pilot country programs to the presentation of legislation to Congress. As yet, however, Shriver had no organization with which to achieve these goals. As one Task Force member told him: "Much of the skeleton has yet to be fleshed out before our creature can walk like a man."[6]

Kennedy's Executive Order had given the Peace Corps governmental authority, $1.5 million from the President's discretionary fund, and some office space on the sixth floor of the International Cooperation Administration's Maiatico building at 806 Connecticut Avenue; this building, a few hundred yards across Lafayette Park from the White House, had also served as the headquarters of the Marshall Plan. Aside from these bare necessities, the Peace Corps had no desks, stationery, organizational plans, or Volunteers. Since there was not enough working space in the Maiatico building for secretaries, typists, and other support staff, additional rooms had to be rented in the nearby Rochembeau Hotel. Shriver wrote his first memoranda on paper borrowed from his last place of employment, the Merchandise Mart in Chicago. Edwin Bayley, the Peace Corps' newly appointed press secretary, described the general chaos of those first few days as "all hell broke loose."[7]

On March 2, Shriver began his search for staff. One of his first recruits was John D. Young, deputy-director of the National Aeronautics and Space Administration (NASA), who had helped set up NASA and other government agencies. NASA granted him a month's leave of absence to help put the Peace Corps together. Young knew his way around the Washington bureaucracy and within a few days he had not only acquired logistical supplies, but had also prepared one of the crucial memoranda in Peace Corps history: "Basic Concepts for Peace Corps Interim Organization."[8]

Sensing that much of Shriver's time would be taken up with

high-level meetings, congressional and press duties, Young first recommended the appointment of a deputy-director to whom Shriver could delegate the day-to day problems of programming, management, and general operation. Next, he urged the creation of a central office for the planning and development of overseas programs. He said that this office should have the power to decide not only where projects would be established, but what their nature and objectives should be. He also advised the establishment of an internal "evaluation" unit to analyze all aspects of operations. He felt that separate divisions would be necessary to deal with private voluntary agency and university participation in the Peace Corps. The all-important recruitment and general publicity functions would be handled by an office of public affairs. Lastly, Young outlined the *sine qua non* of any government organization, the management division. He pointed out that no organization could expect to survive without someone to take care of budgetary, personnel, and administrative matters. He stressed, however, that if these management services were made responsive enough, they could be kept to a minimum.[9] Young's memorandum and line-and-staff chart of March 8 became the touchstone of the Peace Corps' organizational thinking, especially its emphasis on minimal levels of management and bureaucracy. It was exactly what Shriver had wanted: a solid structure that left plenty of scope for individual initiative and creativity.

To help Shriver with the administration of the new agency, several members of the Task Force stayed on. Wiggins took over the essential function of planning and development of overseas programs; Josephson began drafting congressional legislation; Gordon Boyce, capitalizing on his experience with the Experiment in International Living, started contacting private voluntary agencies; and Al Sims, a former director of the International Education Institute's exchange programs, worked on establishing a relationship with universities and educational institutions. Meanwhile, Harris Wofford had taken up a salient position between the Peace Corps and the White House. In early February, Kennedy had asked Wofford to become his special assistant for civil rights. Wofford accepted, but only on the condition that he could continue to devote half his time to the Peace Corps.

Kennedy agreed. With one foot in Connecticut Avenue and the other in Pennsylvania Avenue, Wofford served as an effective channel of communications between the Peace Corps and the President.

Shriver was relentless in his talent hunt for the Peace Corps. When he was looking for a top-class psychologist to develop standards for the crucial function of selecting Volunteers, Nicholas Hobbs (who had served on the faculties of Harvard, Columbia and other universities) was recommended to him. Hobbs, at that time working on a multi-million dollar research project, received Shriver's call in Tennessee. "How much time do I have to decide?" he asked. "Twenty minutes," said Shriver. Twenty minutes later, Hobbs booked a flight to Washington.[10]

Shriver's interviewing style was discursive and provocative. Sometimes he presented interviewees with Max Millikan's report and treated approval of its guarded recommendations as grounds for immediate rejection. Shriver also informed applicants that he had no idea when or how Peace Corps staff would be paid. Thomas Quimby, a successful interviewee, recalled that "Shriver did not want anyone around who was going to be too cautious."[11]

The new Peace Corps Director could be very persuasive. Charles Peters, a state legislator and former worker for the Kennedy campaign in West Virginia, recalled that when Shriver asked him to come to Washington he thought he would "just come up for about three months to share in the exciting task of getting the New Frontier started." Peters stayed with the Peace Corps for five years and, as chief of the evaluation division, became one of the most important figures in the agency's development.[12]

More people applied for staff positions with the Peace Corps than all other federal organizations put together. Shriver's extraordinary style attracted a talented, unusually adventurous group. Among them were Morris Abram, a prominent attorney in Georgia who helped with legal problems; Quimby, chairman of the Democratic National Committee in Michigan who dealt with Volunteer recruitment; Bradley Patterson, an assistant secretary to the cabinet in the Eisenhower administration who established the Peace Corps' secretariat; William Haddad, a prize-winning journalist with the *New York Post* who took on a "special projects" portfolio, with power to research and evaluate all Peace Corps functions; and William Kelly, a former NASA administrator who took on the challenge of how to transport Volunteers from the United States to all corners of the earth. Shriver recruited from inside and outside government circles, ability being the sole criterion. This deliberate policy of using professional bureaucrats like Wiggins, Josephson, Young, and Kelly, as well as uninitiated "laymen" such as Haddad, Peters, Boyce, and Sims, endowed the Peace Corps with a beneficial mix of experience and freshness. It also created no little amount of tension.

At the White House, Wofford heard a rumor that Bill Moyers, the young star of Vice-President Johnson's staff, was eager to get involved with the Peace Corps. Moyers had told Johnson during the campaign that if Kennedy instituted the Peace Corps then that was where he wanted to work. Wofford contacted Moyers and set up an interview with Shriver, thus sparking a minor brouhaha with the White House staff. Moyers was a key man in the Kennedy-Johnson liaison, and the President's aides did not want to lose him. Wofford received an angry call from Kenneth O'Donnell, special assistant to the President. "What the hell are you doing?" O'Donnell exploded. "Moyers is the only man around the Vice-President who we can deal with that we like and trust, and we want to keep him right here."[13]

Kennedy and Johnson went to great lengths to persuade Moyers to stay, but they were unsuccessful. Moyers, twenty-six in 1961, was determined to participate in the Peace Corps. "That boy [Moyers] cajoled and begged and pleaded and connived and threatened and politicked to leave me to go to work for the Peace Corps," recalled Johnson in later days.[14] White House aides regarded Moyers's departure as an act of piracy and throughout the Kennedy years the Peace Corps had the reputation of enticing people away from other government organizations. Named a special consultant to the Peace Corps on March 14, Moyers went on to join Shriver, Wofford, Wiggins, and Josephson as one of the major architects of the new organization. By 1963, he had become deputy-director of the Peace Corps—the youngest official to hold such a high-level position in the history of American governmental institutions.

SHRIVERIZING

To Shriver, the early days of the Peace Corps were "like the campaign of 1960—but with no election in sight." Letters and reports poured in from all over the country and the elevators disgorged constant sorties of "interested persons, newspaper reporters, job seekers, academic figures, and generous citizens offering advice."[15] Some prospective staff members left after a few days of working at the furious pace. Urgency forced the Peace Corps' new administrators to cut through established procedure and, sometimes, to violate regulations. After a mere fifteen days, twenty-two illegal actions had been counted.[16]

Shriver established routine meetings for his senior officials on every Monday, Wednesday, and Friday; on Tuesdays and Thursdays meetings were open to all staff. During those conferences in the months of March and April, Shriver and his team "hammered out basic policies in long, detailed discussions."[17] A wide range of issues had to be decided regarding Volunteers' medical protection abroad, taxes, insurance, and material support. Some favored the idea of a uniform for Volunteers; others suggested a Peace Corps oath should be taken before serving overseas. Regarding Volunteers' accommodation, Shriver was asked whether he was serious about the "mud hut" approach to Peace Corps service.[18]

As far as the Washington organization was concerned, decisions had to be taken on staff ratios, response to mail, information output, coordination with other government agencies, and the form and timing of the Peace Corps' congressional presentation. The question of staff was one of the more sensitive issues. John Kenneth Galbraith, Kennedy's ambassador to India, advised a ceiling of $10,000 on salaries.[19] Shriver agreed in principle that there should not be a huge gap between Volunteers' allowance and staff remuneration. At the same time, he wanted to recruit the best possible staff members; it was likely that many would be married with financial obligations and unable to afford a drastic cut in their income. For that reason, Shriver decided against the low ceiling on salaries. He insisted, however, that overseas staff should forego luxurious housing, ostentatious automobiles, extra allowance for "hardship posts," and the various trappings of diplomatic privilege. Josephson agreed with Shriver that Peace Corps officials should live, and be seen to live, in a simpler manner than their compatriots in the U.S. embassy compound and expatriate clubs. Just the same, he wondered whether a policy of not granting hardship post allowances might not itself be a little hard. He reminded Shriver that in some developing countries the cost of living could be very high. "Toothpaste costs $3 a tube in Conarky," he noted.[20] Shriver stood by his decision.

Meanwhile, Josephson had begun tackling the legal complexities involved in establishing the policies and conditions of Peace Corps service. "There was an enormous amount of work to be done," Josephson recalled, "very dull administrative legal work—writing delegations of authority, getting the fiscal process going, getting the administrative process going, getting the personnel process going, getting the procurement process going."[21] In early March, Josephson and his colleague, Morris Abram, overcame one of the most controversial policy problems: whether Volunteers should be exempt from the draft.

Despite Kennedy's statement on March 1 that the Peace Corps would not be a substitute for military service, the precise legal position remained somewhat fuzzy, and Nixon's earlier remarks about "draft-dodgers" continued to niggle. Josephson and Abram sought to clarify this issue once and for all. Abram arranged a meeting with General Lewis B. Hershey, director of the Selective Service. Noting that Volunteers would be "in service" to their country, Hershey agreed that their deferment from the military draft would be appropriate. According to Josephson, Hershey wrote his decision on a brown paper bag, which was all he had at hand as he traveled with Abram in his car; their discussion took all of two minutes.[22] This quick solution to the draft problem allowed Shriver to make an unequivocal public statement to the effect that Volunteers would be deferred, but not exempted, from military service. This finally killed the draft-dodging charge.

In later years, Josephson claimed that the draft was really a false issue used by Nixon and other critics of the Peace Corps for political reasons.[23] In the early 1960s, few Americans were called up for military service; only when involvement in Vietnam escalated under President Johnson did the pressures on the manpower pool begin to have any bearing on the Peace Corps. In the Kennedy era, selective service deferment was not a substantial factor in motivating young Americans to join the Peace Corps. Much more important to the ten thousand would-be Volunteers who had written to the Peace Corps by the end of March was the new agency's inherently exciting ethos. C. Payne Lucas, a young administrator who joined the staff in 1961, described those early days of the Peace Corps as "a massive orgasm—that was exactly what it was like here. We were dabbling in foreign affairs, catching planes, and learning foreign languages."[24]

This spirit of adventure and informality was personified by Shriver. A newcomer to government himself, he kept the midnight oil burning and encouraged his staff to follow suit. Secretaries refused to send out letters if they contained even the slightest mistake. "That wasn't good enough for Sarge Shriver," recalled Genoa Godbey, a young typist who joined the Peace Corps in March 1961. When a senior staffer suggested a morning meeting "about 10 o'clock," Shriver shook his head. "By ten, the day is half over," he said.[25] In Kennedy fashion, he disliked weakness or failure; he thought of himself as tough-minded. Signs in his office read "Nice Guys Finish Last" and "Good Guys Don't Win Ball Games."

Shriver proposed, prodded, and elicited opinions from all those around him. In this way, ideas became "Shriverized"—a term used by his staff which meant to enlarge, to speed up, to apply greater imagination. Wofford felt that Shriver "empowered people. He released their energies, backed their efforts and drew on their insights."[26] Once an assignment was set, Shriver expected a staff member to run with it, as he would do himself. With his backing, it seemed possible to overcome obstacles which otherwise might have been insurmountable. To many, Shriver's charisma was irresistible. As C. Payne Lucas put it: "There were those of us who came in in the morning just to wait outside the door so we could all ride up on the elevator with Sarge."[27]

THE BATTLE FOR INDEPENDENCE

On March 6, 1961, Undersecretary of State Chester Bowles informed Kennedy that there was "wide agreement on the necessity and importance of the Peace Corps maintaining its own separate identity." Bowles suggested that any organizational plans should be kept "sufficiently flexible so that the Peace Corps may move in the most productive directions which time and experience dictate."[28] As yet, however, there was no consensus within the federal bureaucracy as to the Peace Corps' status. Moreover, such was the ferocity of feeling against the new agency becoming independent of the general foreign assistance program that a bitter bureaucratic battle ensued.

Shriver's Report had warned that "Beginning the Peace Corps as another ICA operation runs the risk of losing its new appeal."[29] He never intended the Peace Corps to be completely separate from the State Department, but, as he told Secretary of State Dean Rusk, he did not want it identified by the public, by Congress, or by foreign countries as just "another foreign aid resource like Development Loans or Food for Peace." Shriver reminded Rusk that when Kennedy had first talked about the Peace Corps he had implied that it would be "an identifiable, visible body of people, a corps in the fullest sense of the word with an esprit de corps all its own." Shriver insisted that it should not be seen as part of existing foreign aid programs but rather clearly identified at home and abroad as "President Kennedy's Peace Corps."[30]

As early as February 19, Josephson had argued strongly that the Peace Corps should not be linked in any way to the traditional foreign aid establishment which was associated with "boondoggles" by many congressmen and with "imperialism" by many Third World leaders.[31] In March, Kennedy proposed to reorganize the entire U.S. foreign assistance program and incorporate all the government's economic and social development initiatives—including ICA, the Development Loan Fund, and Food for Peace—into one huge new bureaucratic unit which he called the Agency for International Development (AID). It seemed logical that the Peace Corps should have its home there. But throughout March and April, Peace Corps officials resisted being subsumed into AID.

Within government circles, a weighty body of opinion felt threatened by the prospect of untrained young Americans going into the Third World. Moreover, as Bill Moyers observed: "The old-line employees of State and AID coveted the Peace Corps greedily. It was natural instinct; established bureaucracies do not like competition from new people."[32] Henry Labouisse, head of ICA, feared that sending inexperienced youngsters into strange cultures would be inviting disaster and embarrassment. He proposed that the Peace Corps should be placed under the firm control of AID where its progress could be strictly monitored.[33] One assistant secretary of state let it be known that not only were many diplomats indifferent to the Peace Corps but that in some quarters there was outright opposition. Career diplomat Elliot O. Briggs described the Peace Corps' team cry as "Yoo-hoo, yoo-hoo. Let's go out and wreak some good on the natives."[34]

This bureaucratic skepticism did not apply to Dean Rusk. He told Shriver that he thought the Peace Corps idea first-class. "The plan is practical, experimental, does not promise the moon to anybody and we should get underway with it right away," he said. Chester Bowles also pledged his assistance "in every possible way."[35] Despite the support of these influential figures, the intransigence of an exceedingly powerful group of experienced bureaucrats had yet to be overcome. Moyers later recalled that "they couldn't outright oppose the Peace Corps because it had such high visibility with the President. So they did the next best thing: they sought to absorb it."[36]

The first real problem arose in late March over Kennedy's proposed special message to Congress on foreign aid. When shown the first draft of Kennedy's proposed speech, Shriver was horrified to note that the President was fully intending to locate the Peace Corps in AID. When Shriver attended a White House meeting on how AID would work, he was shown a large chart of the new super-agency, with control lines to the major operations involving billions of dollars. Over in a small section on the far right were programs called "resources." The Peace Corps was one of them.[37]

Shriver sent a memorandum to the President arguing the case for independence. Kennedy's aides, Goodwin, Dungan, and Sorensen, claimed it was only logical to place all overseas aid, including the Peace Corps, under one umbrella. Kennedy was undecided. Consequently, his speech on foreign aid on March 22 was vague regarding the Peace Corps' organizational status. Citing the Peace Corps as one of the "flexible tools" of the new American foreign assistance program, he said that far from being submerged, its "distinctive identity and appeal" would be preserved.[38] Shriver's petition to his brother-in-law had won the Peace Corps a reprieve, or so it seemed.

On March 24, Shriver wrote to Goodwin and explained that congressional leaders had expressed "strong opinions that Peace Corps legislation should be introduced separately and before the general foreign aid bill."[39] Arguing that the Peace Corps would have a better chance in Congress if it were not tied to foreign aid appropriations, Shriver strongly reiterated the case for independence. It soon appeared that his efforts had been in vain.

On March 30, Kennedy told Shriver that Labouisse had been appointed chairman of a task force which would set about incorporating all foreign aid programs, including the Peace Corps, into AID. Kennedy warned Shriver that he expected Labouisse to be accorded "complete cooperation."[40] The task force on foreign aid met on a number of occasions, but scheduled its final meeting for April 26. On that day, Kennedy himself would decide the Peace Corps' fate. The timing of the meeting could not have been worse for the Peace Corps. Shriver had already been advised by Kennedy that he should attempt to persuade Third World leaders of the Peace Corps' viability by visiting several developing countries; his trip was due to begin four days before the decision on the independence of the Peace Corps.

Throughout April, Shriver lobbied Sorensen, Dungan, and Labouisse and tried to persuade them of the absolute necessity of Peace Corps autonomy. He told them that he wanted to avoid going directly to the President on this issue, but he let it be known that, if he had to, he would. Labouisse objected even to the possibility of Shriver using his personal relationship with Kennedy. He wanted this battle fought under the traditional rules of the bureaucratic game; in his view, an invocation to the President on a personal basis was not fair play. Shriver replied to Labouisse in a strongly worded memorandum:

> I agree that we should, if at all possible, avoid troubling the President at this time. I believe, however, that although organizational, these issues about the future place and role of the Peace Corps are of such fundamental importance that he ought to participate in their resolution. His espousal of the Peace Corps notion in the course of his campaign was an important political commitment, and he has a genuine personal interest in the success of the Peace Corps as well.[41]

Shriver noted that he had consulted with Vice-President Johnson and other legislative leaders and they had advised that "it would be a grave political mistake for the Peace Corps to be authorized at the same time and as but one of the categories of assistance in the new foreign aid bill." He also took a blast against "conceptual and organizational neatness."

Shriver sent a copy of this memorandum directly to the President. Then he embarked upon his journey to the Third World.[42] Shriver had now done all he could to gain independence for the Peace Corps.

Kennedy did not chair the meeting on April 26. All his time at this juncture was taken up with the repercussions of the Bay of Pigs fiasco.* Instead, he designated an assistant, Ralph Dungan, to act for him. Labouisse and David Bell, director of the Bureau of the Budget, recommended that the Peace Corps should be a subdivision of AID. Wiggins and Josephson, representing the Peace Corps, disagreed, and argued that the only advantage of this arrangement was bureaucratic tidiness. Dungan decided in

---

*On April 17, 1961, a force of fifteen hundred Cuban exiles landed at Cochinos Bay in southern Cuba in an attempt to overthrow the government of Fidel Castro. The project was planned by the CIA during the last months of the Eisenhower administration, but was finally approved by Kennedy. The CIA assured him that the Cuban populace would rise up against Castro. No such uprising took place and when Kennedy refused to commit American military forces to support the exiles, the operation proved to be a debacle. By April 20, the invaders had been either killed or captured. Castro's prestige and popularity in the Third World rose, while Kennedy's fell as he accepted full responsibility for the failure. Critics charged that Kennedy's inexperience in foreign affairs was to blame.

favor of incorporation. A dismayed Josephson took notes during the meeting: "Mr. Dungan said that the Peace Corps was not an extra-governmental thing. He said that the Peace Corps could not be favored or given extraordinary treatment at the expense of overall government considerations."[43]

Wiggins cabled a few dispirited words to Shriver, who at this time was in India. "Peace Corps not, repeat not, to have autonomy," he wrote. "Dungan describes himself as acting on behalf of the President."[44] Shriver later recalled his feelings upon reading Wiggins's message as he sat in his hotel room in New Delhi: "I remember just sitting there for some time . . . holding the bad news in my hands and feeling helpless. I was convinced a terrible mistake had been made, that the Peace Corps was about to die a-borning."[45]

Wiggins and Josephson suspected that Dungan had not been an entirely objective adjudicator. There was some evidence that he had intercepted Shriver's memorandum to the President and had prevented it from reaching him. Like Labouisse, Dungan believed the Peace Corps should be part of AID and that the President need not be troubled by the arguments of amateurs. Josephson blamed himself for being "innocent in the extreme" when confronted by wily, bureaucratic infighters. In despair at the defeat, he described the Peace Corps' mood in late April as "neurotic and leaderless."[46] He fired off a memorandum to the President arguing that many Americans would not have volunteered for the Peace Corps had they imagined it was going to be just another part of the U.S. assistance program. Abroad too, he said, leaders like Nehru, Nkrumah, and Nyerere would be willing to accept the idea of a Peace Corps where they would not accept other U.S. international efforts.[47] His words fell on deaf ears.

As a last-ditch effort, Shriver cabled Wiggins and told him to ask Vice-President Johnson if he would intercede on behalf of the Peace Corps. Bill Moyers took on the crucial role here. The Vice-President was fond of remarking that in all his years in Congress he had never had a more capable aide than Moyers. For his part, Moyers knew that Johnson had been a director of the National Youth Administration during the New Deal, had made a speech on a Peace Corps-type program during the 1960 campaign, and had been recently appointed by Kennedy as first chairman of the Peace Corps National Advisory Council (an honorary, bipartisan body consisting of prominent Americans). Moyers played upon LBJ's sympathy for the Peace Corps idea and arranged a meeting for him with Wiggins and Josephson. In later years, Moyers recalled the gist of Johnson's advice against accepting Dungan's decision:

> Boys, this town is full of folks who believe the only way to do something is their way. That's especially true in diplomacy and things like that, because they work with foreign governments and protocol is oh-so-mighty important to them, with guidebooks and rulebooks and do's-and-don'ts to keep you from offending someone. You put the Peace Corps into the foreign service and they'll put striped pants on your people when all you want them to have is a knapsack and a tool kit and a lot of imagination. And they'll give you a hundred and one reasons why it won't work every time you want to do something different."[48]

Johnson agreed that if the Peace Corps became part of AID it would lose its unique appeal to young people, become entangled in red tape, and end up nothing more than "just another box in an organizational chart, reporting to a third assistant director of personnel for the State Department."[49]

Johnson then called Kennedy and asked for a private meeting. It was arranged for May 1. As Josephson later described it, Johnson, on his way to the Oval Office, "picked up Henry Labouisse and Dave Bell by their respective ears and began telling them what the foreign aid program really should do. It should be healing the sick and the lame and the blind—very earthy, pithy stuff . . . very close to what Peace Corps Volunteers could and would do."[50] No formal record was kept of the conversation between Kennedy and Johnson. The story soon emerged, however, that, as Josephson told it: "Johnson collared Kennedy . . . and in the course of the conversation badgered him so much that Kennedy finally said all right."[51]

Kennedy's reversal of Dungan's earlier verdict was confirmed by a terse memorandum from Dungan to Dean Rusk on May 2: "This is to inform you that yesterday evening the President, in consultation with the Vice-President, decided that the Peace

Corps should be organized as a semi-autonomous unit within the Department of State and that the Director of the Corps would have an Assistant Secretary status and would report directly to the Secretary of State."[52] A front-page headline in the *New York Times* sent a much clearer signal: "Peace Corps Wins Fight for Autonomy." Somehow, the whole story of the Peace Corps' battle for independence had been leaked to the press, much to the embarrassment of Labouisse, Dungan, and several other Kennedy aides. "The President's decision followed a two-month tug-of-war within the administration," noted *New York Times* reporter Peter Braestrup. "For Peace Corps officials, it was an important victory."[53]

Harris Wofford rated the winning of independence as "the biggest early decision" in Peace Corps history.[54] Certainly it had far-reaching implications. Dungan, Bell, Labouisse and others who had been opposed to the Peace Corps "independistes" were extremely annoyed at the unusual methods which Shriver and his team had used to achieve their objectives. Deploying Vice-President Johnson was considered particularly sharp practice. A few days after Kennedy's reversal decision, Dungan met with Josephson at the White House and informed him, in no uncertain terms, of his displeasure. Josephson remembered Dungan saying something to the effect of "If we wanted to go it alone — we were really going to go it alone."[55]

From the time of the battle for independence, there was always a certain coolness between the White House staff and the Peace Corps. On the positive side, however, Lyndon Johnson became a staunch advocate of the new agency and took a prolonged and serious interest in its well-being. Referring to Johnson's inestimable contribution to the winning of independence, Shriver praised him as "a founding father of the Peace Corps."[56]

The most significant consequence of independence was that it left the Peace Corps free to develop outside the constricting boundaries of a huge bureaucracy. It was regarded as a "different" type of government body, separate and apart with a life and identity of its own. As Moyers described it, "A remarkable manifestation of a spirit too particular and personal to be contained by a bureaucratic organization."[57] A delighted Wofford praised Kennedy for his decision to preserve the special identity and fresh appeal of the Peace Corps by making it a semi-autonomous agency: "Our best advisers warned against the Peace Corps slipping into the established patterns of foreign aid," Wofford wrote. "The Peace Corps' people-to-people approach and educational emphasis offers an opportunity to create a new pattern. For this it needs the freedom and energy of autonomy."[58]

AMONG THE BELIEVERS—AND UNBELIEVERS

While the Peace Corps battled for its independence within the government bureaucracy, *Life* reported that "the hottest topic on college campuses and among young people generally . . . was neither studies nor panty raids, but President Kennedy's Peace Corps." According to the magazine, the majority of students were strongly in favor of the Peace Corps: "Their earnest debates proved that their generation was not silent, selfish and conformist, as has often been charged, but world-minded, idealistic and responsive."[59] A poll in early April revealed that 68 percent of the public supported the Peace Corps. Another survey undertaken by the American Council on Education showed 94 percent of college students in favor.[60] A few days after the President's Executive Order had made the idea a reality, letters of support for the Peace Corps flowed into the White House from all over the country, nearly five thousand arriving the single day after the Executive Order was issued.[61]

On university and college campuses in particular, the response was ecstatic. The *Guardsman* of San Francisco City College observed: "Campaign platforms, it has been said, are to get in on, not to stand on. Be this as it may, one prominent plank in the platform of President Kennedy is now in the process of becoming reality."[62] The students claimed that the establishment of the Peace Corps proved that Kennedy was not just another politician who used an issue in a campaign and then forgot about it after election day. Fairleigh Dickinson University in New Jersey proposed a plan to offer academic credit and grants for those interested in Peace Corps service. Hundreds of students at New York University sent a 28-foot-long telegram to Shriver requesting that a project be prepared on their campus. By June, over 150 educational establishments and the National Student Association had made similar offers. A conference of twelve eastern colleges decided to send a resolution to the Organization of American States endorsing the Peace Corps.[63]

In the U.S. Senate, Democrat Alan Bible was contacted by the University of Nevada and told of the enthusiasm for the Peace Corps in his home constituency. The American Institute of Foreign Trade in Arizona also indicated its strong interest to Republican Barry Goldwater. Private foundations and industries in New York began to urge Senator Kenneth Keating to back the Peace Corps. In March, Hubert Humphrey told his colleagues in Congress that the twelve thousand inquiries which had already reached the Peace Corps offered proof that public support for Kennedy's proposal was overwhelming.[64]

Shriver claimed that a dozen countries had shown "some interest" in the Peace Corps and the *New York Times* noted that the Washington embassies of Brazil, Nigeria, Colombia, and South Vietnam had given early endorsements. In Europe, Mayor Willy Brandt of Berlin lauded the concept. In Britain, it was praised by both Labour and Conservative members of Parliament. *Newsweek* reported that Prime Minister Harold Macmillan was so enthusiastic about the Peace Corps that he had asked President Kennedy to include a British contingent among the first group to go overseas.[65] Meanwhile, Shriver gave press conferences, wrote articles for national magazines, and worked at keeping up momentum. This was necessary since not everyone had been converted to the Peace Corps. Indeed, a significant element of skepticism remained.

In April, Kennedy received a confidential Harris poll showing that although the balance of public opinion was 2:1 in favor of the Peace Corps, it was a far cry from the overall 10:1 which the administration enjoyed generally. The poll predicted that the Peace Corps would arouse deep divisions within the country; it would attract the support of young people and others sensitive to the Third World's development problems, but conservatives would attack it as "a dead ringer for the National Youth Administration, the Works Projects Administration and several other New Deal experiments." Looking ahead to 1964 and re-election prospects, the poll pointed out that although the Peace Corps would inspire important segments of Kennedy's constituency, it would also "solidify more than any other measure to date, the opposition of support that unquestionably will be lost in a re-election situation in 1964."[66]

Rather than pack off "our evangelical youth" to the developing countries, the New Republic suggested that the United States should send substantial amounts of what really mattered: money. Many skeptics were quick to pronounce the Peace Corps a second "children's crusade," or Kennedy's Kiddie Korps. The Daughters of the American Revolution passed a resolution at their 70th Continental Congress urging U.S. legislators to kill the Peace Corps bill, and the Young Republican National Federation issued a statement strongly objecting to it. Even the generally supportive New York Times warned that the new organization should not degenerate into a public relations exercise aimed at combatting the image of the Ugly American.[67]

At a conference sponsored by the Rockefeller Fund, Peace Corps officials sensed great suspicion of Kennedy's new agency stemming from the behavior of past government programs which had not consulted with the major private institutions. Morris Abram advised Shriver that he must break down this pessimistic attitude by personally talking to foundation heads; in the meantime Abram predicted little help would be forthcoming from that area. Carroll Wilson of MIT also informed Shriver of skepticism and indifference within the academic world. He warned that this would have to be alleviated if the Peace Corps was to function effectively.[68]

More worrisome than the dissenters at home were the unbelievers overseas. President Madibo Keita of Mali commented that while the Peace Corps might be of some value to young Americans, it would probably be ineffective in the help it could offer the developing countries. At a conference on Africa at New York University, Averell Harriman, United States ambassador-at-large, noted that the strong interest in the Peace Corps was tinged with skepticism. Arthur Schlesinger also was informed that labor union delegates from India, Pakistan, Sri Lanka, and Turkey were "skeptical of the Peace Corps' eventual success."[69]

A Burmese student, Khin Khin Kla, wrote an open letter to all prospective Volunteers in the *New York Herald Tribune*. "Will you be able to take all this?" he questioned:

> You will live in a small wooden house, sleep on the floor on a bamboo mat, with a pillow stuffed with rice grain and a mosquito net to protect you from the swarms of bloodthirsty mosquitoes. The heavy, humid heat and the hard bed will not be comfortable . . . you will suffer from the damp weather . . . leeches will cling to you; worms, frogs and snakes will be numerous.[70]

The Washington correspondent of the respected *Times of India* also wondered whether America's mollycoddled youth, accustomed to air-conditioned houses, fast-food, and gas-guzzling cars would be able to "suffer the Indian summer smilingly and, if they go into an Indian village, will they be able to sleep on unsprung beds under the canopy of the bejeweled sky or indoors in mud huts, without writing home about it?"[71] The *Tanzanian Standard* described the Peace Corps as consisting of thousands of ill-trained students who would "pour into underdeveloped countries . . . spreading peace and the American way of life"; a sarcastic editorial suggested that Volunteers could be put to better "educative" use in the corn-growing belt of America's Midwest.

These doubting opinions were reflected in the faint response to the Peace Corps from Third World governments. Despite Kennedy's publicly expressed hope that "those countries which are interested in understanding our country and traditions will welcome these young men and women," not a single formal invitation had come from abroad by the end of March. Shriver quoted the skeptics as saying: "Go ahead with your idealistic ventures; Americans have always oversimplified foreign affairs. The Peace Corps is no exception. Waste your monies and your energies but don't expect us to attach much significance to your effort."[72]

Kennedy and Shriver knew that if the Peace Corps were ever to become a going concern, Third World leaders would have to be persuaded that it was an important American initiative. More than dislike or distrust, Shriver felt the problem was one of indifference. In 1961, the governments of the newly emerging countries wanted capital flows for their development plans. In this context, they simply did not think the Peace Corps very significant. To change this perspective, Kennedy suggested Shriver should go to some of the developing countries and personally inform heads of state about the nature and potential value of the Peace Corps. Kennedy also felt the trip would give Shriver the chance of seeing at first hand the conditions under which Volunteers would live and work and the jobs they might do.[73]

On April 22, Shriver began a twenty-six-day venture in personal diplomacy that took him to Ghana, Nigeria, Pakistan, India, Burma, Malaysia, Thailand, and the Philippines. Accompanied by Harris Wofford, Ed Bayley, Bill Kelly, and Franklin Williams, he conferred at length with leading foreign ministers and cabinet members as well as with American technical assistance officers and embassy staffs. Not all the leaders with whom the Peace Corps' emissaries met were instant converts to the idea.

President Kwame Nkrumah of Ghana, then the leading spokesman for African nationalism, was concerned about the Peace Corps being used for CIA infiltration of his country. However, he was also well aware that Ghana's development depended on having a steady supply of teachers of English, the language of Ghanaian secondary and higher education. There were not yet enough Ghanaians to fill the need. "Peace Corps Volunteers who will teach, but not propagandize or spy or try to subvert the Ghanaian system will be very welcome," said Nkrumah. But he stressed that he only wanted the most highly qualified Americans and was reluctant to accept "ordinary" graduates.[74]

In Nigeria, President Nnamdi Azikiwe also saw a place for Peace Corps Volunteers in his development plans, so long as they were qualified and would behave themselves. There were places in Nigeria's elementary schools for only fourteen thousand children out of the more than two million who were eligible. An official commission had identified a shortage of an estimated seven thousand man-years of teachers for the remainder of the decade. As Wofford later noted: "Great oil resources were awaiting development, and the prospects for the future looked bright if Nigerians could be trained fast enough and educated well enough to know how to manage a complex economy and create a modern society."[75] Azikiwe could build the schools, but he knew that in the short-to-medium-term, most of the teachers would have to come from overseas and speak English, the official language of instruction. Peace Corps Volunteers could fill this need.

In Pakistan, President Ayub Khan wondered whether Volunteers would be able to implement rural public works and irrigation projects.[76] In Burma, U Nu asked Shriver whether he really believed that young Americans could compete with Chinese Communists who had already offered "revolutionary" assistance.[77] But it was India, with its half billion people and leading role among the non-aligned developing countries, that was the hardest and most critical test of the trip. Ambassador Galbraith in New Delhi anticipated great trouble in selling the Peace Corps to Jawaharlal Nehru, the first prime minister of independent India. As in the other countries, however, Shriver's engaging personal style and powers of persuasion overcame Nehru's initial reservations. That Shriver was Kennedy's brother-in-law also helped to win privileges and concessions for the Peace Corps at this early stage which might otherwise have taken months or even years of diplomatic maneuvering to achieve. Galbraith described Shriver's style of diplomacy as "just right . . . natural, uncontrived and sincere." Nehru was so impressed that he asked the Peace Corps to send even more Volunteers than either Shriver or Galbraith had dared hope. Galbraith noted in his diary that he left Nehru's office "a little dazed and with my reputation as a strategist in poor condition."[78]

The aborted invasion at the Bay of Pigs had taken place only a week before Shriver's trip. The Cuban debacle undoubtedly shocked those Third World leaders who had believed that the Kennedy administration's foreign policy would be a real departure from the obsessive anti-communism of John Foster Dulles. The situation would have been much worse, however, had Kennedy gone ahead and used massive U.S. military force to overthrow Castro. His restraint had saved his image in the Third World. "There exists a reservoir of goodwill and hope for you in these countries," Wofford told him. "The high expectations for a new American approach to the world which you have aroused in Nkrumah, Nehru and U Nu, to name three important cases, are a great opportunity."[79] Wofford said that the Peace Corps represented his best hope of taking full advantage of this opportunity.

In May, despite the Bay of Pigs, Shriver returned to Washington with invitations from all eight countries he had visited to send a total of three thousand Volunteers to begin Peace Corps programs. These first few invitations opened the floodgates. Less than one week after Shriver's return from the Third World, Kennedy was able to announce that he had received over two dozen formal requests for Volunteers from various countries.[80] By July, six Peace Corps projects had been announced for Ghana, Tanzania, Colombia, the Philippines, Chile, and St. Lucia; over five thousand applicants had taken the first Peace Corps tests; and soon the first Volunteers would begin training at a field school founded especially for that purpose in Arecibo, Puerto Rico.

Shriver's journey abroad to "invite invitations" was a crucial step in ensuring that the Peace Corps would be successfully established. It not only destroyed the skeptical view that foreign governments would not want young Americans meddling in their internal affairs, but also gave the Peace Corps' organizers an insight into what Third World leaders felt was needed and what they would accept. In the six short months since Kennedy's first announcement of the idea at the Cow Palace, the Peace Corps had found a mission and established an identity.

5

Assault on the Hill

We were determined to make the best impression on
the Congress that anybody had ever made.
—William Josephson, Peace Corps general counsel

POLITICAL SURVIVAL

In the summer of 1961, the Peace Corps' foremost aim was
political survival. If Congress did not make it law and grant
funds, then all would be lost before a single Volunteer got into
the field. To win approval on Capitol Hill, Sargent Shriver would
have to overcome enormous skepticism and even some latent
isolationism. He was highly conscious of Kennedy's political gam-
ble. Many, including Eisenhower and Nixon, had openly derided
the Peace Corps concept; if it failed to pass through Congress,
it would be taken as a sign of the President's inexperience and
reinforce the charge, often made in the campaign, that he was
too young for the job. Despite its noble, international ends, the
Peace Corps' immediate means were inescapably domestic and
political. The jungle of Washington had to be conquered before
any jungles in Ghana or Guatemala.

Democratic Majority Leader Mike Mansfield recalled that
even he had serious doubts about the Peace Corps in the beginning. "I felt that it might be a failure and have adverse repercussions on the administration," he said.[1] The Majority Whip,
Hubert Humphrey, wrote in later years that "while everybody
praises the Peace Corps now . . . anyone who has taken the trouble to look at the votes on the amendments to the Peace Corps

74

proposal at the time we were debating it in Congress or read all the speeches, knows that it wasn't easy."[2]

In his message to Congress on March 1, 1961, Kennedy had emphasized that, at this stage, the Peace Corps was only "temporary," funded from appropriations "currently available for our foreign aid program" and that legislation would follow a "similar approach" to the Humphrey-Reuss proposals of 1960.[3] Despite this cautious and deferential approach, trouble was anticipated for future Peace Corps legislation on the Hill where the very concept of foreign assistance was unpopular. In the same week that Kennedy announced the Peace Corps, the House Committee on Appropriations refused to vote a single dollar of the $150 million in emergency funds that the President had requested to carry out his foreign economic policy.[4]

What made matters worse was that many legislators felt their authority had been usurped by the Executive Order and by the "back-door" funding of the Peace Corps from the President's special contingency supply. "No matter how excellent the Peace Corps idea may be," Senator Wallace F. Bennett, the Republican from Utah, argued, "there is no reason for setting it up in this manner, which evidences such disdain for the constitutional division of powers."[5] A significant number of disgruntled congressmen wrote letters of complaint to the President, and Bill Josephson recalled that there was a "little bad taste in some Committee staff mouths."[6] The Peace Corps had not got off to the best start with Congress and could not afford to be over-optimistic about its legislative chances. To cover the worst of eventualities, Josephson's office prepared, in the spring of 1961, a paper entitled "Authority to Continue a Peace Corps should the Congress *Not* Pass a Peace Corps Act this Session."[7]

SHAPING AND SELLING A BILL

The Executive Order had given the Peace Corps breathing space from seeking appropriations for fiscal year 1961. Between March and June, Shriver and his staff could concentrate on the form of the Peace Corps bill and the congressional strategy to gain appropriations for fiscal year 1962. Josephson remembered the staff's determination to "make the best impression on the Congress that anybody had ever made."[8] In early March, some informal overtures were made to important figures on the Hill. Humphrey and Reuss were the natural choices as floor managers of the legislation in the Senate and House respectively. Humphrey, with his leverage as Majority Whip in the Senate and as an experienced member of the Senate Committee on Foreign Relations, played an especially significant part in nursing the Peace Corps through Congress at delicate moments. His commitment to the Peace Corps ideal was unequivocal and, in his memoir, he described the bill as being "of particular emotional importance to me."[9]

The influential chairman of the Senate Foreign Relations Committee, J. William Fulbright, and the House Foreign Affairs Committee chairman, Thomas Morgan, were also kept well-informed at the early planning stages. On March 5, Shriver paid an essential visit to the office of the Speaker, Sam Rayburn of Texas, the most senior-ranking Democrat in Congress. Afterwards, he wrote Rayburn and thanked him for his advice: "The problem, of course, as you pointed out, is to carry [the Peace Corps] out in such a way that will be constructive and beneficial to everyone concerned. We want it to be a down-to-earth, people-to-people approach that will avoid waste and unnecessary expense and I was glad to get your thinking along these lines."[10]

Shriver recognized that Congress held the power of life and death over the Peace Corps. To give this relationship the attention it deserved, he set up a congressional liaison office. Its functions were to work on the form and presentation of legislation, to reply to congressional mail, to keep the organization informed of congressional visits in Washington and the field, and to report to the White House on legislative developments. Bill Moyers was given charge of this office. Despite his youth, Moyers had gained substantial legislative experience working for Lyndon Johnson (then Majority Leader) on Capitol Hill, and his political acuity was highly valued by the relatively inexperienced Shriver. Josephson, Wiggins, and Wofford also helped with strategy.

In a staff meeting on March 22, Moyers and his team planned the assault on the Hill. The questions likely to prove troublesome were outlined: Will enough people volunteer? Will the Peace Corps move cautiously enough? Will Volunteers be "salesmen" for the American way of life? Will Peace Corps service be more attractive to the wealthy than the poor? Will the government be liable for injuries to, and mistakes by, the Volunteers? Slowly, around the answers to these questions, a congressional presentation evolved.[11]

Meanwhile, discussion of the Peace Corps had already begun in Congress. Republican Frances Bolton of Ohio, a member of the House Foreign Affairs Committee, called the idea "terrifying." Alexander Wiley of Wisconsin, the ranking Republican on the Senate Foreign Relations Committee, felt it was being pushed much too fast. John Rhodes, the Arizona Republican on the House Appropriations Committee, assailed the Peace Corps as an easy target for Communist infiltrators. His colleague from Arizona, Barry Goldwater, added that as far as the Peace Corps was concerned "the bloom is off the rose." On the other hand, a number of Democrats were strongly supportive. Senators Stephen Young, Philip Hart, Edmund Muskie, and Gale McGee spoke enthusiastically of the Peace Corps as an embodiment of the spirit of the New Frontier. Congressman Roland Libonati from Illinois described it as an idea which represented "the pioneer spirit of American youth."[12]

While congressmen geared up for the debate on the bill, Shriver's staff were busily writing it. Based on the "Report to the President," the final product was the cumulative effort of Josephson, Moyers, Wiggins, Abram, and Nelson; Sorensen of the White House staff gave a little advice and Roger Kuhn, a young lawyer who had had some experience drafting legislation for ICA, also helped. Regarding the Peace Corps' authority, Kuhn and Abram argued that it should be vested in the Director or in the Peace Corps as a sovereign institution; but Josephson wanted the Peace Corps directly under the President's authority so it could invoke his name whenever possible. With a view to future bureaucratic battles, he sensed that the Peace Corps would enjoy a better strategic position under the wing of the President than on its own. This meant sacrificing some autonomy, but the long-term advantages of being the President's agency would prove worthwhile. As Josephson explained it: "I felt that we would be in a stronger position if we were able to say these functions are conferred upon the President who will be able to supervise and regulate them and reorganize them if needs be, rather than lock us in institutionally."[13] His reasoning won the day.

Josephson also proposed that the Peace Corps should ask Congress for only one year's appropriation at a time. More experienced foreign aid administrators forecast that such an innovation would cause untold chaos for the Peace Corps and forestall necessary long-term planning. But Josephson argued that by requesting only annual funds, fretful congressmen would be reassured that the Peace Corps would not become a renegade, uncontrollable organization. An element of risk was involved here. In any year it chose, Congress could cut the Peace Corps' money supply. Nevertheless, Josephson believed there was "an absolute utility each year in going up to the Hill. Congress knows that each year it will get at the program, and it also keeps it up-to-date about your program."[14] His argument proved particularly persuasive to reluctant congressmen who were worried that the Peace Corps might become a costly, self-perpetuating government bureaucracy.

By May 11, the final draft of the Peace Corps bill was ready for inter-agency review by the Bureau of the Budget, the State Department, and the White House. The Peace Corps team pressed for this procedure to be carried through on an urgent basis. Wiggins told Dean Rusk that the time was ripe for the passage of legislation since there was "high public and Congressional interest in the Peace Corps."[15] That the new agency was autonomous within the federal bureaucracy and that it was free from being sent to the Hill as part of the administration's general foreign aid package, became crucially important factors; it was axiomatic that foreign aid fared disastrously in appropriations committees.* Shriver had been consistently advised by legislative leaders to take the Peace Corps to the Congress as a separate commodity. As he told Kennedy, Senate Minority Leader Everett Dirksen

---

*The Kennedy administration did particularly badly on foreign aid appropriations. In 1961 (for 1962) the administration's request was cut by 18 percent. In 1962 (for 1963) there was an 18.4 percent cut, and in 1963 (for 1964) there was a 33.8 percent cut.

had recommended that "the Peace Corps should be the subject of separate legislation if we hope to get any prompt and substantial action at this session."[16] This distinctiveness was pivotal to the Peace Corps' success in Congress.

It caused some discomfort, however, in another direction. The President's aides had been extremely displeased by the Peace Corps' fight for independence, and Wiggins and Josephson had been told that they should expect no help from the White House staff on the Hill. Josephson later explained that Ralph Dungan and Larry O'Brien looked upon the Peace Corps' administrators as obstinate "loners" and ambitious "empire-builders."[17] As far as the President's men were concerned, the Peace Corps was on its own in the struggle for congressional support.

Shriver had never held political office, lobbied on Capitol Hill, nor testified before a congressional committee. His chief political experience had been as Kennedy's campaign helper in 1960, and his administrative background was in business, not government. This apparent lack of political know-how seemed a serious barrier to his and the Peace Corps' success with Congress. The committees had to be convinced not only of the feasibility of the idea but also of the competence of the new agency's administrators. Shriver, however, believed that his alleged "innocence" regarding congressional lobbying techniques was an asset. In retrospect, he claimed that "if you don't know how it's supposed to work, then sometimes you do better."[18]

SATURATION BOMBING

Shriver's forte was the personal touch. The usual tactic of a government administrator with a bill before Congress was to concentrate on the "big men" on Capitol Hill—the majority and minority leaders, the Whips, the Speaker, and the committee chairmen. Shriver made sure that he saw these men, but he also talked to three out of every four congressmen. He termed this strategy "saturation bombing."[19] Between March and September 1961, he met with 363 members of Congress. In an enlightening memorandum of September 6 ("from one brother-in-law to another"), Shriver outlined for Kennedy a typical morning on the

Hill. "If you want to know what it takes to get *your* Peace Corps through the House and the Senate, you may find out by looking at the following schedule for tomorrow's activities:

    9:00 – Congressman Avery
    9:45 – Senator Saltonstall
    10:45 – Congressman Bow
    11:30 – Congressman Brown
    12:15 – Congressman Gallagher
    1:00 – Lunch with Senator Ellender and the Senate Appropriations Committee (this is a private luncheon arranged on his own initiative by Senator Ellender)"[20]

In a postscript, the ebullient Shriver claimed that although this had been his routine for two months, "We all love it."

Shriver's meetings with congressmen were unconventional in that they were based on the geographical region which legislators represented rather than party affiliation. Thus, by meeting with Democrats and Republicans at the same time, he carefully cultivated the notion that the Peace Corps was above partisan politics. In later years, he recollected that "I zealously went out to win over Republicans as well as Democrats."[21] As for the congressmen, they felt somewhat flattered when they saw the director of a government agency – and the President's brother-in-law – personally carrying out his own lobbying program. It was a significant factor in persuading many of them to vote for the Peace Corps. As one member of the House Rules Committee explained: "You know why I really voted for the Peace Corps? One night I was leaving at 7:30 and there was Shriver, walking up and down the halls of the House Office Building, by himself, looking into all the doors. He came in and talked to me. I still didn't like the program, but I was sold on Shriver. I voted for him."[22]

Shriver was an able performer in committee hearings, always enthusiastic, always thoroughly prepared. Prior to his appearance before the Senate Committee on Foreign Relations in June 1961, he asked his staff for a complete rundown on some of the Peace Corps' more vital statistics. Thus he could reply to expected questions on expenditure with the precise information that a Volunteer would cost the taxpayer $13,336 for two years service.[23] Before the vote in the Senate Appropriations Committee, Shriver analysed opinion and consulted with Hubert Humphrey regarding the precarious tension within the committee. It seemed the Peace Corps' $40 million budget request would be defeated by a vote of fourteen to thirteen. Shriver felt that the best hope of success was to lobby the two southern Democrats Stennis and Holland; he left nothing to chance.[24]

Shriver reassured congressmen on every facet of Peace Corps operations: training and selection standards would be rigorous, costs minimal, and caution the watchword. He paid meticulous attention to detail. When Senator Homer Capehart of Indiana asked a question about equipment and cost during a Foreign Relations Committee hearing, Shriver's answer ran to exact figures on jeeps (135), horses (20), and outboard motors (1); his figure on cost was to the cent ($10,712,894.58).[25] When necessary, Shriver invoked the President's name. He insisted that Kennedy himself, rather than the secretary of state, should always present the Peace Corps' legislation to Congress. He was also fond of reminding Congress that, to an extent, it was responsible for the birth of the Peace Corps. After all, the House Foreign Affairs Committee had sanctioned Henry Reuss's original proposal for a study of the idea.

Shriver's painstaking efforts paid handsome dividends. Congresswoman Marguerite Stitt Church, a Republican from Illinois on the House Foreign Affairs Committee, remarked that she knew of no government administrator who had "made such an effort to bring his story personally to members of Congress."[26] Dean Rusk echoed this sentiment: "I doubt that any individual or agency has ever had so favorable a situation in the Congress as Sargent Shriver built for the Peace Corps."[27]

Shriver's polished performance on the Hill owed a great deal to the research and planning undertaken by his back-up team. Bill Moyers, in particular, guided him through Congress by anticipating potentially difficult questions and cantankerous members. Knowing that cost would be a critical issue, Moyers worked intensively on the Peace Corps' economic brief. In May 1961, he noted that "There is a certain amount of distrust on the Hill now towards the Peace Corps' expenses, growing out of the use of the Executive Order and Mutual Security fund." Moyers warned that "Congress is not going to want to walk in the dark as far as our administrative budget is concerned."[28] He correctly predicted that Otto E. Passman, the penny-pinching Democrat from Louisiana and chairman of the House Subcommittee on Foreign Operations Appropriations, would prove to be the Peace Corps' strongest single opponent in Congress. Moyers and his staff met formally and informally with Passman and with other congressmen; they established a three-day deadline on replies to congressional mail; phone calls from legislative offices were never delayed or refused; and congressmen were invited to visit training sites in their home states. In early August, Senator Ralph Yarborough saw trainees at Texas Western College in El Paso. During the debate on the Peace Corps bill, he was able to report to his colleagues that "I have never seen a more intelligent, dedicated group of students."[29]

Another of the Peace Corps' ploys was to ensure that a Volunteer from each state had been selected by the time the bill was set for passage. As the first Volunteers were chosen, they became news at the local and state levels, and congressmen in Washington were often required to make at least token statements of acknowledgement on the floor of the House and Senate or via local newspapers and television. This kept congressmen aware that the folks back home were joining the Peace Corps, and that it was a generally popular issue. No time or effort was spared to maintain this congressional involvement and interest. Don Romine, one of Moyers's assistants, recalled rushing to the congressional post office at 4 o'clock one morning in June 1961 just to make sure that congressmen would receive a briefing paper which Moyers had prepared for them for that day's hearing.[30] With this extensive lobbying network in the background, Hubert Humphrey introduced the Peace Corps legislation on June 1, 1961. Senate bill S.2000 sought to establish "a Peace Corps of American Volunteers to carry America's skills and talents and idealism abroad to help other peoples help themselves."[31]

FULBRIGHT AND OTHER DOUBTERS

The bill's passage through Congress was by no means all plain sailing. Many Republicans stressed that in its first year, they would regard the new agency as purely experimental. Outright resistance was strongest in the House. Led vociferously by H. R. Gross, the Republican from Iowa and a member of the House Committee on Foreign Affairs, these doubters viewed the Peace Corps as "a shining example of . . . a legislative pig-in-a-poke" and another "foreign aid boondoggle."[32] The attack on the Peace Corps in the upper chamber was led by Bourke B. Hickenlooper of Iowa who, as third-ranking Republican on the Senate Foreign Relations Committee, was in a position of some influence. George D. Aiken too, the second-ranking Republican on the Senate Foreign Relations Committee, recalled thinking that the Peace Corps offered "an exceptional opportunity to get into difficulty."[33]

Of more immediate importance than the hostility of these Republicans, was the apparent indifference of the Democratic senator from Arkansas, J. William Fulbright. The chairman of the Senate Foreign Relations Committee admitted that, from the start, the Peace Corps was not one of his pet projects. He was dubious about the quality of applicants it would attract, he did not admire its "one-way" approach of sending young Americans to the Third World without reciprocation, and he was concerned about the effect the Peace Corps might have on his own highly successful Fulbright program for educational exchange.[34]

On August 2, 1961, an alarming rumor swept Peace Corps headquarters: Fulbright was about to recommend to his committee that the Peace Corps' authorization request should be cut from $40 million to $10 million. "Peace Corps Bill is Facing Curbs," noted a *New York Times* article, quoting Fulbright as saying that the new organization should adopt a slower approach. The article pointed out that such a deep cut in funds would "cripple the Peace Corps, embarrass the President abroad, and encourage the more conservative House to make even deeper cuts." Minority Leader Everett Dirksen predicted that the Senate Foreign Relations Committee might "completely transform" the Peace Corps' legislation.[35]

Shriver, worried and angry about the lack of pressure being exerted on the Peace Corps' behalf by the White House, immediately fired off a blistering memorandum to Kennedy. "Unless we can build a climate of opinion in which the Peace Corps is considered must legislation," he warned, "we are in trouble—regardless of the general goodwill that surrounds this proposal." Shriver claimed that congressional leaders like Fulbright, Mansfield, and Rayburn were "openly lukewarm toward the Peace Corps—at least in terms of the legislative priority accorded it." He urged Kennedy to provide the necessary leadership on the Hill: "The White House must provide sufficient leadership and pressure so that there will be no doubt in the minds of Congress that the President feels the bill must be passed this session. Unless the White House supplies this leadership, the lateness of the session alone may doom the chances for Peace Corps legislation and appropriations this session." Shriver added that at this stage, he felt thoroughly frustrated. "Bill Moyers and I have been living on the Hill," he wrote. "We may even have laid the foundation for at least the beginnings of a good working relationship with Congressman Passman." However, Shriver told Kennedy that it was now time for the White House to lend a hand: "At this point, the Peace Corps itself has done all it can on the Hill."[36]

Shriver's message had the desired effect. At a news conference on August 10, without being asked a question about it, Kennedy made a strongly supportive statement on the Peace Corps. He outlined the tremendous response which it had been receiving and he spoke of it as one of the most encouraging features of his administration: "It has had a most promising beginning, and we have an opportunity if the amount requested by the Peace Corps is approved by the Congress, of having 2,700 Volunteers serving the cause of peace in fiscal year 1962." With Shriver's memorandum in mind, Kennedy added his weight to the Peace Corps' assault on the Hill. "I am hopeful," he said, "that the Congress will support this effort."[37]

On August 24, when the debate on the Peace Corps began in the Senate, the major issue was whether an amendment proposed by Hickenlooper "to cut $15 million out of the unnecessary fat in this authorization" would pass.[38] The Senate Foreign Relations Committee had previously rejected this motion by eleven votes to six.[39] Significantly, however, Fulbright had voted for the cut and had it not been for some sterling work by Hubert Humphrey, the committee might well have gone the other way.

During the debate on the Senate floor, Humphrey again championed the Peace Corps, noting that the full $40 million request
was less than one-tenth of 1 percent of the 1961 defense appropriation. Majority Leader Mansfield also backed the request for
full funding, although he predicted that the Peace Corps would
run into difficulties in Passman's House Subcommittee on Appropriations. He asked that "at least in getting the program afloat,
we will on this occasion allow the full amount requested by the
Committee on Foreign Relations." The arguments of Mansfield
and Humphrey fended off Hickenlooper's proposed 37.5 percent cut. In a roll call vote the amendment was defeated fifty-
nine to thirty-two. Again, however, Fulbright went on record
as being "not without misgivings," and he, along with seven
other Democrats, voted with Hickenlooper.[40]

The victory on the Senate floor proved somewhat transitory.
As Mansfield had feared, Passman's House Subcommittee made
a deep cut in the Peace Corps' authorized funds. Before it was
finally signed into law, the new agency's budget was reduced
by 25 percent, from $40 million to $30 million. In that respect,
Fulbright and the other doubters had their wish that the Peace
Corps should begin on a more modest level.

THE KAMEN INCIDENT

Aside from cost, Congress's major concerns in 1961 were
that young, unworldly Americans working in foreign countries
would fall prey to Communist infiltrators, and that the Peace
Corps would attract sundry socialists, radicals, and beatniks. The
first fear led to the adoption of another amendment by Hickenlooper which required that Volunteers should receive training
and instruction on the "philosophy, strategy, tactics, and menace
of Communism."[41] To an extent, the second concern was met
by the Federal Bureau of Investigation. It was agreed that J. Edgar
Hoover's agency would carry out investigations of all Volunteers
up to September 1961 (thereafter, the Civil Service Commission
took responsibility for checking Volunteers' backgrounds; only
those deemed "security" risks were referred to the FBI). Shriver
also attempted to mollify worried congressmen by explaining to

them that "We in the Peace Corps share your firm conviction that it is essential for Volunteers to be loyal Americans and to possess a full understanding of, and deep commitment to, the free system."[42] Despite these placatory measures, the fear that the Peace Corps would become infested by radicals was exacerbated in August by a twenty-two-year-old trainee named Charles Kamen.

Kamen had been involved in an incident at a Rotary Club function in Florida in December 1960, when he had dared to laugh during a showing of the anti-Communist propaganda film *Operation Abolition*. Rotarians claimed that Kamen's sense of humor was proof of his left-wing sympathies, and he was forcibly ejected from the club. When it was discovered in the summer of 1961 that Kamen had been accepted by the Peace Corps for training at Pennsylvania State University, a few congressmen, notably Hickenlooper and Gross, took strong exception. "The impression we get is that the Peace Corps is going to be staffed by beatniks and Kamen is a classic example" was one indignant comment.[43]

All evidence suggests that Kamen was an intelligent, responsible, young student, although ultra-conservatives considered his involvement in the nuclear disarmament and civil rights movements indicative of a radical tendency.[44] Many Republicans and southern Democrats were soon calling for Kamen's immediate dismissal from Peace Corps training. Hickenlooper raised the "Kamen incident" during the Senate debate on the Peace Corps bill and Passman grilled Shriver on the subject when he appeared before the House Subcommittee on Appropriations. Such was the furor over Kamen that on August 30, the President was asked by a reporter for his opinion on the subject. Kennedy tactfully replied that he had "every confidence in the judgment of those who make the selections."[45]

This answer did not satisfy the press. *Newsweek* informed its readers that Kamen ("Until recently he was bearded—a fact which his critics have not overlooked") was a perfect example of "going overboard on idealism."[46] The Peace Corps came under tremendous pressure to drop Kamen forthwith. Chief of Public Information Ed Bayley remembered members of Passman's committee telling Shriver bluntly that "If you want $10 million cut—

keep Kamen in."[47] Despite these threats, the Peace Corps permitted Kamen to complete his training course. At the end of his training stint in September, however, he was deemed "unsuitable" for service.

Inevitably, there were suggestions that Shriver had made a deal with Passman to "deselect" Kamen. But if indeed Shriver struck such a bargain, then he certainly got the short end of the stick, for $10 million were cut from the Peace Corps' budget anyhow. It seems more likely that Shriver withstood this early challenge to the integrity of the Peace Corps' selection process and insisted that Kamen be allowed to finish his training, although the eventual rejection of such an apparently able applicant by the Peace Corps' selection officers certainly created the suspicion that Shriver had bowed to the will of reactionary legislators. A *New York Times* editorial criticized conservative congressmen for picking on "irrelevant" issues such as Kamen and praised Shriver for not bending to their whims.[48]

The Kamen incident had two repercussions. First, Congress added an amendment to the Peace Corps bill requiring Volunteers to take a "loyalty oath" in which they had to swear that they neither advocated nor belonged to an organization which advocated the overthrow of the U.S. government. Second, Passman's argument for a large cut in Peace Corps appropriations was strengthened by the great hullabaloo, and the agency lost $10 million from its proposed budget. Thus the unhappy ghost of Charles Kamen was exorcised from the Peace Corps.

A BIPARTISAN EFFORT

On August 25, 1961, the Peace Corps bill passed the Senate by voice vote; on September 14, the House supported it by a margin of 288 to 97. This seemed to confirm that the Peace Corps was an issue which went beyond the narrow confines of party, although it did divide Congress, to some extent, along conservative-liberal lines. Southern Democrat Robert Hemphill equated the political inoffensiveness of the Peace Corps with that of Grace Kelly, Billy Graham, and the Pope.[49] On the other hand, in a memorandum to Shriver of October 1961, Bill Moyers forecast that the Peace Corps would not always escape the murky waters of party politics. He mentioned former President Eisenhower's latest statement which described the Peace Corps as a juvenile experiment. "If you want to send Peace Corps Volunteers to an under-developed area," Ike had said, "send them to the moon!" Moyers told Shriver that Congress would have to be won over again in 1962, and he predicted that the Republicans would make criticism of the Peace Corps "a major issue" in the mid-term election campaign.[50]

This did not happen. Kennedy's Peace Corps had few congressional problems of any consequence after 1961. Once the glowing press reports of the Volunteers' achievements in the field began to filter back to Washington, there was little to be feared on Capitol Hill. Certainly, some irritations remained. The House Subcommittee on Foreign Operations Appropriations persistently attempted to limit the Peace Corps' funds, and Otto Passman continued to be an implacable foe. In 1962 and 1963, however, he could only manage to inflict cuts of 7.5 and 9.7 percent on the agency's rising appropriations ($59 million for fiscal year 1963 and nearly $96 million for fiscal year 1964). In the Senate, criticism virtually ceased.

Despite Passman's appropriations cuts, Fulbright's opposition, and Charles Kamen's sense of humor, the Peace Corps' congressional strategy was a triumph. In 1961 it received the second largest margin of favorable votes of any new non-defense measure sent by Kennedy to Congress and, a few minor changes notwithstanding, the substance of the bill was left as proposed by Shriver and his colleagues. As specified by the Peace Corps Act, the agency's "purpose" was to "promote world peace and friendship."[51] It was to achieve this by: helping the peoples of interested countries to meet their needs for trained manpower; helping to promote a better understanding of the American people on the part of the peoples served; and helping to promote a better understanding of their peoples on the part of the American people. These requirements became known as the Three Goals. They made it clear that the Peace Corps was not just to be a technical assistance agency but that it should also be a means of allowing Third World peoples to learn about Americans and vice versa. The Three Goals were thus consonant with Kennedy's original intention for the Peace Corps and, on Capitol Hill and elsewhere, they were used to gauge its success.

On September 22, Kennedy signed the Peace Corps Act. It was one of the few proposals of his administration which managed to transcend party politics. Thanks to the unrelenting diligence and shrewd tactics of the Peace Corps team, the substantial skepticism which had been evident on the Hill in early 1961 was dissipated. In a sense, it might be argued that Shriver and his colleagues were fortunate in that, with the Peace Corps, they were not dealing in any really hard political currency. Congressmen could not trade opportunities to teach in Thailand or build roads in Tanzania in exchange for votes in Alabama or Arkansas. Thus, the Peace Corps was not subject to the compromises and pork-barrel deals which accompany most legislation. In that respect, the Peace Corps was a politically "clean" issue. Nevertheless, Shriver's achievement should not be underestimated. Many congressmen admitted that they voted for him as much as the Peace Corps. As Senator McGee of Laramie, Wyoming enthused, "If we had ten Sargent Shrivers we could conquer the world."[52]

In later years, commentators liked to describe the Peace Corps' relationship with the 87th and 88th Congresses as a "love affair."[53] In April 1962, Peace Corps legislation was supported in the House by an overwhelming vote of 317 to 70; it passed the Senate by voice. By November 1963, the voice vote formality was sufficient in both House and Senate. In each of those years, Congress substantially increased its funding of the Peace Corps. The *Washington Daily News* adjudged Congress's largesse even more notable in view of its "determination to clamp down on foreign aid spending in general."[54]

With no little pleasure, Shriver charted the conversion of confirmed skeptics to the Peace Corps cause. In March 1962, he sent Kennedy what he jokingly entitled the "Statement-Of-The-Month" from Senator Barry Goldwater of Arizona. At a Harvard-Princeton-Yale Club luncheon, the conservative Republican had said: "At first I thought that the Peace Corps would be advance work for a group of beatniks, but this is not so . . . I have been impressed [and] I'll back it all the way." Shriver also relayed to the President a message from Richard Russell of Georgia, the prominent southern conservative and second-ranking Democrat on the Senate Committee on Appropriations. "I just wanted to say that somebody down there has been doing a good job with a difficult challenge," said Russell. "The Peace Corps seems to be in mighty good shape in Congress." By 1962, Howard Smith, chairman of the House Committee on Rules and leader of the southern bloc in Congress, was so persuaded of the Peace Corps' merit that he permitted his committee to vote unanimously in favor of it in open session. "This is something House parliamentarians tell me is unprecedented," a delighted Shriver informed Kennedy.[55]

At the beginning of 1961, Shriver had gone to Congress with the reputation of a political novice. Upon signing the Peace Corps Act, Kennedy expressed the widespread esteem which his brother-in-law had gained on Capitol Hill. Perhaps reflecting on his own undistinguished record in the area of foreign aid, the President complimented him as "the most effective lobbyist on the Washington scene."[56] Shriver and the Peace Corps had won Congress.

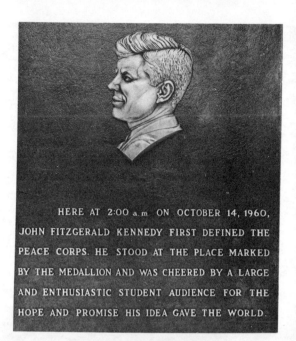

HERE AT 2:00 a.m ON OCTOBER 14, 1960, JOHN FITZGERALD KENNEDY FIRST DEFINED THE PEACE CORPS. HE STOOD AT THE PLACE MARKED BY THE MEDALLION AND WAS CHEERED BY A LARGE AND ENTHUSIASTIC STUDENT AUDIENCE FOR THE HOPE AND PROMISE HIS IDEA GAVE THE WORLD.

JFK proposes the idea of a "Peace Corps" in an extemporaneous campaign speech at the University of Michigan. A memorial plaque on the steps of the Student Union commemorates the historic occasion.

Presidential candidate John F. Kennedy formally announces plan for Peace Corps at the Cow Palace, San Francisco, November 2, 1960.

President Kennedy signs the Peace Corps Act "to promote world peace and friendship," September 22, 1961. Senator Hubert Humphrey, an early proponent at the Peace Corps, is at Kennedy's right.

Sargent Shriver leads first group of Volunteers into the Rose Garden to meet the President before their departure for Ghana and Tanzania, August 28, 1961.

Sargent Shriver presides over a senior staff meeting at Peace Corps headquarters.

JFK meets with Volunteers bound for Ethiopia in 1962.

Only 26 years old in 1961, William Josephson was the Peace Corps' legal sword. No one at Peace Corps headquarters was tougher or brighter.

Charles Peters and his Evaluation Division sent brutally frank reports on Peace Corps programs directly to Shriver.

Warren Wiggins, the experienced foreign aid administrator who planned the Peace Corps' overseas operations, accompanies JFK to a meeting with Volunteers.

Vice President Lyndon Johnson lost his brightest aide, Bill Moyers, to the Peace Corps. Moyers became Deputy Director in 1963.

JFK and Sargent Shriver confer on Peace Corps matters.

6

An Antibureaucratic
Bureaucracy

> The Peace Corps is different from any other large
> bureau in Washington . . . [it] retains those paradoxes
> of style and substance which informed the best inven-
> tions of the Kennedy years; it is expectant, contradic-
> tory, optimistic, innovative and thoroughly frantic.
> — Andrew Kopkind

A DIFFERENT KIND OF ORGANIZATION

"The Peace Corps is a bold, new idea requiring a bold, new
effort," Shriver wrote Secretary of State Dean Rusk in the early
summer of 1961. "The Peace Corps should be and do something
different, different from all other kinds of organizations which
the U.S. has heretofore undertaken abroad." In this early declaration of intent, Shriver stated his aim of making the Peace Corps
a unique kind of government agency. Its winning of independence allowed it the opportunity to develop in the direction chosen
by Shriver, without so much as "asking permission or getting
clearance for anything from the White House."[1] He was determined not to let the Peace Corps fall into the tried and routine
ways of most bureaucracies. Indeed, the most detested word in
Shriver's lexicon was "bureaucracy."

In the early days of the Peace Corps, rumor had it that Jack
Young, who was trying to draft an organization chart, was forced

to hide his line-and-staff drawings from Shriver for fear of incurring his wrath. Young knew that Shriver preferred to "get everybody into the act and then worry about the niceties of how one would manage the enterprise later." Although Shriver had asked him to come up with a formal governmental design for the Peace Corps, Young always had the feeling that this was more for "appearances' sake than from any overwhelming desire to organize and manage."[2] Young's organizational plan of March 1961 had outlined certain rudimentary management processes such as program development, operations, recruitment, and financing which he felt were necessary to get the Peace Corps off the ground and running.[3] But to Shriver, the effective performance of these functions was always of much greater importance than organizational boxes or division of work concepts.

Despite Shriver's thoughts on bureaucracy, the managers under him—Wiggins, Josephson, Young, and Kelly—argued that, from a purely practical standpoint, a minimum level of organizational planning was essential for the effective functioning of any government agency. Josephson joshed Shriver that he too had seen, during the Eisenhower administration, the days when "not much progress was made but, boy, were we organized!" Still, he warned that "while good decisions don't automatically follow from good organization, it is hard to make them without it." Shriver took the point but demanded that the watchword of all plans be "flexibility."[4]

The Peace Corps was headed, in every sense, by its first Director. Shriver was determined to keep control in his hands and, as an outsider to governmental procedure, was not about to become entangled in its convoluted web of red tape. From the beginning, he grabbed hold of the reins of power and never relinquished his firm grip. He was aided by an Executive Secretariat which attempted to formalize the organization's procedures and by a National Advisory Council which made itself available for consultation. Established on March 30, 1961, the council was made up of outstanding Americans from all walks of life and of every political complexion. Its purpose was to help the Peace Corps transcend partisan politics and become a truly national concern. Associate Justice William O. Douglas was ap-

pointed its first honorary chairman and Vice-President Johnson
was its chairman proper. However, since the council's role—
like most advisory councils—was nebulous and its powers undefined, it had no strong policy-making role.[5]

In effect, every policy question was ultimately decided by
Shriver himself, and the Peace Corps revolved around his char-
ismatic personality. Before the end of March 1961, Shriver had
insisted that all policy papers be sent to his office for review.
Bradley Patterson, the first Executive Secretary of the Peace
Corps, recalled that "everybody sent everything up to him for
approval ahead of time before it got sent out."[6] This procedure
became just about the only unthinking bureaucratic response
within the Peace Corps.

Because the Peace Corps was such a small agency, and also
because Shriver had such boundless energy and enthusiasm, it
was possible for him to take a hand in almost everything from
sending out cables to reviewing Volunteers' applications. When
Harvard graduate Newell Flather decided in the spring of 1961
to volunteer, he telephoned Washington to request an application form. He was astounded when he found himself talking not
to a secretary or a clerk but to Shriver himself. Shriver's staff
was amazed at how he coped with all this. "[Shriver's] kids and
his wife didn't see much of him," Patterson said, "but he kept
on top of it."[7]

As the organization grew, Shriver was obliged to delegate
some powers. Even so, he was always liable to inquire into any
Peace Corps matter, from the timing of a press release to which
books should be shelved in the library of the training camps in
Puerto Rico. On one occasion, Shriver took umbrage at a seemingly routine cable sent by a Peace Corps official in Washington
to the embassy in Ghana. The cable outlined what the Peace
Corps overseas staff might need: office space, ancillary staff, a
car, a chauffeur, and so forth. Patterson recalled that Shriver
"took one look at that message and that word 'chauffeur' caught
his eye, and you could pick him off the ceiling he was so outraged." He immediately summoned the staff member responsible and told him that "the Peace Corps wasn't going to have any
chauffeurs, by God." Shriver canceled and rewrote the cable.[8]

STRUCTURE AND STYLE

Patterson described Shriver as "not a systematic person" but rather "a guy who leaps into the breach and gets things done, crossing channels or speeding things up or taking short cuts or cutting corners and so forth in any moment that he feels necessary." His office was like the newsroom of a daily newspaper with groups of people constantly shuttling in and out, others standing arguing in a corner, with pieces of paper flying around between various groups. This unbureaucratic style made it extremely difficult for his administrators, like Patterson, to maintain any semblance of organizational routine. As Patterson later noted, it was Shriver's way of "projecting himself onto his staff and everybody who worked or had relations with the Peace Corps."[9] No organization chart could possibly convey Shriver's all-pervading influence. Since everything important went through him, the image of the Peace Corps and Sargent Shriver became virtually a single entity.

Below the Director, the agency was organized into five major offices, each headed by an associate director responsible to Shriver. These offices consisted of varying numbers of divisions, the chiefs of which also reported to the Director. Responsibility for the selection, training, and general support of Volunteers from the moment of application to termination was vested in an Office of Peace Corps Volunteers. This office maintained communication between Washington headquarters and Volunteers in the field. Lawrence Dennis, educator and journalist, was its first associate director. In reviewing a first draft of the Peace Corps' organizational chart, Shriver noticed that it had neglected to include a place for the Volunteers; he drew a great big box in the center of the chart, channeled everything else toward it and labeled it "Volunteers".

Alongside the Volunteers, the Office of Program Development and Operations (PDO) was at the very heart of the Peace Corps. PDO was responsible for the negotiation and establishment of overseas programs. Warren Wiggins was its first associate director, and it was organized into a general Division of Program Development and Coordination and four regional offices: Latin America, Africa, the Far East, and North Africa/Near East/Asia and Pacific.

Bill Moyers was the first associate director of the Office of Public Affairs which directed recruitment activities and coordinated the agency's relations with Congress. It distributed information on the Peace Corps and responded to the tremendous volume of mailed applications and inquiries.

General review and examination of all Peace Corps activities was carried out by the Office of Planning and Evaluation. Under its first associate director, Bill Haddad, it served as a mechanism for self-criticism within the Peace Corps. Its Evaluation Division sent candid and often scathing reports to Shriver on all aspects of operations and generally advised him on long-term Peace Corps goals.

Last, the Office of Management handled all Peace Corps finances. It also administered personnel procedures: employment, promotion, termination, rating, and security. The associate director of this office had one of the most difficult jobs in the Peace Corps. In an agency committed to unbureaucratic methods, the Office of Management was obliged to be at least moderately bureaucratic. Thus four unhappy associate directors came and went in the first four years.

Other special divisions with direct links to Shriver were established. From the beginning, the cooperation and assistance of private voluntary agencies, universities, colleges, and international organizations was recognized as crucial to the success of the Peace Corps. Accordingly, a Division of University, Private and International Cooperation was set up to maintain a healthy partnership between the Peace Corps and "outside" bodies. By 1963 Franklin Williams had taken control of this division. Responsibility for the actual negotiation and administration of contracts between the Peace Corps and other organizations for services rendered either during training or overseas, was assumed by the Division of Contracts and Logistics, led by the experienced, hard-bargaining Bill Kelly. This division also arranged material support for Volunteers. A Research Division was created to validate and improve the Peace Corps' training and selection methods. Physical and psychiatric examinations of Volunteers as well as health care and instruction were carried out by the Medical Program Division. The General Counsel Division provided legal representation in all matters with other U.S. government agencies, private organizations, and foreign authorities. William Delano was the first official General Counsel, but the real legal sword of the Peace Corps was Bill Josephson (who succeeded Delano as General Counsel in 1963).

Overseas, operations in each country were supervised by a Peace Corps Representative (commonly referred to as "the Rep") and his support staff. These country directors were usually young men in their early thirties who had made a distinctive mark in their respective professions. Shriver told Kennedy that he gave Reps "an unusual degree of responsibility," allowed them to "make many decisions in the field," and urged them to adapt general policies and guidelines to local situations.[10] As Shriver's proxy in the field, each Rep had sole responsibility for the general performance, behavior, and welfare of all Volunteers stationed in his country. There were usually up to twelve people on his staff, among whom would be a doctor, a secretary, and one or more assistant Reps. To facilitate overseas operations, experienced foreign nationals were hired whenever possible.

The Peace Corps' organization chart of 1963 indicated a finely-balanced agency with powers and functions evenly distributed between the various boxes and units. The neat diagram did not show the constant turmoil and intense power struggles which raged within the agency. Underlying the conventional exterior were many competitive elements and several explosive characters. Under Shriver, the Peace Corps was no place for faint hearts. As Bill Josephson, one of the toughest in-fighters, put it: "You had to be capable of taking a knock on the head and come bouncing back."[11]

CREATIVE TENSION

While Shriver was a stranger to government procedure, his running of the Merchandise Mart meant that he was well-versed in efficient business technique. His colleagues were astonished at how quickly and skillfully he handled the complexities involved in establishing a new government organization. "It never ceased to amaze me how well he handled the paperwork," Josephson said. "He had this amazing ability to simplify a complicated problem."[12]

Shriver knew how to get his message across. He could be charming and tactful, but he was always ruthlessly critical of incompetence. He placed little value on bureaucratic etiquette. Rather, he approached each issue on its merits with only one question preeminent: Does it work? In a 1964 political science essay on the Peace Corps, George La Noue—a scholar at the Brookings Institution—ascribed to Shriver "the competitive theory of administration" as outlined by Professor Richard E. Neustadt of Harvard in his influential book *Presidential Power*. Shriver flatly denied following any theory, stressing that his administrative style was strictly empirical: "I am unaware that I have any fixed notions about public administration techniques," he said.[13] However, he did believe in competition and by setting up competing factions, he deliberately cultivated an atmosphere of diversity and, sometimes, contradiction. The toughest fighters, hardest workers, and most persuasive debaters were the winners in the Peace Corps organization. Shriver was the final arbiter.

Professor Robert Textor of MIT, an early Peace Corps consultant, felt that there were three distinct Peace Corps "subcultures": the headquarters staff, the Volunteers, and, in an intermediate position, the overseas Reps. Textor claimed that "Almost any sensitive observer, if given two weeks in Washington headquarters and two weeks at an overseas post, would agree that the separateness of these three is something that is real and demonstrable."[14] The different perspectives of these subcultures contributed to what Harris Wofford termed the "creative tension" within the Peace Corps.[15]

Some headquarters staff tended to regard themselves as the real Peace Corps with the Volunteers viewed as some kind of abstract addendum. On the other hand, the Volunteers in the field considered themselves the true cutting edge of the Peace Corps and were often resentful and sometimes downright hostile towards the paid, professional "bureaucrats" in Washington. In many ways, the Reps were in the worst position. Caught between the major conflicting parties, they were subject to a credibility gap on both sides. However, this tension between the three subcultures had the advantage of helping to achieve one of Shriver's administrative objectives: constant argument and debate over Peace Corps policy. He believed that this would maintain the vitality of the organization both in Washington and overseas.

Within headquarters staff, there were numerous differences of style, character, and opinion. From the start there was an antagonism between the experienced government bureaucrats who had joined the Peace Corps from other agencies—the "insiders"— and the people who were coming into government for the first time—the "outsiders." Most of the insiders had come from the International Cooperation Administration, like Wiggins, Josephson, and Nelson. The outsiders were from diverse backgrounds: Wofford (law), Moyers (staff of Lyndon Johnson), Haddad (journalism), Sims (education), Boyce (the Experiment in International Living), and Peters (local state politics). While Shriver was in theory an outsider, he straddled both fences very well. Patterson said that "Shriver kept all these tigers in check because he was a bigger tiger than all of them."[16]

This conflict between insiders and outsiders stemmed from the Peace Corps' origins. It had begun in an informal, personal way with Shriver, Wofford, and a few friends sitting around a big table in a hotel room, a highly unusual birth for an official bureaucracy. The outsiders were determined that the Peace Corps should not lose that intimate, creative flavor. On the other hand, people like Wiggins and Patterson knew that rules and procedures were necessary for survival. They regarded the committed "antibureaucrats" as incurable romantics. The result was that one group acted as a goad on the other to produce the blend Shriver wanted—"an organization for those who don't want to become organization men."[17]

A job on the Peace Corps staff was not for the timid nor the stuffy. The atmosphere was one of bedlam, the hours were late, the rivalries were fierce and, of course, everyone was playing to Shriver. One new administrator was warned that "You must be prepared to run a hundred-yard sprint for ten miles every day."[18] Offices and individuals constantly fought over plans and policies. In particular, PDO battled with Planning and Evaluation over the latter's "unscientific" methods of assessment. In May 1963, Richard Ottinger, deputy chief of the Latin American regional office, complained angrily to Charles Peters, chief of the Evaluation Division, concerning a report on a project in Peru. Ottinger complained of the short time spent in evaluating the project, the journalistic style of reporting, and the scathing criticism of personalities. On another occasion, when the Evaluation Division submitted a highly critical report on a community action project in Guatemala, Shriver invited Jack Vaughn (then chief of the Latin American region) to respond: "May I have one of your hot rebuttals?"[19]

Peace Corps staff meetings were among the most brutally frank in Washington. Robert Gale, chief of Recruitment, remembered one particularly ferocious debate when an ill-informed staff member fled a meeting in tears and consequently offered his resignation. Shriver accepted it.[20] Even the Director himself was not above censure. In September 1961, Josephson rebuked Shriver and John Corcoran, associate director of Management, for revising an organization chart without prior consultation with the rest of the senior staff. "As I have said to you before," Josephson scolded Shriver, "a substantial amount of the anxiety that reigns around here from time to time stems from bilateral dealings with you on matters of multilateral concern." Josephson advised his boss to think again.[21]

This competitive element was extended to the regional chiefs and country Reps in their quest for the best available Volunteers and resources. Thomas Quimby, Rep in Liberia, admitted "stealing" twelve of the best Volunteers from Harris Wofford's Ethiopia consignment. Don Romine, an assistant to Wofford, recalled taking a leading Selection officer to dinner in order to persuade him to add more Volunteers to the project.[22] One of the most disliked men in the entire Peace Corps organization was John Alexander, the somewhat eccentric but ruthlessly determined regional chief of the Africa Division who also headed PDO's coordination section. This latter unit had the authority to either approve a proposed program or quash it as unfeasible. The meetings over which Alexander presided were known as the "murder boards."

PDO GAINS CONTROL

If the in-fighting caused casualties, personal and organizational, it also produced victors. Wiggins's Office of PDO won one bureaucratic battle after another. In so doing, it gained a prized place at the center of the Peace Corps organization. PDO had the most staff (forty-six out of the first one hundred members), was highly disciplined, manned by "insiders" (mostly foreign aid administrators), and led by the superbly cool and able Wiggins.

From the outset, Wiggins had made an indelible mark on the Peace Corps. Along with Josephson, he had drafted *The Towering Task* and had played a leading role in the winning of the Peace Corps' independence in Shriver's absence. Shriver was impressed not only by Wiggins's intelligence but also by his ability to weave his way through the labyrinthine federal bureaucracy. He was a tough and wily in-fighter who relished a challenge and whose opinion had to be reckoned with on any major issue. Though Shriver often fulminated against "bureaucratic nonsense," he appreciated that he had little knowledge of how to get things done in Washington and that he needed experienced administrators around him. That they were of Wiggins's caliber was a bonus.

Wiggins held, next to Shriver, the most important single position in the Peace Corps. PDO conducted the initial negotiations with host governments, determined Volunteer numbers and skills, supervised coordination with the State Department, AID, and other government agencies, and maintained control over projects. When other offices and divisions wanted something, sooner or later they had to go through PDO and Warren Wiggins.

Well aware that most colleges and universities were generally slow-moving, and more interested in research than action, Wiggins felt it would be disastrous to allow them control of the Peace Corps' overseas programs. He was equally skeptical of the capabilities of private voluntary agencies, whose experience was limited to small projects. Wiggins recognized that educational institutions and private organizations would be helpful on the domestic side of the operation, especially in training Volunteers. But overseas, he wanted the Peace Corps to be the master of its own fate.[23] The "Report to the President," however, had stated clearly that the Peace Corps would directly administer programs only in highly unusual circumstances when reasons of "complexity or novelty or urgency" forestalled administration by private agencies, educational institutions, international organizations, or other U.S. government agencies. "As a high educational venture," Shriver had advised Kennedy, "[the Peace Corps'] proper carriers are our traditional institutions of higher education."[24]

The first organization chart reflected this intention by allocating equally powerful divisions to private voluntary agencies, universities, and PDO. By the end of 1961, however, a much-revised chart clearly indicated that the lion's share of programming would be done directly by PDO, which had been made into a major office, while private agencies, universities, and international organizations remained as mere divisions. By 1963, the further-amended chart showed that the three divisions of private agencies, universities, and international organizations had been merged into a single unit, signaling their significant loss of power. In the struggle for control over Peace Corps programs, the private sector had been defeated by Wiggins's PDO. In February 1964, during an executive session of the House Committee on Foreign Affairs, Josephson confirmed what had been common knowledge within the Peace Corps since the summer of 1961: "Most Peace Corps projects are *directly administered* by the Peace Corps."[25] Behind this terse statement lay the story of a bitter bureaucratic battle fought for control of the Peace Corps' overseas projects.

Most of the early reports on the Peace Corps had recommended that it would best function as a decentralized organization, like the National Science Foundation, operating its programs through grants to private agencies and educational institutions. These reports argued that the Peace Corps would greatly benefit from the skill and experience of the private sector in voluntary service overseas and from the public support these bodies would bring with them. A further rationale was that by using the machinery already available through private means, the Peace

Corps would avoid the administrative elephantiasis of most other government bodies. In March 1961, Gordon Boyce, chief of the Division of Private Organizations, told Shriver that "with appropriate support, private agencies can bring to the Peace Corps a vigor and vitality whose equal will be hard to find. Their resources are deep, their contacts broad, their programs far-flung." Likewise, Professor Carroll Wilson of MIT, working in the Division of University Relations, called for a "sister relationship" between academic institutions and the Peace Corps.[26]

Publicly, the Peace Corps paid homage to this notion of full cooperation with the private sector. On establishing the Peace Corps, Kennedy himself spoke of the "trained men and women to be sent overseas . . . by private institutions and organizations."[27] During Shriver's nomination hearing, when he was asked by Senator Fulbright how the Peace Corps intended to administer its programs, he put "direct administration" at the bottom of a list which emphasized private organizations, educational institutions, government agencies, and the U.N.[28] However, the minutes of one of the Peace Corps' first staff meetings on March 30 revealed that Shriver had told his administrators to concentrate their initial efforts on programs where "the *direct* Peace Corps label and image is engaged."[29]

As a practical matter, Shriver realized that an equal programming partnership between the Peace Corps and the private sector was not feasible. First, most of the major private voluntary agencies were religious-based and any infringement of the First Amendment would have had disastrous political consequences for the Peace Corps. Second, speed was the dominant consideration in 1961. To make an impact on Congress and the public, the Peace Corps simply had to get programs into the field quickly. Shriver knew that if he handed control over to academic "perfectionists" it would take a long time before a Volunteer ever got into the field. As Wofford explained it:

> The great semi-autonomous bodies . . . the Red Cross and things like that . . . don't have a lot of sex appeal in terms of a very fast moving operation. He [Shriver] put enormous weight on speed and the more he saw of the complaints about the State Depart-

ment and AID particularly—how long it takes in their pipeline to get anything done; how, in many projects, the time for them has passed by the time the experts and the money arrive—he was determined that in months we'd be able to produce Volunteers to fill jobs that took fourteen months in the old agencies.[30]

Another problem was that private organizations were unwilling to make a wholehearted commitment to Peace Corps programs. They wanted to help with some parts of the overseas administration but rarely with all of it. The Peace Corps was reluctant to split up its programs in this way. Furthermore, as Shriver told his staff, the Peace Corps intended to go to Third World countries where the United States had "not yet succeeded in making a significant social, economic or political impression."[31] Private American organizations had little expertise in these areas; thus it seemed more practical to let the Peace Corps discover for itself the new challenges to be faced.

Not the least contributing factor to the movement away from the private sector was Wiggins's skeptical attitude. He argued that too often in the past, private organizations and academic institutions had been awarded huge grants by the government only to produce sloppy programs overseas. He was determined that this should not happen to the Peace Corps. Such was his feeling on this matter, it was rumored that Wiggins had told Shriver he would resign unless the Peace Corps was equipped with its own central core programming unit which could fight against the poor administration of projects by outside bodies. Bill Kelly supported the Wiggins view. As chief of Contracts and Logistics, he proposed that the Peace Corps should not give grants to private organizations and academic institutions, but contracts. "Grants do not demand performance; contracts do," he explained. In addition to these considerations, Shriver's personal instincts were inclined toward executive control. Thus he gave Wiggins and his experienced "insiders" in PDO the potential to become the engine-room of the Peace Corps. They seized their opportunity.[32]

Shriver did not intend to emasculate the valuable contribution of the private sector. He was well aware that the Peace Corps depended upon it for its training functions. At the same time, he did not want to relinquish his power over overseas projects. Wofford, who had championed the private sector/university approach, summed up Shriver's thinking on this point: "If it had been parceled out, granted the habits of higher education, the likelihood is that you would have had little pieces of it run by different departments and they'd cut up the pie. It could have been awful."[33]

The programming relationship between the Peace Corps and outside organizations was settled by the summer of 1961. Interim Policy Directive 2.1 made the associate director of PDO (Wiggins) responsible for the overseas administration of "all projects and the coordination and balance of the Peace Corps program." Before all but the first five Peace Corps projects had been approved, PDO had gained control.[34]

In 1963, only sixteen private organizations — including CARE, Heifer Project Inc., the 4-H Club Foundation, the National Farm Union, and the American Association for Health, Physical Education and Recreation — had programming contracts with the Peace Corps. Although these helped administer some thirty projects in twenty-one countries, their participation was peripheral and usually came in the form of providing specialist advisers. Only thirteen colleges and universities were involved as contractors in sixteen projects. They administered barely 10 percent of all Volunteers.[35] Contracts with international organizations also were negligible, although there were exceptions like the project in Pakistan jointly administered by the UN's Food and Agricultural Organization.

By 1963, there was no doubt that PDO was the powerful nucleus of Peace Corps programming. Therefore, it was ironic that the Peace Corps, which prided itself in being unbureaucratic, revolved around its *most* bureaucratic unit: Wiggins's PDO.

THE EXTENDED ORGANIZATION

Although PDO won the battle over programming, between 1961 and 1964 the Peace Corps contracted out some 30 percent of its funds to the private sector for training and other professional support services.[36] Virtually all training of Volunteers was carried out by educational institutions, particularly colleges. This was an extremely important role which, in general, they handled successfully.

In the Peace Corps' first four years, over 450 projects were prepared at eighty-six educational institutions in thirty-two states; nearly five thousand faculty members participated in various ways; and over thirty private organizations helped with training and support. With over 80 percent of Volunteers coming from universities or colleges, the Peace Corps claimed it had over eight thousand "associations" with outside bodies.[37] Educators, linguists, technical advisers, and other experts were hired as consultants. Furthermore, the private agricultural, business, and industrial sectors participated in the Peace Corps by providing advice, equipment, or manpower. In 1962, Shriver reported to Kennedy on the "high degree of cooperation" which the Peace Corps was receiving from the private sector, including IBM, the National Advertising Council, Caterpillar Tractor, and AT&T.[38]

This relationship with outside bodies was of profound significance in the Peace Corps' institutional development. By extending and sharing its responsibilities, it became more like a federation of different entities rather than one monolithic government body. This not only obviated the need for the Peace Corps to hire and train a huge technical staff of its own, but also allowed the maximum number of people from many walks of life the opportunity to participate in it at some level. This established for the agency a strong domestic constituency with roots in the diversity of American life.

Perhaps the most significant gesture of openness on the Peace Corps' part was that it allowed its final product, the Volunteer, to be trained by outsiders—colleges and universities. This leasing of power meant that few procedures within the Peace Corps ever became routine; there was always a different way of doing things, always room for debate. The "extended organization," as it was called in Peace Corps parlance, further provided the essential ingredients which Shriver desired for his "different" government organization: flexibility, vitality, and, most of all, non-bureaucracy.

MAXIMUM FLEXIBILITY

Since, as Shriver said, the Peace Corps was setting out "to do what no government agency had ever done before," he felt that few bureaucratic models served useful precedents.[39] Gerald Bush, an early staff member, recalled that in any policy controversy, "the worst possible argument that could be made was that the Department of State did it that way. The second weakest argument that could be made was that it had been done that way before. The strongest argument was that it had never been done before and let's try it."[40] The lack of an institutional history often meant that decisions had to be made in totally unforeseen circumstances and, sometimes, with little time for discussion. For this reason, Shriver usually made policy as he went along, on an ad hoc basis. The staff nicknamed his policy decisions "Shriverisms." An in-house joke was that whatever Shriver said to the *New York Times* or on "Meet the Press" had to be carefully monitored, in case he made a policy while answering a reporter's question.[41]

Every Peace Corps policy directive was entitled "interim," denoting that it could be changed if necessary. Bill Josephson, who devised this nomenclature, explained that it was meant to indicate that policy was not a "substitute for thought." Since the Peace Corps was dealing with thousands of Volunteers working in many different countries and subject to the vagaries of their particular locale, some elasticity in policymaking was essential. "A routine application of policy to issues raised by Volunteers," said Josephson, "would have killed the Peace Corps."[42]

When the Management Office argued that the Peace Corps, like other government agencies, needed a policy instruction manual, Josephson argued against it: "I knew from my experience in ICA the stultifying impact on the program that would have." Under Shriver, the Peace Corps never printed a policy manual. The closest approximation was a "Peace Corps Representative's Handbook." Collated by Josephson and printed for internal use only, it was a miscellany of documents containing what he termed "bits of written policy": an important letter, a telling memorandum, or sometimes just a cable. Its purpose was to provide some guidance for Reps overseas. But, as Josephson described it, "it didn't tell you the way the government manuals usually do, to take Form 23, and fill in this block, and so on. It told you things that were there really to make you think."[43] Out of necessity, therefore, as much as desire, the Peace Corps' guidelines were flexible and, according to Shriver, "carefully evaluated in each country."[44] This was never better illustrated than when a coup in the Dominican Republic left the Peace Corps in the position of dealing with a government not officially recognized by the United States. After sending a cable to Washington, the Rep maintained the Peace Corps' relations with the new regime; he felt the Volunteers could continue their work without danger to their lives and without becoming politically involved. Soon, the United States recognized the new government, and Shriver commended the Rep on his sound judgment: "You were there, we weren't, and we were relying on you."[45]

Interim Policy Directive 4.6 said the Rep's job was to "provide the imagination and ingenuity necessary to retain the freshness and uniqueness of the Peace Corps and keep its objectives clear and its organization appropriately modest." When a Rep in India wrote to headquarters in Washington with an organizational problem, Josephson's reply was indicative of the Peace Corps' management philosophy: "In response to your question as to whether you are being 'sufficiently bureaucratic,' as you know, the general approach is to discourage this whenever, wherever, however possible."[46] This attitude went a long way to explain Harris Wofford's description of the Peace Corps as "an antibureaucratic bureaucracy . . . an agency of programmed diversity, programmed uncertainty, sufficient unpredictability — just going to the threshold of chaos but not quite reaching it."[47] Even PDO, aside from Management the most bureaucratic component of the Peace Corps, was subject to the stricture that its policy and programming directives should allow for flexibility. "I would like to pass on to you the Director's advice," Wiggins told his staff, "that paper never won a war."[48]

KEEPING THE PUNCH IN THE PEACE CORPS

On paper, the Peace Corps had the appearance of any other line-and-staff government agency with the normal recruitment, personnel, and budget functions. Even the bureaucratese used to describe the Volunteers—"middle-level manpower"—had the ring of a typical federal agency. In early 1961, some feared that such a fate would in fact befall the Peace Corps. John Kenneth Galbraith noted in his diary that he was dissatisfied with the way the Peace Corps was being run. "It should be an amateur enterprise led by dedicated individuals," he wrote. "I fear it will pass under the direction of high-salaried bureaucrats who will inculcate the Volunteers with their attitudes."[49] But Galbraith did not take into account the extraordinary determination of Shriver and his staff to make the Peace Corps a truly "different" type of organization.

"We can't have any negative, efficient bureaucrats here," Bill Haddad wrote Shriver. "No cynics allowed!"[50] Shriver's administrators were always conscious of how Point Four, at one time a bold new program, had become ossified; they were intent that such bureaucratic dinosaurism would not overtake the Peace Corps. "Working with the Peace Corps," Shriver told his staff, "should not be exactly like working with another government agency. We have a special mission which can only be accomplished if everyone believes in it and works for it in a manner consistent with the ideals of service and volunteerism."[51]

The first priority was to keep administrative staff to a minimum. Wiggins informed Dean Rusk in May 1961 that "the Peace Corps does not wish to have a large administrative staff of its own."[52] Bill Moyers also wrote an early memorandum on "How to Keep the Punch in the Peace Corps" in which he argued that the agency had to be a "trim ship" with no frills or extravagances.[53] On March 5, 1961, there were 101 people working at Peace Corps headquarters and no Volunteers in the field. After three years, 647 staff were in Washington with a further 365 in training camps or in overseas posts. Over seven thousand Volunteers were in training or in the field. Despite this rapid expansion, the Peace Corps' sense of smallness was retained. Between 1961 and 1964, there were ten Volunteers in the field for every administrative person in support. The Peace Corps was always happy to compare this figure to the average for the federal government's other international programs—one person in Washington to every four abroad.[54]

The Peace Corps' disdain of bureaucratic procedure led to

friction with the more traditional agencies. The Bureau of the Budget and the Executive Office frequently requested the Peace Corps' projections on future growth, a legitimate inquiry from their standpoint since, acting as bureaucratic mechanisms of control, they wanted to make long-term estimates. For the Peace Corps, the question was absurd. Under Shriver, the agency moved pragmatically from day to day, increasing or decreasing staff and budgets as the situation demanded. Patterson recalled Shriver's reaction when an official asked him to make a long-term budget estimate: "Shriver almost started laughing at him. He said, 'Look, it's a very legitimate question, but how the hell do I know where we're going to be in five years?' "[55] In a virtually unprecedented action for a federal agency, Shriver actually returned Peace Corps appropriations to the Treasury, $1.9 million for fiscal year 1962 and $3.9 million for 1963.

Relishing the opportunity to create something new, the Peace Corps' administrators encouraged risk-taking. "We do not rely upon the rule-book," Wiggins told his staff, "but on the exceptional privileges granted by the rule-book."[56] A new staffer recalled being instructed to "operate fast and stay legal, but if something goes wrong, just operate fast."[57] Shriver had no time for the timid proposal or the bureaucratically inhibited response. He demanded boldness and intellectual daring. "There will be little tolerance of a 'tomorrow' philosophy," he wrote, "or an 'it can't be done because it hasn't been done before' attitude."[58]

Shriver also demanded total commitment. Weekend work and early-morning phone calls became standard for Peace Corps staffers—often to the annoyance of their spouses. So that officials could better identify with Volunteers, Shriver strongly encouraged them to serve in the field at some point. In 1962 Shriver persuaded Harris Wofford to leave the White House to become the Peace Corps' Rep in Ethiopia and Special Rep for Africa in general; other top administrators who served overseas were Tom Quimby in Liberia and Frank Mankiewicz in Peru. By the fall of 1963, Shriver himself had visited thirty-six of the forty-four countries in which the Peace Corps had a program. He wanted to avoid the situation where desk-bound bureaucrats made plans, unaware of the actual conditions under which Volunteers worked. To keep the organization on its toes, he set up an Evaluation

Division. In the words of its first chief, Charles Peters, its function was "to take an independent, no axe-to-grind look at all aspects of the Peace Corps."[59] In effect, Evaluation became Shriver's eyes and ears.

THE CONSCIENCE OF THE PEACE CORPS

The first evaluations were no more than sketchy reports on Peace Corps training methods. Soon, however, a process evolved whereby an individual evaluator or a team of evaluators, often former journalists, went overseas for a two- or three-week period, observed the Peace Corps at work, gathered information through intensive interviewing, and brought back their analyses to Shriver. Their reports were journalistic accounts which concentrated on the problems faced by Volunteers: the appropriateness of the Volunteer lifestyle and living standards, the quality of the job being done, contact with host nationals, personal adjustment problems, host country reactions, and the effectiveness of selection and training methods. They were based on commonsense observations rather than scientific analysis and were designed to impart the mood of a program. They were also extremely candid and classified "eyes only" for the Director.

Part of the rationale behind evaluation was to avoid mistakes or, at least, to discover them before the press did. Shriver described this as "getting the *Time* magazine story before *Time* magazine."[60] Just as important, however, was his desire to have an insider who could be relied upon to be ruthlessly objective. Although the Volunteer was the main concern of the evaluators, every aspect of the organization was open to criticism. There were no sacred cows.

Shriver dispatched these evaluators all over the globe and urged them to cast a cold eye on the Peace Corps. He wanted to know what was good, but more importantly, what was weak or inefficient. "As an evaluator," Peters wrote, "you have a duty to raise hell."[61] To guard against the self-congratulatory tendencies certain to arise in even the most enlightened organizations, Shriver often hired people who had no government ties—journalists, academics, social scientists—to perform evaluations. The hypercritical style and sweeping extent of this process was otherwise unknown in the federal government.

At first, Peters and his evaluators were denigrated by their peers as "Shriver's spies." Every so often, headquarters would rock with news of the latest scandalous exposé from the field. Reps were sometimes dismissed after critical evaluations had been filed. After one particularly devastating report on a program in Pakistan, Peters recalled that the entire overseas staff was sacked. Tom Quimby was once moved to write a twenty-page rebuttal to a critical evaluation report on Liberia where he was Rep. "Frankly, the evaluation reports made me madder than hell," he said.[62]

"Misleading" and "false" were a few of the adjectives hurled at Evaluation by Joseph Kauffman, associate director of Training. In a 1962 memorandum, he was categorical in his denunciation of Evaluation's role "in visiting training centers, of their reports (which are not always seen), of the low level of analysis, colored language and superficiality." The enraged Kauffman said there was "a strong feeling that if the agency had to economize, Planning and Evaluation ought to go first. As presently run, the operation is ineffective at best and an affront to our dignity at the least."[63]

The evaluators cared little for bureaucratic sensitivities. They judged performance by the highest standards and were scathing of even the slightest incompetence. By 1963, Shriver had hit upon the idea of hiring returning Volunteers as evaluators; they especially relished the opportunity to criticize their former bosses. In later years, Peters conceded that evaluation reports were sometimes too subjective and over-reliant on "gut feelings." At one point in 1962, he was sure that he was about to be fired because his reports were proving too disruptive. He recalled Shriver himself being very concerned at the impact of Evaluation's "colorful" assessments. In the fall of that year, however, Shriver visited a broad range of Peace Corps programs in the field. In the middle of his trip, he sent a cable to Washington headquarters which said: "Tell Peters he was right."[64]

In 1963, the Evaluation Division began refining its methods and brought in more technical experts and scholars. Yet, as Bill Haddad pointed out, the scholars, with all their academic training, still produced reports "not significantly different from those produced by the newspaper types we have here."[65] Evaluation meant the loss of many reputations. One assessment of an official read: "While he is a loveable old gentleman, it has never been clear why this individual was hired . . . it would be well not to continue his employment." Another described a Rep as "too pompous, far too church-oriented and too formal." His retainment was not recommended.

In time, no staff member came to be more respected by his peers than Charles Peters. He was bright, irreverent, and farseeing. On every subject, from Volunteers' sexual behavior to possible political scandal, Peters provided the Peace Corps hierarchy with sound advice and gave warning of potential disasters. His critical reports and biting memoranda were hard for administrators to swallow; but if it was difficult not to hate Evaluation, it was equally difficult not to admire Peters's integrity. He was convinced that "if the Peace Corps is to get better—and unless we keep trying to make it better it will surely get worse—we must raise our standards."[66] He was a perennial seeker after excellence who, despite friction with his colleagues, was dubbed by them "the conscience of the Peace Corps."[67]

Evaluation and other reflective mechanisms such as the Research Division, lent credence to Shriver's contention that no one was more critical of the Peace Corps than it was of itself. This self-examining attitude allowed it to escape the ossification endemic in most government bureaucracies and kept it athletic and vigorous. Andrew Kopkind, writing in the *New Republic*, recognized this quality and cited the Peace Corps as "the last, remaining, isolated and beleaguered outpost of the New Frontier. All the other fortresses have fallen to the captains of consensus."[68]

IN, UP, AND OUT

By 1963, the first returning Volunteers were being given administrative positions in Washington. Bill Haddad argued that the Peace Corps staff should eventually consist entirely of "returnees" and thus make the organization thoroughly "volunteer" in nature.[69] While Haddad's dream was never fully realized, by the spring of 1965 returned Volunteers numbered 183 out of a total staff of approximately one thousand. Former Volunteers comprised about 14 percent of the headquarters staff and 27 percent of the overseas staff; a third of all Reps were returned Volunteers.[70] This development added to the process of regeneration within the Peace Corps and formed the seeds of self-revision. The new wave of administrators created a kind of underground movement at headquarters; they got their feet on the rungs of power and became an important force for change and innovation.

The Peace Corps' freshness was further replenished by the "no-career" philosophy which Shriver propounded. In informal, but unmistakable fashion, he made it clear from the beginning that the Peace Corps was a service, not a job, and that the standard emoluments of a career in government—tenure, promotion, retirement schemes—did not apply. Shriver wanted to maintain experimentation, creativity, and risk; he did not want "careerist" types. As Josephson explained, "we almost never made a tenured appointment in the Peace Corps."[71]

On March 6, 1963, in a memorandum entitled "In-Up-and-Out—A Plan to Keep the Peace Corps Permanently Young, Creative and Dynamic," Franklin Williams sought to formalize Shriver's drive against careerism:

> Unless we permanently build in some protections, it is inevitable that the Peace Corps, as a number of other unlamentable federal agencies, will eventually become so bureaucratic, hide-bound, "know-that-this-is-the-way-we-did-it-yesterday-is-the-way-it-should-be-done-today" in our attitudes that all the wonderful vigor, originality, flexibility, etc. that we talk about will slowly disappear . . . This kind of bureaucratic hardening of the arteries can be avoided. The secret is staffing. I propose an "in-up-and-out" procedure for the Peace Corps.[72]

Williams proposed that all Peace Corps personnel should be subject to a limited tenure of five years. Other staff agreed with the Williams thesis that the Peace Corps, in its third year at this point, should do everything in its power to avoid becoming a traditional bureaucracy.

Shriver put Bill Moyers in charge of an internal task force

which had as its mandate "To Keep the Peace Corps Flexible." The task force agreed that some safeguards against careerism were needed, but envisaged a major problem in getting legislation to restrict the number of years a person might work with the agency. Haddad told Shriver that the cut-off date and its implication of "administration by rookies" would cause some concern on Capitol Hill.[73] Shriver also had to take into account the inevitable hostility of the Civil Service Commission, the constant loss of experienced and able people, and the possibility that this controversial piece of legislation might obscure the Peace Corps' more urgent goals in Congress. But he was willing to pay the price necessary to ensure that "new energy, spirit and ideas are constantly injected in the Peace Corps' administration."[74] The long drive for legislation began.

Despite certain reservations about the wisdom of going all-out for legislation, Shriver's staff threw their weight behind what they nicknamed the "five year flush." In a memorandum to Myer Feldman, special assistant to Kennedy, Moyers argued that the Peace Corps was unique among government agencies:

> Why is it unique? A number of reasons could be offered, but the central reason is that most of its people—now totalling about 7,000—are Volunteers. Volunteers are a very special breed. Their idealism, the nature of the commitment they have made, their goals all deserve special respect and require special handling . . . I think Sarge is also concerned to try to create a device which will assure that the Peace Corps will retain its fresh, critical and spirited approach to its business. A five year limitation on employment will guarantee constant injection into the Peace Corps of new ideas and energies.[75]

When Undersecretary of State George Ball warned Shriver of possible congressional intransigence, Shriver responded: "Frankly, I think that anything legislated about this organization is sui-generis almost, even in the minds of Congressmen."[76] As expected, John W. Macy, chairman of the Civil Service Commission, proved an obstacle to legislation. "This approach is so fundamentally in conflict with the concept of the career service," he told Shriver, "that I believe, even under the special cir-

cumstances of the Peace Corps, that this limitation would con-
stitute inappropriate public policy."[77]

As 1963 ended, the "Five Year Limitation" legislation was
mired in Congress. It remained so until October 10, 1965. Effective on that day, an amendment to the Peace Corps Act said that
all professional staff (those at the GS-9 grade or above) would
not be permitted to remain with the organization longer than
five consecutive years. Professor Robert Textor later wrote that
this was "the first time in the history of the American republic
that a federal agency has deliberately moved to limit drastically
the tenure of its own personnel for the specific purpose of
avoiding bureaucratic arteriosclerosis."[78]

The enactment of the five-year-flush was a milestone in the
Peace Corps' institutional history. It was also the most emphatic
symbol of the agency's antibureaucratic tendencies. After five
years, all senior staff had to make way for new people. Accordingly, Sargent Shriver resigned the Peace Corps directorship on
March 1, 1966—five years since his appointment by President
Kennedy.

7

Principles, Policies, and the President

> More than any other agency of government, the Peace Corps personified the whole Kennedy philosophy of "Ask not what your country can do for you, ask what you can do for your country." And all of us believed it and lived it and felt we were part of an enterprise which was the personification of that philosophy.
> —Bradley Patterson,
> Executive Secretary of the Peace Corps

PHILOSOPHY, RULES, AND REGULATIONS

In December 1961, Sargent Shriver outlined for President Kennedy the policies and practices which he considered necessary to implement the Peace Corps program successfully. "The basic philosophy of the Peace Corps," wrote Shriver, "is one of service." He pointed out that Volunteers would be expected to live simply and unostentatiously. They would receive no salaries and would endure "substantial hazards to their health and even to their safety." Since the overseas staff were the Volunteers' leaders, they also would have to live "simply and inconspicuously, maintaining close and continuous contact and identification with the Volunteers." Despite difficult living conditions, Shriver underlined that there would be no special rewards or privileges attached to work with the Peace Corps. "The

116

Peace Corps is not just a job. There are no 9:00 to 5:00 days in our operation," he said. While Peace Corps rules were to be flexible and might not be "uniform for all sections," Shriver was insistent that everyone should not only understand, but fully accept the agency's basic philosophy. "There is no place," he said, "for anyone who disagrees with the goals of service."[1] There was never a clearer exposition of the Peace Corps' *modus operandi*.

Some rules and regulations were easily defined. For example, Volunteers received seventy-five dollars for every month of service. This "termination allowance" was paid in a lump sum at the end of their term overseas. Volunteers were given leave at the rate of two-and-a-half days for each month of service. This leave could be accumulated and travel was permitted outside the Volunteer's host country. Volunteers could resign from the Peace Corps at any time; but to discourage people from just packing up and leaving when they felt like it, Shriver ruled that the federal government would pay for fares home only at the end of the full two years of service.

Other policy matters were not open to such simple definition. In May 1962, General Counsel William Delano noted that the controversial issue of Volunteer marriage had "sharply divided the agency." Bill Josephson added that "no question has been longer discussed within the Peace Corps."[2] Some felt that marriage either before or during service should lead to immediate exclusion from the Peace Corps. They feared that the responsibilities of married life would impair the Volunteers' performance in the field. Delano argued, however, that marriage either to a private American citizen, a host country national, or a fellow Volunteer would not be an irrevocable barrier to service. He believed that if deterrence of marriage became firm policy, "then we may be getting the Peace Corps into many more difficult and controversial situations than would otherwise occur." On legal, ethical, and practical grounds, he feared the Peace Corps would be charting treacherous waters if an arbitrary judgment were made on this deeply personal matter:

> I invite you to put yourself in the situation of a Peace Corps Rep abroad, trying to do a job, probably with too few Volunteers, whose Volunteers are, by and large, very good, mature, dedicated

people, telling one of them who comes to him and says he wants to get married to a non-Volunteer that there is a presumption that his marriage is not consistent with continued service . . . I am not sure that many Congressmen (or women) will understand that point of view . . . [3]

Delano's arguments prevailed. Interim Policy Directive 3.8 (Policy with Regard to the Selection for Training or Service Overseas of Married Volunteers) stated that married couples could be accepted into the Peace Corps and marriages during service would not imply automatic disqualification. By the end of 1963, there were four hundred married couples in the Peace Corps; forty couples had married during their service. As in the vast majority of Peace Corps policies, the main criterion applied in this case was the practical one: would the Volunteer continue to be as effective after marriage as before?

The same question was applied to pregnancy during service. Would the mother and father be able to continue effectively as Volunteers after the birth of a child? "Our policy," wrote Shriver in July 1962, "is to decide each situation on a case-by-case basis."[4] A caveat was that unmarried female Volunteers who became pregnant would be immediately sent home since the Peace Corps could not be expected to take on the maintenance of the child.

On almost every issue concerning the Volunteer it was necessary for the Peace Corps to have an opinion, even if that opinion were not to be regarded as the last word on the subject. For example: that a full-field security investigation of all Volunteers should be conducted either by the Civil Service Commission or, if necessary, the FBI; that Volunteers were not U.S. diplomatic personnel and therefore should not seek the privileges and immunities customarily enjoyed by American officials overseas, especially "PX" facilities (the right to buy in government-subsidized "post exchange" shops); that only essential equipment should be supplied to Volunteers for their work in case they should come to be viewed as "Santa Clauses with handouts." After one Volunteer in the Philippines was discovered carrying a handgun, Shriver demanded that all firearms in the Peace Corps' possession be returned to Washington immediately by classified pouch. "The Peace Corps must never even resemble soldiers," he ordered. "The carrying of firearms by Volunteers may remind some of colonial repressions."[5]

In a letter to Reps on "The Social Behavior of Volunteers," Shriver laid out guidelines on dress, language, drinking-habits, and the use of leisure time. Regarding dress, he pointed out that all Volunteers should be aware that their personal appearance could reflect "credit or discredit upon them and the Corps." The question of beards and their contemporary association with "beat-niks" was a particular problem. "There seems little reason to tell a man who normally wears a neat, regular beard that he should shave it off," Shriver wrote. On the other hand, "a group of Volunteers who suddenly decide to grow shaggy, semi-ludicrous beards as a lark or evidence of 'roughing it,' will bring discredit on the Peace Corps and make it more difficult for all of us to do the job."[6]

Shriver made it clear that he expected every Volunteer to be exemplary in social behavior, including sexual behavior. There was even a policy on contraception. To avoid "Peace Corps babies" in Third World countries, some officials argued that Volunteers should be issued contraceptive devices in much the same manner as GIs were supplied by the U.S. army. Shriver ruled this out, arguing that contraception was a private matter:

> In every aspect of creature comfort needs, we have tried to keep the Volunteers as far from the military approach as possible on the theory that we are dealing with intelligent adults who will live closer to their host country nationals if they cope with food, clothing, shelter and travel on an individual basis. I do not think, therefore, that the G.I. "pro" kit precedent is persuasive in the Peace Corps context.[7]

Within a few years, policy guidelines for the Volunteer had evolved on everything from health precautions to travel during leave periods. After a few Volunteers were discovered to have taken leave in Paris, Shriver prohibited all journeys to Western Europe. "Volunteers are supposed to learn about the Third World," he said, "not the developed, industrialized Western world."[8] Policies also emerged for organizational procedure. The Peace Corps had its own cable series (TOPEC-PECTO) for the frequent and fast flow of information to and from the field. Security classification for certain documents was deemed necessary since the Peace Corps dealt with some highly sensitive personnel information. If a staff member appeared at a function, made a speech, or wrote an article, no payment could be accepted.

By 1963, some staff and Volunteers were complaining that the Peace Corps was becoming policy-laden and that there were too many attempts at "control." But Shriver always emphasized that Peace Corps policies should be seen as flexible guidelines rather than binding laws. He was a firm believer in individual initiative. As he told Kennedy: "Trust and respect will solve more difficult situations than any directive."[9]

THE CHURCH-STATE CONUNDRUM

Only one Peace Corps policy was written in stone: there should be no religious, racial, or sexual discrimination of any kind. In the summer of 1961, Bill Moyers warned Shriver that the religious question was "an emotional controversy with strong political overtones" which could well affect the Peace Corps.[10] John F. Kennedy's Catholicism was adjudged by Theodore Sorensen to have been "the strongest factor against him" in attaining the presidency.[11] The problem was exacerbated for the Peace Corps by Kennedy's choice of his Catholic brother-in-law as its first Director. Moyers explained that if the Peace Corps contracted with religious voluntary organizations, especially Catholic ones, then the charge of government involvement in religious proselytizing and infringement of the First Amendment would inevitably follow. During the early days of the Peace Corps, the problem of separation of church and state was always lurking in the background.

The New York Times advised the Peace Corps to learn from religious agencies working in the development field but not to finance them. "No sectarian religious organization should receive financial support, either direct or indirect, from the Corps," said an editorial in July 1961. "For a federal government agency to

give such assistance would be to violate the constitutional separation of church and state, which should be kept sacred—especially
in these days."[12]

This raised an acute problem for the proposed partnership
with the private sector in overseas projects. If religious welfare
and missionary programs were excluded from Peace Corps participation, then relatively few private organizations would be
left with which to contract. Of nearly twenty thousand secular
American foundations, only twenty-nine had overseas projects
worth more than $10,000. In terms of voluntary work overseas,
the ecclesiastical bodies—Catholic Relief Services, the Church
World Service, Lutheran World Relief, the American Friends Service, and so on—sponsored the bulk of programs.[13] With Peace
Corps projects about to be launched and a bill before Congress,
it was imperative that Shriver should not alienate the support
of organized religion. Yet, as Josephson sensed, the Peace Corps
would have to be very conscious of the President's "understand-
able sensitivity in this area."[14]

Shriver decided that unless directly challenged on its position, the Peace Corps should adopt a public policy of silence.
Presidential counsel Sorensen constantly reminded the Peace
Corps of Kennedy's particular vulnerability in the area of church-
state relations. During a weekend trip to Hyannisport, Shriver
explained to Kennedy the Peace Corps' reasons for its silence
on this matter.[15] In June, Josephson gave the legal opinion that
no Volunteers should be chosen or assigned on a religious basis.[16]
But the nettle of the Peace Corps' direct contractual relationship
with religious agencies had still to be plucked.

Like many Peace Corps decisions, the policy on the religious
relationship was made by Shriver himself in response to a specific
crisis. The problem came to a head in the summer of 1961 while
the first Volunteers were in training at Harvard for a teaching
program in Nigeria. When Nigeria gained independence in 1960,
its new Ministry of Education had incorporated the many colonial mission schools, although these schools retained their
religious base. The question arose whether Volunteers could
teach in these schools without violating the constitutional principle of separation of church and state. Some American private

organizations in Nigeria suggested that Volunteers should be selected according to their religion and sent to respective Catholic or Protestant schools. On July 14, Shriver vetoed this suggestion in a cable to the U.S. embassy in Lagos:

> If U.S. voluntary operated schools in Nigeria are suggesting that religious criteria be applied in selecting Volunteers for programs of such agencies, then it is apparent that failure of communication exists . . . any group of Peace Corps Volunteers will have a great diversity of religious affiliation and non-affiliation.[17]

After consultation with Sorensen, Moyers, and Josephson, Shriver decided that since Volunteers would be employed by the Nigerian government and not by a religious body, the program could go ahead. Volunteers could teach secular subjects in mission schools under the strict condition that no religious instruction would be asked of them. This decision was formalized in a document entitled "The Religious Policies of the Peace Corps." The Peace Corps would consider projects from governments which incorporated religious organizations, provided Volunteers would not be involved in proselytizing. Direct contracts with religious agencies were strictly prohibited. Josephson tempered this latter stricture by explaining that although the Peace Corps would not contract with a private agency in connection with a proselytizing project, a broad spectrum of religiously affiliated private groups remained whose proposals would be considered "on a case by case basis."[18] As ever, flexibility was the watchword.

On December 15, 1961, Shriver publicly announced this policy at a conference of American private voluntary agencies. He used the Nigerian example to illustrate the Peace Corps' religious neutrality:

> In Nigeria we will have 100 people by January—many of them teaching in church schools. It is inevitable that some Volunteers will be teaching in a mission school different from their faith. Some people will write us and say "This is awful." I think it is great. Our basic policy is no religious proselytizing or propagandizing.[19]

Shriver insisted that because of the legal and constitutional question, there could be no direct contracting with a "100 percent church program"; however, Volunteers in the field would work on a practical basis with experienced church professionals.

Despite Shriver's reasoning, many religious organizations were indignant at what they considered to be a snub by a new agency composed of inexperienced amateurs. "The church-related agencies have a tremendous wealth of experience," protested Bishop Swanstrom of the National Catholic Welfare Conference. "I deplore this policy, and we regret, and in a sense, are disturbed that the Peace Corps has set up this policy."[20]

The Peace Corps' religious policy was an important factor in crippling the participation of the private sector in direct administration of overseas programs. The Catholic church was hurt most since it had the majority of denominational projects, especially in Latin America. It had hoped for the Peace Corps' support, in terms of both money and manpower. For several years, Shriver was consistently criticized by the National Catholic Council. Bradley Patterson saw the paradox in Shriver, a prominent Catholic layman, "getting this kind of heat from his own church."[21]

Shriver also recognized the irony. He took pleasure in reminding his brother-in-law that he was defending him and his new agency from the charge of religious bias—toward Catholics or any other denomination. In one illuminating memorandum, he told Kennedy about "a Protestant Volunteer from Kansas, teaching in a Catholic mission school in Ghana (under a Catholic headmaster), who is conducting the weekly meetings of the Student Christian Movement made up of sixty Protestant students attending the Catholic school."[22]

THE RACE QUESTION

When it came to the question of race, the Peace Corps went beyond neutrality. From the beginning, the agency followed a line of positive discrimination in favor of disadvantaged minorities. Shriver explained this policy to the National Conference On Religion and Race in Chicago on January 15, 1963: "We set out deliberately to recruit as many Negroes and representatives of other minority groups as possible for jobs in every echelon.

We knew Negroes would not ordinarily seek out these jobs, so we decided to seek them out."[23]

In his original Peace Corps proposal at the Cow Palace, Kennedy had stressed that service would be open to "every race and walk of life." The policy of deliberately seeking out blacks and non-whites, however, emanated from the convictions of Shriver and Wofford, who together had headed the civil rights section of Kennedy's presidential campaign. Shriver, a longstanding member of the Catholic Interracial Council, had witnessed at firsthand brutal discrimination in Chicago. He had served on the Board of Education there at the time of the Supreme Court's historic Brown decision (which said that the racial segregation of schools was unconstitutional) and had seen the violence and riots caused by racial disharmony. His personal commitment to civil rights was deep and unwavering. Wofford had close ties to Martin Luther King, Jr., and the black community. In 1959 he had edited the first report of the U.S. Commission on Civil Rights to the President and Congress. He had also been the principal force behind Kennedy's famous phone call to Mrs. King when her husband had been thrown into jail in the fall of 1960—a call which probably swung the black vote in Kennedy's favor (seven out of ten blacks voted Democratic). While the Kennedy administration was generally committed to civil rights, the Peace Corps, led by Shriver and Wofford, was far ahead of its time in its strenuous effort to provide equal opportunity for minority groups.

As ever, Shriver's purpose in this area was practical as well as idealistic. He knew that a multiracial Peace Corps would have a better chance of effective people-to-people contact with Africans, Asians, and Latin Americans than a Peace Corps consisting solely of white Americans. In February 1961, Peace Corps leaders planned to use Howard University in Washington, D.C.—a top black American educational institution—to provide Volunteers with "a basic feel and understanding of 'the best' in American Negro culture and thought." In August, Shriver made black recruitment a Peace Corps priority and ordered "a specialized public information attack" on the black community. Wofford circulated a memorandum to staff advocating positive efforts "to

promote equal opportunity within our agency." Franklin Williams
responded that minorities had, in fact, been taken into "the
higher-grade categories" of the Peace Corps and that a special
recruiting drive for blacks was being organized.[24]

 Puerto Ricans were another minority group who found the
Peace Corps "discriminating in their favor." It was felt that they
would add an important texture to the Peace Corps initiative,
particularly in Latin America. Special steps were also taken to
recruit on Indian reservations. In the summer of 1962, Shriver
informed Kennedy that the Peace Corps was doing everything
in its power "to encourage American Indians to volunteer."[25]

During an early Senate Foreign Relations Committee hearing, Shriver made it clear that the Peace Corps would not go
to any country which discriminated against Volunteers on racial
or religious grounds.[26] This issue was raised in 1961 by a request
from Ambassador William Rountree in the Sudan for a Peace
Corps project to be launched there, but on the condition that
no Jewish Volunteers would be included. Shriver flatly refused
and the possibility of a program there died.[27] Universities in the
southern states of America were also refused training and selection contracts because Shriver would not tolerate insults to black
trainees. In July 1962, he publicly protested the refusal of an
inn-owner near Olney, Maryland to serve black Peace Corps
trainees.[28]

Despite the Peace Corps' efforts on the race question blacks
never made up more than 5 percent of Volunteers between 1961
and 1963, a period when blacks were 11 percent of the population.[29] This low figure was attributable to two main factors.
First, many of the most eligible black American youths were beginning to make a commitment to attacking poverty and ignorance at home rather than abroad by enlisting in the ensuing civil
rights crusade. Second, and perhaps more important, most blacks
thought they could not afford the time and the implied economic
sacrifice involved in two years service in the Peace Corps. By
1963, recruiters were trying to sell the Peace Corps to blacks on
positive economic grounds, arguing that after two years of service they would be guaranteed a superior type of job. The argument never proved that persuasive. C. Payne Lucas, the most

outspoken black in the Peace Corps administration, explained why:

> Most of the black kids in the sixties were kids whose parents struggled to get them through college. Suddenly, we were talking about going into the Peace Corps. But black kids finished school and their parents expected them to help them. We offered them 75 dollars a month readjustment pay . . . It comes down to dollars and cents.[30]

Nevertheless, within the Peace Corps administrative staff at least, giant strides in the employment of minorities were taken. In January 1963, 7.4 percent of higher-echelon posts in the Peace Corps were filled by blacks. The comparative figure in other federal agencies was .8 percent. Twenty-four percent of lower administrative positions were occupied by blacks, as against 5.3 percent in other government bodies. By 1964, 10 percent of all Peace Corps overseas Reps were black.[31] In the early 1960s, this was an impressive record.

The effects of this affirmative action program on the countries where the Peace Corps worked were striking. Young white Volunteers openly mixing with black Volunteers and staff—something they could not do in many parts of the still-segregated United States—made a dramatic impact on Third World peoples. "So far as the American image goes," wrote evaluators in a report on Liberia in 1963, "we are probably doing more good on the race issue than any other aspect . . . The race question is still the hottest one going, where Americans are concerned, and the mere fact that we are willing to discuss it with students and others in a reasonable, candid way, makes a solid impression."[32]

WOMEN AND THE PEACE CORPS

Also impressive was the Peace Corps' early emphasis on giving women the same opportunity for service as men in a period when champions of women's liberation and sexual equality were not conspicuous. Kennedy had allowed the Peace Corps the potential to be a leader in this field by stating at the Cow Palace that service would be open to women. In March 1961, Shriver ordered that attention should be given to "opportunities to include outstanding professional women on the headquarters staff." Furthermore, at the first session of the National Advisory Council in May, Shriver pledged his commitment to "women as Volunteers." He also gave major speeches on "Women in the Peace Corps" in which he called for women to work overseas as nurses, teachers, and doctors.[33] Recruitment literature also pointed out that "American women doing Peace Corps work abroad will give a personal nudge to history in terms of improving the status of women in many of the newly emerging countries of the world."

Some early reports on the Peace Corps advised the omission of the "weaker sex" because of the dangers of rape and single-girl pregnancies, especially in the *muchismo* cultures of Latin America. Nevertheless, by 1963 one-third of the seven thousand Volunteers serving around the world were female. During a Senate hearing in February 1964, Shriver admitted that he had not recruited as many women administrators as he would have liked.[34] Even so, Dorothy Jacobsen (chief of Division of Personnel), Ruth Olson (special assistant to the chief of the Division of Volunteer Support), and Alice Gilbert (chief of the Division of UN and International Agency Programs) made it to upper-echelon posts at Peace Corps headquarters. At the Volunteer level, Shriver proclaimed in a speech "On Women" in June 1962 that "the role of women in the Peace Corps is exactly the same as that of the male."[35]

The Peace Corps' nonsexist record was flawed by its position on pregnancy. If a single female Volunteer became pregnant, she was sent home immediately; the father—often a fellow Volunteer—was allowed to remain in the program. Many women Volunteers deemed this a blind spot in the Peace Corps' otherwise undiscriminating attitude toward the sexes.

Even given this bias, however, and the limited success in recruiting minorities as Volunteers, the Peace Corps was visionary in both areas when compared to the deficiencies of contemporary federal agencies. Warren Wiggins went so far as to claim that, for its time, the Peace Corps was "unique in the history of government institutions."[36]

STATE DEPARTMENT RELATIONS

As a fragile new agency, the Peace Corps had to work hard at building relationships with the more traditional federal organizations. In early 1961, there was a good deal of skepticism about sending young Americans overseas as "middle-level manpower." The Peace Corps had to overcome the cynics. In this respect, President Kennedy was of inestimable help. More than any other government agency, his name was associated with the Peace Corps. This relationship was important. As Harris Wofford put it: "In those first years, nobody outside the White House was going to lay a hand on the Peace Corps or Shriver because of his own power and Kennedy's behind him."[37]

Despite this power, there remained a mixture of concern and fear within the federal bureaucracy regarding the Peace Corps. This apprehension was accentuated in May 1961 when the Peace Corps won its independence after some bitter infighting. As Josephson told Shriver, this victory was not exactly "greeted with cheers by the rest of the concerned bureaucracy." Ralph Dungan in the White House and Henry Labouisse, head of ICA, felt that the Peace Corps' use of Vice-President Johnson to exert pressure on the President had been "an end run" and, indeed, that the Peace Corps had behaved "irresponsibly throughout . . . " Some were depicting the Peace Corps as "a ruthless and unruly place." To dispel this image, Josephson advised Shriver to exploit fully his good personal rapport with senior officials.[38]

Although the Peace Corps was semi-autonomous, it was required under law to coordinate its activities with the other official arms of U.S. foreign policy, particularly the State Department. Happily, Dean Rusk sympathized with Shriver's desire for Peace Corps independence. According to Rusk:

> We agreed that the Peace Corps should operate outside of the framework of American foreign policy. That it should not be looked upon as an instrument of the U.S. Embassy in any particular country . . . I told Sargent Shriver that he should not look over his shoulder at me or at the Department of State but that

he should organize and administer the Peace Corps with as much independence as possible.[39]

Rusk personally liked the Peace Corps idea, saying "it was one of my favorite undertakings." He also had "a tremendous respect for Shriver's abilities and talents."[40] He paid Shriver the compliment of inviting him to attend all State Department staff meetings. Undersecretaries Chester Bowles and George Ball also assured Shriver of their early support, and Assistant Secretary William Crockett pledged that "We in the State Department wish to do everything in our power to assure the success of the Peace Corps."[41]

Despite the friendship of high officials, the overall Peace Corps-State relationship was not uniformly cordial. In the summer of 1961, Josephson told Shriver that "carping comments" were still being heard in the middle and lower ranks of State.[42] There was an initial reticence on the part of old hands in the American diplomatic community to accept the Peace Corps. As Chester Bowles described it: "The old-timers didn't want the Peace Corps in their hair. Their thinking was 'Some Volunteer goes out and gets caught in some drug raid, and I, the ambassador, get the blame for it. Keep it away from me!' "[43]

Shriver made strong efforts to allay these fears. In March 1961, he gave a reassuring speech before the Foreign Service Association, the blue blood of the American diplomatic corps. Afterwards, he reported to Bowles that he felt his speech had left State "a little less worried, scared or even terrified at the prospects of Volunteers rushing wildly and aimlessly around the world."[44] Nevertheless, a strong element of mistrust between the Peace Corps and State remained and occasionally led to a blow-up. One such row took place in July 1962, during a State Department-Peace Corps meeting on educational aid to Africa. Bill Haddad described it:

> Immediately, a few of the people at this meeting questioned our competence to select people to teach in African universities. Without the use of four-letter words, I carefully explained to them our selection and training processes . . . This didn't satisfy them . . . they talked about our sudden intrusion into the education

field . . . In checking with the staff, I found that everyone got the same bitter taste in his mouth that I did, and their first reaction was to tell them to go to hell.[45]

Haddad requested Shriver's assistance in dealing with the "pontifical, pompous idiots." Bill Josephson was another who became infuriated with Foggy Bottom's failure to reciprocate the Peace Corps' willingness to allow all its cable traffic to be cleared by State: "Can anyone explain to me why we never appear to see State or AID messages involving major decisions on issues involving countries in which we have programs?"[46]

To some extent, the Peace Corps had itself to blame for its occasionally fraught relations with State. Its insistence on being "different"—abnegating privileges and disdaining the hospitality of the American diplomatic community—led to a certain self-righteousness. Wiggins's remark about the Foreign Service living in "golden ghettoes" overseas, for example, caused enormous resentment. The Peace Corps' ardor in guarding its independent status sometimes lapsed into an arrogance which proved as destructive as the conservatism of some officials at Foggy Bottom.

Overseas, the U.S. ambassador's sanction was required for all Peace Corps program requests. Apart from that formal relationship, the Peace Corps had little contact with embassy staff. While Shriver recommended "courteous and respectful regard for the Ambassador," he advised that Peace Corps offices not be located in the U.S. embassy and insisted that neither Volunteers nor staff should be used for political purposes by the diplomatic corps. Shriver was willing to suffer the charges of Peace Corps "aloofness" which this raised because he felt it essential to avoid congregation in the areas where Americans lived and association with formal diplomatic efforts. "Separateness from other overseas operations of the U.S. is important to achieving the desired image," he wrote. "These policies may come as a blow, but they must be applied."[47]

In its first year of operation the Peace Corps' leaders regularly complained about the lack of cooperation from the American overseas community, diplomatic and business, toward the Peace Corps. In time, however, this situation improved. As assistant secretary for Cultural and Educational Affairs, Philip Coombs, put it: "Once the young people got out there and predominantly favorable reports began to flow back, it became clear that they were a unique and significant new asset, and the misgivings sharply subsided."[48]

Ambassador Charles Baldwin in Malaysia at first told Shriver that he wanted no more than thirty Volunteers; but later, as the program expanded, he admitted that it was "very successful." In the Philippines, Ambassador William Stevenson resented the "foolishness" of the Peace Corps Volunteers' refusal to use the embassy or the expatriate club; yet he admitted that "When I would visit a governor say in Palavan—which is a far-off area— his first words to me would be that he wanted more Peace Corps people." Likewise, Ambassador Charles Cole thought the Peace Corps a "great success" in Chile, while Ambassador William Mahoney in Ghana assessed it as "the only effective thing we're doing out here." Once established in a country, the Peace Corps usually went its own way and handled its own affairs. Ambassador Baldwin described this arrangement:

> I tried insofar as possible to keep hands off the Peace Corps people—to refrain from interfering. I had a compact with my Peace Corps supervisor that while I recognized my responsibility as Ambassador for the Peace Corps activities, I felt it was desirable to play down as much as possible the official aspect of the Peace Corps, to emphasize the people-to-people aspect. We carried out that policy. While I provided office space in the Embassy chancery for the Peace Corps for a while, it later moved out of the chancery completely. This was part of the agreement between me and the Peace Corps supervisor, that they should function physically outside the Embassy.[49]

The distant cordiality which characterized the Peace Corps' relationship with the U.S. official mission was not evident in its dealings with the Agency for International Development (AID). Many AID officials had felt betrayed by the Peace Corps at the time of its battle for independence within the federal bureaucracy; this antipathy prevailed throughout the Kennedy era. In July 1961, Bill Moyers reported that some AID trainees in Washington had made caustic criticisms of the Peace Corps.[50] Ty Wood, AID chief in India, noted "a vast suspicion of Peace Corps generally at that time." In Bolivia, evaluators noted "an undercurrent of ill-will towards the Peace Corps" from AID officials who felt that the Volunteers should drop their pretensions and "get on the team." Lawrence Fuchs, Peace Corps Rep in the Philippines, wrote of the constant "bickering and politicking between the agencies."[51]

The problem was a fundamental one of approach. The Peace Corps proclaimed itself people-oriented whereas AID concentrated on the supply of needed capital and equipment and was technically-oriented. The Peace Corps sought to do the special "personal" job that AID or other technical assistance programs would not attempt. This caused resentment. Sometimes Peace Corps and AID undertook successful cooperative ventures, such as the educational television project in Colombia. In general, however, as Peace Corps staffer Robert Carey wrote, "The early relationships between the Peace Corps and AID were dismal."[52]

THE TREATY

The Peace Corps' relationship with the Central Intelligence Agency (CIA) was even more sensitive. Throughout the Kennedy era, leftist governments accused the Peace Corps of being a "cover" for American espionage. As early as March 16, 1961, Radio Moscow attacked the Peace Corps as a plan for "the collection of espionage information for Allen Dulles's agency."[53] A year later, it was broadcast that "U.S. agents are sent to Afro-Asian countries under the U.S. Peace Corps label. The plan to organize the Corps was jointly prepared by the U.S. State Department, Pentagon and CIA. Director of the Corps, Shriver, is an old employee of the CIA."[54] Radio Peking joined in, as did Fidel Castro and the Eastern bloc press. One of the more ludicrous propaganda pieces appeared in an article in the Polish press in March 1963. Alongside photographs of female Volunteers in training, the caption read: "The Americans consider all means acceptable. Where other means do not succeed, sex may be very useful. Girl members of the Corps on the exercise field." Tass also had a flair for misconstrued sexual innuendo. It charged that a woman Volunteer teacher in Somalia corrupted her pupils by demonstrating the "indecent movements" of the pop dance, the Twist.[55]

Not a single case of CIA infiltration of the Peace Corps, or use of CIA resources by the Peace Corps, has ever been substantiated. No investigation—including the thorough search in 1976 of Senator Frank Church's Select Committee to Study Governmental Operations with Respect to Intelligence Activities—has turned up the slightest evidence of use of the Peace Corps as an arm of U.S. intelligence. Shriver knew that any such association would destroy the Peace Corps' credibility. Hence he took the strictest precautions. Most important, he was assured by the President that the CIA would not attempt to infiltrate the Peace Corps and would not enlist former Volunteers until at least ten years after their Peace Corps service. Kennedy personally relayed this message to Allen Dulles and John McCone, the two CIA directors of the period. This understanding on the inviolability of the Peace Corps was referred to in Peace Corps circles as "The Treaty."[56]

On February 28, 1962, the CIA's assistant director, Stanley J. Grogan, reassured the White House that the "CIA has nothing whatever to do and wants nothing whatever to do with the Peace Corps. Nothing could be more fatal to the Peace Corps than to have a CIA connection."[57] In a National Security airgram to all U.S. embassies in the Third World, Dean Rusk reiterated the principles of the treaty. "From the beginning of the Peace Corps, I have considered it understood that Peace Corps Volunteers would not be used as intelligence sources in the countries in which they are serving," he said. He continued:

> Because of the geographic dispersion of Volunteers and the access which they have to the people of the country, some members of your staff, through either unfamiliarity with the policy or over-zealousness, may be tempted to regard the Volunteers as instruments of foreign policy designed to serve the particular ends of the staff members' jobs. In order that there should be no misunderstanding as to the role of Peace Corps Volunteers, I wish to state the relevant policy: Peace Corps Volunteers are not to be regarded or utilized as official members of the Mission and

in particular they are not to be requested to undertake any formal or informal intelligence functions.[58]

To a great extent, the true role of the CIA in the early 1960s—an era when it was rapidly expanding its counterinsurgency capabilities in the Third World—remains unknown. Such was the nature of its operations that almost every American working abroad could have been accused of being an "agent." Moreover, historian Herbert Parmet has written that AID missions were "often heavily infused with intelligence operatives." Given this background, there may have been instances of over-zealousness by CIA agents in the field, and some Volunteers could conceivably have been recruited. The evidence, however, is negligible. Peace Corps evaluation chief Charles Peters recalled only one incident, when a military intelligence operative tried to recruit a Volunteer in Thailand. Once discovered, a message was sent directly from the White House putting an immediate stop to it.[59]

The U.S. ambassador in Liberia once ordered Peace Corps Rep Thomas Quimby to make reports to him on field situations. Quimby refused, and when he protested to Washington, the erring ambassador was severely reprimanded. Bradley Patterson knew of only one occasion when the Peace Corps asked the CIA for help, and that was to seek advice on how to deal with the problem of loneliness and frustration facing the Volunteers in the field, and hence possible entrapment by Communists. Even this mild example of collaboration was inconsequential since the Peace Corps never used the CIA's preferred instructions.[60]

Within the Peace Corps, formal policy regarding the CIA was established on September 6, 1961. No former employee of the CIA and no one who had worked in intelligence up to ten years previously would be employed. Even someone married to an intelligence officer was excluded. This directive, "Employment of Personnel who have been Employed in Intelligence Work," was unequivocal: "We do not want the Peace Corps publicly identified in any way with intelligence work and we do not want the Peace Corps used as a vehicle for intelligence work."[61]

The Peace Corps' chief of public information, Ed Bayley, confirmed that "we would screen out any person connected with the CIA, just as we would screen out a Communist . . . We considered them in about the same class as far as the Peace Corps was concerned." Excellent people were refused entry into the Peace Corps, both at the staff and Volunteer level, if they had the slightest intelligence connection. William Delano had the special portfolio on this problem. He remembered two first-class secretaries being turned down because they had done some part-time typing for the CIA years earlier. He also noted that Volunteers were warned during training about possible CIA infiltration. They were told that the slightest hint of solicitation should be reported immediately to their Rep.[62]

All available evidence indicates that, in the Kennedy years, the Peace Corps and the CIA had a perfect relationship: they stayed as far away from each other as possible. This understanding worked to the advantage of both agencies. Notwithstanding Communist assertions that Shriver was a "bloodthirsty Chicago butcher and sausage-maker" and the Peace Corps "a nest of spies," Bill Josephson recalled "a lot of generalized charges, but no specific charges naming specific people." Subsequent revelations in the 1970s concerning assassination plots and plans for political destabilization in a number of countries indicated that the CIA was something of a rogue institution in the early 1960s. But there is nothing to suggest that it did not honor its treaty with the Peace Corps. In later years, Senator Christopher Dodd of Connecticut, who had been a Volunteer in the 1960s, testified before Congress on the point:

> Last year at about this time I was in Cuba with a delegation from the Congress and spent 6 hours with Fidel Castro. In our conversations, he learned that I was a former Peace Corps Volunteer and had worked on a neighboring island, the Dominican Republic. He was fascinated with the program and what it had done. He said something to me that I thought was quite revealing. He said, "In all the years I have been in office, despite rumors that have flowed from all sources, we never once have had one piece of specific information to ever link any Peace Corps Volunteer or any person who worked with the Peace Corps with any foreign intelligence operation." He said that on his own free will. I didn't probe him on it at all. I think it was an interesting point.

Thus it seems that even Fidel Castro, despite his own allegations in the early 1960s, was persuaded that the CIA left the Peace Corps alone.[63]

THE SHROUD OF THE PRESIDENCY

In many ways, the Peace Corps' most crucial relationship was with the White House and the President himself. There rested the ultimate source of its power and prestige. Shriver recalled that Kennedy "never ever turned down anything we asked him to do."[64] Whenever he was requested to greet Volunteers in the Rose Garden, announce a new program, or sign a letter of congratulations to those serving abroad, Kennedy willingly complied. Shriver, for his part, kept up a constant stream of personal letters and memoranda to the President on various issues pertaining to the Peace Corps: the warm reception given to the first Peace Corps contingent in India, the dangers Volunteers faced from rebels in the outback of North Borneo, or the news that Kennedy's alma mater, Harvard, was participating in a training program.[65] One newsy letter from Shriver in Colombia informed Kennedy that "your Peace Corps is proving to be an asset in Colombia . . . The Volunteers are in towns where *no* North Americans are living or have lived." On the sensitive religious question, Shriver wrote:

> Our Volunteers are *not* living in the homes of priests (as reported in *The Washington Star*.) They have their own private accommodations which are shared in every case with a Colombian counterpart. But cooperation from Church and local priests is essential to success. We're getting it.

Shriver also told the President that Volunteers "have your photo affixed to a map of the U.S.A. in many of their rooms."[66]

These personal messages were not usually substantive. They were more a reflection of Shriver's desire to keep the President informed and interested in the progress of the Peace Corps. However, Shriver also made an official weekly report to the President on Peace Corps activities and these reports hit a more serious note: difficulties with a Senate committee (usually Appropriations), a critical article in the press, or an analysis of early terminations from Peace Corps service. Occasionally, a piece of bad news was related; for instance, that the Governor of Rio Grande do Sul in Brazil, in an attempt to embarrass the United States, had ordered the Peace Corps out of his area.[67] More often than not, the reports glowed with achievements: a record number of Peace Corps applications, a word of praise from a Third World leader, or an extraordinary job done by a Volunteer. After reading one such report, Kennedy remarked to an aide that "Sarge is really on the ball."[68]

In a memorandum to the President, Harris Wofford dubbed the Peace Corps Kennedy's "special baby, and in a sense the first offspring of the New Frontier." Extending this metaphor, presidential assistant Fred Dutton said that the rest of the federal bureaucracy was well aware that the Peace Corps was "a favorite child." Aide Dave Powers recalled that the President loved to meet and talk with the Volunteers. When Ambassador Baldwin met with Kennedy, the President asked him to tell the Tunku in Malaya that he was "very pleased indeed that he is interested in what I think will be a very important program, the Peace Corps." Ambassador Galbraith noted that whenever he returned from India and met with Kennedy, the President would ask: "How are Sarge's kids doing?"[69]

Although Kennedy always displayed his interest in the Peace Corps — and it was a crucial factor in its success — he paid little specific attention to it; with few exceptions, Shriver used the presidential relationship only for cosmetic or publicity purposes. As Wofford put it, "Shriver only went to Kennedy to add juice to the Peace Corps."[70] Certainly, Kennedy signed the Executive Order which gave the Peace Corps an auspicious beginning, and he also helped protect it from the cloak and dagger of the CIA. For the most part, however, he took no direct hand in Peace Corps affairs. During the all-important fight for independence, for example, Vice-President Johnson was much more active on the Peace Corps' behalf than the President.

Some Peace Corps officials attributed Kennedy's apparently inattentive attitude to a lack of serious regard for the Peace Corps. But Wofford saw it more in terms of the President's preoccupation with crises — Berlin, Cuba, civil rights — rather than indif-

ference. Presidential aide Ralph Dungan acknowledged that the
Peace Corps was not central to Kennedy's thinking. "It was not
often discussed or debated in the White House," said Dungan.
"It was nice but it just wasn't that important." Fred Dutton
described Kennedy's perspective on the Peace Corps as "a bright
speck on a general picture of problems and politics." While Kennedy liked to remind his staff that he was fond of the Peace
Corps, he was quite happy to leave its management to Shriver
and his associates. "They paddled their own canoe," said National Security Adviser McGeorge Bundy.[71]

The fact that some White House staff did not take the Peace
Corps very seriously had its upside for Shriver and his administrators, for it left them free to develop the agency in the
direction they chose. Nevertheless, some of Shriver's staff were
disappointed that there was such little White House response
to the Peace Corps' progress. "Nobody ever called me up and
said this was good, or we want more of this," said Bradley Patterson. Bill Kelly believed that the White House staff ignored
the Peace Corps because they were certain it would prove an
impractical flop, and they did not want its failure directly
associated with the President.[72] This analysis certainly shed a
different light on Shriver's wisecrack that Kennedy only chose
him as Peace Corps Director because "no one thought it could
succeed and it would be easier to fire a relative than a friend."
Shriver's more serious view was that he should make the Peace
Corps a success without troubling the President. He told Patterson that he did not want to "bother Jack with problems . . . I
don't want to wash my dirty linen in front of him."[73]

Shriver's approach camouflaged a coolness between the
Peace Corps and certain White House officials. This had its roots
in the 1960 campaign when there had been some friction between
the Shriver wing of Kennedy's staff and the experienced, professional wing—O'Brien, O'Donnell, and Dungan—known collectively as the Irish Mafia. The latter group felt that Shriver's
team was not hard-headed or realistic enough. They nicknamed
Shriver "the boy scout." This friction increased during the transition when some of Shriver's talent hunt choices—Bundy, Rusk,
McNamara—were favored by Kennedy over those of the Irish
Mafia. According to Wofford, O'Brien was especially "sore at

Shriver for shoveling all these people in that hadn't done anything in the campaign and he was particularly sore when some
egghead who hadn't done anything in the campaign was being
treated more respectfully than somebody that he was recom-
mending."[74] The Irish Mafia were further irritated by the Peace
Corps' determined stand over the independence issue in the
spring of 1961.

Philosophically also, the presidential aides were very different from the people who tended to join the Peace Corps staff.
Shriver attracted confirmed idealists. Peace Corps officials sometimes joked about "working for Hallelujah." The more skeptical
members of the White House staff deemed them insufferable
romantics. Fred Dutton found the Peace Corps' "we-can-walk-
on-water" attitude intolerable.[75]

There was no doubt that the Peace Corps had its share of
hubris. The institutional pride was overwhelming and there was
some arrogance and insensitivity. These bright young people
were supremely confident in their own ability and the success
of their undertaking. On discussing traditional foreign aid programs during one of the first Peace Corps staff meetings, the
twenty-six-year-old Bill Moyers proclaimed: "We can do it better."[76] This was the Peace Corps' credo and, not surprisingly,
other officials—including some White House staff—resented it.

This coolness between Peace Corps and White House staff
was not helped by the fact that Shriver and Kennedy were quite
different in terms of personal style and, to some extent, political
outlook. Shriver had always been much more liberal than Kennedy, especially in the area of civil rights. Indeed, Shriver was
regarded as the "family Communist" by the Kennedys. Moreover, Shriver's effusive brand of idealism went against the grain
of John Kennedy who was, wrote David Halberstam, "at least
as skeptical as he was idealistic, curiously ill-at-ease with other
people's overt idealism, preferring in private the tart and darker
view of the world and of mankind." Wofford also noted that
Kennedy was "put off by too-far-reaching ideas . . . Certainly,
idealism or liberalism in any conventional sense was uncongenial
to him."[77] Kennedy's existential sense of irony was the polar opposite of Shriver's unbounded idealism and optimism.

The insinuation that Shriver owed his position to his family ties to Kennedy was another sensitive spot. When a reporter asked Shriver about his kinship with the President, he replied curtly: "It's a fact of life, why think about it at all? I'm perfectly capable of looking after myself."[78] A rebuff suffered by Shriver at the hands of his brother-in-law in May 1961, did nothing to assuage this sensitivity. Shriver, inexperienced with Congress, was due to take the Peace Corps legislation to Capitol Hill. Worried about the lack of help coming from the White House congressional liaison office, he took advantage of a weekend trip to Hyannisport to ask the President for some advice and cooperation; his wife, Eunice, acted as intermediary. Referring to the fight for independence, Kennedy told his sister that Shriver and the Peace Corps had wanted to be on their own and now they were *completely* on their own. It was as if Kennedy was telling Shriver that it was time to face the harsh realities of political life. In later years, Shriver recalled that from that moment on he vowed never to ask the President for as much as "a light for a cigarette."[79]

Despite their differences in style, there was tremendous mutual respect between Kennedy and Shriver. In typical fashion, Kennedy peppered his public expression of admiration for his brother-in-law with a quip. "I don't think it is altogether fair to say that I handed Sarge a lemon from which he made lemonade," he said. "But I do think he was handed one of the most sensitive and difficult assignments which any administrator in Washington has been given in this century." In a more private manner, Jacqueline Kennedy Onassis confirmed the high regard which the President held for Shriver. On a photograph of Kennedy talking with Shriver she wrote, "Jack always said that no one could have made the Peace Corps work but Sarge."[80]

There is little doubt that Kennedy looked upon the Peace Corps with an endearing eye. It was a bright idea which he had thrown out in the heat of the campaign, and it yielded unexpectedly high returns. Once ensconced in the White House, however, it was not one of his principal concerns. Shriver ran it so efficiently that it did not have to be. For the President, there was only ever the question of political priorities; the Peace Corps was not one of them. But in terms of public perceptions, and perhaps in terms of his own personal feelings, Kennedy was closer to the Peace Corps than any other government agency. As he told a group of Volunteers in 1962, "The White House belongs to all the people, but I think it particularly belongs to you."[81]

In Washington, Peace Corps administrator Jack Young noted that "the ever present shroud of the Presidency . . . set an environment where things got easier to do once the bureaucracy understood Kennedy was truly behind the Peace Corps."[82] Overseas, Kennedy was even more closely identified with the Peace Corps. In Tanzania, the local peoples referred to Volunteers as "Wakina Kennedy"—followers of Kennedy. In the town of Bassari in Togo, the locals nicknamed the lone Volunteer there "Kennedy in Bassari." In the Dominican Republic, the Volunteers were called "los hijos de Kennedy"—Kennedy's children.[83]

But perhaps Kennedy's affinity with the Peace Corps was best described by a young Volunteer in Africa who wrote to Peace Corps headquarters shortly after the President's death. "Being in the Peace Corps we all here felt we had a special attachment to him," he wrote. "Hell, most of us felt we were working for *him* and would refer to him as Jack—as if he were a Peace Corps Volunteer."[84]

8

Volunteers for Peace

From the very start the question of motives was raised i.e. "Why did you join the Peace Corps?" Everyone seemed to want to know . . . Invariably we gave these queries an unfriendly response – partly because they soon acquired the hollow ring of a cliché, partly because the reasons were complex, profound and personal and partly, perhaps, because we weren't quite sure of the answer ourselves.

— John Demos, Volunteer in Ghana

ANSWERING THE CALL

Shortly after the Peace Corps had been launched, Vice-President Lyndon Johnson took Sargent Shriver aside and gave him some advice on the selection of Volunteers. "Do it like I did the Texas Youth Conservation Corps," said Johnson. "Keep out the three Cs." "The three Cs?" asked a puzzled Shriver. "The three Cs," Johnson repeated: "The communists, the consumptives and the cocksuckers."* In his own inimitable fashion, the Vice-President was telling Shriver that if the wrong type of person were selected to go overseas, the Peace Corps would face embarrassment at home and abroad.[1] Yet Shriver had to recruit, train, and select thousands of young people to go to exotic Third World countries and perform tasks which few Americans had attempted before. The only way of learning was by trial and error.

*CCC was the acronym for the Civilian Conservation Corps established by Franklin Roosevelt in the 1930s. Johnson administered a youth program in Texas.

142

Shriver's "Report to the President" of February 1961 had left the opportunity for service open to any American over the age of eighteen. Within early Peace Corps councils it had been argued that service should be restricted to skilled technicians and to those with specific academic qualifications. Shriver disagreed; he felt that many useful jobs in the developing countries could be done by the average, well-motivated American. In the area of people-to-people contact, he believed that an unskilled but enthusiastic generalist could do at least as well as a skilled but diffident technocrat. "There was no point in having Ph.D.'s in the boondocks," he said.[2]

Shriver's sentiment reinforced Kennedy's original aim of giving as many young Americans as possible the chance to serve at a grassroots level in Third World countries. As a traveler himself, Kennedy realized the potential benefit of crossing cultural frontiers. His Cow Palace proposal had been aimed primarily at the college senior completing a liberal arts degree — bright, healthy, interested in world affairs, and well-educated in a general sense. B.A. generalists would also be more likely to sacrifice two or three years of their lives to service in a developing country than technicians already embarked upon a career. Nevertheless, critics were skeptical of the abilities of the inexperienced generalists and of the wisdom of Shriver's decision to build the Peace Corps around them. Shriver told Kennedy he was certain that the Peace Corps could attract "cream-of-the-crop, talented, fit, well-adjusted and devoted American men and women."[3]

Despite Shriver's confidence, the Peace Corps experienced some initial difficulty in finding sufficient numbers of suitable applicants. In those early, frenetic days when an organization had to be built, programs developed, and Congress faced, recruitment had been left to take care of itself. The popular interest in Kennedy's new idea had been such that Shriver and his colleagues had assumed that Volunteers would appear in droves without an intensive recruitment campaign. Indeed, the Peace Corps' policy position was that it did not "recruit" but merely supplied information to prospective applicants. Shriver did not want the Peace Corps to become engaged in a "we need recruits" campaign; accordingly, he issued a stern warning that the Peace

Corps should never attempt to enlist people in the manner of the U.S. Marine Corps.[4] The agency waited and hoped that enough people would answer Kennedy's call.

Answering that call was not as simple as it first appeared. To become a Volunteer, anyone interested had to fulfill the rigorous requirements established by Dr. Nicholas Hobbs, the psychologist who became the Peace Corps' first chief of Selection (he had helped develop U.S. Air Force selection methods in World War II). Hobbs decided that applicants should initially take written tests rather than interviews since he felt the latter had little or no predictive efficiency.[5] Thus applicants had to go through a lot of paperwork before being accepted by the Peace Corps.

A comprehensive Volunteer Questionnaire dealt with the applicant's personal history, from medical record to criminal convictions. Next, six references had to be nominated whom the Peace Corps then asked to supply information on the applicant's maturity, character, and relations with other people. Then a six-hour exam consisting of general aptitude and language tests was conducted. The applicant also had to undergo a thorough medical examination, although physical problems, of themselves, were not disqualifying factors.* Having run this gauntlet of testing, applicants deemed suitable were invited to training. The success rate was not high. Between 1961 and 1963 only one out of five applicants was selected for training.[6]

This careful and protracted procedure meant a world of difference between the expression of good-natured interest in the Peace Corps and the time-consuming process of finding references, answering difficult, personal questions, and actually applying. Peace Corps administrators did not at first appreciate this difference. The error of their ways was soon driven home.

RECRUITING VOLUNTEERS

In March 1961, the Peace Corps received ten thousand letters of interest from would-be Volunteers. By the end of that

---

*The Peace Corps made it clear that there were opportunities for the handicapped to volunteer. Each case was judged on its merits depending upon the availability of assignments compatible with an applicant's abilities.

month, application forms had been printed and distributed to U.S. post offices all over the country. It looked like the Peace Corps was about to be overwhelmed by an avalanche of eager applicants. By the end of April, however, although letters of interest continued to pour in, it was clear that instead of the fifteen thousand applications which Shriver had expected, only half that number had actually returned questionnaires. This shortfall was made worse by Shriver's absence on a trip to the Third World where he was busy informing governments of the supposed vast numbers of young Americans anxious to serve. Warren Wiggins cabled Shriver, telling him that obtaining even an adequate supply of Volunteers might be a problem. The rate of returned questionnaires was less than two hundred a week and going down.[7]

"With each day it is becoming clearer," wrote Wiggins, "that recruitment is as important a Peace Corps task as program development." He proposed that immediate energies should be concentrated on recruitment and that Bill Moyers should be placed in charge. Accordingly, the Recruitment Division was transferred from the Office of Peace Corps Volunteers to the Office of Public Affairs under Moyers. Still, thousands of applicants could not just be conjured up overnight.

In early May, the *New York Times* criticized the Peace Corps for not providing the public with enough specific information. It also reported that applications were lagging far behind expectations. Despite Shriver's prediction that seven thousand people would take the first Peace Corps tests on May 27, officials were forced to admit that only half that number had participated.[8]

In public, Shriver said that while numbers had fallen below expectations, he was pleased with the high caliber of those who had applied; in private, he admitted his disappointment.[9] He was worried that he would be unable to honor his commitments abroad, and he feared the adverse impact which the mild response might have on Congress. He plunged into the recruitment drive, asking businesses to grant leaves of absence to those willing to volunteer and urging labor unions to guarantee reemployment rights to workers who joined the Peace Corps. Subway and bus cards carrying information on Peace Corps service were printed, an information booth was set up in Times Square, and advertisements were run on radio and TV stations. By the end of June, these efforts had yielded ten thousand applications — enough to select an adequate number of Volunteers to meet the first year's requests. After June, however, the daily rate of applicants dwindled again. If the Peace Corps were to reach its proposed target of ten thousand Volunteers in the field by 1964, more productive recruitment techniques would have to be found.

The Peace Corps publicity machine churned out stories for newspapers and magazines. Numerous brochures describing opportunities for service were aimed at specific groups: teachers, farmers, doctors, architects, and engineers. At the same time, Shriver wrote hundreds of letters to college presidents, education boards, and captains of industry, coaxing them to endorse the Peace Corps. His efforts did not go unrewarded. In 1962, New York City's education board was only one of many which allowed teachers leaves of absence for Peace Corps service without loss of job or increment. At Shriver's request, Harvard's president, Nathan Pusey, publicly encouraged his students to join the Peace Corps (next to the University of California, Harvard became the biggest source of Volunteers in the Kennedy years).[10]

To establish the crucial recruitment relationship with universities and colleges, Moyers brought in Samuel Babbit, former dean of Vanderbilt University. Adopting a low-key approach, Babbit set up a single Peace Corps faculty contact on campuses all across the country with instructions to conduct a continuous but unaggressive information program. Babbit hoped to win the Peace Corps a reputation for honesty and thoroughness which, in the long run, would produce a consistent flow of high-quality applicants. He refused to indulge in a mass, hard-sell campaign which might bring immediate results but would eventually damage the Peace Corps' image and attract the wrong type of applicant.

In 1962 the Peace Corps received twenty thousand applications, compared with thirteen thousand in 1961. Even so, recruitment could hardly keep pace with expansion. During 1962, the Peace Corps went through its most staggering period of growth. Established in nine countries in 1961, it moved into another thirty-two in the following year, thus putting tremendous pressure on recruitment.* Moreover, the early months of 1963 saw a drastic decline in applications, and the agency suffered one of its worst shortfalls. With more and more countries requesting Volunteers, the Peace Corps needed recruits.

THE WISCONSIN PLAN

During a staff meeting in March 1963, Robert Gale (then chief of Special Projects) criticized the Peace Corps' recruitment methods as amateurish and argued that efforts on college campuses should be intensified. He advocated an in-depth, professional "sales" campaign. Attacking previous methods as too timid, Gale said there was little point in having a lone recruitment officer on campus who put up a notice from time to time and then sat waiting for interested students to appear. He proposed that teams of well-briefed, enthusiastic Peace Corps officials should engage in "blitz" recruitment drives on campuses all over America. Shriver gave Gale the job of organizing this effort.[11]

In the spring of 1963, Gale took several of the Peace Corps' most outgoing staff members to the University of Wisconsin and began his experiment. "The aim," he told his colleagues, "is to raise all kinds of hell without being idiotic." Literature was handed out in bulk, classes were interrupted for Peace Corps seminars, a colorful information booth was set up in the middle of campus, and every senior student was openly solicited as a potential recruit. Gale's methods were forceful and aggressive, the opposite of Babbit's. They were also immediately effective. After one week, 426 Wisconsin students had applied for Peace Corps service, approximately 10 percent of the senior class.[12]

All available hands were pressed into service for a huge national recruitment drive. In 1963 and 1964, "Wisconsin plan" teams visited some two thousand colleges from New York to California. Simultaneously, a stream of information flowed from Bill Moyers's Office of Public Affairs. Over fifty Peace Corps "ser-

---

*On June 30, 1961 there were 124 Volunteers and trainees; three years later there were 10,078.

vice councils"—composed mainly of friends and relatives of Volunteers—were established to assist the Peace Corps by giving talks at junior colleges, high schools, and local community meetings. Gale estimated that over seven hundred speeches on the Peace Corps were given monthly.[13] This effort produced an unprecedented number of applicants. In 1963, nearly thirty-five thousand Americans volunteered, while letters of interest came in at the rate of seven thousand per week. Shriver estimated that a further fifty thousand applications would arrive in 1964.[14]

Despite this astonishing success, not everyone was gratified at the Peace Corps' zealous pursuit of recruitment targets. Some officials warned of the evils of excess and the grave danger of becoming over-eager to "sign up" people for two years of service. "Under cover of an information campaign," wrote evaluator David Gelman, "the Marines had long since landed." Gelman felt the mass recruitment drives too often lacked taste and restraint. "The final failure of team recruiting is that its effects on our great uncaptured mass of potential Volunteers are about as enduring as those of a traveling circus," he wrote. "Once the sawdust is swept up, there's nothing left but the odor of performing elephants." Such was the neurosis about big numbers that the Recruitment Division was accused of trying every advertising device in the book short of "dropping questionnaires from aeroplanes."[15] One young applicant expressed his disappointment at the Wisconsin plan style of recruitment: "I thought we were something special. Then I saw that they were just pulling people off the street and testing them later."[16]

QUANTITY AND QUALITY

At Peace Corps headquarters, some staffers called for the complete abolition of recruitment or, at least, for a return to Sam Babbit's subtle approach—building small, year-round Peace Corps support constituencies on campuses. Gelman warned that unless quality was given priority over quantity, the Peace Corps would not only acquire too many "high-risk" applicants but would drink dry the well of potential recruits. The latter prophecy came true. From 1964 (when forty-six thousand applications were received), the level of Peace Corps applications steadily declined. By 1965, Gale was forced to admit that "With few exceptions, we are coming back from schools with fewer and fewer numbers. Results from team recruiting are down 22 percent from last year."[17]

A more general criticism of recruitment was that all too often it succumbed to "Madison Avenue hoopla" and took to "selling the Peace Corps the way ad-men sell Volkswagons." Volunteers consistently criticized the travelogue style and holiday brochure-type content of some of the recruitment literature. In early Peace Corps advertisements, Nepal was depicted as "The Land of the Yeti and Everest." Potential applicants for programs in hot climates were sometimes told by recruiters to "Bring your bathing suit, the swimming is great." One report accused Washington's "you-too-can-be-a-world-saver" approach of misleading the public and the prospective recruit.[18]

On his return to Washington after two years overseas, Volunteer Roger Landrum advised Shriver to make radical changes in recruitment procedures and in the tone of Peace Corps publicity. Landrum contended that current methods lost the Peace Corps the very people it needed most:

> The literature that is being distributed does not . . . create the proper image of the Peace Corps to the people that we should want as Volunteers. Some of my friends have said that after reading various Peace Corps brochures, they felt that the Peace Corps was too superficial an organization. A solution to the problem would be to add more insight and a fuller picture to the Peace Corps' informational material and to cut the Madison Avenue approach.[19]

Bill Moyers, a fighter against publicity gimmicks, emphasized that the Peace Corps could not draft anyone: "and if we set up appeals ('opportunity to learn about other people,' 'travel,' etc.) beyond the basic desire of an individual to involve himself in this program simply because he feels it is worth doing, we will fail."[20]

This sort of criticism had the desired effect. By 1963, the Peace Corps had begun to remedy some of its recruitment weaknesses. A new poster stressed sixteen-hour days, monotony, mosquitoes, and "one fraction of the results you'd hoped for." A heightened sense of realism entered pamphlet literature. "This is how the Peace Corps measures success," proclaimed a picture of one inch on a ruler. Another caption beneath a photograph of a solitary shovel read: "The Peace Corps brings idealists down to earth." Young Americans were told why they should *not* join the Peace Corps: "You were expecting romance? Glamor? Then forget about the Peace Corps." One huge poster showed two identical photographs of a village: one was titled "Before Peace Corps," the other, "After Peace Corps." The blurb went on to explain why Volunteers should not expect to change the world overnight.

Despite the flaws in the Peace Corps' recruitment process in its first years, it did achieve its most important goal. Between 1961 and 1964, about 112,000 Americans applied for service overseas.[21] As for the charge that the Recruitment Division sought big numbers at any cost, in the Kennedy years only about 20 percent of all applicants were deemed of a high enough caliber to be invited to training. Quality was given preference over quantity.

TRAINING: A PARTNERSHIP WITH HIGHER EDUCATION

While recruitment was a serious challenge, devising an appropriate training process was even more difficult. A number of options were available. The Peace Corps could set up its own training centers around the country, establish a central Peace Corps academy in Washington, or use the facilities of private organizations like International Voluntary Services and the Experiment in International Living. Alternatively, it could use the services of higher education. After heated discussion, the latter expedient won the day.

Although colleges and universities seemed the obvious choice to prepare Volunteers for programs overseas, some Peace Corps staffers, notably Warren Wiggins, were worried that academics might push training in a theoretical rather than a practical direction. After all, the whole point of the Volunteer was to be more a "doer" than a "thinker." It was indisputable, however, that colleges and universities had the resources, staff, and the space to accommodate Peace Corps trainees. Furthermore, they could begin training without delay. By striking up an immediate partnership with higher education, the Peace Corps could save valuable months during that hectic summer of 1961. During the following two years, training programs were established with over seventy academic institutions.

This extension into the world of higher education had an important domestic impact. Not only were thousands of students and their families made aware of the Peace Corps' presence but, as Dr. Virgil Hancher, president of Iowa State University noted, training programs also had a beneficial effect on faculties:

> The members of our faculty are having to come together across disciplines. They are having to think through old problems of education freshly and to tackle new ones. Along with the Peace Corps trainees, they are learning, learning how to teach languages in the new method, how to teach area studies better . . . The project is increasing the international dimension of the State University of Iowa.[22]

By involving colleges and universities in its experiment, the Peace Corps' international dimension came to be shared by a broad spectrum of Americans.

The educational institutions undertook training programs mostly during the summer months when teachers had time to devote sufficient attention to the Peace Corps, and trainees could take up rooms in the dormitories vacated by regular students. Thus the Peace Corps gained the knowledge and advice of academia's area experts, linguists, and psychologists. Like all marriages, the Peace Corps' relationship with universities and colleges was subject to breakdowns of communication. Yet, in time, it developed into one of the most mutually enriching and profitable partnerships ever established between the federal government and higher education.

At Peace Corps headquarters, staff debated whether training should be brief and relaxed or lengthy and competitive. Since Shriver wanted Volunteers in the field as soon as possible, the shortest method had obvious attractions. Some private voluntary agencies—such as International Voluntary Services and

Voluntary Service Overseas—had worked quite successfully without rigorous training procedures, although these were small-scale programs. Shriver felt it would be courting disaster to thrust large numbers of young Americans into developing countries without adequate preparation. During a staff discussion of the training needs of the first group of Volunteers bound for Tanzania and Ghana, he decided upon roughly an eight- to twelve-week intensive training period. From this decision there developed a three-phase pattern for all training programs: eight to ten weeks at a college or university in the United States; two to four weeks field training at one of the Peace Corps' outdoor camps (located in Puerto Rico, Hawaii, St. Croix and St. Thomas); finally, a brief one- to two-week period of in-country training overseas.

THE TRAINING SCHEDULE

Realizing that each educational institution had its own distinctive character, the first training chief, Dr. Joseph Kauffman (a former president of the University of Rhode Island) decided that the Peace Corps should assign its own training officer to each campus to bring at least a degree of uniformity to the process. He also designed eight core components for all programs: technical studies gave the trainee a grounding in the skills needed to do a specific job overseas; language studies concentrated on conversation practice and technical terms germane to the work assignment; area studies dealt with the cultural aspects of a host country; international relations and the danger of Communist subversion were studied in a world affairs course; American studies focused on U.S. history and contemporary socioeconomic problems; recreational studies included physical education and learning about a host country's sports and pastimes; medical studies advised the trainee as to basic health care in a developing-country environment; finally, a general orientation course encompassed the aims of the Peace Corps and the role of the Volunteer. While these components were adapted to individual projects and countries, they ensured that all Volunteers shared something of the same training experience.[23]

A typical campus schedule had the trainees in class from 7:00 A.M. to 10:00 P.M. six days a week. Some Volunteers complained that the trainees had less autonomy than a college freshman: "He was bedded in a dormitory, tumbled out at an arbitrary hour, fed in a prescribed place at a prescribed time . . . he hardly had time to sleep far less to think—it was like boot camp."[24] Outdoor training programs, which sought to give Volunteers a feel for the situation they would face overseas, were even more demanding. Trainees bound for social work in Colombian city slums were given on-the-job training in New York's Spanish Harlem. A group going to Nepal was trained in mountainous Colorado. New Mexican Indian reservations and Spanish-speaking villages provided environments for trainees assigned to community development projects in rural areas. The island of Hawaii, with its multiracial population, remote valleys, and varied economy, performed a similar function for Volunteers headed for Southeast Asia.

The Peace Corps' own two training camps in Puerto Rico were modeled on the British "outward bound" school camps.[25] Dawn rises, two-mile runs, half-day hikes through the wilderness and obstacle courses were standard fare. Some trainees, particularly older ones, complained that this extreme physical exertion was unnecessary. But Shriver argued that the strenuous exercise was beneficial to those trainees who had never lived an outdoors life. "We will use physical training as a vehicle to measure a man's stamina, courage and resourcefulness," said William Sloane Coffin, the former Yale chaplain who ran the Peace Corps' first training camp.[26]

Since training was the most visible domestic aspect of the Peace Corps, it had an important impact on the American public. It seemed that everyone wanted to see or read about this new breed of American. Reporters filed into the Peace Corps' field camps to see trainees swinging through trees, scaling sheer cliffs, and being thrown into rivers bound hand and foot (presumably the sort of tests that would await them in the jungles of the Third World!). As Gerald Bush, a staff training officer put it: "The ten-hour day, six-day week with calisthenics at 5:00 A.M. became a part of the Peace Corps image."[27] Unstinting praise was given to these adventurous training techniques; they seemed a step in the right direction, away from the boring Foreign Service manuals and the stultifying procedures of the State Department and AID. The *Nation* forecast that Peace Corps training would imbue Volunteers with "visions of what they could do for the underdog, the torch of learning they would carry to remote and illiterate settlements, the prosperity they would spread with their American knowledge and skill, the sanitary latrines and clean water supplies they would create, the misery they would erase."[28] Training for the Peace Corps, however, was never that simple.

Since the Peace Corps was charting new territory, some of its early training programs suffered from vague country information, imprecise job descriptions, and ambiguity regarding the structure within which Volunteers would operate overseas. Only when Volunteers actually got into the field could the Peace Corps start to learn how it might improve its training methods. Given these beginnings, it was not surprising that early programs were patchy. As Peace Corps consultant Robert Textor wrote: "The quality of training ranged from very good to very poor."[29]

Charles Peters and his colleagues in the Evaluation Division consistently complained that Volunteers were not being given the realistic preparation necessary for going overseas. Seventy percent of Volunteers worked in other than isolated, rural communities; yet most training programs were oriented toward the traditional image of the Volunteer working alone in a remote village. The majority of Volunteers went overseas as teachers and, for most of them, it was their first classroom experience; yet early training programs provided very little teaching practice. Too often, trainees were led to expect well-planned jobs and immediate results; this rarely proved to be the case. One early evaluation report pointed out that "much more emphasis should be given in training to convince the Volunteers that they are workers in the vineyard and that they might not be around to see the crop harvested."[30]

The failure to prepare Volunteers for the frustration that often accompanied success overseas became the most consistent criticism of training. "Given the hopeful American nature, its naiveté, lack of experience and susceptibility, we are just not training our Volunteers well enough," wrote David Gelman in 1962.[31] Training courses tended to emphasize constant activity and job satisfaction. Many Volunteers found that boredom and frustration could be just as common. As one disgruntled teacher in Sierra Leone put it:

> They just don't tell it to you the right way in training. It's not romantic. It's hot, sweaty and tedious. It's not the challenge of the mud hut and all that—that would be too easy. It's the challenge of the principal changing schedules on you every day and sending two teachers to the same class. It's the unruliness of the students, the indifference of the other teachers . . . That's what they ought to tell you in training.[32]

To a great extent, the problems which bedeviled the early training programs could be laid at the feet of academia. The universities and colleges were geared toward research and theoretical discussion in the classroom, not hands-on work in the field. Since the higher educational institutions—like everyone else—were not quite sure of what the Peace Corps was trying to do, they played it safe and sought to supply their usual academic product. In most cases, this was exactly what the Peace Corps did not want.

TO SPEAK AS EQUALS

The faults of academia notwithstanding, some of the Peace Corps' early problems with training were of its own making. The most blatant mistake was the failure to concentrate on languages. Six weeks passed before the trainees bound for a project in Malawi had an instructor who knew the native tongue; to trainees going to a teaching project in Morocco it seemed that French instruction at the California Polytechnic Institute was "squeezed into odd spots in the program . . . for teachers, they scrounged around among the student body and found some Lebanese students whom they used"; Volunteers destined for an agricultural project in Brazil felt that their training in Portuguese had come as an afterthought to their instructors.[33] In 1963, Eugene Burdick and William Lederer, authors of The Ugly American, surveyed several Peace Corps projects and reported their findings to Shriver. "We are convinced," they wrote, "that a successful Peace

Corps operation is dependent upon language facility more than any other single factor. The Volunteers we found to be operating at a high degree of capacity, accepted in the barrios and integrated into their communities, were those who had mastered the language."[34]

To some extent, the Peace Corps' early weakness in this field was inevitable. It had to teach scores of exotic languages more rapidly and intensively than had ever been attempted in the United States. In some cases, the languages needed were so new to America that the Peace Corps had to write its own textbooks and dictionaries for them; Somali, Tshi, Malay, Twi, and Hausa were in this category. In Nigeria alone there were 250 different dialects. To prepare a comprehensive language program on all of these would have been impossible. However, the problem was exacerbated by the Peace Corps' initial failure to recognize the absolute necessity of language proficiency if Volunteers were to be successful overseas.

In later years this deficiency was remedied. By 1963, language instruction had become the central focus of training programs, with over three hundred hours of every course devoted to it. After only two years of operation, the Peace Corps had given instruction in forty-seven languages, half of which had never been taught before in the United States. When a 1963 evaluation report on a program in Afghanistan informed Shriver that not all Volunteers were fluent in Farsi, he ordered the staff in Kabul to "get into action on this language situation." He followed this up with a letter to Peace Corps missions all over the world demanding "continued efforts to upgrade language competence."[35] Charles Peters urged Shriver to go even further, advocating that all staff as well as Volunteers who did not maintain an adequate language facility should be dismissed. "We talk a lot about Peace Corps service being tough," he told Shriver, "let's make it tough by giving language tests every six months and throwing out all Volunteers and staff who fail to show reasonable improvement."[36]

This intense focus on languages improved the quality of the training programs immeasurably. Indeed, in the countries where they worked, Volunteers gradually began to erase the most egregious characteristic of the Ugly American: he was no longer tongue-tied. As language training chief Allan Kulakow put it: "Volunteers are trained to speak as equals with people throughout the world."[37] This was especially significant since those people remembered only too well the disdain and deprecation expressed in the linguistic ethnocentrism of the old colonial powers.

WEAKNESSES AND STRENGTHS

Between 1961 and 1963, a plethora of deficiencies plagued Peace Corps training. Agricultural extension Volunteers in Uruguay complained that their training program had put too much emphasis on "how we grow this in Iowa" instead of concentrating on how various agricultural techniques could be adapted to Latin American farms. Instructors for a recreational project in Sierra Leone were not aware that the national sport there was soccer; thus Volunteers went overseas prepared to establish contact in their local communities by encouraging basketball practice. At Utah State University, trainee teachers going to Iran were given little idea what to expect; instead of being prepared for the complex social structure and the undercurrent of political unrest, they were shown slides of gazelle hunts and private swimming pools.[38]

A further failing of the early programs was their lack of detailed cross-cultural instruction. On joining his teaching program in Afghanistan, a Volunteer reported that his deepest disappointment was the widespread apathy and lack of incentive among the local students; he was also angry that he had not been warned about "people spitting or blowing their noses in public — sometimes on you — the tendency not to plan but to live from day-to-day, and the widespread homosexuality." A training program for the Dominican Republic left Volunteers ignorant of the fact that men often raised four or five families simultaneously and that the illegitimacy rate was near 70 percent.[39] For African programs, training generally overlooked the clash of tribal tradition with industrial modernization in the burgeoning cities.

No part of training was more disliked by Volunteers than the euphemistically entitled "World Affairs" courses which sought to instruct them on how to counteract possible Communist attempts to subvert them overseas. Congress had insisted that Volunteers should be trained in the "history and menace of communism" and, in the early days, too much time was devoted to this.[40] Trainees preparing for the first overseas teaching project, in Ghana, spent less time learning Twi than they did the theory and practice of Marxism.

Every trainee received a pamphlet entitled *What You Must Know About Communism*. Most adjudged it a waste of time and advocated that this part of training should be replaced with more relevant information on the topics which really interested their Third World hosts: civil rights, Hollywood, living standards in the United States, and America's foreign policy. Charles Peters recommended that anti-Communist training should be completely abolished. Shriver knew from his experience on Capitol Hill that any such suggestion would only enrage conservatives in Congress; but by 1963 the amount of training time allocated to "World Affairs" had been quietly scaled down to a few hours.

Despite the over-emphasis on Communist subversion, the lack of detailed cross-cultural analysis, and other deficiencies, the Peace Corps' training process had more strengths than weaknesses and most Volunteers deemed it a highly useful tool in preparing them for their overseas experience. Trainees bound for a community development project in Peru praised their program at Cornell University highly; they had been given a practical technical training and, since almost all their instructors had lived in Peru, the area studies course was first class. Volunteer nurses going to Tanzania felt that their training at Syracuse University had been excellent; the language instruction in Swahili had been effective and analyses of local conditions were full and accurate. An evaluation report noted that trainee teachers bound for Ghana gave the faculty at Berkeley "rave notices . . . it can be said that nearly all volunteers feel they were well prepared for the Ghanaian situation by the training program."[41] Joe Walsh, a native of Massachusetts training at the University of New Mexico for an agricultural extension project in Guatemala, felt his instructors had given him the best possible preparation. He was taught how to vaccinate pigs, raise chickens, and dig wells, and he described the outdoors field training on an Indian reservation as "an eye-opener."[42] In fact, most Volunteers appreciated the outdoors training courses, whether carried out in Puerto Rico or some other location. Notwithstanding the minor complaints about extreme physical exertion, many considered the outdoor camps an essential part of the training schedule.

Most of the failings of the early training programs stemmed directly from the dearth of relevant experience in what the Peace Corps was trying to do. In 1961 few Americans understood the complex cultures of the developing countries. In that respect, the Peace Corps was flying blind. Moreover, it had to fly at great speed in order to get Volunteers into the field and make the Peace Corps a going concern, operationally and politically. In the face of these constraints, the achievements of the Peace Corps' early training programs were considerable. Moreover, by 1963 the training period had been extended to a minimum of three months and, as Volunteers began returning from their overseas assignments, their first-hand knowledge was incorporated into the training process. Training was still not perfect, but as Shriver argued in an angry riposte to a critical report, "After all, we've only been doing this job for 30 months!"[43] In that short time, nearly ten thousand American men and women had been moved from their sheltered home environment to a foreign country, had been taught a basic skill and, most important, had learned a language.

The Volunteers themselves realized that training could not prepare them for every aspect of their overseas service. "Everyone should expect at least a couple of months of floundering around," wrote a young Volunteer in Malawi. "There are some things which unfortunately can't be learned in the training program." Another Volunteer in Ethiopia encountered difficulties which he felt "no American experience and no amount of verbal orientation can prepare one for."[44] Even so, William Hutchison, an early trainer who had administered U.S. Foreign Service programs, reckoned that the Peace Corps' methods were top-notch.[45]

Compared to other countries' voluntary service programs, Peace Corps training seemed to be superior. In Ghana, a 1964 evaluation report comparing American with Canadian and British volunteers noted that the Peace Corps came off very well. "The Canadians and the British have to spend an awful lot of time finding out things about Ghana they feel it is essential to know if they are to operate effectively," said the report. Peace Corps Volunteers seemed to know more about Ghanaian politics, geography, history, and culture. They also spoke the language. All in all, the report concluded, the Peace Corps displayed a "special superiority in training."[46]

SELECTION AND DESELECTION

The most important ingredient in the general success of Peace Corps training was the quality of the trainees. To a great extent, they selected themselves. That is, Volunteers *asked* to join the Peace Corps. Although only 20 percent of all applicants were invited to training, roughly half that number chose to decline the invitation because of career choices, emotional commitments, and other concerns.[47] Those who accepted the invitation were reminded that selection for training was not a guarantee of selection for overseas. "Do not sell your home, furniture or car, or cut your ties completely, when you accept an invitation for training," invitees were advised. "Before reporting, and during training, make arrangements for these things but try to postpone final action until you are sure you are going overseas."[48]

Prior to final selection, applicants had to withstand the rigors of a Peace Corps training program during which they were continuously assessed. Poor performance during training, health problems, psychological instability, or general unsuitability were all potential grounds for "deselection." Trainees were also subject to a check—sometimes by the FBI—into their background. The discovery of a major misdemeanor or serious indiscretion could lead to the trainee being requested to withdraw. Each case was judged on its merits. In 1961, Bill Josephson successfully defended a trainee who had been given a $35 traffic ticket a few years previously.[49] Charles Kamen's controversial gaffe at the Rotary Club in Miami was not of itself deemed an act meriting deselection. On the other hand, the FBI discovered a confessed homosexual among the first group of trainees at Iowa State University; he was deselected. Another man in training at Rutgers had concealed a larceny conviction; he also was asked to leave the program.

Dr. Joseph Colmen, the leading psychologist in the Selection Division, felt that his unit had the most important job in the Peace Corps, for the agency was ultimately dependent on the personnel it selected to go overseas. "An ounce of selection is worth a pound of training," he told Shriver.[50] If the applicants were of poor quality, then no amount of training would make them into first-class Volunteers. To ensure the highest possible standards, Shriver set up a process of selection by continuous testing and review. He told his staff that, "In case of any serious doubt regarding a trainee's suitability for overseas duty, it is advisable to resolve the doubt in favor of the Peace Corps and the project."[51]

By the time an applicant arrived at his designated training site, an assessment summary—an analysis of the information from the Volunteer Questionnaire, personal references, and assorted tests—had been compiled. This was the first part of a cumulative record on the prospective Volunteer. Throughout the training period an ad hoc selection board (usually made up of the training officer, the project director, a doctor, a psychologist, a host country national, and sometimes, the country Rep), observed the trainee's progress. Trainees themselves contributed peer evaluations. All this material was reviewed in selection board conferences held halfway through the training period and again at the end. Trainees were rated on an ascending scale of 1 to 5. Obviously unsuitable candidates were "selected out" at the halfway stage; others who scored below an average of 3 were deselected at the meeting of the Final Advisory Selection Board.

The most controversial deselection of the early years centered on Mrs. Janie Fletcher, a sixty-five-year-old Texan in training for a home economics teaching project in Brazil in May 1962. Mrs. Fletcher alleged she was not selected because she had been unable to run a mile before breakfast, do push-ups each morning, and swim with her feet tied and her clothes on. Her Republican senator, John Tower, took up her case and accused the Peace Corps of physical cruelty toward an elderly citizen. "She fell while swinging from a rope on an obstacle course where she was expected to participate along with those in their early 20s," Tower told the Senate.[52]

With Peace Corps appropriations just about to pass Congress, the brouhaha came at an awkward moment for Shriver.

He suspected that Tower, an ambitious new member of the Senate, was playing politics with the Peace Corps. The easy option was to have the Selection Division reconsider its decision on Fletcher. But Shriver stood by the Peace Corps' process and explained that Mrs. Fletcher had been deselected because of her poor language facility, not her inability to withstand the physical exercise schedule at Puerto Rico. The Senate Foreign Relations Committee was satisfied with Shriver's explanation and took the matter no further. However, the incident indicated the serious attitude which trainees took toward the selection decision. Shriver realized that those not selected were "greatly disappointed and sometimes indignant."[53] He also knew that an indignant trainee was less of a liability for the Peace Corps than a poor quality or ineffective Volunteer.

In the early 1960s, an applicant from a small town who had been invited to Peace Corps training often left home with brass bands playing and his picture on the front page of the local newspaper. If not selected, his homecoming could prove a humiliating experience. Most trainees were haunted by the fear of deselection. One Volunteer explained:

> It was in the front of everybody's mind. "I've got to be selected" was a constant, desperate refrain in the mind's ear. If you sat in the coffee shop and the psychologist or one of the staff came in, you became self-conscious of everything you did. People were scared to death they wouldn't make it. Most of them had left their small towns like returning heroes, with the flags flying and the drums beating, and you could hardly face not making it. You tried to avoid any action or word that might prevent selection.[54]

Some found the tension unbearable. A Volunteer in Sierra Leone recalled that during training "we weren't worried about Sierra Leone, we were worried about selection. It always felt like you versus Washington until you were finally selected."[55] The sessions with psychologists were particularly detested.

Since the factors governing selection were variable and often intangible, Shriver ordered that no attempt should be made to explain assessment methods to trainees. Trainees selected out at the halfway stage sometimes disappeared overnight from their program. In these circumstances, it was inevitable that trainees criticized selection as clandestine, inhumane, and arbitrary. Sometimes there was a gap of a few weeks between the end of training and the final decision on selection. Trainees at Georgetown University waiting for confirmation of their selection for a teaching project in Ethiopia described this period as "limbo-haunted." At the University of Pennsylvania in 1962, trainees bound for Sri Lanka told of the "torture and hellish apprehension" they endured before the final selection decision.[56] Between 1961 and 1963, 22 percent of all trainees were deselected.

THE AVERAGE VOLUNTEER

Like recruitment and training, Peace Corps selection had its faults. Decisions on the quality of Volunteers were by no means foolproof. A project in the Dominican Republic included one man who was an alcoholic and a gambler; his main prowess was "shooting one-handed pool," and he had "close connections" with known underworld figures. Another Volunteer in the same group had been selected despite a history of psychological instability. In a rural public works project in Pakistan, a report noted some Volunteers of the highest quality, but also remarked that "the general level is not high enough . . . there are probably a good 30 who shouldn't have been sent in the first place." In Guatemala there was felt to be only one absolutely top-class Volunteer among a "barrel-scraped crew" who were judged to be much too young and immature.[57]

On the other hand, an evaluator in Uruguay described the Volunteers there as "the right group for the right project in the right country." Charles Peters ranked the first group of Volunteers to go to badly programmed assignments in Bangladesh as "one of the great Peace Corps groups. Not one quitter when most of them had every excuse to quit. We may have screwed up in every other way with them, but we sure as hell didn't when we selected them." Likewise, Volunteers in Costa Rica were a "top-notch group", while selection for Malawi had been "excellent, with only a few who are not first class."[58]

Evaluators' major criticism of selection was that too many Volunteers rated as 3s—qualified trainees but not outstanding ones—were allowed through the Peace Corps net. The ability or potential of these 3s was the subject of constant debate within the Peace Corps. Charles Peters maintained that if 3s were not outstanding in training then they would not be outstanding in the field. Volunteers in Panama were described as "mediocre . . . unobtrusively ineffectual." An evaluation report attributed this to the inclusion of eleven 3s in the program. In a biting memorandum to Shriver, evaluator Timothy Adams wrote: "We are inviting disaster when we load a group with trainees who are assessed as 3s . . . Too often when the Peace Corps has found itself forced to make a choice between shortfall (or cancellation of a program) and a dip in selection standards, we have gone for the dip."[59] Adams concluded that the results of such a choice were not happy. He claimed there was a direct correlation between the weakness of projects in Guatemala, Sri Lanka, and Pakistan, and the high percentage of 3s in those programs (55 percent, 68 percent, and 59 percent respectively). In an attempt to provide a certain measure of quality control, the Evaluation Division proposed that there should be a 20 or 25 percent ceiling on the number of 3s in any Peace Corps group.

In a spirited reply, Shriver denied that there was a direct link between 3s and weak programs:

> I disagree enthusiastically with this approach which implies that 3s are automatically weak. Overseas, 3s have done as well as 4s and 5s. Under your theory we should take only 5s. But even then I doubt whether we would improve overseas performance by more than 5 percent.[60]

Shriver had a point. In Venezuela some of the best Volunteers in the field had been assessed as 3s in training. Another report on Jamaica noted that of the nine 3s in a program of thirty-eight Volunteers, one was "outstanding," five were doing "good work," two were "marginal," and one had been dismissed. On this evidence, the report acknowledged that it was difficult to generalize that 3s should never be selected.[61]

Shriver believed that the relationship between performance in training—on which selection was based—and performance overseas, was imprecise. No matter how meticulous the Selection Division was, there was a dramatic difference between the training site and field conditions. This lent an air of unpredictability to the entire selection process. The Volunteers themselves, more than a little skeptical of the psychologist's contributions to final ratings, felt that selection was often a "hit-or-miss affair."

One Volunteer in St. Lucia had been dropped from another program bound for Latin America because of a poor language rating; his undistinguished academic record almost got him selected out of the St. Lucia project. Once overseas, he was rated by evaluators as "the best of a good lot in the field. He came to St. Lucia to help and he doesn't see anything stopping him." One of the best Volunteers in Iran was a woman who had been judged "beatniky" in training. Instructors had warned her about social niceties such as crossing her legs and not slurping her soup. Yet she was one of the most effective Volunteers in Tehran. She taught English in girls' vocational schools as well as in government offices and in the University of Tehran's medical institute; at night, she supervised home economics and handicrafts classes for Iranian women.[62]

A Volunteer in Belize who had been assessed as a 5 in training, turned out to be a "plain phoney" overseas. "He left the project early," noted an evaluation report. "He tried to get others to leave with him, and now he writes them letters about the easy life back home." A Volunteer teacher in Somalia, described as intellectually brilliant by the training staff at New York University, took to heavy drinking overseas. "And when he drinks, he gets nasty," reported evaluator Richard Richter. At a Somalian party the Volunteer accused one guest, a Somali education official, of sleeping with the girls in the school where he taught. "That the incident didn't lead to at least a minor explosion is due to the official's good humor," wrote Richter.[63]

When Burdick and Lederer reviewed Peace Corps projects, they found that "no necessary connection existed between those Volunteers who seemed the best in training and those who turned out to be the best in the field." More important, they concluded that it was the "average" trainee, not necessarily the brightest or most talented, who often made the best Volunteer. They outlined their picture of those who were most effective overseas:

> They were neither the brightest nor the best educated; they were less rather than more interested in politics, and they were

motivated by a mixture of reasons for joining the Peace Corps rather than being driven to the Peace Corps by a compelling desire to get away from it all (whatever "all" may have been) or an intense commitment to service. Overall, they were more average than extreme.[64]

That the average Volunteer was the best became a common finding of evaluation reports. The quiet, hard-working Volunteer often fulfilled the aims of the Peace Corps more satisfactorily than the multi-talented, brilliant one who was always visible. Burdick and Lederer advised selectors to be wary of the "all-American, cheerful, rah-rah, outgoing, extroverted campus hero or heroine." They warned equally against the introverted graduate student, buried in his books and thoughts. Early experience overseas indicated that college graduates were generally more amenable to language-learning and to establishing social relationships in a foreign community than were brilliant academics or skilled technicians. Hence, college seniors were regarded as prime Peace Corps material. It should be added, however, that Americans from many walks of life volunteered, were selected, and went on to prove themselves overseas.

The Peace Corps was well into refining its elaborate selection procedures by 1963. Application forms had been simplified and the number of psychological tests reduced. Shriver realized that these could not take enough cognizance of the changes that might affect a Volunteer under the hot-house conditions of service in a developing country. Quirks or strengths of character were bound to emerge which no amount of testing could predict. It gradually became apparent, therefore, that the best selectors of Volunteers were the Volunteers themselves. Nicholas Hobbs explained that since only a very select type of American volunteered for the Peace Corps in the first place, "the elaborate screening apparatus that was developed was not appropriate and was rather quickly abandoned on the research evidence that the tests were not making any difference . . . [applicants] had already been self-screened so that the screening tests had no real function."[65] Burdick and Lederer underscored this point in their reports to Shriver. "Just as very few men come out of the military forces better than they went in," they wrote, "so too we think the Peace Corps can do little more than reinforce those personal qualities the Volunteers already have."[66]

WHO VOLUNTEERED AND WHY

By 1963, seven thousand Americans were sharing the Peace Corps experience; but there was no such thing as a "typical" Volunteer. Shriver believed that anyone who decided to give up two years of his or her life to service in a developing country was extraordinary. There were, however, several characteristics which many Volunteers had in common. He or she (the male to female ratio was 3:2) was usually a recent graduate in the liberal arts, unmarried, and aged between twenty-two and twenty-eight. Volunteers were sometimes referred to as the "in-betweeners." Most had just finished college but were as yet undecided whether to pursue a career or continue on to graduate school. Some were already involved in further education. For others, immediate job prospects were uncertain and the Peace Corps provided a useful breathing space at a critical juncture in their lives.

Although no degree was required and there was no upper limit on age, applicants who had not attended college or who were over thirty-years old were in the minority. In fact, 86 percent of all Volunteers had a degree and less than 1 percent were over sixty. Relatively few blue-collar workers joined the Peace Corps. One critic contended that the twelve-page Volunteer Questionnaire was enough to put off "almost everyone but college types."[67] In 1964, forty thousand application forms were sent out to automotive workers in Michigan in the hope of getting skilled mechanics for programs in Latin America. Only three hundred applications were returned, producing about twenty-five Volunteers. The two years of economic sacrifice which Peace Corps service entailed proved a disincentive to young, skilled workers who could earn good money in American industry. Economics also partly explained the vast under-representation of minority groups in the Peace Corps, despite the agency's repeated specialized recruitment efforts and its outstanding record of non-discrimination.

Two-thirds of all Volunteers were Democrats rather than

Republicans, reflecting the Peace Corps' liberal ethos.[68] The large number of Republicans, however, was indicative of the agency's bipartisan political appeal. In terms of regional appeal, the West Coast always led in the number of Volunteers (evidence of Kennedy's sound political intuition in choosing San Francisco for his first public espousal of the Peace Corps). Next to California came the big industrial states of the East and Midwest—New York, Illinois, Pennsylvania, Ohio, Massachusetts, and Michigan. The Southern states lagged far behind. The segregationist policies of many of their colleges prevented the Peace Corps from using them as recruiting or training grounds.[69] By the end of 1962, not a single college or university in the South had a Peace Corps training contract. The Peace Corps did contract with black universities in the North.

The reasons why Volunteers chose to join the Peace Corps was one of the questions most commonly asked of them. Since their motivations were usually complex, the question was not easily answered. A 1962 study analyzed applicants' responses to a question in the Volunteer Questionnaire: "What do you hope to accomplish by joining the Peace Corps?" Answers were widespread ranging from: to help the poorer countries; to develop or improve as an individual; to get to know and understand other countries; and to further my career. Few applicants gave just one reason and most claimed their motives were mixed. The most recurrent answer was "to help people and humanity in general"; next was "to improve international relations and promote international understanding." At the bottom of the list were "to travel and have an adventure" and "to fight communism."[70]

Although these sets of reasons were sometimes at opposite ends of the spectrum, applicants often combined both types in their answers. Moreover, after some experience in the field, Peace Corps officials preferred to see a mixture, believing that Volunteers who were too single-minded in their motivation had to be looked at carefully. As Burdick and Lederer explained:

> Better a Peace Corps Volunteer with a capacity to admit his mixed motivations. Such Peace Corps Volunteers may be better able to adjust to the realities of life in the Peace Corps than those who say they come primarily to the Peace Corps for purely altruistic

motives. In addition, too strong protests of commitment may be covering up less desirable characteristics.[71]

One sixty-year-old Volunteer got tired of being constantly asked why she had joined the Peace Corps. Finally, when a reporter again wondered why she would want to travel to Africa after teaching school for thirty years in Kansas, she responded: "Young man, have you ever taught school for 30 years in Kansas?"[72]

A major factor in persuading young Americans to join the Peace Corps was the special affinity which many of them felt with John F. Kennedy. "Here was a man with whom I, and all young people could identify," wrote Duncan Yaggy, who volunteered in the summer of 1961, "a man who suddenly made being an American an exciting idea." Paul E. Tsongas, who volunteered in 1962 (and went on to become a Democratic senator for Massachusetts), recalled that Kennedy's influence was the "major factor" motivating him to overcome all obstacles in his path — including the grave doubts of his Republican father.[73] In the early 1960s, the President inspired many others to join the agency which he had created. On the day after Kennedy's assassination, the Peace Corps was flooded with requests from young people on college campuses all over America. In the week after Dallas, the all-time record number of applications was received: 2,550. This response led one young Peace Corps official to conclude that Volunteers were really "the last of the old-fashioned patriots," answering Kennedy's call to do something for their country.[74]

Aside from these broad generalizations about motives, few Volunteers cared to pinpoint any single reason for their decision to join the Peace Corps. Volunteer David Schickele said that a "favorite parlor sport" among trainees was to dream up "cocky answers to a question that was put to us 17 times a day by the professional and idly curious alike: why did you join the Peace Corps?"[75] Most Volunteers considered it a simplistic and infuriating question. Lyndon Johnson deliberately avoided asking it when he met a group of trainees at the Peace Corps' Puerto Rico camp in July 1962. Instead, he suggested that the next time someone asked them the question, they should turn it around, "like Thoreau turned Emerson's question around. Emerson had paid a visit to his friend in the Concord jail. 'My dear Thoreau,' Emerson said, 'Why are you here?' To which Thoreau replied, 'My dear Emerson, why are you not here?' "[76]

9

Programming for Peace

> One of the curses of colonialism is its tendency to make the ruled people look up to a superman, the colonial master, for all their needs. This tendency . . . should and can be replaced with self confidence and genuine pride that the Peace Corps can generate by working with, not only for our people.
> —Nene Mate Kole, Ghanaian statesman

THE PEACE CORPS AND THE THIRD WORLD

As the 1960s began, dozens of countries in Africa and Asia were emerging from their long night of colonial domination. *Uhuru!*, the Swahili clarion call for freedom reverberated throughout the Third World. "It was natural to be romantic and believe that independence would solve all our problems," said Leopold Sedar Senghor, Senegal's first president.[1] In reality, the Western powers had left their former colonies with fragile political, economic, and educational systems, and with a dearth of trained manpower.

Africa was particularly hard hit. In Senegal, Niger, the Ivory Coast, and other countries of West Africa, French technicians held virtually all senior positions; in Kenya, Tanzania, and other East African countries, British expatriates were dominant, with fewer than 25 percent of high-level civil service posts in national hands. Zaire (the Belgian Congo) was left without a single African doctor, lawyer, or engineer. Trade and industry throughout the continent were almost entirely foreign-owned; only 3 percent of highschool-age students received a secondary education.[2] As

171

the ambitious leaders of the newly independent nations looked to the future, they knew that mass education and training were essential to their countries' long-term social and economic development. To help meet this need, they turned to the Peace Corps.

In one of the Peace Corps' first staff meetings, the economist John Kenneth Galbraith advised Shriver and his colleagues on the role which young American college graduates might play in the Third World. Since African and Asian leaders wished to pursue the ideal of mass education and to expose their populations to modern ideas, he said that Peace Corps Volunteers who could teach languages, science, and math would be in demand. In Latin America, where countries had been independent for some time (and where literacy rates were much higher than in the other regions) Galbraith believed the most urgent requirement was change in the rigid social stratifications which, in many places, prevented all but the rich from participating in the decisions which governed the lives of the majority. Volunteers who could work in the villages and slums, organizing cooperatives and sparking community ventures could make a significant contribution.[3]

This analysis of the potential demand for Volunteers fitted perfectly with Shriver's sense of what the Peace Corps would be able to supply. He believed that thousands of motivated young liberal arts graduates could be trained quickly to teach and perform general community services in the Third World. Between 1961 and 1963, more than half of all Volunteers went overseas as teachers; another 30 percent worked in the sector which became known as community development.

By focusing on these two sectors—although another 20 percent of Volunteers worked in agricultural extension, health care, public works and administration, and other areas—Shriver believed the Peace Corps would be able to meet its three objectives as legislated by Congress: (a) to provide a needed skill to an interested country; (b) to increase the understanding of Americans by other peoples; and (c) to increase American understanding of other peoples. Kennedy's original idea for the Peace Corps was not that it should be just another technical assistance agency or a mini-AID. He wanted Volunteers to be able to impart a needed skill but he also wanted Third World peoples to learn about ordinary Americans and he wanted young Americans to gain first-hand experience of what life was like for the 75 percent of the world's population that lived in the developing countries. Shriver felt that a focus on human resource development through teaching and community organization would allow the Peace Corps to meet all three goals. He liked to say that rather than being in the business of making money or manufacturing goods, the Peace Corps was in the biggest business of them all, "the people business."[4]

DESIGNING THE FIRST PROGRAM

The challenge facing Warren Wiggins and his staff in the Office of Program Development and Operations (PDO) was to design programs which could meet these adventurous people-to-people objectives. Without becoming bogged down in the red tape and bureaucratic procedures traditionally associated with aid agencies, Wiggins had to get Americans overseas who would be, in Kennedy's words, "wanted by the host country, have a real job to do and who would be qualified to do that job."[5] On his trip around the Third World in April 1961, Shriver had promised the leaders of Africa and Asia that the Peace Corps would be up to this task. But no precedent existed for a federal program which would utilize the B.A. generalist for development work overseas. PDO had to start from scratch.

The initial planning and development of programs was done on an ad hoc basis. This was epitomized by the way in which the first Peace Corps project—road surveyors for Tanzania—was designed. It was negotiated almost single-handedly by Lee St. Lawrence who was to become chief of the Far Eastern region in PDO. St. Lawrence, a former ICA program officer, had worked in some of the most turbulent Third World countries of the 1950s—Laos, Vietnam, and the Belgian Congo. He had the reputation of being both an astute programmer and something of a swashbuckler. Bill Josephson described him as "foolishly courageous." During a staff meeting in March 1961, St. Lawrence suggested that Tanzania might be an appropriate place for the Peace

Corps to begin a program.* Shriver gave him the task of finding a feasible project. St. Lawrence left the meeting, caught a flight to Dar-es-Salaam and vanished. "We didn't hear a word from him for weeks—literally," Josephson recalled.[6]

In the first few weeks of April, St. Lawrence "bushwhacked" Tanzania (a nation the size of France, Belgium, and Germany combined) from end to end. He discovered less than eight hundred miles of paved roads. This meant that during the rainy season, there were long periods when villagers could not get their crops to market. Since agriculture was Tanzania's primary economic sector, its nine million people needed to get their crops transported if they were to make a living. St. Lawrence started designing a road surveying and engineering project. He checked out possible sites, consulted with local officials, investigated the living conditions which Volunteers would face and, finally, he met with President Julius Nyerere, who confirmed that roads were one of his country's development priorities. St. Lawrence then returned to Washington with the first tentative Peace Corps contract in his pocket. In terms of speed, first-hand knowledge of the field, and audacity, his bushwhacking in Tanzania set a remarkable precedent for Peace Corps programs. With enough determination and imagination, it seemed anything was possible.

The thirty-five trained engineers, surveyors, and geologists who made up the first project for Tanzania were a much celebrated group. The first Americans to enter Peace Corps training, they were showcased at home and abroad. After training at Texas Western College and being introduced to basic Swahili, they were flown to New York to visit the United Nations and on to Washington to meet President Kennedy. Taking his cue from St. Lawrence's bushwhacking trip, Kennedy told them that "There is nothing more important in Tanganyika than the development of roads to open up the country."[7]

St. Lawrence's example contributed to the establishment of some ground rules for programming. In particular, an in-country appraisal of every proposed project by either an official from headquarters or by the Peace Corps Rep in that country became standard procedure. The potential benefits and liabilities were

*Tanganyika was due to become the independent Tanzania in December 1961.

assessed by PDO's Coordination unit (the "murder-board") and a decision was made whether or not to go forward with the project. A formal working agreement was then signed with the host country. Under the aegis of the designated regional chief (of Africa, Latin America, Far East, or North Africa/Near East/Asia and Pacific), the Peace Corps Form 104—the detailed description of the proposed assignment—was written. Based on the 104, training and selection procedures got underway. On average, the entire programming process took between sixty to ninety days. In the first two years, when there was tremendous pressure to produce programs quickly, some were set up in an even shorter time.

Programs originated from many different sources: a meeting between Shriver and a foreign head of state, a suggestion by a U.S. ambassador, an AID official or a Peace Corps Rep, or a direct request from a host country institution. The specific details governing each project varied. Some host governments insisted on maintaining an element of independence by paying part of the cost of the Volunteers' service; Ghana, for example, provided Volunteers with their living allowances. A few projects were partly administered by an American private organization. In Colombia, CARE helped direct the Peace Corps' community development program. A consortium of Indiana universities, led by Notre Dame's Fr. Hesburgh, helped implement a rural action program in Chile. Some host institutions, like the education board in the Philippines, assigned a native counterpart who worked side-by-side with Volunteer teachers in a reciprocal learning process. In dealing with these new, sensitive, foreign governments programming policy had to be flexible.

There was, however, one broad precondition for any project: it should meet the "felt needs" of the host country and be wanted by the local people. Volunteers were at the service of their host government, not the United States. As Shriver put it: "The Volunteers go to work with people, not to employ them, use them or advise them. They do what the country they go to wants them to do, not what we think is best."[8]

Preference was also given to projects involving maximum contact with host country peoples rather than those which required a finely honed skill but minimal participation in the local community. Wiggins said that if a choice had to be made between a project calling for thirty laboratory technicians and thirty physical education instructors, the latter should be given priority. He explained this decision:

> Although the lab technicians might make a more apparent contribution to the social and economic development of the host country, the physical education instructors would have an opportunity to relate more closely to more people of that country and the direct results of their work would be more obvious.[9]

In short, Wiggins said that the physical education instructors would have more chance of meeting all three of the Peace Corps' goals.

PROGRAMMING GENERALISTS

In the main, Volunteers did not have specialized skills but rather were capable of doing, and of teaching their hosts to do, a basic job. The bureaucratese for this was "middle-level manpower"—in a category between the few highly trained experts and the completely untrained masses. At first, however, many aid experts questioned whether there was a "middle-level" role for the inexperienced B.A. generalist. Another major question was whether Peace Corps jobs should be structured (like formal education, agricultural extension, engineering and construction) or unstructured (community organization work dependent on personal initiative and improvisation). Although less than a thousand Volunteers actually took up overseas assignments in 1961, they helped resolve both these issues.

During that first year, five basic models for Peace Corps projects were set up: skilled technicians (the road surveyors) in Tanzania; teachers of math, science, history, and geography in Ghana and Nigeria; teachers' aides in the Philippines; English teachers in Thailand, and general community action workers in Colombia and St. Lucia. The early reports on these projects confounded those who had doubted the use of generalists. There were, of course, adjustment problems for the Volunteers involved in teaching in Africa and community development in Latin

America; but there were no complaints from their hosts about a lack of skills or a failure to participate in local communities.

On the other hand, the original Tanzanian program experienced some difficulties. The skilled surveyors and engineers had no problem finding work. They helped to design a network of farm-to-market roads and worked on plans for harbors, water lines, sites for airports and even entire towns. However, an unexpected cut in the road development budget by the Tanzanian authorities rendered much of their work ineffectual. Government economies meant that the Volunteers' planning and surveying did not culminate in much actual road construction by their hosts. Most important, the itinerant nature of the surveyors' work prevented them from establishing many close, personal relationships with their hosts. George Carter, one of the first Peace Corps Reps in Africa, recalled that the first Tanzanian project demonstrated that "the provision of technical skills was no guarantee of success."[10]

The lessons of these first few projects had a salutary effect on both the size and nature of all future programming. In particular, Warren Wiggins decided that the Peace Corps would never do another "Tanganyika."[11] In terms of satisfying the three goals of the Peace Corps Act, the early programs seemed to indicate that the trained generalist could well be more effective than the technician, in either structured or unstructured assignments. The generalists did not have the expertise of the technicians, but they seemed to have a greater aptitude for language-learning and to be more receptive to training in a wide range of basic skills. The relatively short training period could not transform the generalist into an expert, but it could make him proficient in a skill such as teaching literacy and numeracy, elementary public health, and agricultural extension methods. Brent K. Ashabranner (a Rep in India and later a deputy director of the Peace Corps), described this process for a poultry-breeding project in India:

> The generalists spent their time on just one thing: learning the rudiments of starting and taking care of small poultry units in India. They learned about the right kind of mud chicken houses by actually building them; they learned the deep litter, close confinement system of raising chickens . . . They learned the right

feed formulas and how to improvise with ingredients available in India. They learned to vaccinate, debeak and kill diseased chickens.[12]

After several months of training, the Volunteers were not experts on farming or animal husbandry. But they had acquired one basic skill: how to house, raise, cull, and keep healthy a small flock of chickens. They could impart this skill to their hosts.

The early reports on the first projects also seemed to indicate that the generalist was more adaptable to working conditions in the developing countries. Thomas Quimby, Rep in Liberia, explained that the B.A. generalist often proved to be more resilient than the skilled expert who tended to "climb the wall" on discovering that his host country coworkers could not always grasp sophisticated theories or complex instructions.[13] More important—at least in terms of the Peace Corps' three goals—the generalist usually tended to have a more effective social interaction than the technician. The generalist did not rely on his technical skill as the sole means of communication with his hosts. No matter what his specific assignment was, he was usually prepared to participate in his local community in as many ways as possible. Thus, the early projects convinced Shriver and his staff that the promotion of mutual understanding—a quintessential Peace Corps aim—would be better achieved by generalists than by technicians.

This finding was not displeasing to Shriver. Although the first few programs, especially in Tanzania, included a fair proportion of technicians, relatively few skilled workers applied for Peace Corps service. Most technicians tended to establish themselves in jobs, marry early, and generally take on commitments which prevented them from joining the Peace Corps. The first year's recruitment figures made it clear that the Peace Corps' principal catchment would be B.A. generalists. Four out of the five model projects set up in 1961 consisted mostly of this group. Had these projects been outright failures, the future of the Peace Corps would have been problematical. At the very least, Shriver would have been obliged to rethink *The Towering Task's* notion of a large Peace Corps. As it happened, the opposite was true. The one project (in Tanzania) which had relied almost totally upon technical expertise, had proven to be only a mixed success in terms of its people-to-people impact. An evaluation report described it as a "junior AID" technical assistance program where the highly skilled Volunteers had only an employer-employee relationship with their hosts.[14]

The programs consisting of generalists seemed to be thriving. In early 1962, an evaluator reported on the "outstanding group" of young generalists working in community development in Colombia. They were taking on diverse tasks such as helping to build bridges, sanitation systems, agricultural marketing boards, and handicraft cooperatives. "To those who think there is no such thing as the practical do-gooder," the evaluator concluded, "that helping mankind is the work of evangelists and cranks, I suggest the catharsis of a visit to Colombia."[15] Reports like this were a signal for the Peace Corps, based upon the B.A. generalist, to expand. By 1964, over ten thousand Volunteers were in forty-four countries.

EDUCATION: THE NATURAL PEACE CORPS PROGRAM

Teaching was the natural Peace Corps program, from both the host countries' and the agency's standpoints. For the emerging nations of Africa especially—where the illiteracy rate was 85 percent in 1960—education was regarded as the key to their political and economic independence. It was given priority in their requests for Volunteers. On arriving in Nigeria in 1961, the first group of Peace Corps teachers there were urged by the country's first president, Nnamdi Azikiwe, to help "Africanize" his country's educational system and move it away from the colonialist British influence.[16]

So intense was Ethiopia's concern for education that Emperor Haile Selassie personally directed the Ministry of Education; he asked the Peace Corps to send five hundred teachers. In Tanzania, President Julius Nyerere, himself a former schoolteacher, felt that the liberal arts education which Volunteers could provide would help the young citizens of his new nation to think critically. (During his years in a colonialist prison cell, Nyerere had translated Shakespeare into Swahili.) "It is no use the teachers giving to their pupils the answers to the existing problems of our nation," he argued, "because by the time the pupils are adults, the problems will have changed."[17] Nyerere wanted the Peace Corps' education programs to teach Tanzanians to solve problems for themselves.

For the Peace Corps, teaching was the optimal Volunteer assignment. It provided a relatively structured environment, was well suited to young college graduates, had a direct people-to-people impact, and it allowed the agency to get off to a dramatically fast start. In 1961, 34 percent of the first 763 Volunteers went into education programs, setting a pattern of heavy emphasis on this sector. By 1963, nearly four thousand Volunteers were in education, accounting for nearly 60 percent of all Volunteers. The percentage of education Volunteers in each region was 80 percent for Africa, 61 percent for NANEAP (North Africa/Near East/Asia and Pacific), and 22 percent for Latin America.[18] The Peace Corps' primary focus in the sector was to fill teacher shortages in order to expand access to schooling. The majority of education Volunteers were assigned to secondary schools; English and the humanities were the most widely taught subjects. However, Volunteers also taught at the primary, teacher-training and university levels, and across the full range of subject matter.

If providing trained manpower in education can be equated with success, then the Peace Corps' teaching programs were, by and large, eminently successful. As developing countries requested Peace Corps teachers in increasing numbers, the Volunteers assigned to them allowed governments to open new schools, expand schooling into remote areas, add college graduates to marginally qualified school staffs, and undertake curriculum reform. Volunteers also provided modern educational methods and helped to break down the colonialist rote system of learning and Third World students' fear, instilled by colonialist teachers, of attempting anything beyond their textbooks' rigid instructions. As the development economist Barbara Ward Jackson noted: "The Peace Corps is a valuable effort to provide in developing countries the massive numbers of teachers needed to carry out modernization"[19]

The Peace Corps had a particularly dramatic effect on a large number of African school systems. In Ethiopia, where the Peace Corps ran its largest teaching program, the need was overpowering. Before the arrival of the Volunteers in 1962, there were less than five hundred secondary school teachers serving a nation of 21 million people. The four hundred Volunteers assigned to Ethiopia by 1963 increased the country's secondary school capacity by 80 percent (to twenty-five thousand students), the largest single increase in the number of people educated in Ethiopian public schools since the school system was established in 1908. In 1964, the Ministry of Education requested six hundred additional Volunteers.[20] The government even established its own counterpart volunteer teacher service (the Ethiopian University Service) under which all Ethiopian college students went out into the provinces to help develop the country's educational resources.

In addition to requesting Volunteers to meet teacher shortages, African Education Ministries also expressed their strong interest in receiving "American methods of instruction . . . as contrasted to the more formal approaches characteristic of the past, which offer few economically useful skills and attitudes."[21] In meeting these requests between 1962 and 1963, Peace Corps teachers took up posts in 40–50 percent of all secondary schools in Ghana, Sierra Leone, and Somalia; in Nigeria, 442 Volunteers taught over forty thousand pupils, 35 percent of all Nigerians enrolled in secondary schools and teacher training programs; the Peace Corps helped Malawi push its number of secondary school teachers up to 227, an increase of 77 percent; in Niger, Volunteers taught the English language in French to 30 percent of the country's secondary school students; and in Guinea, Volunteers represented 40 percent of all teachers of English in the country. By 1963, the term "Peace Corps teacher" was well known in nineteen African countries.[22]

Despite the popularity of the Peace Corps' education programs in Africa and elsewhere (in 1963 there were twice as many requests for Volunteer teachers than the Peace Corps could fill), there was a serious internal policy debate as to whether the agency should be involved in the sector. A number of evaluation reports argued that a formal education was useless to Third World children, many of whom were going to drop out of school before graduating, go back to their villages, and spend their lives trying to make a living out of the soil. In particular, there was argument as to the value of teaching English in the Third World, especially in Francophone Africa. Evaluators were also critical of Volunteers who lived in neat houses in the school compound, sometimes with cooks and stewards in attendance. In short, critics questioned whether teaching programs had sufficient development impact in the sense of producing more goods and services to boost a country's GNP.

Shriver, a former Board of Education chairman in Chicago, was a vigorous proponent of the Peace Corps' role in education. Intuitively, he sensed what development experts were to confirm in later years: that countries with higher literacy rates enjoyed faster economic growth, that education contributed to greater agricultural and industrial production, and that it was linked directly with improved health and nutrition.[23] Shriver was no development theorist, but he firmly believed—along with Alfred Marshall and the classical economists—that "Knowledge is the most powerful engine of production."

In terms of specific contributions, Shriver noted that the Peace Corps enabled Education Ministries in the Third World to make substantial savings in teachers' salaries and in other indirect costs such as revising curricula; that Volunteer teachers often taught in the bush schools that were avoided by local teachers; and that Volunteers in teacher-training positions had a multiplier effect on the number of host national teachers graduated, thus contributing to the country's eventual self-reliance in educational resources. For these reasons, Shriver did not agree that the Peace Corps' focus on the education sector was misplaced. Besides, it was what the developing countries wanted. He argued that it would have been imperialist for the Peace Corps to tell them that they should limit their education efforts to certain segments of their populations or to certain subjects.

In this context, he defended the Peace Corps' largest education program: the teaching of English. From his discussions with Third World leaders, Shriver knew that English was regarded as an important subject, especially in the former British colonies where English was the language of instruction, government, and development. They believed that knowledge of the industrialized world's major language was a key to their countries becoming more fully integrated with the world economy and in providing access to untranslated technical information. As for English-teaching programs in Francophone Africa, Shriver pointed out that it was the host countries themselves which requested them as a form of defense against Charles de Gaulle's attempts to force them into closer and more subordinate relationships with France. In Gabon, the Peace Corps' involvement in the education system was significant enough (Volunteers helped construct many Gabonese schools) that de Gaulle pressured the Gabonese government to expel the Volunteers in his effort to maintain and expand French influence in West Africa. President Leon M'ba insisted that the Peace Corps should remain.[24]

In addition to the strictly technical benefits of education programs, Shriver knew that they were most suitable to helping the Peace Corps fulfill its people-to-people mandate. As Roger Landrum, one of the first Volunteers in Nigeria (he taught African literature to his students) later explained, the role of the Peace Corps teacher was not just confined to the classroom:

> Classrooms lead out into the world beyond for both the students and the Volunteers; into the atmosphere and operations of the local school and national school system; into the complexities of life in a local community; into the larger forces and issues governing the economic and political progress of the host country.[25]

Many Volunteers carried out "secondary" projects in addition to their official teaching assignment. They helped to establish local libraries, demonstration gardens, craft cooperatives, and adult literacy programs. These secondary projects, often based on Volunteers' personal interests or special skills, allowed the Peace Corps to establish a network of social relationships which extended far beyond the classroom.

Nigeria's Minister of Education and Economic Development, Alhaji Waziri Ibrahim, confirmed that the Peace Corps' education programs provided "something extra" to their host communities. He cited the wide variety of extracurricular activities in which Volunteer teachers were involved:

> They have organized libraries. They have given radio lessons. They have created science laboratories. They have produced

plays. They have brought a new dimension to physical education in our land. They have led school excursions. They have undertaken research in local history.

More important, Ibrahim said that the Volunteers—unlike the colonialists— "identified themselves with the future progress" of his people, "and in such a manner that lasting friendships have been formed."[26]

ACCIÓN COMUNAL: A REVOLUTIONARY FORCE?

While Shriver actively encouraged Peace Corps teachers to go beyond their classroom duties and mix with their host societies in many different ways, the philosophy of "participation" found its fullest expression in the other major activity of the Peace Corps: community development. In contrast to most education jobs, community development was often completely unstructured and could be used to describe any action which helped "better" the lives of the local community. For example, many children in developing countries had distended stomachs caused by a parasitic germ in their drinking water. Since their parents regarded this condition as normal, they paid little attention to it. Volunteers could help simply by giving the example of sanitizing water by boiling. No great skill was needed, just elementary scientific information and a friendly approach. With this type of basic contribution in mind, Shriver deemed community development an ideal assignment for the B.A. generalist.

His staunchest ally in the espousal of community development was Frank Mankiewicz, first Peace Corps Rep in Peru and later regional chief for all Latin American programs. He saw community development as much more than the limited imparting of basic information on hygiene and nutrition. To Mankiewicz, it was a revolutionary force: "the ultimate aim of community development is nothing less than complete change, reversal— or a revolution if you wish—in the social and economic patterns of the countries to which we are accredited."[27] In Latin America, where Mankiewicz estimated 97 percent of the population had no say in the political, social, and economic decisions affecting their lives, he deemed it the Volunteers' duty to "teach Democracy at the community level." He instructed Volunteers to encourage and inspire, by their example, apathetic villagers and dispirited slum dwellers to participate in the development of their own community. While in most projects host peoples worked with Volunteers to alleviate physical poverty, *acción comunal* was aimed more at the poverty in men's minds.

Community development was often the source of greater food production, purer water and cleaner streets, but its effects were not measurable solely in those terms. It also sought to change attitudes in such a way that the poor would grasp an understanding of collective action and its power to solve their problems. As Mankiewicz put it: "If the aims of community development, as the Peace Corps sees it in Latin America, can be summed up in one sentence, it is that success is in sight not when the economic statistics have reached a certain level, not when a certain number of miles of roads or cinderblock houses have been built, but when the forgotten and ignored have been invited to join in society."[28]

By 1963, nearly three thousand Volunteers had been "parachuted" into the urban *barrios* and remote *campos* of nineteen Latin American countries. They were told to spend their first few months getting to know the people, identifying potential junta leaders and discovering the community's "felt needs." Gradually, the Volunteers were to become active in community affairs, culminating in their organizing the first community meeting. At these meetings the Volunteers would "lead the people into discovering their problems and finding solutions." After the community decided on its priorities, the program entered the "doing stage," constructing village wells, digging latrines, or establishing cooperatives and community councils. In this phase, the Volunteer was to "act as a general supervisor at times, and often as a common laborer."[29] Once the initial projects were completed, the newly organized community would go on to bigger problems on its own. This at least was the theory.

Mankiewicz acknowledged that community development was desperately difficult either to define or to do well. Yet, after a few months general training, the Volunteers were plunged into a strange, new environment and told to "participate." One Volunteer described the great potential for failure and frustration inherent in such an assignment:

The community developer comes into town and takes up resi-
dence with a local family. For weeks he seemingly does nothing.
He plays with the children, talks with the shopkeepers, drinks
in bars. His Spanish or his Quechua is a little halting and quaint.
It takes quite a while before the people see that he sincerely wants
to help them tackle a few problems. In any event, the Volunteer
is faced with the task of making himself acceptable and he remains
guilty (or at least suspect) of all types of contrived motives until
he proves himself innocent.[30]

Many host officials were disappointed by the Peace Corps' community development programs. "We were told that Volunteers
would be trained and fully capable of helping farmers with their
crops," said one *campesino*. "We received nothing of the kind.
They are nice young men and women, but they know nothing
about agriculture." In the cities, there were similar expressions
of disappointment about the Volunteers sent to work in the
slums: "They do not understand our people or our problems,"
the head of an urban self-help housing program said. "And they
bring no skills with which to help."[31]

In criticizing a community development project in Panama,
an evaluation report noted that:

The project's aims were not clearly understood in either Panama
or Washington because the Panamanian Health Service does not
seem to have a clear conception of community development. To
what degree the project was to emphasize community development as against public health and sanitation has never been resolved. The selection and training of the Volunteers reflected this
confusion.[32]

In Venezuela, inadequate preparation led to disaster for the
community developers working in rural areas with the 4-H Foundation. The project had been planned by a Peace Corps official
who had never strayed from an air-conditioned office in Caracas.
Not surprisingly, nobody in the host community seemed to know
that the Volunteers were coming, and they had no jobs. Evaluators ranked the project with "many of AID's smaller fiascos . . .
everything that could possibly go wrong has gone wrong." Likewise, in El Salvador by September 1963 only ten Volunteers (out

of twenty-three) remained in a community development program which evaluators described as a "swamp of imprecision and generalities."[33]

Charles Peters claimed that imprecision characterized the programming for most community development projects in Latin America. Even Frank Mankiewicz admitted in later years that community development's major flaw was that it had been applied too quickly in too many countries. He felt the Peace Corps had been a little over-optimistic in its belief that nearly every "red-blooded young American" could make some sort of material contribution to the developing countries without a basic skill and a definite job.[34] Other critics were even more severe. C. Payne Lucas and Kevin Lowther (two former Peace Corps staffers) maintained that most programming for community development was "pure fantasy" and that only one Volunteer in twenty was effective.[35] "You know what really got me?" asked a Volunteer working in El Salvador. "I realized one day they had a name for me. It was 'vago' . . . that means vagabond. They weren't being mean or anything; but I didn't have a job or even a government title, so that's just what I was—a vagabond."[36]

While the frustration rate was extremely high among Volunteers working in community development, the projects were by no means all failures. "The community development program in Peru is healthy," noted a 1963 evaluation report. "There appear to be no big or dramatic problems. In general, the program exhibits vitality, maturity and stability." Volunteers were in structured nutrition and medical projects and the local Peruvian agencies eagerly put them to work in helping to feed four thousand children during the school year. "The question in Peru is not so much of going from bad to good—but from good to better," concluded the report. "We are in Peru, we are accepted and we are wanted. The Peace Corps idea is working."[37]

The largest community development program, in Colombia, was also basically sound. By January 1964, over six hundred Volunteers were working in various projects and, despite the huge size of the program, it was a significant success. Evaluator Meridan Bennett claimed that "the Peace Corps' ability to work in community development has been proven in Colombia." Since much of the work was undefined, the Volunteers were free to tackle everything. This they did with a vengeance as they took on literacy-teaching, arts and crafts classes, agricultural extension, and ante- and post-natal care. Female Volunteers working in the machismo-dominated *campos* proved as effective as males, and Bennett concluded that the fear—held by some Washington officials—that women could not function as community developers, should be banished forever.[38]

In 1962, Charles Peters described the community development program in the Dominican Republic—consisting of chicken-breeding, well-digging, and market-gardening—as "a successful project . . . making good use of the Volunteers' talents and meeting the real needs of the Dominican Republic." Likewise, the rural action program in Chile (led by the University of Notre Dame) was "faring well" and had endowed the Peace Corps with a good reputation.[39] Community development in Bolivia was another effective program. Jack Vaughn, (a former ICA official and Shriver's successor as Peace Corps Director) recalled that the Peace Corps had approached a community development project in the high plains near Lake Titicaca with trepidation because of the hostile attitude of the Indians there. "They were all armed, they seemed resentful, didn't speak Spanish and didn't change," said Vaughn. After three years of a Peace Corps presence there, Vaughn visited five villages in the area. He found the change in attitude astounding:

> They had all built a new school, the first school in a thousand years. They all had a clinic for child deliveries, the first clinic in a thousand years. They all had potable water piped in, and they had done it themselves. They had made more physical progress in a couple of years than they had made in the previous thousand. But more important was the attitude, the openness, the willingness to look you in the eye and tell you about who they were and what they had done, and the pride and self-respect of citizenship.

Vaughn concluded that much of this change was due to the Peace Corps. "What the Spaniards and the Incas and the Western miners and the diplomats and the AID people couldn't do in a thousand years," he said, "the Peace Corps had helped to do in about three years. This is real revolution."[40]

Whether the Peace Corps' community development programs were "revolutionary" is an open question. The experience
and effect varied according to each individual project and each
Volunteer. While there was enough evidence to suggest that the
Peace Corps was mistaken to implement community development so quickly and on such a large scale, there were sufficient
successes to confirm that many Volunteers were catalysts of
positive change in previously neglected villages and slums. *La
Nacion*, the Bolivian government's newspaper, underscored this
notion: "These Volunteers are formidable ambassadors direct
from the soul [of our] North American neighbors. They come
in contact with the people when they arrive and they awaken
their initiative; they understand them . . . " The editorial concluded that while the Volunteers' technical skills were not all that
had been hoped for, "they leave behind them a thirst for improvement and for a better life."[41]

THE NUMBERS GAME

The major criticism of Peace Corps programming in the Kennedy era was that it played a numbers game: in order to make
an immediate impact on Congress and the public at home and
on foreign governments overseas, it pushed too many unskilled
Volunteers into too many countries—to the detriment of both.
Noting that Volunteer numbers rose from several hundred in
1961 to over fifteen thousand in 1966, Brent Ashabranner wrote
that "commitment to growth dominated all other thinking."[42]

The philosophy of "bigness" originated with Warren Wiggins's *Towering Task*. However, Wiggins's idea of having groups
of thousands of Volunteers first in one country and then in
several others, never materialized. Rather, relatively small groups
ranging from twenty to six hundred were assigned to forty-four
countries.* Still, the concept of bigness was there, even if not
in the sense that Wiggins had originally intended. In early 1961,

*Successive Peace Corps projects in individual countries were often aimed
at different sectors—education, community development, agriculture—and they
were numbered in sequence. Thus Volunteers identified themselves as Ghana
I, India V, or Brazil IX, and so on.

Shriver told his staff that "The world will not wait while we attempt to fill an ocean with an eye-dropper." Firmly against the cautious approach, he warned that "To anticipate our limits before we must would be a disastrous error."[43] Thus the Peace Corps began with a quantum jump.

The first numbers game was played in the Philippines, the country Wiggins had used as his test-case in *The Towering Task*. The historical relationship between the United States and the Philippines suggested a conducive atmosphere for a spectacular program and hundreds of generalist Volunteers were quickly channelled into vaguely defined jobs as "teachers' aides." Rep Lawrence Fuchs recalled that "The Philippines was the place where you could get the largest number of bodies most quickly, because you had the fewest intergovernmental problems." In the Peace Corps' first year of operations, three hundred Volunteers were in the Philippines; after eighteen months, there were six hundred. "The first year we had one third of all the Volunteers in the world in the Philippines," said Fuchs, "but people didn't know this generally; we talked about being in 15 different countries."[44]

Charles Peters and his evaluators uncovered other examples of the numbers game. A 1963 report hit out at PDO's proposal to assign 150 additional teachers to Liberia where there already were 300. With the country's total population under one million, the evaluators felt that any enlargement of the program would make Liberia top-heavy with Volunteers. PDO's Form 104 had justified expansion in terms of the United States' "historic commitment to Liberia." The report suggested that it more probably reflected the Peace Corps' "present commitment to wedge a thousand more Volunteers into Africa by hook or by crook."[45]

In Pakistan, the Form 104 for a salinity project called for 240 Volunteers in one fell swoop, while a technical school project proposed assigning 150 Volunteers to one small area. Evaluator Timothy Adams described these plans as at best, "hyperbolic examples of the numbers game," and at worst, "grandiose and dangerous." Another report on the community development project in Ecuador was concerned that there were far too many underemployed Volunteers in the program. The report warned that while big numbers of Volunteers might please the Ecuadorian government and make "good reading in the U.S.," it was nonetheless "a sham and a delusion to 'sell' it as either necessary or desirable."[46]

"When one sees the Peace Corps idea being prostituted by an attempt to play the numbers game," Peters told Shriver angrily in a 1963 memorandum, "one's blood pressure tends to rise . . . you've got to make clear to the people in Washington how demoralizing the numbers game can be when witnessed by unemployed Volunteers."[47] It was not just the numbers that infuriated Peters, but that the Volunteers involved were often unskilled generalists for whom PDO had not provided definite jobs. The Form 104 for an agricultural extension project in Panama had called for a dozen agronomists; only three Volunteers turned up with the required skills. Perfirio Gomez, the Panamanian director of agrarian reform, was resentful at having been made a victim of the numbers game: "Next time if I ask for 30 who know agriculture and you have only ten, please send only ten." A frustrated Volunteer victim of the numbers game in Pakistan wrote: "I'm not contending that numerically we have too many people, but for Pete's sake get jobs that exist and are needed. Then get people that have needed skills and have the character to take them into their positions. The main thing missing in developing countries is skills, skills, skills."[48]

The numbers game stemmed partly from the empire-building tendencies of the Peace Corps' leaders. They wanted the agency to make an immediately favorable impression on the world. And in the America of the early 1960s, bigger was always better. From Shriver's point of view, political considerations also had to be taken into account. A small, slow, expensive Peace Corps would probably not have won support on Capitol Hill. Congressmen reading a quick summary of Peace Corps achievements before a vote looked at the number of Volunteers and countries. Evaluators tended to ignore this fact. "Our basic strategy for Congress," advised David Gelman, "needs to be nothing more complex than excellence and service. Numbers have little to do with either."[49] However, as Peace Corps Director, Sargent Shriver could not afford to view the world in such simple terms. Besides, a miniscule, cautious Peace Corps would not have been consonant with Kennedy's order to "create a New Frontier image abroad."[50]

But while he wanted the Peace Corps to be a significant size, Shriver denied that he was committed to numbers for their own sake. "We have no such expansionist policy," he told evaluators. His response to the numbers game charge was that a Peace Corps of twenty-, fifty-, or even a hundred thousand would do no more than scratch the surface of the gargantuan development problems confronting the Third World. He argued that if he had heeded "numbers game" critics in February 1961, then the Peace Corps would never have got off the ground. "There were also arguments in those early days about saturation of the foreign country, either in terms of jobs or the psychological impact of the American presence," he wrote. He did not agree that the ten thousand Volunteers who served with the Peace Corps in the Kennedy years constituted an excessive number. "Our country and our times have had plenty of experience with programs that were too little, too late," he said, noting that the Peace Corps managed to respond to only a fraction of both those at home who applied for service and those abroad who requested Volunteers.[51]

Shriver was right that, after the initial pump-priming from Washington, the pressure for increased numbers came mainly from the developing countries. But this demand, together with the great need for speed, locked the Peace Corps into a mode of operation by crisis. This sometimes led to vague programming and inferior projects. In 1961 and 1962 especially, officials from Peace Corps headquarters rushed in and out of Third World countries, setting up programs which sometimes proved unfeasible. Such was the poor quality of some of the early project plans that critics described them as "literary documents bordering on fiction."[52] A major difficulty was that Peace Corps programmers, along with everyone else, did not have an exact idea of what Volunteers could or could not do overseas. This confusion was reflected in the early "shopping list" programs which assigned Volunteers to do everything, from teaching to public health care, agricultural extension, and physical education in a single project.

A hurriedly produced or badly written Form 104 took its toll on every other component of the Peace Corps operation. The selection and training functions were directly affected. If the 104 were vague or mistaken about a given project, selection and training could be rendered virtually irrelevant. Ultimately, the Volunteers and the host country nationals suffered most from what evaluators referred to as "spilt-milk" projects.

"Only innocents continue to rely on the 104 as some reflection of reality," wrote evaluator Dee Jacobs in a highly critical report on a school construction project in the Dominican Republic. The 104 had stated that, along with the host country counterparts, the Volunteers would be helping to construct low-cost, "self-help" school houses. When the Volunteers arrived, however, they found that they were actually expected to build the schools on their own. In addition, it soon became obvious that several key host government officials had no interest in the project. It collapsed after a few months and the Volunteers moved into general community development. Jacobs blamed PDO for the superficial planning which had pushed Volunteers into ill-conceived work situations: "The pressure to produce was on and it shows in the 104s and in the field. Not enough time was spent to investigate carefully the need for and feasibility of various projects."[53]

Worse was the project for the Ganges-Kobadak valley in Bangladesh, ambitiously described in a 104 as "irrigation management." Volunteers arrived to discover that they had been assigned to an irrigation project which lacked one essential ingredient: water. The 104 had not reflected the grave doubts voiced by those familiar with the area as well as the gloomy forecast of a Harvard Study Group. An evaluation report pointed out that the result was "a pitiable operation, sloppily researched, unrealistically planned and, thus far at least, poorly executed." Charles Peters counseled Shriver that this critique of the Ganges-Kobadak project should be read by all programming officers as a guide to "how we don't want things done."[54]

Haste, inexperience, over-optimism, and big numbers were among many factors contributing to the weaknesses of some early Peace Corps projects. But weaknesses were only one side of the story. The accomplishments of Peace Corps programming far outweighed its mistakes. "This is a country where the Peace Corps looks almost too good," wrote evaluator John Griffin in Thailand. The Volunteer teachers had been well prepared and most were well placed in structured jobs in the secondary schools. The program was tightly administered, there was close cooperation with Rep Glenn Ferguson, and not one Volunteer resigned or was sent home. Such was its success, the report recommended that the Peace Corps should expand into university teaching where an impact could be made on Thailand's future leaders. "This program deserves its reputation as one of our best run and anyone looking for real trouble will be disappointed," the report concluded.[55]

In Gabon, the school construction project was "one of the most successful programs the Peace Corps has ever put into the field . . . meeting a direct and immediate need of the Gabonese government." The Volunteers were enormously popular with their hosts, they had personal contact with at least thirty local Gabonese communities, and local counterparts were plentiful and enthusiastic. Evaluator Philip Cook was ecstatic:

> The Gabon project, to date, proves that the Peace Corps can make effective use of young, low-octane Volunteers in structured assignments . . . one can certainly conclude that the Peace Corps can put nineteen and twenty-year-olds together in groups of ten or fifteen, show them how to do a relatively complex job, and then leave them to continue the performance with little direct supervision.[56]

Volunteers working in English teaching, nursing, and mechanical engineering in Afghanistan were all busy performing needed tasks and were described by evaluator Thorburn Reid as "excellent . . . not a word, not even a suggestion, of criticism of the Peace Corps program did I hear in Kabul." Despite the mysterious Afghan environment and a delicate political situation, their work presented a good example of a "small, well-directed Peace Corps project with high standards of programming."[57]

Evaluators noted that the home economists and agriculturalists in Uruguay had scored a "definite, if unspectacular, success in meeting all three Peace Corps goals." And the physical education and sports program in Belize—as in almost every country—was an outstanding success. Evaluator Richard Elwell saw it as a great force of social education which gave the Peace Corps its "greatest exposure." Nor were there any major problems for the solid agricultural extension project in Costa Rica which in July 1963 was already "good . . . with prospects of becoming better."[58]

Even where projects did not of themselves appear very successful, Volunteers often made significant contributions outside of their specified assignments. Volunteers in the Philippines, disappointed with their ill-defined "teacher's aides" jobs, participated in numerous kinds of community projects in the *barrios*. Although evaluators Burdick and Lederer criticized the vagueness of the original program, they sensed that the reservoir of goodwill which Volunteers were building was a "key achievement." There was a "genuine feeling of warmth" for the Peace Corps, and there was no doubt that it had taken on a special meaning for the Filipinos:

> Perhaps most Filipinos are still convinced that all Americans are rich and live in big houses but they are also convinced that these rich American youths are willing to live in *barrios*. The children, especially, will always carry this memory with them: in the long run, perhaps this alone makes the whole effort worthwhile even if it might be done better in some important ways.[59]

In 1963, the Filipino president, Diosdado Macapagal, presented the Peace Corps with Asia's equivalent of the Nobel prize, the Ramon Magsaysay Award for International Understanding. It was the first time the Award had been made to non-Asians.

DOING SOMETHING RIGHT

Long before the first Peace Corps program was implemented, Shriver knew there would be mistakes. Before going overseas, he warned all Volunteers that "No matter how good a job of programming the Peace Corps has done, the job to which you are assigned may turn out to be quite different from the way it is described to you." He told Volunteers to be prepared to "adjust to the new circumstances or even be reassigned to a new position within the country. In many cases, we ask the Volunteer to help in the development of the job to its full potential."[60] Shriver knew that in the newly independent countries of the

Third World there were many imponderables; it would have been foolish to expect programs to work out exactly as planned. In a number of cases, there turned out to be a gap between the glowing promise of a host government's support in the project agreement and the weak back-up provided in the field. "You can do everything," said a frustrated Volunteer in Colombia, "but if you can't get a two-peso bag of cement when you need it, everything goes to pieces."[61]

With such vicissitudes in mind, Shriver said that project descriptions should not be treated as more than rough outlines upon which "felt needs" perceived in the field could be transposed. Shifting and searching for jobs and personnel characterized the first few months of even the best projects. In this context, Shriver gave enormous power to Peace Corps Reps and placed his faith in the initiative and versatility of Volunteers. Sometimes performance fell below expectations. Still, Shriver resisted the temptation to establish a new overseas bureaucracy like Point Four, ICA, or AID, staffed by various levels of program officers. Despite the arguments of Peters and other evaluators, Shriver was not persuaded that highly priced program experts and time-consuming economic appraisals would, in the final outcome, produce better projects than PDO. Replying to a critical report on this subject, Shriver predicted what would become of the Peace Corps should it succumb to the regimental charms of "efficiency" and stifle individual initiative:

> We create "programmers" . . . They will be "experts." They will issue forth from a program "office." They will zoom around telling the overseas staff what is permissible—huge "program documents" will be prepared in the field at huge expense in time and money. Secretaries will type them with copies for five different Washington offices, all of whom will have to "sign-off" . . . The Peace Corps will receive an award for clean-cut, hard administrative efficiency from Forbes Magazine and the Director of the Peace Corps will move from his post to an Executive Vice-President's post in a large industrial concern in Dayton.[62]

Shriver knew Peace Corps programming was not faultless. The range of Volunteers' skills and the quality of their performance were inadequate to the needs of the developing countries; given the magnitude of those needs, that was inevitable. All the same, the Peace Corps' skill contribution to Third World countries was not inconsiderable. In the field of education especially, Peace Corps teachers who learned the languages of their host nation—Ibo, Quechua, Luo, or Urdu—and who involved themselves and their students in the lives of their local communities, often struck a blow for social and economic freedom. Besides the specific, technical subjects which they taught, Peace Corps teachers often had their greatest impact simply by encouraging their students to challenge the status quo and apply the question "Why?" to their poverty-stricken societies.

Nor should the contribution of those Volunteers involved in community development programs be underestimated. Any judgment of success depended very much on which individuals were involved, when, where and how. Evaluators were highly critical of community development because they felt it involved too many unskilled generalists in undefined programs. However, as Frank Mankiewicz argued:

> In communities where a significant step upward towards a better life is the opening of a seed store, or the entry of a literate person . . . or the formation of a credit union, or the distribution of a two-page weekly newspaper—where the United States is as far away as the moon and the idea of self-government as unlikely as flying to the moon—Peace Corps Volunteers are a powerful force.[63]

Evaluators often forgot that the provision of trained manpower was but one of the Peace Corps' three goals. Building social relationships with host peoples was at least half of the Volunteer's job. In this respect, energy and friendliness were as important as technical expertise. The Volunteer's attitude toward his hosts was as significant as the task he sought to perform with them. During a 1964 staff meeting on the perennial "skills" versus "people-to-people" question, former Volunteer Roger Landrum could say with a conviction derived from his teaching experience in Nigeria, "If a technical job is all that the Peace Corps contributes, it makes no profound impact either for social change or in person-to-person relations . . . if the Volunteer is only a technical assistant, then the Peace Corps' days and contribution in these countries are limited and will wash away with the rising tide."[64]

Under Shriver, the Peace Corps strove for success on both the technical assistance and the people-to-people fronts. Toward the end of 1963, it was learning more and more about how better to go about this. For one thing, the Peace Corps was established in many countries and additional projects could be programmed from the field with relevant experience and support. "Shopping list" programs were dispensed with and "pyramid programming"—placing at least a few technically skilled Volunteers at the base of generalist groups—was introduced. The Peace Corps also began to realize that its most useful programming commodity was the advice of its returning Volunteers. They were employed in PDO, in the Evaluation and Training Divisions, and as overseas staff. At last there were people in the Peace Corps administration who had actually had the Volunteer experience.

Perhaps the most important factor affecting programming was that by 1963 the Peace Corps had established and proven itself; it could afford to slow down. The agency continued to expand, but not at the breakneck speed of 1961 and 1962. Between 1964 and 1966, Peace Corps expansion was limited to two countries: Kenya and Uganda. "Where do we go from here?" Bill Moyers asked Warren Wiggins in the summer of 1963. "The answer is not in the numbers of people you ask for, not 'from 10,000 to 13,000' but in the nature of the programs you develop." Moyers raised the questions to be asked if these programs were to improve: "Do programs make it possible for the Peace Corps seriously to affect the development of a country? Do they provide Volunteers with real possibilities for creative service on Peace Corps terms?"[65]

While these questions continued to be the subject of debate within Peace Corps headquarters, the developing countries had already answered with a resounding affirmative. Edward Seaga, Jamaica's young Minister of Manpower and Development who signed his country's first agreement with the Peace Corps, believed that the Volunteer teachers who arrived in 1962 would have a multiplier effect on the minds of their young students. To Seaga, the Peace Corps was "an assault on the social barriers and skill shortages" which faced his newly independent state.

He was further heartened that the Peace Corps seemed to be a step toward reversing the flow of educated people from the developing countries to the industrialized nations.[66] Along with most other Peace Corps recipient countries, Jamaica asked for an increased number of Volunteers in 1964. This demand did not convince Shriver that he had overcome all the problems of programming for peace. But it helped reinforce his view that, whatever its shortcomings, the Peace Corps "must have been doing something right."[67]

10

A Special Group
of Americans

For what should a Volunteer be prepared? He should
be prepared for a delightful, warm, friendly, apprecia-
tive and fun-loving people, and for the nerve-racking
frustration that arises out of incomprehension and consistent failure. He should be prepared for a rewarding
experience which will live with him as long as he is
on this earth.
— A Peace Corps Volunteer in Sierra Leone

THE FRONT LINES

Sargent Shriver was fond of reiterating that "The front lines
of the Peace Corps are overseas."[1] He knew that in the final outcome, the agency would stand or fall by the talent, maturity,
and commitment to a set of ideals of its chosen representatives
overseas. "Learn the language of the people," Shriver told them,
"make up your mind that the work of the developing nations
is worth the price of personal sacrifice; anchor yourself in the
customs and traditions of the country where you are serving . . .
and believe in the power of personal integrity, humility and
determination."[2] These basic guidelines notwithstanding, as the
first group of Volunteers left for Africa in August 1961 no one
could predict whether the Peace Corps experiment would be a
spectacular success or a dismal failure.

Meeting with the first two Peace Corps groups (road
surveyors bound for Tanzania and teachers assigned to Ghana)

in the Rose Garden just before they left, President Kennedy called them "a special group of young Americans." He knew that for many of them, their Peace Corps service would be their first overseas experience of any kind. He reminded them that they would be viewed as the personification of America: "There are of course a great many hundreds of millions of people scattered throughout the world. You will come in contact with only a few, but the great impression of what kind of country we have and what kind of people we are, will depend on their judgment . . . of you." Thus Kennedy bade the young Americans farewell, shaking their hands and telling them, "We put a good deal of hope in the work that you do."[3]

Hopes were also raised in the developing countries as Volunteers arrived at Accra airport in Ghana on August 30 (the Volunteers bound for Tanzania did not arrive until a day later). The choice of Ghana as the first Peace Corps destination was symbolic. It had gained its independence only four years earlier and it was regarded as the most militant Third World nation; its dynamic leader, Kwame Nkrumah, was the self-appointed "savior" of African freedom movements. A number of high Ghanaian officials, including Minister of Education A.J. Du-wuona Hammond, watched closely as Peace Corps Volunteers set foot on foreign soil for the first time.

The fifty-one Americans who stepped onto the airport's tarmac were not loud or jazzily dressed, they did not chew gum or endlessly take photographs—as some Ghanaians might have expected. Instead, the Volunteers quietly formed themselves into a group and began to sing the Ghanaian national anthem in Twi. This had a stunning effect. Radio Ghana taped their performance and replayed it over the air many times. The broadcast announced that here were some Americans who had enough interest in the land where they would be living for the next two years to take the trouble to learn the local language.

Their dramatic arrival over, the Volunteers traveled to their assignments in different parts of Ghana. On September 12, 1961, Tom Livingston of Wood Dale, Illinois became the first Peace Corps Volunteer to begin working overseas when he took up his post as an English teacher at Ghanata secondary school in Dodowa. With Kennedy's words still on their minds—"These

Peace Corps Volunteers will learn far more than they will teach, and we will therefore have another link which binds us to the world around us"—Livingston and his colleagues set to work.

HEALTH AND ATTRITION

In the Peace Corps' first months of operation, a subject of major concern was the health of Volunteers. The Peace Corps represented the largest single group of Americans who had ever tried to live in the developing countries at "grassroots" levels. More Americans had been sent overseas during World War II, but the troops had been in organized units with safe food, clean water, and medical care. Such comforts would not always be available to Volunteers. Critics predicted that the young Americans would soon be the victims of deadly diseases in "Darkest Africa" and that they might even find themselves butchered by "the natives." Such prognostications caused Shriver nightmares:

> I used to wake up in the middle of the night with the question tearing at me: How are we ever going to protect the health of the Peace Corps Volunteers? Could we go to the parents of this nation and say to them, yes, we want your sons and daughters, and admit at the same time that for two years they would be overseas—many of them in primitive and remote towns and villages—with no medical assistance?[4]

Dr. Luther Terry, surgeon-general of the United States, solved Shriver's problem. Since the Peace Corps was a public service, he proposed that Public Health Service doctors should be assigned to each Peace Corps country. Under Dr. Leo Gehrig, first chief of the Peace Corps' Medical Program Division, a service was created whereby general preventive health measures for Volunteers were provided by American doctors, while the unique illnesses and diseases which developed in individual Third World countries were handled by host country doctors. It was a system suited to the Peace Corps' needs and consonant with its ideals. It was also effective. Of the first 117 early terminations from the Peace Corps, only 20 came back for medical reasons.[5]

Inevitably, there were cases of hepatitis, amoebic dysentery, and malaria, as well as rare fevers and multifarious skin ailments. There were also five accidental deaths between 1961 and 1963. In 1962, David Crozier and Lawrence Radley became the first Volunteers to die in action when their plane crashed in Colombia.* However, no Volunteers died of malaria or beri-beri or were killed by "savages" in the bush. Indeed, that this caused such concern in the first place reflected the rather primitive view which most Americans had of the Third World. In the early 1960s, the "underdeveloped" countries remained shrouded in mystery and their peoples were often regarded as hostile.

That less than 10 percent of the first ten thousand Volunteers came home before the end of their two-year stint overseas helped to break down these attitudes.[6] The Peace Corps experience also helped debunk the myth that Americans were too soft to live in African villages or Latin American slums. The young Americans who more often than not dressed in T-shirts, Levi jeans, and tennis shoes were widely regarded as being idealistic; they soon won a reputation for being tough as well.

CULTURE SHOCK AND FATIGUE

To Volunteers, the problems of "culture shock" and "culture fatigue" were much more troublesome than physical illness. Culture shock was experienced by Volunteers shortly after arrival in their host countries. It could be triggered by a combination of various factors: loneliness, strange food, pervasive disease, extremes of climate, dire poverty, or indigenous class and caste distinctions. One Volunteer in the Philippines admitted that, "When I arrived here nothing appealed to my sense of taste —not sights, nor sounds, smells, foods . . . I felt completely cut off from everything I had ever known, and came as close as possible to having a nervous breakdown without actually cracking up."[7]

---

*The Peace Corps' two training camps in Puerto Rico were named Camp Crozier and Camp Radley in memory of the first Volunteers to die during their service overseas.

Life in the developing countries could never be adequately described before the Volunteer's arrival. Neil Boyer, a Volunteer in Ethiopia, wrote that "it is a baptism by fire . . . a collision of different values and different expectations, of values that are never wholly transferable, of expectations that are never fully realized."[8] A female Volunteer stationed in the Far East agreed that when faced with "rotten teeth, foul breath, smells, sores, filth, rags, I couldn't take it. I was astonished to find that my reactions were so diametrically opposed to my ideals . . . I simply and truthfully hated it and wanted to go home."[9]

Many Volunteers were shaken and depressed on initial contact with their host culture. Once their initial feelings of exhilaration and excitement subsided, their expectations and motivations were severely tested by the raw physicality of an alien environment. "I spend much of my time looking for places to urinate and being angry with the presence of mosquitos," said a Volunteer in one of his first letters from the *barrios*. "I am constantly annoyed by spitters and careless coughers. I request napkins in vain and eat and drink the most disagreeable concoctions sometimes until I can explode."[10] The rate of early returnees was always highest during these first few months of service. Tom Carter, an able and sensitive Volunteer in Peru, described the horrible feeling of culture shock:

> I get a lot of letters from people saying "how exciting your work must be" or "how picturesque" or "how much you must enjoy it" . . . But there comes a day when things are no longer picturesque, they are dirty, no longer quaint but furiously frustrating and you want like crazy to just get out of there, to go home. This is called culture shock and you don't find it mentioned in recruiting papers. It happens to one and all, usually about the third or fourth month. How hard it hits you and for how long depends largely on this problem of false motives. More Volunteers quit and go home at this stage than any other. Unhappy, with a lot of time out of their lives wasted, full of bad memories of their experience, they fell victims to their own imagination.[11]

The vast majority of Volunteers overcame culture shock and went on to complete their two-year term. Most said that once they got over their initial sense of isolation, the actual physical conditions of their host surroundings were the least irritating aspects of their service. Volunteer Patricia MacDermott in the Philippines claimed that although "absolutely nothing is familiar and I feel totally alone, the physical difficulties actually help, as they take my mind off myself and the feeling of suddenly being cut off from the rest of the world."[12]

Moreover, as Volunteers came to know their host countries better, they also came to love them. "This is probably the most beautiful place on earth," wrote Volunteer David Roseborough in Malaysia. More than the rice paddies and groves of rubber trees, he felt drawn to "a very basic joy with life here that I wish I could take back and inject into America."[13] Volunteer Paul Theroux said that he had never dreamed of a place as beautiful as his Peace Corps host country, Malawi. On being told he had been assigned there, he had difficulty finding it on the map. When he did, he described it as "like a small worm clinging to a blue leaf." Speaking longingly of his time there, Theroux said that "I wouldn't have known the place existed if it wasn't for the Peace Corps."[14]

In most of their letters home, Volunteers marvelled at the natural beauty of their environments much more than they complained about strange sights, sounds, and smells. Despite the initial shock of life in a remote African village, a Volunteer said that "the beauty of Africans and the fascination that comes in trying to understand the complexities of their culture and their hopes and fears as human beings is always sustaining."[15]

More debilitating than culture shock was the culture fatigue that set in after nine months to a year of a Volunteer's service. It was a term used to describe the psychological and emotional exhaustion that invariably resulted from the Volunteers' gradual discovery that their efforts, no matter how laudable, were ultimately not going to be enough to satisfy the mountainous needs of their host communities. "I sat for a long time tonight just thinking of all the things I'd seen," wrote Volunteer Mary Seberger in Venezuela. "What can I—one person—do in two years that will help reduce in any way, the problems that I've seen?" Another Volunteer in Colombia wondered "just how beneficial our project is and if we could ever make a dent in the situation."[16] After some experience in the field, training instructors tried to warn Volunteers that they should not expect to be world savers. Nevertheless, as Volunteer Neil Boyer in Ethiopia perceived, "Even when your expectations are low, they may be too high."[17]

When asked how she rated her impact on the *barrios*, a Volunteer in the Philippines commented: "It's rather like pouring water into a sieve."[18] A major philosophical difficulty was that the Volunteers came from a fast, profit-oriented, high-achieving society; it was painful for them to adjust to the often slower pace of many Third World countries. As one Volunteer serving in a Moslem society put it, "We're in competition with Allah," a reference to his hosts' apparent passive acceptance of their poverty-stricken lives.[19] Volunteers who complained to Peace Corps headquarters of being underemployed were often considered over-industrious by their more relaxed hosts. As one Volunteer in Morocco noted: "To avoid frustration . . . you kind of have to gear yourself down."[20]

One of the main causes of culture fatigue was that the Volunteers' hosts did not necessarily want to be "Americanized." Many Volunteers went overseas expecting to find willing converts to the traditional American work ethic. Instead, what they sometimes found was monotony and indifference. A Volunteer teaching in the Ivory Coast found himself confronted by this stark cultural gap:

> The fight is primarily against what we will feel is African indifference . . . In speaking of the African character, I think many things must be taken into account. Not the least of these is the incredible monotony of the climate. Twelve hours of day merge into twelve hours of night, and the very birds and beasts move with their own inner clocks! The cocks crow (or begin to crow) at 4:00 *du matin*, and the songbirds start at six sharp in the winter, and ten minutes earlier now that the sun has moved back on our side of the equator. The temperature during the year may vary as much as twenty degrees, but I have yet to see it. And I have had dreams, glorious dreams, of Minnesota winters or Vermont lakes in the early mornings. The monotony of life here is difficult to understand or believe if you have never been exposed to it. There is only the endless joyless sun (as Conrad put it) and the

rooms full of fractious kids, so used to the "cash-register" system of French education that they are going to fight it for all they're worth! It is quite a heartbreaking thing from time to time.[21]

Quite unconsciously, most Volunteers expected that everyone naturally yearned for the material aspects of American culture: money, luxury gadgets, plenty of food, and the other trappings of the American work ethic. It took time to understand that these were not universally valued. As Burdick and Lederer wrote in a report on the Philippines: "The psychic underpinnings of the puritanical American which have seeped into the Volunteer — whether he knows it or not — are outraged in day-to-day life."[22]

The realization that their hosts were sometimes not self-motivated and, worse, that bribery and corruption were often accepted as the natural order, came hard to most young Americans. A disenchanted Volunteer in Togo complained that "What we have accomplished seems insignificant. We are tired, a little bored and discouraged by the lack of cooperation." He admitted that he felt like quitting mainly because "the people we came to help don't act as if they needed or wanted any help."[23]

In St. Lucia where, as a Volunteer noted, 75 percent of the children were undernourished and even the most basic methods of hygiene were often ignored, the major constraint on progress was an unshakeable conservatism: "Everyone is positively afraid to try anything new," he wrote. "Often an idea is rejected not because it is bad or impractical or too expensive but solely because it has never been done before."[24] In a small town in Colombia the Peace Corps was frustrated by the intransigence of local bureaucrats. After their fourth visit to the local mayor in the town hall, two Volunteers were finally promised a much-needed bulldozer. But they were skeptical that they would ever receive it. "As we walked down the hall," said one, "we looked at each other and laughed because we knew the son-of-a-bitch was lying — just as he lied before."[25] An evaluation report on Morocco noted that while the Volunteers were annoyed by flies, dirt and the steaming climate, their real frustration came from "the corruption, the indifference to suffering in animals and people, petty bureaucratic obstructionism, and the lack of trust and cooperation."[26]

A different set of cultural values was the problem at the heart of every Volunteer's culture fatigue. The various other relatively minor hardships did not help: the tedious diet of fish and rice, the lack of amenities such as hot running water, indoor toilets, accessible transportation, and the embarrassment felt at being constantly stared at and pointed out as the "yanqui" or the "gringo." But the real challenge was the difference in cultural attitudes. A Volunteer in the Philippines, described by her Rep as "extremely dedicated and determined," admitted that she too had gone through the period of frustration when she had felt "very small and weak in the light of this thing called culture."[27]

Most Volunteers were well-balanced and resilient enough to accept what they could not hope to change, and by their second year had managed to shake off any ill-effects of culture fatigue. They became more settled, more accepting of their limitations, and more understanding of their hosts' mores. A Volunteer in North Africa summarized the more philosophical approach: "There are times when one needs to look to a power greater than oneself in order to overcome the loneliness and frustration and to persevere long enough to be able one day to bask in the warmth of a job well-done, a smile genuinely returned or a friendship and trust well-merited."[28] To teacher David Schickele in Nigeria, the challenge of the cultural frontier was the real meaning of the Peace Corps. "It is the call to go, not where man has never been before," he wrote, "but where he has lived differently; the call to experience first hand the intricacies of a different culture; to understand from the inside rather than the outside; and to test the limits of one's own way of life against another."[29]

Uncompromising idealists tended to be hurt most by the contrast between their cultural attitudes and those of their hosts. In their earnest efforts to bridge the cultural gap, some went "native"; that is, they went through a phase of trying to live as much like their hosts as possible. They would not boil their water, use mosquito netting, or take precautions against the sun. One Volunteer in the Philippines died after he had refused medical treatment for an intestinal complaint, because he wanted to be "like the natives."[30] At the other extreme, some Volunteers became cynical and allowed themselves to get sucked into the "expatriate syndrome," spending too much time with Americans in the embassy compound or in exclusive private clubs. Frustra-

tion and underemployment were always factors that could entice a lonely Volunteer to fraternize more with fellow Westerners
than with his hosts. One of Sargent's Shriver's few iron laws
was that Volunteers should forego the pleasures and privileges
of the expatriate community; but sometimes, during a bout of
homesickness or culture fatigue, even the best Volunteers were
tempted. As an evaluation report pointed out, this was only
natural; after a few hard weeks work in the bush, Volunteers
could not be blamed if during a weekend in town they wanted
nothing more than "drinks and darts at the pub or 'chercher la
femme.' "[31]

Few Volunteers broke through all the cultural barriers in
their host countries, but most at least made a beginning. In the
process, they reaped the full benefit of the Peace Corps experience: learning to speak another language, becoming intimately
aware of another culture, and establishing friendships with people with vastly different life experiences and expectations.

Volunteers in Uruguay lived with the locals, paid rent to
them, and developed such close relations that they referred to
their host family members as "my father, my mother, my brother
or sister." In Belize, an evaluator noticed that Volunteers could
not walk down the streets without becoming involved in con-
versations with clusters of local folk. The Volunteers in Thailand
"disappeared" among the locals and worked with what an evaluation report described as "a quiet earnestness." When Volunteers melted into their host society in this way, it was a sure sign
they had established effective cross-cultural relations. Senegalese
villagers took note of how Volunteers lived simply in their midst,
an indication that these were white people who had come to help
rather than exploit. "Unlike the French," observed evaluator
David Hapgood "the Volunteers mix with the people instead of
staying aloof; they work with their hands with the Senegalese
instead of handing down orders." When Volunteer teachers in
Sierra Leone made their way to work, the local children ran after
them chanting "Peace Corps, Peace Corps." When a Peace Corps
official asked them why, they replied: "Because no other white
people would do this."[32]

David Espey, a young Volunteer teacher in Morocco, established a warm rapport with his host students whom he found

friendly, cooperative, and grateful. "I have no trouble getting in contact with Moroccans," he wrote, "since I live and eat with the students. It's amazing how much help is needed, can be so easily given and is so greatly appreciated." A young Volunteer building water filters in the schools of Togo received a "terrific amount of cooperation . . . from all parts of the community, and the remarkable amount of work the kids did was encouraging and very satisfying." He felt he had broken through the cultural barrier and established a base for mutual respect. The concept of self-help—working to ameliorate problems in the community with no promise of remuneration—was strange to the Togolese. "Yet, once they see it in action," he wrote, "they pitch in with far greater enthusiasm and goodwill than I ever expected. This is surely one of the answers to progress in Africa."[33] In Iran, a Volunteer who married a local girl was described as having a "superb affinity for the culture, ably abetted by his attractive wife . . . one of the best Volunteers in terms of relating to Iranians." A female Volunteer working in Asmara, Ethiopia became something of a legend both to her hosts and her fellow Volunteers. She taught herself the local language (Tigrinya), visited her students in their homes, and was known to "every urchin in the streets."[34]

Similarly, two married couples of Volunteers teaching English in the small town of Bolu in Turkey were known by just about all of the fourteen thousand local people; their adult education classes were looked upon as one of the town's highlights and were very well attended. Evaluators in the Dominican Republic came across a robust sixty-year-old Volunteer who was "respected, even loved, by nearly everyone." His hog-breeding, rat-eradication and water-filtering projects had become the talk of La Vega, noted evaluators Dee Jacobs and Philip Hardberger. They described him as "opinionated, straightforward, demanding, honest and shrewd." They also said he had "fantastic energy and ingenuity . . . although he is a threat to those who want things done 'manana.' " Another Volunteer in Afghanistan mixed so well with her hosts that two mullahs asked her to give them English lessons. "This is a breakthrough," noted Charles Peters, "roughly equivalent to Hubert Humphrey being asked to lead a John Birch study group."[35]

There were many such examples of Volunteers slowly and sensitively adapting to their hosts' cultural mores and, at the same time, promoting an understanding of Americans. For many, their students became their best friends; their host country became their home. "We aren't tourists," wrote one Volunteer, "I live here. They ask me what my family life is like, what kind of work I do, the kind of life I have in the States. And I describe my farm life, for example. They can picture it. They have a concept of an American as a human being. They've discovered that, after all, our human needs are not so different from theirs."[36]

This was a reciprocal lesson. David Szanton, one of the first Volunteers in the Philippines, agreed that despite culture fatigue and its accompanying frustrations, many of his colleagues came to learn and accept that the American way was not the only way, that bigger was not always better. "After some while in the field," he wrote, "many Volunteers did finally begin to accept emotionally the idea—and its extraordinary implications—that a people could be equally human, could be equally entitled to consideration, while at the same time they were significantly different in their values and behavior."[37]

THE JOB

As well as coming to terms with living in an alien society, the Volunteer had to learn how to work in it. Although never entirely independent of the ubiquitous cultural dynamic, the Volunteer's job engendered its own problems. In the summer of 1962, after the Peace Corps had been one full year in the field, Nicholas Hobbs, chief of the Research Division, reported to Shriver that the major problem facing the Volunteer was not culture shock, disease, or physical hardship but rather the difficulty in finding "meaningful work to do."[38] Volunteers did not often gripe about cross-cultural differences per se; but they did complain about underemployment and frustration with their jobs.

Given the weaknesses of early Peace Corps programming, the Volunteer's role could only ever be what each individual made of it. To some, especially in community development, the vague nature of their jobs was the biggest single source of frustration. They did not relish the prospect of adapting to new situations or of introducing themselves to strangers and inviting themselves along to work sites. For them, the loosely structured assignment was little more than a license to be miserably underemployed. Others loved the opportunity to create a role for themselves. To the dedicated, imaginative Volunteer, an ill-defined or even badly-programmed assignment could be an asset, since it offered a challenge to exercise social skills and overcome cultural barriers. Any Peace Corps program usually consisted of various combinations of both types. A report on India noted:

> A remarkable number of Volunteers in India know precisely what they are doing, and are doing it well. It hasn't been automatic, a good percentage of Volunteers arrived to find either a non-existent job or a small fragment of one. A number of Volunteers did nothing for the first three months and then found work for themselves. Many others enlisted the assistance of the staff. Some have acquired lots of small jobs that add up to full employment. A few Volunteers have many small jobs that add up to nothing.[39]

The community development project in Peru started out on a shaky footing. The government was tardy in giving support and many of the initially assigned jobs fell through. The Volunteers proved versatile, however, and most managed to adapt to the trying circumstances. "Everything has not worked out as they expected it or wanted it," commented an evaluation report, "but where the Volunteers have been overcome by their problems, they have not surrendered. They have fought back or they have moved on to other work on different Peace Corps projects." Four Volunteers around Puno had begun a small nutrition program which, by the summer of 1963, was helping to feed ninety-five thousand students in thirteen hundred schools. In Panama, a young Volunteer began to participate in his local community by helping them tend their livestock. Through this work he came in contact with local farmers and, after a few months, he won their confidence to the extent that they became willing to experiment with his ideas for new types of rice plants, fertilizers, insecticides and seeds. They even allowed him to inoculate their cattle. Another Volunteer in Chile gradually helped develop *campesino* cooperatives to the point where 1200 host families were involved. He had not been specifically assigned to this task, but he was resourceful, and according to evaluators, he had "an integrity about him and a dedication to his work."[40]

Not all Volunteers were as resourceful. A number working in community development eventually surrendered to frustration and created tight, specific jobs for themselves where they could see each day that they were producing something concrete. To counteract local indifference to their schemes, Volunteers sometimes fired ahead on their own. In a way, this defeated the purpose of community development, which was to persuade the local people to do things for themselves. The Volunteers felt more fulfilled when they were constantly active but, in the long run, their individualistic efforts were not conducive to the nurturing of the self-help principle. Volunteers in Chimbote, Peru refused to put a roof on a local school building until the local community offered to help. "It would be a $10 project and about one day's work for two or three Peace Corpsmen," noted one of the Volunteers. "Yet, we don't do it. If we gave that school a roof, it would always be a gift, the 'gringos' roof. When it needed fixing no one would fix it. If it takes a year to talk our neighbors into putting on that roof, it will be worth it. Because it will then be their roof on their school."[41]

In the course of two years in a foreign setting, it was inevitable that even the most exciting, time-consuming job would have its frustrating, even boring interludes. "If someone had told me I'd be bored sitting at the foot of Kilimanjaro with elands galloping around me, I would have said, 'You're out of your mind,'" reported one bored Volunteer. A group of Volunteers working in the outback of East Africa lived the kind of vibrant life that many restless Peace Corps teachers dreamed of. Yet, as an astonished evaluator reported, not only were the "adventurous" Volunteers bored but "the majority are convinced that teaching must be the only satisfying and useful work a Volunteer can do."[42]

Certainly the structured nature of their assignments made it easier for Volunteer teachers to feel a sense of satisfaction. "For a long time I was 'the American physics teacher' and was sniffed and prodded accordingly," wrote a Volunteer in West Africa.

"But luckily I found I enjoyed teaching . . . there are few things more satisfying than to see students suddenly understanding."[43] Another Volunteer in the Ivory Coast described his rewarding experience on visiting one of his students after school-hours:

> The poverty one sees here is almost inconceivable to an American. Students who go to the *Cours Complementaires* come from all over the Ivory Coast, for it is the idea of the government to mix them up and get the members of one tribe thoroughly used to the members of another. Well and good. I went to visit one of my students not long ago. He is here from Sassandra, a fishing village about 400 kilometers away. He lives in a mud hut where he shares a pallet to sleep on, a table, a single chair, and a lamp à petrol which had no petrol when I was there. There is a single little petrol stove, too, on which he cooks his rice. Food prices for anything better here are exorbitant. The diet is not calculated to make consecrated students. And if you take a walk after the sun has gone down, you'll find under the street lights of the town, those youngsters who . . . have some interest in their schooling, learning-memorizing by ear their dear little lessons.[44]

The structured teaching jobs also had their drawbacks. Some Volunteers, especially in West Africa, found it hard to break away from their school compounds and make contact with a thicker slice of African life. Maintaining discipline in rowdy African classrooms was another problem for young, inexperienced Volunteers. African teachers freely wielded the cane to discipline pupils. Once the students realized that the Americans were not accustomed to using corporal punishment, they took advantage. At least one Volunteer broke under the strain and resorted to using the paddle (a wooden stick) to reprimand an unruly Liberian youth. On another occasion, a Volunteer in Malawi was not quite sure of what action to take when he caught his pupils smoking marijuana at the back of the classroom.[45]

Some Volunteer teachers also had to overcome temperamental headmasters. In Sierra Leone, Volunteers came across an eccentric British headmaster who went around all day hugging a chimpanzee to his chest. Others had to deal with an African principal who would not permit electricity to be installed in his school because it would attract "the devil." Old-fashioned teaching methods such as rote-learning and out-of-date syllabi were additional bugbears. In one textbook a Volunteer found sentences such as "a nurse is pushing a pram across a zebra-crossing on her way home to afternoon tea." He wondered what sense this could possibly make to children living in the bush in Togo.[46]

COLONIALISTS, DIPLOMATS, AND MISSIONARIES

The Volunteers came to associate such irrelevancies with the school system in Africa as established by the British and French who, as one Volunteer put it, had only wished "to produce automatons for the colonial civil service."[47] Many Volunteers claimed their greatest culture shock was not in coming face to face with Africa and Africans but, rather, having to live and work in a remnant colonial society. Volunteer teachers often found themselves in uncomfortable situations vis-à-vis their host communities because they taught in a school system, set up by colonialists, which actively discouraged any extracurricular contact with Africans. The rules of the old colonial game sometimes made adjustments and adherence to Peace Corps philosophy extremely difficult.

As the sun set on the British empire, many expatriates retained teaching and administrative posts in the decolonized lands. They were often hostile toward the young "amateurish" Americans. Professionally qualified British schoolteachers looked down their noses at U.S. college degree-holders. At the same time, they felt jealous or threatened that America was about to fill the void left in the developing countries by a Britain rapidly declining as a world power. Volunteers in Nigeria also sensed that resentment still lingered from the days of World War II when the British description of American troops in England had been "overpaid, over-dressed, over-sexed and over here."[48]

Volunteers angered the British because they would not accept the colonial interpretation of the "African mentality": that Africans were ignorant, greedy, violent and hence had to be kept in their place. "The vanishing colonialist is a bitter fellow," noted a Volunteer. "He came not to help but to exploit; most of them sought the prestige—the white shorts, the white socks, the club, and the household servants—they could not attain in the U.K. . . . many of them would not give an African the right time of day."[49] The British applied strong pressure on the Peace Corps to conform to colonial patterns of behavior. The colonial education system was based on the Cambridge exam; the economic system provided luxury housing and black stewards for Europeans; and the social system dictated that whites should remain distant from blacks.

When the Volunteers did not conform to these colonialist standards, they often found themselves ostracized and maligned by the expatriates. Female Volunteer teachers in Malawi had to contend with rumors, spread by their British colleagues, that they were only there to relieve the U.S. unemployment problem, that they ran around naked at night, and that they had become pregnant by African men. British doctors were highly indignant that Peace Corps nurses were not qualified in midwifery, a standard part of the British nurse's training. Yet, despite what an evaluation report described as the "spit-and-polish first, patients last" attitude of the British surgeons, Volunteer nurses were always in great demand in the Third World, and they had a significant impact on both the technical and human values of hospital service.[50] The expatriates were sometimes forced to acknowledge the Peace Corps' positive contribution. In 1962, the British government announced its pleasure at the way Volunteer teachers were "fitting into Africa."[51] A crusty ex-colonialist in Tanzania even conceded that "I don't know how we did without you chaps before this."[52]

The British were not the only expatriates with whom the Volunteers had to contend. They sometimes found their American compatriots in the diplomatic corps to be as great a nuisance, and relations between the Peace Corps and the Foreign Service were strained in several countries. The problem was not so much the diplomatic community's objection to the Peace Corps' operations, but rather a resentment at the style in which they were carried out. American diplomats consistently accused Volunteers of being self-righteous and downright unfriendly. The difficulty stemmed from Shriver's policy that Volunteers should avoid the P.X. club, the embassy restaurant, swimming pool, and so forth.

"They [the Volunteers] came with stars in their eyes . . . they thought they were going to fix the Philippines in eighteen months," recalled Ambassador William Stevenson. "This, I thought, was absolutely foolish, that they had to take this attitude, that they knew the right way to handle people, that we were all wrong and all that business."[53] Had Stevenson had his way, however, he would have stationed the Peace Corps office on the same floor of the embassy as the CIA. The consequences of such a maladroit arrangement would have been disastrous for the Peace Corps' image and impact.

Officials of other U.S. agencies in the Third World were quick to point out that not all Volunteers or Reps lived at the grassroots level, despite the Peace Corps' sometimes pontifical statements about American diplomats living in "golden ghettoes" overseas. Embassy staff in Morocco derided the luxurious housing rented by Peace Corps officials, "especially after all this bullshit about the Peace Corps image and the new kind of American."[54] Shriver recognized that not all Peace Corps staff or Volunteers lived up to the organization's ideals, but he deeply resented expatriates or diplomats poking fun at Volunteers who were at least trying to make sacrifices, no matter how small, like shopping in the local bazaars or taking the bus instead of using a U.S. vehicle. "Why don't they do so?" asked a furious Shriver. "It would save taxpayers some money if all U.S. persons abroad did likewise."[55]

AID officials in Guinea were "openly hostile" to the Peace Corps; they offered no help by way of logistics or equipment. "There must be well over a thousand hard-core Communists in Guinea," noted evaluator Philip Cook, "but they are no match for the U.S. embassy/AID contingent when it comes to making trouble for the Peace Corps." In Morocco, the official mission formally criticized the Peace Corps' operations as "slap-dash, emergency style, grandly indifferent to costs, ungrateful for help, impatient with the red tape imposed upon those who gave the help and hoggish for the credit."[56]

In the early days, Shriver had worried that the Peace Corps would be identified with big-money U.S. foreign aid programs; he constantly stressed that "we deal in people not materials." In one of the first projects in Colombia, Volunteers were mistaken for officials of the Alliance For Progress, Kennedy's ambitious economic aid program for Latin America. They found that a typical greeting was for the locals to ask: "Where's the money?"[57] This was exactly what Shriver was determined to avoid. However, Volunteers soon came to realize that it was to their advantage to work closely with the "Kennedy cum Alianza" organization. Since Kennedy was associated with the Alliance, the Volunteers also reaped the harvest of its resounding popularity. Besides, Alliance officials were much more thoughtful about the placement and disbursement of funds when the Volunteers did not treat them like social lepers outside of working hours. In 1963, Bill Haddad advised Shriver that it was high time the Peace Corps relaxed its policy toward its fellow agencies overseas. With a view to changing the self-righteous attitude which Volunteers sometimes adopted, Haddad proposed that "we should now work more closely with other agencies, while still maintaining our apartness."[58]

The problem of "apartness" cropped up again when Volunteers were assigned to religious schools or had to work in the *campos* with missionaries. Notwithstanding the Peace Corps' policy of avoiding any organization or assignment that involved direct religious proselytizing, Volunteers were advised that in a variety of field situations a certain amount of flexibility would be required. Peace Corps officials were well aware that in Latin America the Catholic church had the power, if it wanted to use it, to block all community development projects. Therefore Volunteers were often told in training that they should approach the local padre upon first alighting in their community. They were wary of being used as religious propagandists but, where necessary, they worked hand-in-hand with activist priests.

In Tamopata, Peru an American priest helped Volunteers teach mechanical skills; in Guatemala, the local priests helped Volunteers establish agricultural cooperatives. In some areas, the Volunteers came dangerously close to appearing as if they were working through the Catholic church. Volunteers in Ecuador taught in Catholic schools, worked in agencies directed by priests, and one Volunteer even lived in a rectory. The Peace Corps Rep was careful to ensure that the program was kept free of direct religious entanglements, but he was realistic enough to recognize "the necessity of working with things as they are in Ecuador." In its milk distribution, health care, and agricultural extension programs in Bolivia, the Peace Corps took a further risk by working with Catholic Relief Services (Caritas); but again, these projects were free of proselytizing.[59] In Senegal, however, evaluator David Hapgood thought that Volunteers teaching in mission schools beside monks were actually "aiding a proselytizing effort." To avoid a charge of infringement of the First Amendment, he advised that the Volunteers should be immediately transferred from mission schools to the government's public schools.[60]

Missionaries could also prove troublesome to Volunteers, especially in African countries where they sometimes viewed the Peace Corps as a competitor rather than a helper in the field of education. Missionaries trained in the old methods of education sometimes deemed young Volunteers neither strict enough with their students nor religious enough in themselves. For their part, Volunteers found some missionaries imbued with much the same educational zeal as the British and French colonialists. One Volunteer teacher in Liberia described his religious colleagues as being "full of contempt for the Liberians—they think they're dirty and cheat and steal, and they beat them." Another exasperated Volunteer in El Salvador finally resorted to the tactic of dissuading the good friars from beating pupils with sticks by beating the good friars with sticks.[61]

Some Volunteers working in mission schools experienced awkwardness with the faculty over the question of religious participation. A Volunteer assigned to a Presbyterian mission in Cameroon was told bluntly by her colleagues that she was not wanted because she was a Catholic; the mission had to relent when the Cameroon government insisted she be allowed to take up her appointment. When Volunteers working in the Evangelical United Brethren and the United Brethren in Christ mission schools in Sierra Leone refused to attend religious services, they were chastised by their British headmasters.[62] In the majority of cases, however, religious resentment was finally overcome, and Volunteers worked effectively in schools of every denomination. An evaluation report on Ecuador, for example, noted that Protestant Volunteers were managing to work intimately and successfully with Catholic padres in the highlands of Ecuador.[63] By

1963, Volunteers of every religious persuasion were established in both Catholic and Protestant schools all over the Third World without too much injury to either private conscience or constitutional principle.

A MOST DIFFICULT PROBLEM

Sargent Shriver claimed that, in many ways, the "most difficult problem" for Volunteers overseas was racial disharmony in the United States.[64] In Africa especially, Volunteers were continually being asked probing questions about racial discrimination back home. Racial incidents in America were widely broadcast in African countries. In a letter to Peace Corps headquarters in June 1963, Volunteer Jim Crandel in Niger described the effect the civil rights conflict in the United States could have on an overseas project:

> Our time here in Africa has really opened our eyes to many problems of the U.S. and given us a look at our country from a different viewpoint. Peace Corps in Africa is very important, not only from the standpoint of educational, technical and agricultural help, but to show the Africans that not all American whites are anti-Negro . . .

The Volunteer added sadly that "It sure is a funny feeling attending a show with some close African friends and have a newsreel show those white bastards in the South hosing, turning dogs loose on people and men beating colored women."[65]

Some African officials expressed disappointment that only 4 of the first wave of 124 Volunteers were black. Despite the Peace Corps' efforts to recruit blacks for service in Africa, Asian-Americans for service in Asia, and so forth, approximately 95 percent of all Volunteers in the Kennedy era were white. The few black Volunteers that there were often felt that their color was an advantage in establishing people-to-people contacts in Africa. Tanzanians treated Volunteer Jerry Parsons as a hero. "I was hailed as 'My Brother,' 'Watangayika,' and 'Negro Bwana,' " he said. His village tried to entice him to stay with them by offering him a wife and a small farm. Parsons remembered that one of the questions most commonly asked of him was: Why did more blacks in the United States not return home (Africa) "to help their brothers?"[66]

Black Volunteers had a profound impact not only on their host societies, but also, on occasion, on their fellow Volunteers. A white Volunteer from Alabama who admitted he had been guilty of racist feelings at home, was shocked when the Peace Corps assigned him to Liberia. It proved to be an enlightening experience; for the first time in his life he worked with blacks. By the end of his service, he said that his attitude "towards the Negro race" had been revolutionized. Another Volunteer in Nigeria found that his association with the locals had given him a profound insight into the problems faced by blacks in America. He felt that "What was before a rather distant, ideological commitment to civil rights . . . has become a very personal one."[67]

Inevitably, Volunteers found that some Third World countries had developed their own brand of racial hatred. In Belize, Volunteers were criticized for consorting with blacks. A local white barman told a Volunteer that the blame lay with "all that Kennedy business in the U.S."[68] To change such attitudes was one of the Peace Corps' objectives. President Kennedy helped. In Africa and in the Caribbean his speeches and general stance on civil rights had won him a reputation as an advocate of black equality. It was somewhat ironical that, at least in the Caribbean, the other champion of black aspirations was Kennedy's nemesis, Fidel Castro.

VOLUNTEERS AND STAFF

While the Volunteers were glad to have Kennedy's popular image behind them, they tended to regard the Washington officials who ran the Peace Corps as "bumbling idiots who don't know what the heck they are talking about."[69] The Volunteers' attitude was similar to that of front-line soldiers toward the general staff; the individuals who worked and sacrificed in the field did not feel kindly toward their bosses whom they imagined making policy while sitting in their comfortable Washington offices. Once overseas, the Volunteers formed their own exclusive "subculture" and most preferred to have as little to do with Peace Corps/Washington as possible. According to one evaluation report, the Volunteers' feeling of being pitted against Washington "begins in training and never lets up. The Peace Corps administration to them is a bureaucratic bungler. The inadequacies of training cultivate this feeling. Selection methods heighten it, then breakdowns in field support, wrongheaded publicity etc. . . . all add to it." The report concluded that "most Volunteers feel they succeed despite Washington."[70]

Ironically, no one espoused the Volunteers more than the chief official in Washington: Sargent Shriver. He traveled tens of thousands of miles to every corner of the world to congratulate and encourage them. Volunteers wrote long, personal letters to him; he always replied. When one disgruntled Volunteer in Colombia asked an evaluator to "Tell Sargent Shriver not to make promises he can't keep," Shriver commented, "That's right!"[71] He then wrote to the Volunteer asking what promises were being referred to and what could be done about them. Volunteers were sometimes deprecating of Shriver's lightning visits to the field and his effusive pep-talks. However, as Burdick and Lederer noted when Shriver visited the Philippines:

> All the Volunteers went to considerable trouble to get to the places where Shriver was talking, analysed his talk in very great detail and were somewhere between bemused and admiring about his appearance—even when this attitude was carefully buried under cynicism. And when he did not arrive as he had been scheduled to do, they were openly disappointed.

They concluded that Shriver was "an important element in Volunteer enthusiasm."[72]

Although he spent a good deal of time in the field, Shriver was never as sensitive to the Volunteers' problems—cultural, logistical, or personal—as they would have liked. When he visited some disgruntled Volunteers in Niger, an evaluator recorded that "they accosted him like the English barons cornering King John at Runnymede."[73] Whether any leader could have lived up to the Volunteers' lofty expectations is doubtful. As Burdick and Lederer told Shriver: "It is inevitable that there will be hostility from people in the field directed at whatever administrative headquarters are set up."[74]

A major difficulty was that neither Shriver nor his staff had undergone the Volunteer experience. No matter how hard they tried, they could not possibly be aware of all the complexities involved in living and working at a grassroots level in the Third World. Volunteers detested the manner in which Peace Corps officials paid flying visits to their projects, asked some elementary questions, and then sped off with reports back to Washington. At an end-of-term conference on Colombia, one Volunteer described how a staff person came "whizzing through his town, stayed for a quick meal, asked 'How's your sex life?', gave me a whack on the back and told me to keep up the good work."[75]

The sometimes over-exuberant messages relayed to the field from headquarters which began "You are the pioneers . . ." were treated scornfully by the Volunteers. "I was prepared for urinating in the streets, for rats, fleas, malaria, leprosy," said one disdainful Volunteer, "but I was not prepared for slow as molasses response from Washington."[76] Often the "bunglers" in Washington failed to get the Volunteer's sea freight delivered on time or took months to assign him to a new job or forgot to send his monthly subsistence allowance. At the same time, Volunteers complained that the Washington bureaucrats were encroaching far too much on their individual initiative. As the Peace Corps developed, policies and regulations were imposed on dress, travel during vacations, social activities, and use of vehicles. Volunteers claimed that while headquarters staff preached self-reliance and individualism, they practiced a form of paternalism.

Volunteers valued their independence highly. The feeling of being on their own in a faraway country gave them a sense of adventure and responsibility. They did not consider themselves to be federal employees. By 1963, some had begun to fear that the regular check-ups from Washington, the conferences and evaluations (in the interests of research and assessment), and the proliferation of rules would eventually erode their autonomy. In 1963 a Volunteer claimed that "The Peace Corps attracted more bold adventurers in its early days—before it was safe." Another moaned that "Big Daddy Peace Corps is too much."[77]

The Peace Corps administration's difficult task was to strike a balance between support and interference. If headquarters did not provide enough information or equipment, it was accused of being indifferent to the Volunteers' needs; if it provided too much, then it was doubting their maturity. Each Volunteer had his own idea of where the golden mean lay. Some Volunteers in Bangladesh who had set up an ad hoc medication center were deeply resentful when Peace Corps/Washington ordered them to shut it down because, technically speaking, they were not qualified to deal with medical problems. "We're becoming the typical American bureaucracy," opined one Volunteer.[78]

The in-country administrators — the Reps and their staffs — had to bear the brunt of the Volunteers' resentment of Peace Corps officialdom. This was slightly ironical since, as Shriver pointed out, most Reps shared the Volunteers' feelings of being "out of touch" with headquarters. Situated between the Peace Corps hierarchy and the Volunteers, the Reps and their staff formed their own unique "subculture." Their job was all-encompassing. As the head of the Peace Corps mission in the field, the Rep had to deal with host country nationals and with other American agencies. Although somewhat removed from official protocol and routine, the Rep had to be skilled in the arts of diplomacy. He also had to be a vigorous administrator. Endowed by Shriver with an enormous amount of responsibility, the Rep had to be capable of delegating and exercising power in strange circumstances with very few procedural guidelines.

The long distances separating the Rep's country headquarters (usually in the capital city) from the various regions where the Volunteers worked complicated the administrative picture even more. Communication became difficult and confusion almost inevitable. It took a Volunteer stationed in the backcountry of Brazil three days to reach the Rep's office in Rio where he had been told an urgent telegram awaited him; when he arrived he discovered the cable was for someone else.[79]

Given the youth of most Volunteers, their inexperience in foreign countries, and their idealistic commitment to the Peace Corps, it was natural that they would look to their Rep not only for guidance but for approbation. The Rep had to win their confidence, fuel their enthusiasm and, simultaneously, enforce discipline when necessary. Somehow the Rep had to avoid being regarded as a "tyrant" but also had to beware of becoming overly-permissive. As Rep Roderic E. Buller in Venezuela put it: "You've got to give them [the Volunteers] a kick in the butt when they need it and still make them like it."[80]

Volunteers often became disappointed if the Rep did not measure up to their own expectations, even though these were sometimes unreasonable. Reps soon understood that everything about their lives—whether their living quarters were austere or luxurious, whether their children went to local or expatriate schools, whether their wives shopped at the local market or the P.X. commissariat—was under the continual and critical scrutiny of the Volunteers in their programs. The Rep's proximity to the field meant that his time and his home always had to remain open to Volunteers; a private life was impossible.

Despite the difficult nature of the job, the Peace Corps produced many highly successful Reps. At Washington headquarters, Frank Mankiewicz had a reputation for being disorganized. As Peace Corps Rep in Peru, however, evaluators noted that he was liked and respected by the Volunteers there, and that he was constantly involved in negotiations with Peruvian agencies to improve and adjust program deficiencies. An evaluation report estimated that Mankiewicz reached "about the best possible mix between leadership, guidance and free-rein in programming Volunteer projects." Likewise in Costa Rica, Rep Frank Appleton provided a first-class example of how to build effective and mutually amicable Volunteer-staff relations. "It would be hard to find a man more personally concerned with the welfare and success of his Volunteers," reported evaluator Dee Jacobs.[81]

Robert Steiner in Afghanistan was another model Rep. "Very soft-spoken, Bob works in a gentle, smooth, soft-sell way that is equally effective with Volunteers, Afghans and the USOM," a report commented. "Patient, good-humored, understanding and perceptive, there is little to fault him." Steiner set his Volunteers an excellent example by speaking fluent Farsi, hiring Afghans among his staff, and by living modestly. Of a weekend, Steiner was to be found in the local bazaars shopping and bargaining for various items such as rope beds for his Volunteers. In Togo, Rep C. Payne Lucas covered thousands of miles in his Peace Corps jeep to maintain communication with his far-flung Volunteers. The roads were bumpy and dangerous and Lucas had many accidents. However, he broke through some serious bottlenecks and kept in touch with his Volunteers, while managing to uphold an uneasy truce with a somewhat hostile U.S. embassy staff. As evaluator Philip Cook pointed out, Lucas was "young, frenetic, and a bit unsteady in his management, but he has generally done a super job."[82]

Shriver constantly stressed to his in-country staffs that they were there to support the needs of the Volunteers. "Let it be clear," he wrote, "not one staff member is more important to the Peace Corps than the freshest, most apprehensive Volunteer in the field."[83] Shriver's principle on this matter was not always followed to the letter. The most serious shortcoming among Reps was a failure to maintain communication. In some countries, Reps' reluctance to visit Volunteers in faraway projects contributed to their general lack of awareness and understanding of Volunteer attitudes, problems, behavior, and jobs. Some Reps overemphasized the Peace Corps' diplomatic relationship with the U.S. embassy and the host government—at the expense of the Volunteers. Others acted as if the field was an annoying nuisance which interrupted the important work of administration and organization.

A Rep in Sierra Leone did not make a habit of traveling long distances to see his Volunteers. "He makes it pretty clear that he likes his comfort," wrote evaluator David Gelman. "He likes the gracious life, he likes his leisurely lunch on the verandah." A staff member in Morocco obviously regarded the Volunteers as "pains in the neck that cause her to get up earlier than she likes." A Rep in the Ivory Coast was reported to Shriver as being "not exactly warmly human with the Volunteers." In Brazil another Rep was just "too nice" to be effective.[84] Between 1961 and 1964, Shriver ordered a number of Reps to "take a purgative." Indeed, attrition was greater among overseas staff than among Volunteers.

LIVING CONDITIONS

Despite the popular image of the Peace Corps Volunteer living in a "mud hut" in the developing countries, few Volunteers suffered extreme physical hardship. They were paid a monthly subsistence allowance from which they had to feed, clothe, and shelter themselves. The amount of this allowance varied according to the general standard of living in different countries, but it was usually in line with the salaries earned by their host counterparts. In a few places, over-generous subsistence payments to Volunteers led to over-comfortable living conditions and, more seriously, social separation from the poorer host peoples. A Volunteer in Venezuela was able to afford a new motor bike on which, according to evaluators, he clocked up "5,000 fun-filled miles" far away from his host community.[85]

Almost all Volunteer teachers had reasonably comfortable accommodations—sometimes deemed too comfortable by evaluators. In Africa, Volunteer teachers usually employed native stewards, houseboys, and cleaners who could be hired for a few dollars a month. To some extent, the Volunteers were pressured into this situation. African teachers were expected to have a comfortable abode and at least one servant. Had the Volunteers refused, they would not only have been guilty of contravening an important social custom but would have found it difficult to win the respect of their host counterparts and students alike. Thus Volunteer teachers reluctantly accepted what they found personally repugnant, although most admitted that it was extremely helpful to have someone who could do the day's shopping while they taught in school (no refrigerators were available) and protect the house from thieves. Evaluators, however, continually urged Shriver to prohibit Volunteers from hiring stewards and houseboys. "It's important to show that the Volunteer can do the dirty work around the house," wrote Charles Peters.[86]

The most prominent sign of what evaluators sarcastically referred to as the "Cuerpo de Tourista" image of the Volunteers was the Peace Corps' blue-colored jeeps. A few of these vehicles were automatically provided to each Peace Corps program in the early days. In the poorer countries of Latin America, evaluators Philip Cook and Thorburn Reid pointed out that "Peace Corps vehicles stand out like President Kennedy's white Lincoln with the armor plate."[87] By 1963, the worst health hazard to Volunteers had proven to be not tropical diseases, but Peace Corps jeeps. Some Volunteers tended to drive the jeeps on the dirt roads of Africa and Latin America at much the same speed as they would have driven them in New York City. There were a number of accidents involving Volunteers, local peoples, and livestock. In the Dominican Republic, evaluators counted three major and thirteen minor accidents in two years.[88] In some countries, lawsuits resulted over injuries to host nationals and animals. By and large, the jeeps were a menace. They cost the Peace Corps money in gasoline and repair bills, and wayward Volunteers were inclined to use them for unscheduled vacations and visits to fellow Volunteers in faraway towns. Moreover, it was not the best advertisement for the Peace Corps when, as in Venezuela, the blue jeeps were sometimes spotted parked outside the local brothel.[89]

In some countries vehicles were necessary. In Peru, they were essential for getting Volunteers to the coastal areas; and in Malawi, an evaluation report underscored the moderate and level-headed way in which jeeps were being used. In general, however, most evaluators reckoned that the fewer Peace Corps jeeps in a country, the better it was for the program. In September 1963, Charles Peters recommended a policy to Shriver of "no Peace Corps-supplied vehicles" for Volunteers. "Of course," he concluded, "we should continue to supply motor bikes, bikes and horses where necessary."[90]

Access to jeeps notwithstanding, most Volunteers did make a significant physical sacrifice during their Peace Corps service. Volunteers rarely had to go hungry, or sleep out in the open, but there were varying degrees of discomfort. A subsistence allowance which was comfortable by Third World standards was still meager. Each Volunteer managed finances in his own way. Some saved their money for travel during vacation, others used their allowance to invest in materials for their projects—like the Volunteer in Brazil who bought food with her own money to supplement the diet of local children.[91]

Volunteers were usually the severest critics of the relatively comfortable life which they led compared to their poverty-stricken hosts. One Volunteer in Liberia chided himself and his colleagues that "We're not living as the natives live. We have plenty of clothes, we eat better and ride around and drink Fanta and have lots of books."[92] But when evaluator David Gelman visited this Volunteer and his colleagues, he reported that they were living very stringently. While few Volunteers had to suffer abject poverty, they usually had to do without access to clean toilets, safe drinking water in their homes, refrigerators, and other amenities that were taken for granted in the United States.

To most Volunteers, "luxury" soon came to be defined as a cold beer and a hot shower.

The American press tended to associate physical deprivation with a successful Peace Corps program. This was a simple-minded distortion of the Peace Corps' purpose. The Peace Corps Act said Volunteers should be "willing to serve under conditions of hardship if necessary." Discomfort, as such, was not a goal. Shriver insisted that Volunteers had to show a willingness "to share the life of another people, to accept sacrifice when sacrifice is necessary and to show that material privilege has not become the central and indispensable ingredient in an American's life."[93] Although most Volunteers did not live in mud huts, the majority fulfilled those objectives.

The happiest Volunteers were often those with the most difficult living conditions. Many Volunteers seemed to enjoy jobs in the outback rather than big city work. In a city, with many expatriates, the Volunteers could easily become just another face in the crowd; it was difficult for Volunteers to make a contribution that was distinctly their own. While they had the company of each other in the city, there was the danger of social clan-nishness and that contacts with their hosts would become limited. Volunteers could congregate for "bull" sessions where they could gripe, gossip, and generally waste time. Up-country assignments lacked social amenities and conversation with Americans, but they held the attractions of a freer, more infor mal style of life, increased contact with the local folk, and greater opportunities to make a personal impact.

Naturally, not all Volunteers preferred to be on their own, and the best results were not always produced working "à la Schweitzer." The needs of different projects varied, and many demanded the application of a group of Volunteers working in close harmony. However, Volunteer morale was almost always higher in the up-country programs. These were studded with characters who thrived on the freedom and responsibility that isolation allowed them. In Panama, a young Volunteer working with the Caribbean coastal Indians did not visit his Peace Corps office in Panama City for ten months; every few weeks he took a boat upstream to deliver fish, rice, and pig-meat to local com-munities. A Volunteer working in the Liberian bush became so

popular that he was adopted as a son of the local tribe and had
a baby named after him. In Pakistan, a lone Volunteer taught
agricultural classes, organized a local parent-teacher association,
set up demonstration gardens, and coached the school basketball team; he was even given seven hundred rupees by the town
council to develop a farm. An arts and crafts worker in Peru
helped the Indians of Arequipa with their designs and took advantage of the great love of music in the *barriadas* to organize
a local choir. In Ethiopia, Paul Tsongas not only taught math
but, with the help of his students, cut down trees and built foot-
bridges over muddy streams and ditches. During his vacation
he remained alone with his students to construct a school dormitory for the village of Ghion. An evaluation report noted that
Tsongas, like many other Volunteers working alone in isolated
areas, had achieved "a close relationship" with his hosts.[94]

INDISCRETIONS

Not all Volunteers were as exemplary. As might have been
expected, some were guilty of both public and private indiscretions. One Volunteer in Nigeria was dismissed ("terminated" in
Peace Corps parlance) for taking a completely unauthorized fifty-
day vacation in Europe. In Ethiopia, evaluator Richard Elwell
noted that some Volunteers' manners had deteriorated so badly
that "they fart out loud at meal-time." A Volunteer in Indonesia
spent most of his working day writing up his Master's thesis;
another was described as having "the experience and most of
the attributes of a Californian beach-boy."[95] Some Volunteers in
Latin America were dismissed for getting involved in the local
black market; others for showing "poor judgment" in joining a
public demonstration against their school administrators. A
Volunteer in Brazil, a welder, ordered and received two thirty-
pound clamps for use in his work; but he preferred to use them
as bar-bells. He was reported as being "passive, doesn't relate
well with nationals, doesn't want to work—and has tremendous
biceps."[96]

In the early 1960s, few Volunteers were involved with drugs,
although a couple were sent home for smoking marijuana. Some

Volunteers over-indulged in alcohol. The most outrageous incident occurred in 1963 when a group in Bangladesh visited a bar in downtown Dhaka. When the party broke up, one Volunteer had to be carried out of the place; meanwhile, his colleagues commandeered the bicycle rickshaws at the curb, put the local drivers in the passenger seats, and raced each other through the streets.[97] The locals were not impressed at this particular form of "people-to-people" contact. This drunken group were among about 120 Volunteers who, between 1961 and 1963, received the "Braniff Low Achievement Award," the Volunteers' facetious euphemism for an early plane ticket home.

SEX AND THE VOLUNTEER

Sexual relations presented Volunteers with some of their most sensitive personal dilemmas overseas. Peace Corps headquarters established some general policies: cohabitation was forbidden, contraceptive devices were not supplied, brothels were off-limits. During training, Volunteers were told that while the Peace Corps wanted them to have maximum freedom in their personal lives, going overseas was not a license for sexual adventure. They were left in no doubt that any conduct which endangered either the success of their program or the reputation of the Peace Corps would result in instant dismissal. However, it was impossible to regulate the sexual behavior of thousands of young men and women, especially under the lonely and often frustrating circumstances they faced overseas.

In Togo, an evaluator reported "affairs involving female Volunteer teachers and Togolese men. There are affairs involving female Volunteer teachers and Peace Corps men. There are affairs involving Peace Corps men and Togolese women. And there is a bit of V.D." Charles Peters emphasized to Shriver that these Volunteers had to be made to understand that "even though their particular hosts might not object to nightly orgies, a worldwide reputation for such behavior could get the Peace Corps un-invited in a lot of other places and unsupported in the U.S. Congress."[98]

Peace Corps Reps tried to guard against imprudence, but

not always with complete success. Despite the ruling against cohabitation, the problem of "mixed housing"—male and female Volunteers sharing the same accommodation—persisted in several countries. When evaluators in Venezuela discovered a male Volunteer and a female Volunteer living together alongside a Venezuelan couple doing the same, they described the situation as "the ultimate in counterpart relations."[99] In Pakistan, several Volunteer households contained two single girls and a single man. These "ménages à trois" had become the subject of a good deal of Pakistani gossip and had strengthened the already prevalent feeling that Americans were immodest and immoral. As an evaluation report pointed out:

> In a Moslem country where separation of the sexes is so strictly observed, it is curious that we Americans should import a living arrangement that is opprobrious even in our own relaxed society . . . To be sure, the relationship between male and female Volunteers in such households is quite clearly that of a brother and sister. But the housing arrangement has the appearance of a greater intimacy than that, and in Pakistan the appearance is the reality.

In the margin of this report Shriver ordered immediate action to be taken on this "inexcusable situation."[100]

While the vast majority of Volunteers behaved with modesty and tact, there were a few embarrassing incidents. One Volunteer in a Latin American country went around throwing herself "literally and figuratively at the opposite sex." Another woman whose sexual proclivities had already got her transferred from Nigeria, again brought herself to the brink of scandal in Liberia.[101] A number of female Volunteers became pregnant and there were cases where native women filed paternity suits against male Volunteers. A few Volunteers became fathers to "Peace Corps babies"; there were also instances of "marriages of necessity" between Volunteers. In some Far Eastern countries, even the most casual relationship with a native female was regarded as a prelude to marriage. Several impressionable young men found themselves married to local girls after only a few months of Peace Corps service. One twenty-one-year-old Volunteer in Colombia was sent home after it was discovered he had married a native grandmother.[102]

Most Peace Corps programs suffered at least a few cases of venereal disease. In Thailand, the staff were concerned that only three cases of V.D. had been reported among the more than sixty male Volunteers. The concern was that others might be getting inadequate or no treatment. "But before I left," wrote evaluator John Griffin in February 1963, "other reports came in, building the number up to what the Peace Corps doctor called a 'healthy average.' " Griffin noted that some U.S. army units in Thailand suffered 100 percent infection.[103]

Most of the Volunteers' sexual quandaries stemmed from cross-cultural differences. In some Moslem countries, male Volunteers felt that as far as sexual relations were concerned, they "might as well have been eunuchs." An exasperated Volunteer in Indonesia claimed that not only was "dating impossible, but even visiting a native girl was difficult."[104] In countries such as Turkey, Iran, and Sri Lanka, male Volunteers had to come to terms with the extensive homosexuality. As evalutor Arthur Dudden noted in Sri Lanka, the widespread homosexuality was "an alarming challenge to some Volunteers."[105]

The complications raised by a different culture's approach to sexuality were often exacerbated for female Volunteers. In some Near Eastern societies, only a certain type of woman walked alone in the streets and took active part with men in community life. In other countries, it was against social etiquette for an unmarried woman to be seen alone with a man. Female Volunteers had to overcome these predicaments and, at the same time, avoid offending racial and cultural sensitivities.

Early training courses did not give women Volunteers enough warning of the sometimes aggressive sexual attitudes of African and Latin American men. In many developing countries, the image of the American woman was that projected by Hollywood: glamorous, empty-headed, and promiscuous. An evaluation report noted that, in Turkey, American films had given the impression that "the American woman jumps from bed to bed." As a result, female Volunteers were regarded as "fair game" by their male hosts. In Ecuador, evaluator Richard

Elwell warned Peace Corps women that they would have to be careful because "an unescorted female is very likely to get raped after dark in Guayaquil." In the Philippines, many female Volunteers had been either "pinched, grabbed, abused, attacked, raped or near-raped."[106]

Although difficulties and temptation abounded, few Volunteers chose to over-indulge their sexual appetites. Most proved to be healthy personalities who held a responsible perspective on their own moral priorities. Volunteers were rarely holier-than-thou types. They did pride themselves, however, on being different from the swaggering, loud-mouthed, macho American often on view overseas. If a Volunteer were in danger of disgracing his program, his colleagues usually reprimanded him before headquarters did. In Thailand, an evaluator noted one case where a Volunteer had started living with a prostitute; the other Volunteers had a serious talk with him to the effect that he was spoiling the Peace Corps' impact by behaving like a GI. After a few days, the Volunteer returned to live with his fellow Peace Corpsmen.[107]

EXTENDING THE HAND AND THE HEART

Despite the many problems facing Volunteers overseas, most managed to make some kind of tangible contribution to their host societies. They also left a favorable impression of Americans. Evaluation reports, written from a critical standpoint, were freighted with stories of the positive impact made by Volunteers. "On the job, most of them resemble Al Capp," wrote Philip Cook in Gabon. "Bearded, sweaty, the few clothes they wear dirty or torn, they are a frightening sight . . . but Volunteers are providing sound, on-the-job training in carpentry and construction to unskilled Gabonese villagers." In the Toledo district of Belize, Volunteers "blazed romantic trails through the bush" moving from village to village teaching handicrafts. A Volunteer in Peru, in addition to his teaching job, helped the local Indians manufacture a skin cream from the water left over from their wool-making operation, and thus initiated a new cottage industry.[108] In a community development project in the Dominican Republic, evaluators singled out a Volunteer who would leave behind as evidence of his presence, a town council already convinced that it can bring about civic improvements by utilizing its own resources. He will leave behind scores of farmers using modern methods of feeding and breeding their animals, along with others who realize the advantages of prime seed, fertilization and use of insecticides. Unless we miss our guess, he will also leave a model home construction and agrarian reform project to be admired and copied.[109]

In criticizing Kennedy's Peace Corps, Kevin Lowther and C. Payne Lucas argued that the agency surrendered to "benign mediocrity" and retained "non-performing" Volunteers in order to give the American public the impression that the bold experiment was succeeding. They described the majority of Volunteers as "do-gooders and dilettantes . . . the unmet hope of the Peace Corps."[110] With so many young people being sent overseas for the first time, there were bound to be programming problems and personal indiscretions. But while weak links existed, it would be simplistic and wrong to condemn generally the quality of Kennedy's Peace Corps.

Every program contained at least three very broad levels of Volunteers. A number of absolutely outstanding Volunteers were effective in achieving all three Peace Corps goals; they had a useful skill, showed real empathy with their hosts and colleagues, relished the experience, and were the epitome of capable Americans striving for understanding of another culture. In the middle was probably the largest group, who made a contribution in terms of providing knowledge and exchanging cultural values, but—because of difficult local conditions or shortage of a skill, energy, or empathy—did not have first-class, all-round impact. At the lower end of the scale were a small minority of Volunteers who, for various reasons, ended up frustrated, defeated, and perhaps even embittered. Evaluators observed both strong and weak Volunteers in every project, and often the pendulum swung between the two. As Charles Peters pointed out, the most consistently effective Volunteer was not the brilliant innovator or the tireless adventurer, but rather the "dependable, self-reliant, feet-on-the-ground man."[111]

There were many Volunteers in that category. They worked hard, lived modestly, and made friends where they could. Most of their efforts went unrecorded. Often the Volunteers' most satisfying work was done during vacations when they traveled up-country and came in contact with remote communities. Sometimes their successes were achieved in unconscious moments when they taught their hosts, by "doing," how to put a fence around their chickens, or cover the juncture in electrical wires, or sterilize water before drinking. Volunteers probably made their strongest impression on the minds of children: teaching them, laughing with them, showing them that not all Americans were "Yanqui imperialists."

These subtle forms of impact were not easily or immediately discernible, and the Volunteers' work often did not seem exceptional. But to host country people, especially in the newly decolonized lands, there was something special about the young Americans who came to live and work with them. As a Peace Corps teacher in Sierra Leone wrote, "The appreciation we have been getting from people on all levels is no less than outstanding." Some of his students wondered why he would give up the luxuries of the United States—"the good jobs, the money and the conveniences"—to come and work in West Africa. "But," he said, "they are glad to have us. One student said to me, 'I really don't know why you want to do this, but welcome.' "[112] When Bertha Evosevich had to tell her Nigerian pupils in late 1963 that she was returning home to Pittsburgh, a little girl began to cry: "Madame, you can't do that . . . we love you so much."[113]

Such moments of satisfaction often alternated with feelings of frustration. Evaluator Timothy Adams wrote that a Volunteer needed "the imagination of Leonardo, the patience of Job, the courage of Sergeant York and the hide of an elephant."[114] A community developer in Peru commented that "A really good Volunteer receives little credit—keep that in mind when you read Peace Corps success stories. I have a lot of failures, a few tangible successes and a great deal of frustration . . . Now, all things considered, I think I'm doing something worthwhile. I don't think I'll sign up for another stretch, but you can't drag me away from this one." Another Volunteer in Tunisia complained that "The red tape, inefficiency and lack of comprehension seem insurmountable walls blocking any progress . . . but, if I had the chance to do it over again, knowing what I do now, I would not hesitate. It is a remarkable experience."[115]

What made the experience remarkable varied according to each Volunteer. For teacher Carol Fineran in Venezuela, it was when "an awfully bad kid finally shapes up or an insolent teenage girl hugs you and says 'thanks.' " To a young Volunteer in sub-Saharan Africa, his Peace Corps service brought him the "personal peace to salve my conscience that I and my peers were born between clean sheets when others were issued into the dust with a birthright of hunger." A Volunteer in the Philippines said it was the "little things" that brought her most satisfaction: "like attending the barrio elections, showing interest in the barrio council meetings, playing ball in the town plaza with the kids." To another Volunteer in Sierra Leone, the rewards of the Peace Corps went beyond "abstract philosophical arguments and platitudes" to "the poverty, the illiteracy, the sub-standard educational opportunities which are rampant in this as well as many other countries." These were "reasons enough for anyone," he said, "to want to extend his hand and heart in order that these plights might be at least partially effaced."[116]

Despite the many frustrations that all Volunteers endured, 94 percent said that they would go through their Peace Corps experience again; 10 percent extended their service for an extra year.[117] "Our Volunteers have had many difficulties and bad moments," wrote a Peace Corps Rep in Chile, "but they have also had a million laughs, and all of us have stored away enough memories to last a lifetime."[118] In a letter to Sargent Shriver, Mike O'Donnell, a Volunteer in Morocco, underscored that the positive aspects of his service far outweighed the discouragements:

Peace Corps Morocco I is, at the very least, typical of projects everywhere insofar as it has had its share of work shortage, partial success, entanglement in bureaucratic red tape, and so on. But these negative factors have been in the minority, a minority richly interwoven with success in personal contact at the grassroots level, with the satisfaction of having passed on technical knowledge, though basic, to Moroccans who will do the job when the Peace Corps is no longer here.

The Volunteer was heartened that "we are part of a vital and growing community of goodwill ambassadors to developing countries throughout the world."[119]

For young Americans in the early 1960s, the Peace Corps was the great adventure of their times. It was the courageous, the daring thing to do. Through the Peace Corps they stormed their own cultural frontier and discovered the world. Some learned the words of Sierra Leone's national poet, Abioseh Nicol:

> Go up-country, they said,
> To see the real Africa . . .
>
> You will find your hidden heart,
> Your mute ancestral spirit.[120]

By going up-country with the Peace Corps, Volunteers saw the real Africa, the real Asia, and the real Latin America. In return, this special group of Americans extended the hand of help and friendship—and the Third World caught a glimpse of the heart of the United States.

Potential Volunteers: trepidatious young men and women prepare to take the Peace Corps' first written test, May 1961.

The Peace Corps sought to give trainees skills useful for the Third World. Here they learn basic agricultural techniques.

Harris Wofford and Volunteer Douglas Mickelson (with sunglasses) chat with the children of Rus Desta school in Ethiopia. Wofford, an inexhaustible source of ideas, was the Peace Corps' philosopher-king.

Volunteer teacher Carol Waymire catches the school bus with her Ghanaian students.

Volunteer Dolores Tadlock, who with her husband Larry initiated a poultry development project, greets a child in Habra, India.

Volunteer Norman Tyler and his coworkers built Sierra Leone's first A-frame dwelling, a school near the town of Kenema.

In Anecho, Togo, Volunteer Michael Ruggiero put to good use the trawling skills he had learned in Gloucester, Mass.

Volunteer teacher John Gallivan with enthusiastic Turkish students. Globetrotting Sargent Shriver sits in to observe the class.

Volunteer Elaine Willoughby trained teachers and worked with children in "head start" programs in Jamaica.

Modesto Ortiz-Rosario, a Volunteer in Uba, Brazil, inspects his hosts' poultry.

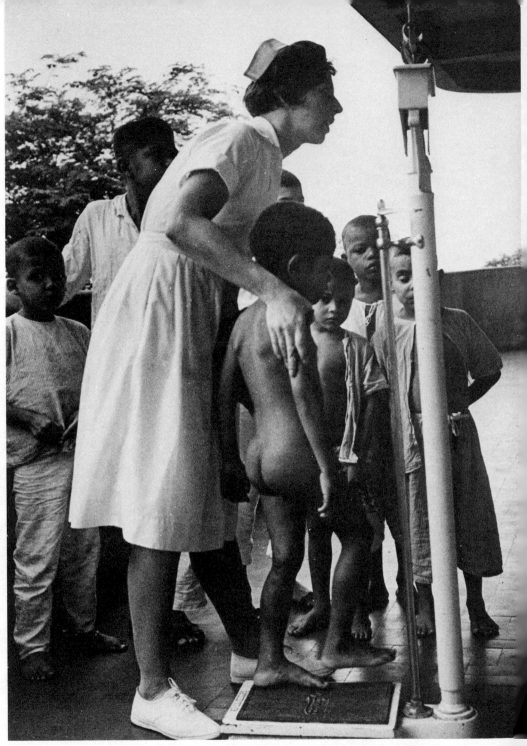

Nancy Conway of Foxboro, Mass., was a Volunteer nurse in the favellas of Rio de Janeiro.

Phil Silver (left) and Paul Tsongas, Volunteer teachers in Ghion, Ethiopia, built a school dormitory for their students. Tsongas was elected U.S. Senator from Massachusetts in 1978.

Peace Corps doctor Rick Van Rheenan attends to his Nigerian patients.

Volunteers Jess Stone (left) and Bernard Barela (right) discuss development projects with a local official in Boni, the Dominican Republic. The graffito reads: "Away with reaction. Down with the Yankees."

Volunteers Bill and Myra Ilson ran a teacher-training program in Kingston, Jamaica.

11

The Image

The American image of the typical Volunteer is pretty
distorted. I guess the image depends on whether you
read the jokes in *Playboy*, the *New Yorker*, the *Saturday
Evening Post* or the various editorials in the syndicated
newspapers.
— Chuck Guminer, Volunteer in Senegal

LIFE IN A GOLDFISH BOWL

"What person can really believe," asked the *Wall Street Journal* "that Africa aflame with violence will have its fires quenched because some Harvard boy or Vassar girl lives in a mud hut and speaks Swahili?"[1] Reading this editorial in early 1961, Sargent Shriver was aware of a thousand suspicious eyes peering over his shoulder. "Some of them were the eyes of friendly critics," he wrote, "but many belonged to unfriendly skeptics."[2] From the beginning, the new agency was the subject of constant media exposure. Shriver cautioned Volunteers and staff that life in the Peace Corps was akin to living in a goldfish bowl. At the same time, he avidly sought publicity. Shriver knew that the Peace Corps would be especially vulnerable to criticism in its early days; he also recognized that without popular support, at home and abroad, the venture would surely fail. Accordingly, he deliberately encouraged media interest, knowing full well that the fourth estate had the power to make or break the Peace Corps.

At first the Peace Corps was received by the American media with a mixture of enthusiasm and skepticism. The *New York Times* saw it as "an experiment in international brotherhood," and an editorial cited the hero of *The Ugly American* as the prototype for the Peace Corps Volunteer.[3] According to the *Nation*, this Volunteer would give the lie to the notion that Americans were dedicated only to "the suburban split-level, the dry martini, and the vice-presidency of the company."[4]

The more popular newspapers and magazines latched onto the glamor of the Peace Corps. "Telephones jangled, the switchboard blinked and drifts of incoming mail accumulated . . . The Peace Corps has captured the public imagination as has no other single act of the Kennedy administration," reported *Time* magazine. Romantic images were conjured up of "emotionally cool and dedicated workers" with "ever-youthful dreams of forging a better world." They would be "idealistic, patriotic, freedom-loving, adventuresome youths [with] the patience of Job, the forbearance of a saint and the digestive system of an ostrich." *Newsweek* wondered whether Volunteers should have an official uniform, slogan or song. In a gushing editorial on Kennedy's meeting with the first group of Volunteers, *Time* effused: "It was just like a wedding . . . A long line of young men and women stood among the rosebushes in the White House garden . . . and everyone was smiling and chatting amiably—sometimes in Swahili and sometimes in Twi . . . For brains and looks and verve, those chosen so far would rank high in any enterprise."[5]

As well as the enthusiastic if somewhat facile reports, there were also the cynical. The *New York Daily News* envisioned "hordes of well-meaning youngsters, sticking their snoots into people's private lives telling them how to bring up their children and what or what not to eat and drink." The conservative *National Review* wondered why American youths were "so caught up in the enthusiasm for bringing electric dish-washers to the Angolese?" Headlines such as "Crew-cut Crusade" and "Brownie Troop Do-Gooders" introduced articles which described prospective Volunteers as "pony-tailed co-eds and crew-cut Jack Armstrongs playing Albert Schweitzer—an appalling army of innocents abroad."[6]

The *New Yorker* conceded that while the Peace Corps had fired the imagination of American youth, "a distressing number of Asians and Africans are saying that they want no help from it, and some of their leaders have predicted that it will turn out to be nothing but a youth division of the C.I.A." Humorist Art Buchwald offered to serve as a Volunteer on the French Riviera where, "people went around half-naked, lacking shelter, and many still don't have their own boats." Spoofing Kennedy's address to Congress on the Peace Corps, Mr. Buchwald promised, "to live the way they do, share their homes, eat the food they do, and show them that an American is not too proud to become one of them, no matter what hardships he has to face."[7]

A more serious editorial in the liberal *New Republic* suggested that a voluntary service would have been more sensibly begun at home, where Volunteers could be tested before going overseas. It questioned the ability of young Americans to adapt to Third World cultures and doubted their resolve to live at the "grassroots" level: "The first time one of them has an attack of appendicitis in say, Nigeria, we shall see how conditional this resolve is." The skeptics awaited the first catastrophe.[8]

Shriver and his staff knew there would be blunders, but they worried that a spectacular calamity in the early days—a death, a rape, or a case of Communist infiltration—would completely destroy the agency's credibility. After only one month in the field, disaster struck, but in a most unlikely manner. In October 1961, a young female Volunteer in Nigeria lost a postcard and brought the Peace Corps its first crisis.

THE DROPPED POST CARD

After seven weeks training at Harvard, Margery Michelmore, a twenty-three-year-old *magna cum laude* graduate of Smith College, was assigned to a schoolteaching post in Ibadan. The daughter of a wealthy Massachusetts manufacturer, Michelmore was shocked on encountering slums, squalor, and open sewers in the Nigerian city. She wrote a postcard to a boyfriend in the United States describing her new environment.

> I wanted you to see the incredible and fascinating city we were in. With all the training we had, we really were not prepared for the squalor and absolutely primitive living conditions rampant both in the city and in the bush. We had no idea what "underdeveloped" meant. It really is a revelation and after we got over

the initial horrified shock, a very rewarding experience. Everyone except us lives in the streets, cooks in the streets, sells in the streets, and even goes to the bathroom in the streets.[9]

Unfortunately, Michelmore dropped her postcard on the way to the post office and it fell into the hands of some students at the University of Ibadan. They distributed copies of the card and staged an anti-American demonstration. Volunteers were denounced as "agents of imperialism" and "members of America's international spy ring." The protest made front-page news in Nigeria and it sparked a minor international incident. As the Nigerian Ambassador to the United States explained: "No one likes to be called primitive."[10]

Shriver met with the President as a flurry of cables passed between Peace Corps headquarters and Rep Sam Proctor in Nigeria. It was decided that it would be best for all concerned, including Michelmore, if she were brought home. She came back to Washington and worked in the Division of Volunteer Support. "I regret very much my part in the unfortunate affair at Ibadan," she wrote to Kennedy. "I hope that the embarrassment it caused the country and the Peace Corps effort will be neither serious nor lasting.[11] She need not have worried. Five weeks after the postcard incident, a second contingent of Volunteers arrived in Nigeria to be greeted warmly by Prime Minister Abubakar Balewa.

The American media, however, were not as forgiving as they pounced on the story. "From the moment of its inception, despite laudable aims, the Peace Corps was bound to run into trouble," commented *Time. U.S. News and World Report* condemned the naiveté of the entire concept and claimed, "this is only the first big storm."[12] The Associated Press reported that thousands of Nigerians had taken part in the "Communist-inspired" protest. Former President Eisenhower fueled the furor by claiming that there was now "postcard evidence" of the worthlessness of Kennedy's new idea.[13]

Other press commentary treated the misadventure in a more balanced manner. "The problem involved is really bigger than the Peace Corps," noted a *Commonweal* editorial, "for it reflects the gap that exists between the wealthy U.S. and most of the rest of the world. Given this fact, incidents like the postcard affair are bound to happen." The *New York Times* pointed out that only 150 to 200 students had joined in the demonstration, not thousands, while the *New Republic* made it clear that the protest was not Communist-inspired but merely an expression of sensitive African nationalism.[14] Columnist James Wechsler of the *New York Post* pleaded for sanity in the media's coverage of the incident:

> Nothing in the card was sinister. It contained the instinctive expression of horror of an affluent American girl in her first direct encounter with the gruesome squalor of Nigeria (which might have been East Harlem). She was neither patronizing nor self-righteous in her comment; yet, whoever found the lost card managed to stage a big production. Like many other people, the Nigerians need and want help; but they do not like to be told how desperate is their need.[15]

Tai Solarin of the *Lagos Daily Times* agreed: "If Michelmore was out to ridicule the country, she would be intelligent enough to protect her stings with an envelope." He added that "not a single Nigerian who knew this part of Nigeria would suggest that she was sending home a made-up story." The Nigerian press was generally kinder to the Peace Corps than the popular magazines in America which ridiculed the episode. "Why," asked James Wechsler, "is there so much desire to burlesque the Peace Corps?"[16]

The "dropped postcard" proved to be somewhat fortunate for the Peace Corps. Its first mishap, whatever it might have been, would have attracted a disproportionate amount of publicity. The relatively innocuous nature of the Michelmore mistake was a blessing in disguise. In later years, there were much more sensational incidents—rapes, murder trials, political entanglements—but the media paid little attention. To the press and the public, the Peace Corps' first set-back was its greatest: a dropped postcard.

The incident also had its benefits for Shriver and his staff in terms of experience. Under the full glare of the public spotlight, they were not panicked into withdrawing the Peace Corps program from Nigeria or even requesting Michelmore's resignation.

"Margery was as sensitive and as intelligent a Volunteer as we ever had in the Peace Corps," wrote Charles Peters to Shriver; but the lesson to be learned was that "even the best young people can be damned silly at times."[17] In training progams, heavy emphasis was placed on the need for Volunteers to be sensitive to the conditions of poverty in the developing countries and to the proud nationalist feelings of their host peoples. Volunteers were also advised against writing postcards.

The President's personal support helped the Peace Corps weather its first storm. He sympathized with the young woman's predicament and felt that, to a great extent, she had been a victim of circumstance. In a handwritten note to Michelmore during her ordeal, he told her, "We are strongly behind you and hope you will continue to serve in the Peace Corps."[18] Kennedy also maintained his sense of humor regarding the affair. As a group of Volunteers left for Africa a year later, the President wished them good luck and bade them to "Keep in touch . . . but not by postcard!"[19]

THE EXOTIC AND THE BIZARRE

After the Michelmore episode, the American media viewed the Peace Corps with a relatively uncensorious eye. "From the front porches of the U.S.," said *Time* in July 1963, "the view of the Peace Corps is just beautiful." Volunteers were seen as " a battalion of cheery, crew-cut kids who hopped off their drugstore stools and hurried out around the world to wage peace." To the popular press the Peace Corps was virtuous and wholesome. It would show the Third World that America was "a loving country," said *Vogue*. "Goodbye to the 'Ugly American,' " proclaimed *Parade* magazine. *U.S. News and World Report* described how Volunteers would demonstrate that "the U.S. is determined to build a peaceful world and that Americans oppose any government that tries to make war and spread tyranny." Broadcaster Howard K. Smith told his television audience that the Peace Corps was "America's answer to Moscow's possession of local Communist cadres in all emergent countries." Comparing the Cold War to a football game, *Newsweek* called the Peace Corps America's "freshman team."[20]

While the media certainly supported the Peace Corps, its coverage was usually superficial. Articles were not balanced or well researched. Emphasis was on adventure, hardship, and exotica. *Time* praised one Volunteer who walked eight miles every day to and from the school where he taught; another was reputed to be living in a hut along with goats and snakes. One female Volunteer in Chile was said to have "revolutionized" her community by giving local women the recipe for apple pie.[21] A typical story, headlined "Peace Corps Life Is Rugged," appeared in the *Baltimore Sun* in the summer of 1962:

> Wading hip-deep in swamps with hippos snorting behind a curtain of tall grass, riding the river in a dugout canoe, palavering with tribal chiefs at sunset after a long day on Safari, sleeping under thatch-roof shelters, getting up in the morning to find a crowd of natives wanting to join the hike because there is safety in numbers in elephant country. Such is the rugged outdoor life that enlistment in the Peace Corps has brought.[22]

The American press approved of the Peace Corps, but preferred its romantic, quaint, and lighthearted aspects to the more complex and realistic story. There were tales of great works performed. In Pakistan, Volunteers were reported to have invented a new machine to par-boil rice; in Colombia a loom was invented to weave bamboo. According to *Time*, the Peace Corps' greatest achievement in St. Lucia was to teach the local peoples how to dance the Twist. In the Punjab, a young Volunteer's achievement was that he had persuaded his Indian counterpart to remove the hammer and sickle emblem from the top of his chicken coop. Two Volunteers in Accra "proudly won" second place in a Ghanaian "High Life" dance contest. There were reports on romance and marriage in the Peace Corps and lush descriptions of evenings in the Andes.[23]

Sometimes the more bizarre stories printed by the American press caused great embarrassment for the Peace Corps overseas. In a letter to friends back home, Volunteer Richard Lipez in Ethiopia described the national dish, *injera-watt*, as "a terrifying assault on one's innards by tomatoes, peppers, eggs, chicken, sheep's intestines and a murky sponge-rubber-like bread." He added whimsically "and maybe a few, fat pussycats." Four months later, a letter from Peace Corps headquarters informed him that an Associated Press article entitled "Peace Corps Diet: Fat Pussy Cats" had appeared in nearly two hundred newspapers across the United States. A front-page headline in the *Voice of Ethiopia* read: "Peace Corps Volunteer Says Ethiopians Eat 'Fat Pussy Cats.' " An indignant editorial accused the Peace Corps of telling "Damned Bad Lies" and wanted all Volunteers thrown out of the country.[24]

Fortunately, Rep Harris Wofford was able to pacify Ethiopian officials and persuade them of the trivial nature of the matter. Ethiopians accepted his apology and a nasty incident was averted. The Volunteer, dumbfounded to find himself at the center of the controversy, was allowed to remain in service. However, by its silly distortion of a Volunteer's innocent observations, the press had placed the Peace Corps in an extremely difficult situation.

Rarely were the Peace Corps' real problems mentioned by the media. Instead, in the summer of 1963, *Time* reported on some minor "Foul-ups" overseas. *Newsweek* also carried a story on a Volunteer in Ghana who lived in luxury and spent his weekends "surfing and sun-bathing in the company of a most delightful blonde." In March 1963, *U.S News and World Report* heard "whispers" that young Volunteers were "running wild" in Venezuela. In a critical piece in the *Washington Star*, journalist Eric Sevareid acknowledged that given the media's almost euphoric coverage of the Peace Corps, any critical questions raised would receive the same treatment as "a doubt expressed about virginity." All the same, he was highly skeptical of the "jazzed up publicity that surrounded the birth and recruitment of the original Peace Corps, the romanticizing of their missions, the lionizing of individuals in the glossy magazines."[25]

By 1963 Sevareid was almost isolated in his criticism of the Peace Corps. "[It] has won the envy and the enmity of the communists, and the admiration and affection of 46 countries," said the *New York Herald Tribune*. The *Los Angeles Times* praised it as the most effective U.S. agency overseas. "What is amazing is that the adverse incidents have been so few," claimed the *Washington Post*, "indeed only the famous affair of the postcard is worth mentioning at all." In an editorial congratulating the

Peace Corps on reaching its "Second Birthday," the *New York Times* stated: "Now and then, some new agency of government clicks from the start—mark this one down with a plus sign." The foreign press followed suit. Britain's liberal *Guardian* believed that "John Kennedy's Peace Corps has restored some of the decency in patriotism, regenerated some warmth in our reluctant alliance and, above all, for all our poor sakes, has revived a little of the romance of America."[26]

In another article in the *Guardian*, however, Alec Dickson— founder of British Voluntary Services Overseas—warned the Peace Corps of the dangers of being lulled into a false sense of security by glossy magazine stories. He suggested that success did not necessarily lie in spectacular individual achievements and that failure often came "in the apparently placid projects where Volunteers may feel themselves completely superfluous."[27] But the American press was in no mood for Dickson's informed analysis of the realities of Volunteer existence. The American public was never told that most Volunteers were teachers, many lived in cities and towns in relative comfort, and that most suffered periods of extreme frustration. Rather, Volunteers were described as happy-go-lucky kids, living in mud huts and working with picks and shovels in the jungle. In short, the press image of the Volunteer was a simplistic stereotype.

CREATING A STEREOTYPE

To some extent, the stereotype was fostered by Shriver and his staff. They sensed the intense public interest in the Peace Corps and they decided to make the most of it. To inspire and harness public enthusiasm, Shriver established the Office of Public Affairs under Bill Moyers. Shriver also set up a Division of Public Information which produced stories and news releases on the Peace Corps and dealt directly with the media. In 1961, Shriver told Kennedy of his plan to "dramatize as widely as possible" the Peace Corps story.[28]

Sponsorship by the Advertising Council (a non-profit voluntary organization established by American advertising agencies) meant millions of dollars of free advertising for the Peace Corps. The New York advertising agency, Young and Rubicam, advised the Peace Corps on how to plan and execute a media campaign.

By 1963 it was at the top of the public advertising list. At the same time, the Division of Public Information formed an excellent rapport with the press. Articles appeared in almost every kind of magazine and newspaper, from national sellers like the *New Yorks Times* and *Time* to small-town rural dailies. The Peace Corps fed articles on all Volunteers to their hometown papers. Shriver informed Kennedy that between three hundred to four hundred editorials, articles, and special features on the Peace Corps appeared in the national press each week.[29]

Ed Bayley, first chief of Public Information, estimated that 98 percent of all newspaper stories and 80 percent of editorials were favorable to the Peace Corps. "Publicity regarding all aspects of the Peace Corps has been lavish," he noted. "Almost no phase of our operation has been considered too small for public notice . . . Most of the reporters with whom we deal, both in Washington and elsewhere, are sympathetic to the idea of the Peace Corps and anxious to help it along."[30] Shriver was particularly pleased to tell the President that the black press, though skeptical at first, "has now generally endorsed the Peace Corps."[31]

The Peace Corps' public relations exercises were slick, professional, and effective. Television cameras were invited into training camps; Volunteers appeared as guests on "What's My Line"; celebrities' visits to overseas programs made national headlines. The President's association with the Peace Corps was particularly well publicized: meeting Volunteers in the Rose Garden as they left for overseas or congratulating them on their return. Sometimes Kennedy wrote to journalists or broadcasters who had been particularly kind to the Peace Corps. In April 1962, he thanked Stephen Riddleberger, president of the American Broadcasting Company, for the "significant help the ABC-owned radio and television stations have been to the Peace Corps . . . Much is said and written about radio and television public service time, I think this is an example of public service at its best."[32]

There were several former journalists within Peace Corps ranks: Bayley, Haddad, Moyers, and Douglas Kiker. Even Shriver had been a stringer for *Time* in the 1930s and an assistant editor of *Newsweek* in the 1940s. This allowed the Peace Corps informal as well as formal ties to the media. Peter Braestrup, a journalist with the *New York Times*, was particularly friendly with

Haddad. At propitious moments—at the time of the battle for independence, on the Peace Corps' anniversary, and so forth— very positive articles tended to appear on the front page of the *New York Times*; they were usually under Braestrup's by-line. As Bayley noted: "We have a considerable number of former re- porters among our staff members—this has made hay for us on many occasions and saved our necks on others."[33] Peace Corps officials, with their inside knowledge of the media, knew exactly how to sell a story.

Many Peace Corps stories were planted. "We have been told to steer the direction of news," Bayley wrote. Referring to the informal links with the media, he felt that "Most of our best work has been done on the telephone and in conversation with re- porters." He concluded it would be possible, "if done deftly, to subvert the press by playing up to its prejudices, its traditions and its own values."[34] Since the media seemed to value glamor- ous, albeit superficial, news, that was what the Division of Public Information sought to provide. Little attempt was made to ex- plain the complexity of Volunteer life or the frustration and failure that often accompanied success. Instead, Peace Corps releases stressed one magnificent accomplishment after another.

A few officials attempted to quell this penchant for self- congratulation. Reviewing the Peace Corps' 1963 *Annual Report*, General Counsel Bill Josephson complained that there was far too much emphasis on the glib "Jack-the-Giant-Killer" type of success. He noted that a few congressmen and almost all Volunteers already felt the Peace Corps "brags too much about itself" and he called for a more modest tone in press releases: "Let us say what we have done and let that speak for itself."[35]

Most staffers, however, worried that if the agency became too candid and admitted too many weaknesses, then the public might become confused about what the Peace Corps was doing and even turn against the idea. As Douglas Kiker, appointed chief of Public Information in 1962, explained: "We are neither in the business of publicizing our mistakes nor of hiding them. Our obligation is to state what the Peace Corps is doing simply and authoritatively . . . and without raising an unnecessary ruckus by the failure to explain properly or emphasizing those parts of our operation which are matters of delicacy. When asked, it is necessary to respond; it is not necessary to raise issues ourselves." Kiker argued that if "enough goofs" became known in the press, the Peace Corps would soon be out of business.[36]

MR. CLEAN

Shriver himself played a central role in the creation of the Peace Corps' public image. Indeed, he became the epitome of that image. He was young, handsome, athletic, always well groomed and photogenic. The press soon built up a picture of a superbly cool but enterprising executive. To save money, he traveled tourist-class; to save time, he took cat-naps on the floor during long plane journeys. Unlike other U.S. officials, he never carried a tuxedo on his overseas missions. Sleepless nights, pre-dawn telegrams, and constant action were associated with the Director of the Peace Corps. "He never stops," said the *New York Times*, "even in his pajamas." *Look* magazine described him as "A combination of Billy Graham and Tom Dooley—with a dash of advertising salesman thrown in."[37] The media soon nicknamed him "Mr. Clean."

Shriver took considerable care to ensure that he and the Peace Corps were seen in the best light. In March 1961, he gave Bayley the following instructions:

> In connection with all releases, I believe we should play up the fact that I was President of the Chicago Board of Education, a businessman, and have been active in interracial matters. Over-seas, the brother-in-law relationship is probably very important to emphasize, but domestically, at least, let's focus on the educa-tion, civil rights and business background.[38]

Hundreds of articles appeared under Shriver's name, he became a regular guest of television and radio interviewers, and by July 1963 he had even made the cover of *Time*. Shriver was the ideal public relations man, ever ready with an amusing anecdote, sophisticated under pressure, and invariably congenial. "Sarge was never much of an administrator," said Bayley, referring to Shriver's unique management style, "but it wasn't an ad-ministrator that was needed at the outset, it was a person like Sarge who was a promotions man really."[39]

Shriver's enthusiasm for promoting the good name of the Peace Corps was boundless. He suggested to staff, in Washington and overseas, that they should be willing "at all times, to respond to newspapermen's requests for information [and] provide them with Peace Corps stories and literature."[40] He always sent notes of thanks to editors and journalists who had expressed confidence in the Peace Corps. At the same time, he reacted strongly to criticism. Through the pages of the *Saturday Review*, he waged literary battle with journalists Eric Sevareid and George Sokolsky. He rebuked a television show for mistaking IVS workers in Vietnam for Peace Corps Volunteers. He also chastised the editor of the *Washington Star* for printing an "inaccurate" story that government officials in India had complained about the inexperience of Volunteers assigned there.

Shriver was in Colombia when he read about Eisenhower's criticism of the Peace Corps as a "juvenile experiment"; he immediately sent a copy of the report to Kennedy. "Articles like this which greeted us upon our arrival in Bogota are creating great obstacles to acceptance of the Peace Corps in Latin America," he told the President.[41] When "The David Brinkley Journal" television show featured a "Disenchanted Volunteer," Shriver explained to Kennedy that the Volunteer in question was completely atypical, "one of the weakest of all Volunteers . . . persistently troublesome and a loud-mouth." He concluded that "It's incredible how the press, radio and T.V. can always ferret out this kind if they are around."[42]

Despite the Peace Corps' generally excellent press, Shriver suspected that the media was always looking to publicize something disparaging or seamy about the agency. After it was discovered that a reporter had got a Volunteer drunk in order to get a story, Shriver told Bradley Patterson that sometimes he thought the American press was the Peace Corps' real "enemy."[43] As a result of this fear, Shriver tended to be over-protective of Peace Corps operations. He clamped down on leaks to the press and was prone to exaggerate the Peace Corps' achievements. He rarely admitted a mistake or a problem. "I sometimes say the Peace Corps is like a Volkswagen," he told "Meet the Press," "we continue to improve it all the time inside, but it remains just about the same externally." Shriver presented the romantic image of the Peace Corps. Occasionally verging on the trite, he depicted Volunteers as all-Americans leading a physically tough but spiritually rewarding life in the boondocks. "The first law of the Volunteers," he wrote in *National Geographic*, "seems to be: the rougher it is, the better we like it." Volunteers referred to this kind of hyperbole as "Shriver's hair-shirt stuff."[44]

THE CREDIBILITY GAP

Between 1961 and 1963, Volunteers consistently complained about the "phoney image" and "fake glamor" projected by the Peace Corps' public relations machine and the American media. Almost unanimously, Volunteers resented the stories of physical hardship, self-sacrifice, and devotion to duty. From their point of view, there was a huge credibility gap between what happened in the field and how it was reported back home. One angry Volunteer in Chile vowed that when he returned home, "if there's one thing I'm going to do, it's destroy the Peace Corps' image."[45] He and his colleagues rebelled against the bland newspaper reports about mud huts, suffering, and fighting communism in the Third World. As far as the Volunteers were concerned, the media was far away from understanding what the Peace Corps was about. "This is most obvious in the mud-hut and forces-of-light-marching-into-darkness picture," wrote Volunteer Roger Landrum in Nigeria.[46]

As well as the media, Volunteers attacked the image-making proclivities of Peace Corps headquarters. "I just wish they'd stop trying to make us something we're not," said a Volunteer in Brazil.[47] The publicity machine devoted a disproportionate amount of attention to community development programs because they provided more "exciting" news than teaching programs. Yet most Volunteers were teachers and they resented the fact that their quiet, unobtrusive efforts were often ignored. Volunteers complained of the "Mickey Mouse tone" of internal publications like the *Volunteer* and *Peace Corps News*, printed by the Division of Public Information. A Volunteer in Tanzania criticized Peace Corps officials for promoting an image of "American kids going around the world and putting their finger in the dyke."[48]

Shriver was regarded as the biggest PR culprit. Volunteers in Africa recalled him visiting them with photographers in tow who wanted "mud hut" pictures. One of Shriver's most oft-repeated anecdotes concerned a mob in the Dominican Republic which allegedly broke off from chanting "Yanquis go home" to explain to a Volunteer, "We want Yanquis to go home, not you." Volunteers in the Dominican Republic knew that the episode had actually involved an American priest, not a Volunteer. Some Volunteers felt that no matter what difficulties Shriver saw in the field, he retained his own, rather pristine image of the Volunteers. Without doubting Shriver's personal sincerity and belief in that image, most wished that "we could work without publicity, as missionaries have done for many years."[49]

Volunteers acknowledged that there was some truth in the popular image of the Peace Corps. While the majority of them did not live in mud huts, few had the usual comforts of their American homes. Relatively speaking, they did endure hardship. Morover, a significant number of them did genuinely live on the romantic edge of the Peace Corps. In Tanzania, for example, an evaluation report described Volunteers "living rather like white hunters, operating out of a tent in the bush . . . walking through vast herds of zebra at sunrise with gentle winds bending the brown grass."[50] Volunteers did not object to the glamorous stories because they were false, but because they were representative of only one aspect of Peace Corps service.

WISHING FOR A SUCCESS STORY

Perhaps the glamor was the only aspect that the American public wanted. In the early 1960s, the influence of Burdick and Lederer's *The Ugly American* was pervasive. It had said that Americans were not liked overseas. Reacting to this, Americans desperately wanted to believe that their country was capable of doing good. They looked to the Peace Corps. In the process, they invested it with a degree of virtue and idealism which could never have been matched by the realities of the operation. But Americans wanted something that would outstrip reality. The image of their young people dressed in T-shirts and sneakers, living in hovels, and feeding African children provided the psychic gratification which the public craved.

A 1963 Harris poll showed that the Peace Corps was the third most popular act of the Kennedy administration (behind "national security" and "Berlin").[51] A massive 75 percent of all Americans approved of it. "We older, squarer citizens love our Peace Corps," wrote journalist Ira Mothner in *Look* magazine. "It is homey as a hound dog, healthy as vitamin D. And it's a success—because we just couldn't bear for it not to be. The Peace Corps is our dream for ourselves and we want the world to see us as we see the Volunteers—crew-cuts and ponytails, soda-fountain types, hardy and smart and noble."[52]

One report blamed the unrealistic public perception of the Peace Corps on "the sloth of the Washington press corps."[53] Sloth notwithstanding however, American journalists found themselves in a difficult position in covering the Peace Corps. They had to write about an organization involved in complex cross-cultural and development issues. At the same time, they had to disseminate an impression of that organization which would be readily understood by a public which had already made an emotional investment in its "good image." This made it almost impossible to write objectively about the Peace Corps. Besides, the problems and more subtle aspects of Volunteer service were not always amenable to mass consumption. Therefore, difficulties were not reported and the Peace Corps was not treated in a serious manner.

Volunteers, of course, felt exploited by all this image-making. They accused Shriver and the Division of Public Information of demeaning Peace Corps service by supplying the American press with trivia. In 1961, however, the new agency had badly needed support from Congress and the public. To achieve this, it was necessary to have a relatively straightforward image which could be readily identified and accepted. Shriver conceded that the glossy aspects of that image expanded out of all proportion, but it had helped to satisfy the Peace Corps' domestic constituency.[54] The Volunteers concluded that their leaders simply did not understand the realities of field conditions. It was not quite that simple.

By 1963 the Peace Corps had, in fact, begun to publicize

some of its weaknesses. Press releases, congressional presenta-
tions, and articles written by staff became more balanced. "The
Volunteers have many discouragements," noted the Peace Corps'
own publication, the *Volunteer*, in September 1962; "success or
failure is difficult to measure." Shortly after Kennedy's death,
Shriver informed President Johnson that the Peace Corps' news
releases were beginning to move toward "realism," with as much
emphasis on frustration as achievement.[55] Shriver also recalled
that in 1963, when he offered an article entitled "Failures in the
Peace Corps" to *This Week* magazine, the editor refused it. He
told Shriver that his readers did not want to know about the
Peace Corps' mistakes.[56] Since the American public regarded the
Peace Corps as an embodiment of their personal ideals, there
was no market for exposés of weak programs or Volunteers'
peccadilloes.

In the early 1960s in general there was no great zeal for the
investigative journalism so characteristic of the American media
in the wake of Vietnam and Watergate. In the Kennedy era, the
nature of the press and public reading habits were simpler and
more innocent. In that sense, 1960 was the perfect time for the
Peace Corps to be established. America wanted a success story.

The irony of this success story was that, to a great extent,
it was based on a distortion of what Peace Corps life was really
like. Despite the overwhelmingly favorable impression which
the Peace Corps made on the American public, few people had
any accurate perspective on what Volunteers were actually doing.
They only read about dropped postcards, sultry days in exotic
climates, and survival amid mud huts. Most Americans were not
aware of the Volunteers' painstaking efforts to break down often
imperceptible cross-cultural barriers or make a contribution to
economic development. Instead, the Peace Corps was regarded
as something quaint, inoffensive, and wholesome. "Not many
people took the Peace Corps seriously," wrote Harris Wofford
in later years. "In the American mind it took its place somewhere
between Boy Scouts and motherhood."[57]

12

Politics and Ideals

Should it come to it, I had rather give my life trying
to help someone than to give my life looking down a
gun barrel at them.
—David Crozier (the first Volunteer to die in service)*

THE COLD WAR COMPLEX

As John Kennedy assumed the American presidency in
1961, the Cold War was nearing what he termed its " hour of
maximum danger." On January 6, Nikita Khrushchev, the Soviet
Premier, predicted that Communist world victory would be
achieved through wars of national liberation. The Third World
was to be the main battleground. Khrushchev's belligerent speech
reaffirmed Kennedy's belief that communism continued on the
offensive.[1] During his State of the Union address on January 30,
in which he announced the formation of a "National Peace
Corps," Kennedy forecast that the struggle between communism
and democracy would reach its climax in the 1960s. "I speak today
in an hour of national peril," he said. "Before my term has ended,
we shall have to test anew whether a nation organized and governed such as ours can endure. The outcome is by no means
certain . . ."[2] In this atmosphere, any foreign policy initiative was
certain to have Cold War connotations. The Peace Corps was
no exception.

*David Crozier died in a plane crash in Colombia in 1962; he wrote these
words in a letter to his parents.

Launched in the spring of 1961, the Peace Corps coincided with America's biggest-ever armaments budget and the Bay of Pigs invasion. This context led some critics to believe that the new agency was nothing more than another weapon in America's Cold War arsenal or a "daring stroke in the ideological contest between Western democracy and the socialist doctrines for the allegiance of the post-colonial world." Historian Charles J. Wetzel wrote that the Peace Corps was a direct "product of American anti-Communist foreign policy."[3]

Certainly the anti-Communist argument was used by early proponents of the idea. Congress's original study of the Peace Corps in 1960 was authorized under the terms of the Mutual Security Act which sought to "maintain the security of the United States and the free world from Communist aggression and thereby maintain peace." One of the Peace Corps' founding fathers, Hubert Humphrey, told his Senate colleagues that "This program is to be part of the total foreign policy of the United States . . . to combat the virus of Communist totalitarianism."[4]

Kennedy's first formal espousal of the Peace Corps at the Cow Palace in 1960 was also spiced with Cold War rhetoric. He spoke of Soviet geologists, electrical engineers, architects, farmers, and fishermen working in Ghana, and of "Castro-type or Communist exploitation" in Brazil.[5] He called for skilled and dedicated Americans to compete with the Soviets. *Newsweek* described the Peace Corps as "America's latest weapon in the Cold War"; *Reporter* magazine compared it directly to the Soviet Union's Institute of Africa (which trained Russians in the languages and customs of developing countries). *New York Times* journalist David Halberstam inferred that the pervasive sense of competition with the Soviets, in politics, economics, and ideas, was an important factor in persuading "bright young men off the Eastern campuses" to join the Peace Corps in the early 1960s.[6]

To win the support of Congress and the public, Sargent Shriver realized that it was necessary to imply that the Peace Corps would make a contribution to the anti-Communist cause. "Either we do these jobs or the Communists will," he told an audience in 1961.[7] Nevertheless, Shriver always insisted that the Peace Corps should not be thought of, or used, as a means of achieving the short-range political aims of the United States. In a memorandum in the fall of 1961 entitled "The Shape of the Peace Corps Program," he emphasized that the Peace Corps would not just go to countries deemed politically favorable to the United States. Moreover, the Peace Corps would avoid states ruled by small, militaristic elites unresponsive to the will and needs of the majority; it would also avoid countries where massive financial and military assistance had served only to identify the United States with an unpopular ruling circle. At the same time, Shriver was realistic about the Peace Corps' position vis-à-vis American foreign policy. "We cannot shut our eyes to the realities of world conditions," he wrote. "The Peace Corps is a part of the United States foreign policy effort even though it has a special role and separate identity."[8]

This was the paradox at the heart of the Peace Corps. It never attempted to persuade its host countries of the merits of U.S. foreign policy. Yet, precisely because it engaged in no such activity, it became a uniquely significant asset to the United States. By treating local peoples according to their own needs and customs, without undue reference to their ideological beliefs, the Peace Corps built the kind of goodwill that did, ultimately, have considerable political effect. A few foreign policymakers appreciated this. As Secretary of State Dean Rusk told the Peace Corps National Advisory Council on May 22, 1961, "The Peace Corps is not an instrument of foreign policy because to make it so would rob it of its contribution to foreign policy."

The staff and the Volunteers, of course, saw themselves as distinctly non-political. But they were sponsored by the U.S. government and, as such, they had certain responsibilities to it. Besides, foreign observers were bound to see Volunteers as representatives of American foreign policy in its broadest sense. Thus the Peace Corps could not escape the times into which it was born; whether it wanted to be or not, it was caught in the Cold War complex.

WALKING A FINE LINE

In his "Report to the President" of February 1961, Shriver had asked Kennedy to take steps to ensure that the Peace Corps would not be seen as an attempt to export surplus American political zeal. In particular, he urged the President to propose that all member nations of the UN should establish their own versions of the Peace Corps to work alongside American groups overseas:

> You could propose that the United Nations sponsor the idea and form an international coordinating committee for all Peace Corps work underway. You could express your hope that Peace Corps projects will be truly international and that our citizens will find themselves working alongside citizens of the host country and also volunteers from other lands.[9]

Shriver hoped this would show that the Peace Corps was not merely an initiative of the Cold War. During an early staff meeting, he reiterated that Volunteers were not to be regarded as instruments or agents of American policy:

> They are not expected to represent official American views on current affairs; they are not "instructed"; they are, of course, to be prudent. They are rather free men and free women, the products of a free society, sent abroad to serve and to do their assigned work with such dedication and such skills that their hosts will, by this example, be brought to reflect on the nature of the society that produced them.[10]

Shriver had no hesitation in sending the Peace Corps to so-called "neutralist" states like Ghana, Guinea, India, and Indonesia. "The fact that a country might vary back and forth from friendly to not-so-friendly, should not mean we move the Peace Corps in and out like an accordion," he told a "Meet the Press" panel.[11]

He stressed this point to Third World leaders. For example, the mercurial but highly influential president of Guinea, Ahmed Sekou Touré, was reputed to have set his country on a Communist course. In offering the Peace Corps to Touré in early 1961, Shriver told him the United States recognized that each country had to choose the political system most suited to its needs. Shriver explained that there were no political strings attached to the Peace Corps. It was not concerned with whether there were "one, two or four Communists in the government or outside it," he told Touré, "[but with] the desire of the people of Guinea for a better society and a higher standard of living."[12]

Interim Policy Directive 2.1 attempted to define the Peace Corps' role in this difficult sphere: "A project must not be inconsistent with U.S. foreign policy. However, in order to make the maximum contribution to the foreign policy effort, a project should maintain the unique role and separate identity of the Peace Corps."[13] This claim to a separate identity did not preclude all political considerations. Shriver ordered that special efforts should be made to establish Peace Corps programs in countries where the United States had not yet succeeded in making a significant "social, economic or political impression."[14] He knew that if the Peace Corps was to win credibility as a force for change, it would have to prove its worth not only in friendly, pro-Western states, but also in turbulent, uncommitted ones. Accordingly, the Peace Corps outlined "high-priority" countries in the developing world in terms of specific socio-economic needs and broad U.S. foreign policy objectives.

In Africa, most importance was placed on Ghana, Guinea, Nigeria, Tanzania, Mali, and Senegal. In the Far East, Indonesia and the Pacific Trust Territories (Micronesia) were said to be of particular value. Indonesia had "a tremendous development potential," wrote director of Programming Warren Wiggins, "and its size, location and leadership make it a key to much of the Far East." The Trust Territories, in which Wiggins envisaged an education program, were "of high priority in terms of American foreign policy as a result of their status as one of the last U.S. trusteeships. All American activity there will be closely scrutinized by the rest of the world." Wiggins also argued that a proposed English-teaching program for Japan—not yet the economic giant which it was to become in the 1970s—would be of vital concern to both the United States and the Peace Corps. "To a great extent," he said, "that country will determine the future of America in Asia."[15]

The entire Latin American region was given very high priority, with Argentina singled out as "significant for political reasons." Mexico's unique relationship with the United States was also stressed. In the Near East and South Asia, Wiggins suggested that Iran, Afghanistan, and Nepal had "a political importance resulting from their geographic locations." He also mentioned "local political considerations" in Greece, Turkey, Cyprus,

India, Pakistan, and Sri Lanka. Finally, he included Yugoslavia and the United Arab Republic because of their "particular political priority." Wiggins noted that Yugoslavia might open the door to an eventual Peace Corps presence in Eastern-bloc countries.[16] Shriver even claimed that he would send Volunteers to the Soviet Union and China, if requested.

These programming strategies, which showed above all else that the Peace Corps was eager to have a program in most developing countries, were not driven primarily by political considerations. Social and economic need, as well as an indigenous desire to have the Peace Corps, were always more important. Because of the latter, the Peace Corps never entered Japan, Argentina, Mexico, Yugoslavia, Greece, or the United Arab Republic. Nevertheless, that these countries were discussed in a foreign policy context, indicated that the Peace Corps was walking a fine line in its relation to U.S. strategic objectives.

In their reports from the field, evaluators noted that the Peace Corps was not always completely non-political in its program choices. In Sri Lanka, for example, a number of Peace Corps teachers found themselves superfluous in a country which had one of the highest literacy rates in Asia, a large class of trained intellectuals, and nearly one thousand unemployed local teachers. Evaluator Arthur Dudden could only conclude that the Peace Corps was there for reasons of political prestige: "U.S.- Ceylon* relationships on the matter of the Volunteers' presence seem to be a mixture of package deals, coercion and reluctant acceptance on the part of the host country."[17] Indonesia was another politically attractive country where the host government was courted by Shriver and the Peace Corps. One evaluation report claimed that "The fact that we are there is more a tribute to our persistence and patience and to political considerations than to any sudden recognition of our potential value."[18]

Another report seriously questioned whether the Peace Corps should be in Uruguay, since it had advanced social welfare programs, educational levels were high, and half the population lived in cosmopolitan Montevideo. "Certainly, it is not an underdeveloped nation," wrote evaluator Dee Jacobs. Yet

*On gaining independence in 1972, Ceylon renamed itself Sri Lanka.

the Peace Corps began making overtures to the Uruguayan government in 1961; eventually, in 1963, eighteen Volunteers were accepted. Jacobs suggested that the government's "neutral-to-mildly-hostile stance" towards the United States was an important element behind the Peace Corps' eagerness to begin a program there. The American ambassador was even more explicit, saying that the Peace Corps had a vital role to play in combatting Communist pressures in Uruguay:

> Ambassador Coerr says he feels the Volunteers are already fulfilling "a political purpose." He says the United States "needs their presence" especially in the northern and western areas where the Communists and far-leftists are concentrating attention on the rural sugar workers.[19]

The ambassador concluded that, in his view, the presence and activities of the Volunteers definitely helped to weaken the Communists' "anti-American and anti-democratic stand."

OUTSHINING THE SOVIETS

The Peace Corps' leaders were well aware of the presence of thousands of Soviet teachers all over the Third World. In Guinea, evaluator Philip Cook felt that this provided "an especially appealing challenge . . . if we can continue to recruit, train and find proper assignments for the right categories of Volunteers in Guinea, the Peace Corps may succeed in upstaging the Chinese and Eastern Bloc technicians now working there." The Soviets were also making persistent efforts to penetrate Togo. The Peace Corps contingent and the American diplomatic staff combined did not total the numerical strength of the Soviet embassy in the capital city, Lomé. Cook was again pleased to report that the Peace Corps was making a "substantial impact" in Communist areas.[20]

In Ghana, one of the most volatile of the non-aligned states, evaluator Richard Richter described how the arrival of ninety-eight Soviet teachers had "spiced up" the Volunteers' experience:

> There is a Volunteer in almost every school where there is a Russian teacher. In fact, the Volunteer without a Russian pet feels

cheated. The presence of the Russians, while perhaps somewhat distressing politically, can be viewed favorably in just about every other respect. It adds unusual dimension in the Volunteers' experience and gives us an opportunity to influence some Russians.

Richter underscored the Peace Corps' political potential. "So far," he reported to Washington, "we have outshone our Cold War antagonists both in and out of the classroom."[21]

While Volunteers recognized the element of competition between themselves and their Russian counterparts in the developing countries, they never engaged in narrow, anti-Soviet activities. In Ghana, the local people tended to be disparaging about "those Russians" who often did not speak Twi and who usually seemed cold and aloof. But the Volunteers avoided any comments that might lead to tension. "They [the Russians] know who we are and they're the Russian equivalent of the Peace Corps," said one Volunteer. "Last year one of them was convinced we were spies. Later we used to joke about this with him."[22]

When working together, the Volunteers usually enjoyed cordial relations with their Soviet colleagues. There was often a good deal of professional and, sometimes, non-professional fraternization. In Guinea, sick Volunteers were occasionally attended by Soviet doctors. In Ghana, Volunteers invited Russians to dinner, went out for drinks, and played sports together. One Volunteer was allegedly friendlier with a Soviet teacher than any of the other Volunteers in his town. In some cases, there were even signs of incipient romance. One report described the scene at a Ghanaian Ministry of Education party to which Volunteers and Soviet teachers had been invited:

> One male Volunteer, spotting a fair-haired lovely across the crowded room, asked a Russian official if he might have permission to date the girl. The official very emphatically said the girl was free to do as she wished. The implication was clear: why should anyone suppose that Russia would want to keep a tight rein on the actions of their bright young teachers? It is somewhat disappointing to report that our hero never did date the lass, but he did find another Russian girl teaching in his school.[23]

Peace Corps officials in Ghana reportedly had a recurring nightmare about a Volunteer and a Russian falling in love and wanting to marry.

Sargent Shriver's view of the Cold War was more refined than that of most Americans in the 1960s. While he felt that the global Communist challenge had to be met with a vigorous U.S. response, he did not believe that that response should be limited to financial or military means. He was convinced that, in addition, the United States had to find an effective way of demonstrating to the poor peoples of the world that it supported their economic progress and freedom. In this context, he told Kennedy that "the impression we [the Peace Corps] could make on the neutralist nations could be profound."[24] He added that the Peace Corps represented Kennedy's best opportunity to show that his approach to the Third World was different from that of his predecessors. After meeting with Sekou Touré, Shriver told Kennedy that the Peace Corps, in its unique fashion, could help to steer Guinea and other developing countries away from Moscow:

> Here we have an opportunity to move a country from an apparently clear Bloc orientation to a position of neutrality or even one of orientation to the West. This is the first such opportunity I know of in the underdeveloped world. The consequences of success in terms of our relations with countries like Mali or Ghana, or even Iraq or the United Arab Republic could be very good indeed.[25]

While in Latin America in September 1961, Shriver informed Kennedy that the "leading Commie in Colombia" had just returned from Moscow along with 280 Colombian students whom the Soviets had sponsored on a three-month educational trip. "To make a real dent in the Colombian situation," Shriver wrote, "we should plan on 500 Volunteers." He proposed that, ultimately, Volunteers should be assigned to at least half of the twelve thousand small towns in Colombia.[26] In March 1963, he told Kennedy that in the Cuzco province of Peru, Communists had infiltrated all the *campos* except one; the pocket of resistance was a village where Volunteers had set up a medical clinic and were working in irrigation and public health.[27] In 1962, Shriver relayed his delight (in a letter to his wife, Eunice) that he had been invited to Indonesia to discuss the possibility of a Peace Corps program with President Achmed Sukarno. "Sukarno has been very pro-Soviet," he wrote, "and this is the first time since Jack has been President that Sukarno has invited any operating agency of the U.S."[28]

But while Shriver recognized the Peace Corps' political potential, he always stressed that supplying much-needed skills and establishing people-to-people contact came first. No project was set up for purely political purposes. Even in Uruguay where, as an evaluation report noted, "the political overtones weigh heavier than usual," the Peace Corps' primary objective was to improve the country's economic situation through helping to develop the agricultural sector.[29]

Time and again Shriver insisted that Volunteers were not on the front lines of the Cold War, and he often reminded Kennedy that the Peace Corps should not be classed with standard U.S. foreign policy initiatives. He pleaded with the President not to send military "civic action" teams—like the Special Forces— into the Third World to carry out projects such as digging roads and building bridges because he was concerned that the Peace Corps would become confused with military units doing Peace Corps-type work. "This could kill the Peace Corps," he warned Kennedy. "Past experience shows that large numbers of U.S. armed forces, stationed abroad, tend to accelerate a general militarization of less developed countries . . . which is something we should prevent, not encourage."[30]

Shriver also kept the Peace Corps in countries which had broken off relations with the United States. In the Dominican Republic and Honduras in 1963, and in Panama in 1964, the Peace Corps remained in service despite military coups which had caused the breakdown of formal communication with the U.S. government. He even persuaded Congress to legitimize such unusual behavior by passing an amendment to the Foreign Assistance Act of 1963. Proposed by Hubert Humphrey and Kenneth Keating, the Republican from New York, the amendment authorized Peace Corps programs to continue even in countries which nationalized or expropriated American property without compensation.[31] This seemed to confirm Shriver's assertion that, while the Peace Corps might help the United States outshine the Soviets in some Third World countries, its primary objective was not to bring them over to America's side in the Cold War. "What we are seeking is not the support of these nations, but their success," he said. "If they succeed in their plans for economic, social and political progress, it will not matter much whether they agree or disagree with us, even whether they like us. If they become healthy, democratic societies in their own right, they will not become threats to world peace."[32]

STRATEGIC CONCERNS

While the State Department occasionally requested Shriver to give priority status to some pivotal, non-aligned nation, Secretary of State Dean Rusk believed that the Peace Corps would best operate "outside of the shadows and struggles of the Cold War . . . outside of the constant sense of national advantage which pervades diplomacy."[33] Like Shriver, Rusk felt that the Peace Corps would best serve American foreign policy by remaining distinctively separate from it. He believed that the United States would profit, in terms of political goodwill, from the Peace Corps' initiatives. He acknowledged, however, that any foreign policy benefits would simply be a "by-product to be cherished but not an aim to be deliberately sought."[34]

McGeorge Bundy, Kennedy's national security adviser, did not recall the Peace Corps ever meriting formal discussion in the National Security Council. Harris Wofford suggested that this was because the "Cold Warriors" in the White House and the National Security apparatus did not consider the Peace Corps important enough to use as a weapon against communism, even had they wanted to do so.[35] On the rare occasions when political pressure was exerted from the top, Shriver fought doggedly to preserve the Peace Corps' neutrality.

Between 1962 and 1963, the foreign policy establishment urged the Peace Corps to move into Algeria. The ostensible reason was to help with rural rehabilitation projects; but there was a strong political desire to maximize the American presence in the newly independent North African state led by the socialist

Ahmed Ben Bella. Shriver persistently refused to send the Peace Corps where it was not invited. Irritated by this stubbornness, Harold Saunders and Robert Komer (two national security staff members) asked Bundy to give Shriver "a gentle straightening out" on this matter. Saunders was skeptical of the Peace Corps' argument that it was "independent of strategic concerns." He pointed out that, as a foreign policy priority, Algeria outranked most other countries in which the Peace Corps was working. "Shouldn't we quash this nonsense that the Peace Corps is independent of U.S. policy interest?" Saunders asked.[36]

Bundy tried to persuade Shriver to initiate a program in Algeria. "I know you don't like to get into nasty international political considerations," he wrote, "but nevertheless there are only two or three countries in Africa that are as important, and none more so for the long run." Bundy also suggested that the Peace Corps presence in Algeria would be "mildly irritating to some of those in Europe who are giving us most trouble at the moment" (an allusion to the French, from whom Algeria had gained independence in 1962 after a bitter war). He concluded that "Ben Bella is impressed with the Peace Corps, with you, and with the President. And a little help here might butter a lot of parsnips."[37]

Shriver was unmoved. "I really see very little evidence of the Algerian government's interest in having a Peace Corps project," he told G. Mennen Williams, assistant secretary of state for African affairs. "If the government were really interested, I believe that we would have had a specific request by now. Ben Bella's ambassador is free to come and see me here in Washington at any time."[38] The Peace Corps did not go to Algeria. Nor did Shriver bend to President Johnson's later request to send Volunteers into Vietnam. Indeed, he infuriated Johnson by insisting that the Peace Corps would never go to a country where the United States was actively waging war.[39]

As for John Kennedy's view of the strategic importance of the Peace Corps, he believed that when it came to resisting Communist subversion "you cannot separate guns from roads and schools."[40] He often spoke of halting the Communist advance by developing agriculture, industry, and educational resources in the Third World. To this extent, his perception of the Peace

Corps was influenced by his staunch anti-communism. Yet, while Kennedy clearly saw the United States as "the great and chief guardian of freedom all the way . . . from the American soldier guarding the Brandenburg Gate to the Americans now in Vietnam, or the Peace Corps men in Colombia," he had no illusions about what a few thousand young Americans could achieve overseas in strategic terms.[41] When asked whether Kennedy had ever indicated that he considered the Peace Corps to be strategically important, Shriver answered bluntly: "He never said anything like that to me."[42]

The Peace Corps helped Kennedy in his desire to place a more informal, adventurous emphasis on American foreign policy. He wanted to replace "protocol-minded, striped-pants officials by reform-minded missionaries of democracy," wrote Schlesinger.[43] Kennedy instructed this new breed to make people-to-people contact, speak native languages, eat the same food, and participate in the community life of the uneducated and the needy. "Peace Corps Volunteers will give a fresh, personal meaning to our diplomacy," he said, "by building human relations."[44]

Kennedy rarely interfered in the Peace Corps' affairs. Occasionally he made a suggestion to Shriver or asked a question. In August 1962, he hinted that the Peace Corps should "keep in mind the importance of Latin America, which I think should be a primary area." When he asked in June 1961 why there were no Volunteers going to the Ivory Coast, a newly independent and politically important state in West Africa, Shriver replied matter-of-factly: "I have looked into this matter and find that Houphouet-Boigny [the president] has made no overtures to us requesting the Peace Corps."[45]

Kennedy's primary concern was with the educational impact the Peace Corps might have on Americans and Third World peoples. He was determined to break down the tremendously insular outlook characteristic of America in the early 1960s. At the same time, he knew that in the eyes of many developing countries, the United States appeared as a "harsh, narrow-minded, militaristic, materialistic society." Kennedy was particularly worried that young Third World peoples never got the opportunity to view the more idealistic side of America. "There may be only a thousand Volunteers scattered thinly around through millions of people," he said, "but they give us a chance to call attention to this side of our life which is extremely important and which is so frequently ignored."[46]

Schlesinger remembered Kennedy remarking wistfully about Cuba: "Each weekend 10,000 teachers go into the countryside to run a campaign against illiteracy. A great communal effort like this is attractive to people who wish to serve their country." He saw the Peace Corps as a means of tapping a comparable fund of idealism in Americans. He stressed that this physical representation of American altruism was the most valuable and enduring advantage of the Peace Corps: "[It] gives us an opportunity to emphasize a very different part of our American character, and that which has really been the motivation for American foreign policy, or much of it, since Woodrow Wilson, and that is the idealistic sense of purpose which I think motivates us."[47] Kennedy felt the Peace Corps' value to his foreign policy was as a symbol of this moral impulse.

CHARGES OF IMPERIALISM

Paradoxically, one of the charges levelled against the Peace Corps by contemporary leftist critics was that it went against the American moral impulse and in fact functioned as an arm of American imperialism—economic, cultural, and political. Revisionist historian Marshall Windmiller claimed that Volunteers acted as "advance men" for American capitalism. Arguing that the Peace Corps softened up Third World markets for American business, he wrote that "The more I examine the Peace Corps, the more it seems that its essential role is this kind of public relations work on behalf of American power and influence in the developing world."[48]

Shriver deemed this charge absurd, noting that the Peace Corps had no ties whatsoever to big business.[49] Furthermore, the Peace Corps went to some of the most poverty-stricken countries in the world where people did not have enough money to buy basic food, let alone sophisticated American products. Many Volunteers worked up-country where locals were not likely to be subject to advertising campaigns and Western sales techniques. The predominant Peace Corps objective was not to persuade Third World peoples to buy American goods, or any other goods; on the contrary, the Peace Corps aimed to encourage citizens of developing countries to be self-sufficient and to produce for themselves what their communities needed. In this context, the Marxist critique of the Peace Corps is unconvincing.

Windmiller also charged that the Peace Corps' major function was "to assist in the expansion of American cultural values to develop pro-American, English-speaking elites, and to make America's role in world affairs more palatable." Comparing the Peace Corps to the nineteenth-century British colonial civil service, he argued that it forced Western education, arts, and morals on Third World peoples with the express aim of keeping a firm grip on their political sympathies. British journalist Henry Fairlie agreed that Kennedy sent the youth of America to "the outposts of the empire, to exercise the right to the moral leadership of the planet." He claimed that the Peace Corps fostered the idea that empire-building was an "exciting moral adventure, good for the character."[50]

There was a hint of cultural imperialism about the Peace Corps in the Kennedy years. Endemic to that era was the idea that the export of American values and traditions, of themselves, would be of inestimable benefit to the rest of the world. "Much more than most," noted Lawrence Fuchs, Peace Corps Rep in the Philippines, "Volunteers believed in America's historic mission to spread the value of freedom of choice . . . they agreed with President Kennedy that it is 'the American people who should be marching at the head of the worldwide revolution.' "[51]

Some Volunteers were guilty of acting in a self-righteous, patronizing manner; and in some of the more sensitive of the developing nations, the slightest non-native act — eating canned food, for example — could be regarded as a form of cultural imperialism. For the most part, however, the Peace Corps assiduously sought to avoid association with any form of cultural imperialism. In the "Report to the President," Shriver had stressed that the Peace Corps would contribute to America's education. "This must be a truly international and mutual venture," he told Kennedy. "Our aim must be to learn as much as we teach." Shriver constantly reiterated what the Peace Corps did not want to do: "We do not want to send people abroad who think they are carrying the 'white man's burden' to civilise the rest of the world in their image."[52] The irony was that the more Volunteers tried not to be cultural imperialists, the more attractive—and more influential—they became to their hosts.

For most Volunteers, the overseas experience led to an awareness and a serious questioning of their own customs and beliefs. In effect, the Peace Corps took Americans away from American values. Puzzled by the mores of a different culture, Volunteers were often forced to ask themselves whether they had any right to attempt to change them. One Volunteer in Bangladesh described the problem:

> If you're going to do the job right, it often means being insubordinate. But by being insubordinate you can be accused of cultural imperialism because you're trying to change the system towards something that seems obviously right to you, but may seem only "American" to them. On the other hand, if you just fit yourself into their way of doing things, you feel guilty because you don't think you're contributing much to them or to the Peace Corps. So you end up doing a little of each.[53]

The Peace Corps originated in a culture which placed a greater importance on social change, efficiency, and material well-being than many cultures of the developing countries. To varying degrees, Volunteers were bound to reflect these values overseas. This left them open to the charge of cultural imperialism. Yet, as Evaluation chief Charles Peters argued, "The cultures of the world are so far along the road to getting mixed up with one another that the relevant question is not should this happen, but how can we help the best values win out . . . The point is that there are different ways that our culture and our hosts' are superior to one another and our aim should be to see that the exchange we encourage is of the best elements in each."[54] That was the Peace Corps' objective.

Another persistent charge against the Peace Corps was that it served as an instrument of American political imperialism. At the United Nations, the Soviets made much of the Cold War context in which Kennedy had proposed the Peace Corps, and they constantly attacked this "army of ill-prepared youngsters engaging in nefarious activities in far-off places." Windmiller also cited the Peace Corps as part of America's attempt to police and protect its interests and to establish a Pax Americana over the Third World. "The Peace Corps made Pax Americana seem legitimate and benevolent," he wrote, "counterinsurgency in a velvet glove."[55]

Shriver denied that the Peace Corps ever forced itself on the Third World. In June 1961, in a letter to national security official Walt Rostow, he explained that if people had the impression that thousands of young Americans were about to invade the developing countries then "they did not get it from anything the Peace Corps or the President has stated." Giving specific examples of the Third World's interest in the Peace Corps, Shriver emphasized that the first Volunteers were going to Ghana and Tanzania because both countries had invited them. Nkrumah had called the Peace Corps "a bold, splendid idea," noted Shriver, and Nyerere had expressed his "strong support." Shriver stressed that while the Peace Corps could offer itself to countries, it was those countries' leaders who decided whether they wanted a program, how many Volunteers there should be, and what those Volunteers would do.[56]

In the summer of 1961, the question of imperialism arose regarding the Peace Corps' planned program for Nigeria. Responding to this charge, Ambassador Joseph Greene in Lagos cabled Dean Rusk to emphasize that there would be "no question of Nigeria's sovereign rights as an independent nation being infringed" by the Peace Corps. Nigerian government officials had been consulted at "all stages of negotiations," they had decided where the Volunteers were needed, and they had ensured that the "full employment" of local peoples would not be endangered. Greene assured Rusk that the Peace Corps venture was a "general partnership between the two governments" and that there was no question of political pressure being exerted.[57]

While explaining how the Peace Corps would function to Sekou Touré, Shriver said that it would go "only where needed and wanted; it would be imposed on no one. If it was not wanted, the United States' feelings would not be hurt." Shriver added that Volunteers would be "responsible for their work to the people of Guinea and to their government." Sensitive to the fears of newly independent states, Shriver declared that the Peace

Corps was "not a part of any new colonialism, imperialism or attempt at Americanization."[58]

The Peace Corps' community development projects ran the highest risk of becoming involved in internal politics. The claim of Latin American regional director Frank Mankiewicz that the Peace Corps was a "revolutionary force" was subject to much misinterpretation.[59] The Peace Corps' community development programs were aimed at social reorganization; that is, encouraging people to take the action necessary to secure their community welfare and democratic rights. On occasion, this had political consequences; for instance, the shake-up of the privileged aristocracy in various parts of Latin America. But the principal role of the Volunteer was not in leading a revolt against the mayor or the *alcalde*, but rather in advising and teaching communities about the means available for action. Unavoidably, some political apple-carts got overthrown in the process. "Our job," wrote Mankiewicz, "is to give [local peoples] an awareness of where the tools are to enable them to assert their political power. By that I don't mean register them to vote; obviously, we don't mean to say that the way to a better life is through the Christian Democratic Party or the Socialist Party or the Conservative Party or whatever it may be. When I talk about political power I am talking about the ability to be noticed and to be taken into account."[60]

In fact, Volunteers were strictly forbidden to engage in any kind of political propagandizing or subversive activity overseas and the Peace Corps was meticulous in its avoidance of the slightest involvement in political or military affairs. In Ecuador, when the U.S. embassy tried to persuade Volunteers to distribute anti-Castro leaflets, Shriver put a stop to such solicitation. On another occasion, when he discovered that a political science course taught by Volunteers in an Ethiopian university was being taken by local military and diplomatic personnel, he ordered it to be immediately discontinued. In an unequivocal statement in June 1963, Shriver reiterated that the Peace Corps had no truck with imperialism of any kind:

> The Peace Corps Volunteer goes to a foreign country to work within the country's system; he helps fill their needs as they see

them; he speaks their language; he lives in the way they live and under their laws; he does not try to change their religion; he does not seek to make a profit from conducting business in their country; he does not interfere in their religious, political or military affairs.[61]

CAUGHT IN THE MIDDLE

Many of the Peace Corps' difficulties overseas stemmed from its political naiveté. Young Americans in the early 1960s came from a political environment based, essentially, on consensus. A sharing of fundamental views on property, social structure, language, foreign policy, and so forth, could usually be taken for granted, and election issues generally revolved around questions of degree, detail, and personality. By contrast, many Third World nations were seething cauldrons of sharply defined political antagonisms and ancient social arrangements based on ethnic and class distinctions. But since the Peace Corps' administrators intended Volunteers to be above politics, training programs often neglected these local political conditions. It came as a shock to many Volunteers when they arrived overseas and found that they had to contend with many tension-filled situations.

Peace Corps teachers in Sri Lanka discovered that all educational matters were the subject of intense political debate. "The newspapers are filled by controversies over teachers politicking or being victimized by politicians," noted one report. "Banishments to rural areas are political punishments meted out to teachers and school administrators alike. Promotions and better assignments are more likely to come from interfering M.P.s than from within the educational system." The Volunteers there soon realized that despite their non-political stance, they were the subject of ministerial and parliamentary controversy. An evaluator noted that most Volunteers had tended to see themselves as "some sort of free souls armed with a mission to teach and tied to the U.S. only by financial support."[62] To their chagrin, they learned that Peace Corps life was not that simple.

Peace Corps officials had also hoped that Volunteers would circumvent countries' Cold War posturing and jockeying for strategic favor. Overseas, however, Volunteers could not help but be affected by the tensions inherent in a country's geopolitical position. In some countries, Volunteers were welcomed as prestigious tokens of the government's friendly relationship with the United States. In Nyasaland (which was to become independent Malawi in 1964), evaluator Richard Elwell reported that "Politically, the project has been a smash."[63] The timely arrival of the Peace Corps in 1963 gave a dramatic boost to Dr. Hastings Banda's hopes for nationhood. Banda pointed to the Volunteers as proof that an independent Malawi could get assistance outside the sphere of the British Colonial Office. On the other hand, President Kenneth Kaunda of Zambia refused to invite Volunteers to his country because he feared they would be taken as a sign that he had committed himself in the East-West struggle. He did accept British VSO workers.

Volunteers sometimes found themslves treated as political footballs in their host countries. The Tanzanian government periodically criticized the Peace Corps simply because it wanted to make an anti-American statement which would appease the Soviets and ensure that aid would continue to flow from East as well as West. In Indonesia, the Peace Corps was attacked by the local Communist party not because it was unpopular or inefficient, but because it was American. An evaluation report predicted that, such were the Cold War pressures being brought to bear on Sukarno, the Peace Corps might "get kicked out of here for reasons unrelated to its efforts."[64] This happened in 1964.

Afghanistan, with its government intent on playing the USSR off against the United States, was another place where the Peace Corps found itself in a delicate position. A highly developed grapevine system in Kabul meant that the locals were well aware of the Volunteers' presence. As a Volunteer was cycling to work, he was astounded to hear one camel-driver remark to another: "Oh, he's one of the Americans teaching here now." A policeman was assigned to each street where Volunteers lived to report on their activities. "One slip," said evaluator Thorburn Reid, "and the Peace Corps may be through in Afghanistan."[65]

In Pakistan, America's provision of military assistance to neighboring enemy India in 1962 led to Foreign Minister Ali Bhutto's decision to tilt his country toward China and the Soviet Union. Despite Pakistan's almost total dependence on U.S. economic and military aid, by 1963 America was regarded as a foe. The Peace Corps was caught in this crossfire. In 1961 Pakistan had requested over a thousand Volunteers; two years later, the number had dropped to a handful and those already there were accused of being spies. They were watched carefully, their mail was intercepted, read, and crudely resealed.

Pakistani suspicion was heightened by the innocent, but ill-advised curiosity of a few Volunteers during the communal strife between Moslems and Hindus in 1963. Two Volunteers left their posts to look into rumors of fighting near the Indian border. Shortly after their return from this trip, they were abruptly transferred by the provincial government. For a time, Volunteers were forbidden to travel to India on leave. The Pakistanis feared that they would publicize the wholesale slaughter of Hindus which was then taking place. As tension reached fever pitch, one Volunteer's house was burned down. The local police claimed that it had been used to store weapons, although there was no evidence to substantiate this change. An evaluator's report back to Washington was bleak:

> We have entered what one Volunteer aptly called the "Era of Active Non-Cooperation" and it can be felt at many levels of the government, from President Ayub Khan down to the Sub-Divisional officers, principals, hospital administrators, and other supervisors for whom our men and women work . . . 55 percent of our troubles are attributable to the mutual disenchantment between Pakistan and the U.S. . . . The more frost there is in the air, the less Volunteers are able to do; the less they are able to do, the less they try to do. And the less they try to do, the more we are blamed for poor performance. It is a knot that gets tighter and tighter."[66]

Even when the political winds had been blowing sweetly, Volunteers had had to tread warily in Pakistan; the increasing hostility between Islamabad and Washington made their lives virtually impossible. The evaluation report concluded that "The future looks gloomy both for U.S.-Pakistani relations and for the Peace Corps in Pakistan."

Ghana was another country where the Cold War atmosphere was intense, with Kwame Nkrumah intent on straddling the fence between East and West. He saw his importing of Soviet teachers and technical experts to match Peace Corps Volunteers as a brilliant tactical coup. However, his brushes with the United States over issues such as the Congo, Angola, and South Africa made him appear Bloc-oriented to Americans. Nkrumah was likewise suspicious of the United States. He was convir.ced that the CIA had assassinated Patrice Lumumba, leader of the Congo, in 1961. He was later to blame the CIA for the murder of Kennedy in 1963. Evaluators warned that if there were a serious altercation between Nkrumah and the U.S. government, "he may need a scapegoat, and he may have to turn on the Peace Corps."

For the Volunteer in Ghana, perseverance meant shrugging off the question, "You're not a spy, are you?" Ghanaian students attending the Nkrumah Ideological Institute were told to beware of foreigners from "neo-colonialist nations" (a euphemism for the United States and Britain) because they were all intelligence agents. Volunteers were regularly vilified in the local press. "The chances for any improvement in the political climate are exceedingly slim," reported evaluator Richard Richter in 1964. His warning was underscored by the comment of the American ambassador in Accra, William Mahoney. He cautioned that there should be no more than two hundred Volunteers in Ghana because any more than that would "make the Peace Corps conspicuous."[67]

Flashpoints in the Cold War provided Volunteers with some of their most uncomfortable moments. During the Cuban missile crisis in October 1962, Volunteers all over Latin America were taunted as "imperialists" by students who had been listening to the latest developments on Radio Havana. When a Peace Corps staff member visited Ayacucho, Peru at the height of the crisis, a mob surrounded his hotel chanting, "Peace Corps, War Corps," and "Cuba, Yes! Yanquis, No!"[68]

Most Volunteers resented being included in the Cold War dialogue. "We're not here to plant the flag and give democracy a hard sell," protested one Volunteer in Tanzania.[69] Yet, despite the beneficial work which they performed, Volunteers were often associated with the United States and its backing of unpopular governments. In some countries, Volunteers became much more radically-minded in reaction to militaristic, repressive regimes which had Washington's official blessing. Iran was one example. "Some of us feel we are in an ambiguous position because we are not convinced that our government is pursuing a morally justified policy," a Volunteer said in 1964. "The U.S. government supports the Shah, yet most of the teachers and doctors I work with are very dissatisfied with the Shah's policies."[70] The Soviet Union's Iranian radio outlet exploited this situation and tied the Peace Corps to America's sanction of the Shah.

Not all the Peace Corps' political difficulties were linked to the Cold War. In Arab lands, because of the highly emotional climate surrounding all initiatives by the United States or any other non-Moslem country, the Peace Corps was involved in controversy from the start. Jewish Volunteers, in particular, encountered deep hostility. In Africa, the residual colonial influence presented political problems when Volunteers were confronted by resentful British and French expatriates. Moreover, the new nations were extremely sensitive to the slightest lack of political tact. Two bemused Volunteers in Tanzania found themselves arrested for innocently leaning against a fence during the playing of the national anthem.[71]

Other Volunteers were guilty of more intentional political indiscretions. One young man in Sri Lanka was sent home for actively participating in a local election campaign. When a female Volunteer in a Latin American country became romantically involved with the leader of a local political faction, an opposition group attacked the Peace Corps; the girl's service was terminated. In Ethiopia, a few Volunteers became sympathetic to Eritrean separatism and engaged in criticism of the official church and government. In the Philippines, evaluators noted that some Volunteers, shocked and frustrated at the injustice prevalent in a society dominated by the land-owning aristocracy, were in danger of falling under the influence of professional Marxist organizers.[72]

Sometimes Volunteers had no choice but to play active parts in political imbroglios. In Tanzania, North Borneo, and the Dominican Republic, Volunteers were taken hostage by local rebel gangs. All were freed unhurt. But Reps always had to be aware of the possible political consequences of elections, assassinations, civil strife, and revolutions. Accordingly, most prepared tentative evacuation plans for their group.

In March 1964, the Peace Corps was obliged to leave Cyprus when war broke out between Greece and Turkey. It was the first time the Peace Corps had been forced out of a country. Military or political pressures pushed it out of Sri Lanka, Indonesia, and the Dominican Republic within the next year. In the vast majority of countries, however, the Peace Corps survived most political upheavals and retained its unique identity. While it could not avoid entanglement in all political snares, it was never regarded as a run-of-the-mill U.S. foreign policy initiative, even by the most sensitive of Third World governments.

In Guinea, a report noted Sekou Touré's "special interest in the Volunteers." He was intensely critical of AID, but not of the Peace Corps. Volunteers were allowed a remarkable amount of freedom, and Touré requested an increase in numbers because, he said, "Volunteers comport themselves properly [and] behave themselves well in political matters." In Togo, despite a government coup and the assassination of President Sylvanus Olympio (who had extended the original invitation to the Peace Corps), Volunteers managed to retain a neutral course. "The Togolese confide in them," wrote evaluator Philip Cook, "but do not insist that they take sides or become involved." Cook estimated the Peace Corps to be "the most welcome and commendable U.S. activity in Togo." Even in Ghana, where political nerve-ends were extremely frayed, the local people seemed genuinely to like the Volunteers and to prefer them to the rather standoffish Soviet technicians. Moreover, an evaluation report noted that "For all his irrationality, Nkrumah likes the Peace Corps." Although prone to frequent anti-American outbursts, the Ghanaian leader never expelled any Volunteers. "[Their] contribution is fully realized," wrote evaluator Richard Richter. "The people realize the importance of education. They realize they've gotten their money's worth from the Peace Corps."[73]

THE POLITICS OF PEACE

To Shriver, the Peace Corps was the best example of Kennedy's "new politics of peace."[74] It was also one of the President's outstanding political successes, at home and abroad. There was some criticism on the domestic front from extreme right-wing groups like the John Birch Society who claimed that the Peace Corps was "soft on Communism." But Kennedy fought fire with fire: "If they [the John Birch Society] really want to do something about Communism . . . they will encourage their children to join the Peace Corps," he said.[75] America's general response to the Peace Corps was overwhelmingly favorable. "The Peace Corps is in high gear," Harris Wofford told Kennedy in January 1962. "It can be a big thing going for us politically in the years ahead."[76]

As Wofford pointed out, however, the Peace Corps' greatest impact was overseas. Here, he suggested to Kennedy that it would help restore the sparkle to a foreign policy badly tarnished by the Bay of Pigs fiasco. "You may underestimate the degree to which doubts have been building up since Cuba," wrote Wofford. "There is a growing feeling . . . that there is little new, aside from the Peace Corps and our position on Angola, and that the Democratic foreign policy is in danger of becoming merely a more elegant version of Foster Dulles's." Wofford advised Kennedy that while more needed to be done, "the Peace Corps strikes the note the developing nations are waiting for."[77]

In 1961, a Bolivian government official characterized the Peace Corps as "the point of the lance" in Kennedy's attempt to win a new image and a new respect in countries long neglected by the United States.[78] In 1960, America appeared monolithic rather than pluralistic to the developing nations. Most Americans in the Third World were either diplomats or soldiers. Peace Corps Volunteers gave the emerging nations an indication of the diversity of American life. This had a tremendous effect.

In Gabon, on the West African coast, peasants living in remote villages, where newspapers and radio were not available, asked government officials when the Americans would arrive to help them build schools. The Minister of Education was overheard at a government reception telling President M'ba about the Volunteers he had seen "swinging machetes and carrying heavy loads." In the Dominican Republic in 1964, evaluators contrasted the popularity of the Peace Corps with the rampant anti-American sentiment they had encountered there in 1962. "There is little doubt," they reported, "that having personable, hard-working Volunteers scattered throughout the Republic has favorably and significantly influenced the attitude of the Dominican people towards the U.S."[79]

The Peace Corps was not always responsible for such sweeping changes in attitude. With the United States represented overseas essentially by the State Department, the military, and the CIA—as well as the Peace Corps—it was inevitable that a composite image would be presented. But, the Peace Corps was seen as a distinctive part of that composition. This was exemplified during the anti-American riots in Panama in January 1964 when the local people protected Volunteers in their homes because they were regarded as "gringos who are different."[80]

The step from liking these individual Americans to accepting U.S. foreign policy as a whole was a long and tenuous one. The Peace Corps' more significant effect was to demonstrate to non-aligned, often suspicious countries that the United States was capable of idealism. Thanat Khoman, foreign minister of Thailand, expressed his surprise that the Peace Corps idea was born in the United States: "Many of us . . . thought of this great nation as a wealthy nation, a powerful nation endowed with great material strength and many powerful weapons. But how many of us knew that in the United States ideas and ideals are so powerful?"[81]

In 1961, Ambassador Galbraith in India told Shriver that the Third World would welcome the Peace Corps as "an affirmation of American idealism. It is particularly important in rubbing out the impression that we are excessively prone to military solutions."[82] A young Volunteer in Tunisia relayed a similar message in 1962: "The Peace Corps . . . exhibits to the world the fact that the U.S. is interested, and in a personal, direct and humanitarian way."[83] To Volunteers, their Peace Corps service was a declaration of their faith that they could escape becoming pawns in the Cold War.

This idealistic spirit allowed the Peace Corps to transcend the often murky waters of international politics. Certainly, the Peace Corps emerged in part from America's intense feeling of competition with the Soviet Union. But neither Kennedy nor the U.S. foreign policy establishment attempted to mold it for political purposes or push it in particular directions. For it was almost universally recognized that the Peace Corps had less to do with governments and their foreign relations than with peoples and their human relations.

Speaking before the U.S. Foreign Policy Association in 1963, Shriver asked, "In this world of the Cold War and many little hot wars, of the hydrogen bomb, the Atlantic Alliance and the Sino-Soviet split, what room is there for a Peace Corps?" The day before Kennedy's assassination, a *New York Times* editorial gave the answer: "In a little over two years, the Peace Corps has come to be recognized as the most idealistic arm of our foreign effort and one of its most successful expressions."[84]

13

The Three Goals

I consider the Peace Corps the best gift the United States has made.
— President Diori Hamani of Niger

WIDENING CIRCLES

Sargent Shriver compared the Peace Corps' impact to a series of widening circles, "Like the expanding rings from a stone thrown into a pond." The inner circle represented the Volunteers' immediate accomplishments overseas in terms of technical assistance, skills imparted, and social contacts and friends made. The second ring was the effects the returning Volunteers had on American society: "on institutions and people, on the creation of a new sense of participation in world events." The last circle was more intangible than the others but nonetheless important: "a declaration of the irresistible strength of a universal idea connected with human dignity, hope, compassion and freedom.[1]

Shriver's analogy of the expanding rings roughly corresponded with the three goals of the Peace Corps Act: to provide the developing countries with trained manpower, to help promote a better understanding of Americans on the part of the peoples served, and to help increase American knowledge of other peoples and cultures. "The Peace Corps touched many lives and made them better," Senator Hubert Humphrey said, "yet critics ask what visible lasting effects there are, as if care, concern, love and help can be measured in concrete and steel or dollars." Humphrey contended that "education, whether in mathematics, language, health, nutrition, farm techniques, or peaceful coexistence may not always be visible, but the effects endure."[2]

Not everyone agreed with Shriver and Humphrey's wide-ranging, positive assessments of the Peace Corps' impact. In 1962, journalist Eric Sevareid argued that while Volunteers might have been responsible for "some spot benefits in a few isolated places," they had little to do with the "fundamental investments, reorganizations and reforms upon which the true and long-term economic development of backward countries depend."[3] A more damaging criticism came from C. Payne Lucas and Kevin Lowther, two former Peace Corps administrators. As they saw it, "There was no overall purpose to the Peace Corps' presence in a country . . . Thousands of Volunteers were committed to vaguely conceived and marginal projects that had little or no impact on people's lives or on national development."[4]

Shriver, his colleagues, and most Volunteers disagreed with the view that the Peace Corps did not affect people's lives. Only two years after the first Volunteers went overseas, Shriver claimed the Peace Corps had brought learning to "tens of thousands of children, opened up new worlds for hundreds of villages, brought new meaning and perspective into the lives of thousands of Americans and showed the face of an America which many never dreamed existed."[5] Immersed for two years in the humbling task of helping to satisfy the Third World's development needs, Peace Corps Volunteers were well aware of their limitations. All the same, they deeply resented being treated as wholesome, but essentially insignificant, do-gooders. "Our relevance to the world is not that we are a nice bunch of people offering low-paying overseas fellowships," said Warren Wiggins.[6] Volunteers went overseas to work.

THE FIRST GOAL: MAKING A DIFFERENCE

The Peace Corps put a good deal of emphasis on its first goal: providing trained manpower. Objective studies underscored this. A survey of the Peace Corps' development impact on the Philippines conducted by the Social Research Institute of the University of Hawaii in 1966 reported that:

> Our research teams found palpable evidence of the Volunteers' impact. Thus in 92 percent of these places our interviewees established that educational facilities and new teaching techniques had indeed been introduced. In 53.1 percent of the Peace Corps communities, scholarships had been instituted and material aid given to help the residents improve themselves one way or another. Slightly smaller percentages of communities showed other Peace Corps innovations: community development projects (51.3 percent), voluntary organizations of various kinds (42.3 percent) and recreational facilities (38.9 percent).

The report concluded that "Volunteers definitely made a difference to their communities."[7]

Cornell University studied fifty Peace Corps Volunteers and their impact on villages in the Peruvian Andes. A major finding was that Peace Corps communities were progressing much faster than those without Volunteers. "The Peace Corps program did achieve a measurable impact upon its target communities," this report stated, "and the Volunteers fulfilled one of the three missions defined for the Peace Corps by the Congress in establishing the organization—by contributing to the development of a critical country in the South American region." The study's indices ranged from setting up garbage disposals to helping publish daily newspapers. One town, for example, gained a point with the acquisition of a potable water installation inspired by two Volunteers.[8]

Not all Peace Corps projects lent themselves to this type of statistical analysis. A Volunteer in Senegal observed that there was no way of quantifying whatever benefits he may have brought by "convincing a mother to give protein foods to her child, taking someone with inflamed eyes to a hospital to get his possible trachoma diagnosed and operated on, or giving a shot that saves a life."[9] When returned Volunteers were asked what effect they felt they had had on the development of their host country, they usually preferred vague or non-committal answers. Some said it would be years before they could even begin to judge their contribution. Others said their contribution had been marginal or intangible, resulting primarily from their mere presence in the community and their example of initiative, hygiene, and so on. Some suggested that whatever effect they had had would be lost unless another Volunteer replaced them in their host community.

In terms of development impact, the Peace Corps' contribution was almost always at the micro- rather than the macro-economic level. Studies of the Peace Corps usually concluded that while its people-to-people approach helped alleviate the poverty of the local communities in which it worked, there was little evidence of its leading to a growth in the national economy. Shriver acknowledged that "We could send 500 Volunteers into Borneo and do a good job and the Gross National Product (GNP) might still go down."[10]

When he appeared before congressional committees, the Peace Corps Director could reel off an impressive list of material accomplishments: six inland fish farms begun in Togo, two hundred miles of road laid in Colombia, a 1,790-foot pipeline built in Morocco, a million eggs produced in four poultry cooperatives in India, seventeen bridges erected in Sierra Leone.[11] Such achievements notwithstanding, Shriver admitted that the Peace Corps' major impact was at the local rather than the national level.

The exception to this general rule was the Peace Corps' education programs. These did have a broad and important effect on nations' development. In Africa especially, the presence of nearly three thousand Volunteers in nineteen countries between 1961 and 1964 greatly increased educational opportunities in that continent. The Peace Corps' valuable development contribution was to give tens of thousands of Third World children and youths the chance to go to school. Although critics questioned the value of the Peace Corps' concentration on the education sector, development institutions were to confirm the importance of this effort in later years. "Most of the fastest-growing developing countries without oil have had well-educated populations," stated the World Bank's *World Development Report* in 1980. "More education can help the poorest people climb out of their poverty."[12]

Taking a broader view of education, the Peace Corps' contribution was by no means limited to the classroom. Shriver often argued that the Volunteers' people-to-people approach had widespread educational value, regardless of the specific job they were doing. Evaluators noted that even where projects were unsuccessful or collapsed after the Volunteers left, "they had accomplished something merely by introducing, enunciating and clarifying ideas for the first time."[13] In nutrition projects in Latin America, children were required to wash their hands before they were served any food, line up in an orderly fashion (giving respect to others), wash their plates after dining and store them. Thus Volunteers not only gave the children one square meal a day but taught them basic hygiene and some organizational discipline.[14]

Objective observers tended to agree with Shriver that the Peace Corps' greatest impact was on people's attitudes. When anthropologists from Cornell evaluated the effects of the Peace Corps on the villages of the Andes, they noted the afforestation of eucalyptus trees, the potato-graders built, the agricultural extension projects carried out, and the athletics programs devised. Their conclusion, however, was that the Peace Corps' principal contribution had been in "reinforcing the modern institutions established during the previous decade and in helping to lay the groundwork for others in the future."[15]

Besides its "educational" impact, the Peace Corps did not make deep inroads into Third World poverty at the national level. Unlike larger organizations — the World Bank, the UN, AID — the Peace Corps was not in the business of transferring massive economic resources. Rather, it concentrated on increasing productivity and encouraging self-reliance in the villages and towns often ignored by the more well-endowed development agencies. "In the face of the staggering problems confronting the people of the developing world," Peace Corps official Jack Vaughn wrote, "the economists ask us: Does it really make a difference what a handful of Peace Corps Volunteers accomplished in a small, forgotten village in the Andes?" To Vaughn, and to most Volunteers, the answer was obvious: "Yes," he said, "it makes a difference to that village."[16]

In the 1970s, development experts came to recognize that, in too many cases, the massive transfer of capital to the governments of Third World countries—the traditional form of aid—had failed to "trickle down" and ameliorate the condition of the people at the lowest socio-economic levels. A "grassroots" approach, aimed at directly meeting the basic human needs of the poor was proposed as an alternative. Kennedy's Peace Corps was a forerunner of this approach. From the beginning, Volunteers confronted poverty at the lowest levels.

Because of the many uncertainties associated with this work, Volunteers usually chose to describe their "impact" in personal terms. A Volunteer in Liberia felt his major contribution had been to persuade his pupils to wear shoes, thus helping to reduce the incidence of worms acquired by barefoot children. Another Volunteer in a health program was satisfied that she had persuaded the women of her village to boil water. "In my estimation," said a Volunteer teacher in Bangladesh, "I have accomplished one change: I have gotten the kids to ask questions." In Peru, the Peace Corps' contribution was assessed in terms of:

> The small people, the endless parade of the impoverished ones, the little old ladies who came to the meeting on the wrong day at Calda, the kids on the Volunteer-made swings at Chimbote, the radical University student at Cuzco who wanted to meet me, the Vicosinos, who call a girl Volunteer "Momita," the waiter who often serves Volunteers at a little hotel in Huarez, a police captain who rode in the back of a pick-up truck with me after the bus broke down, a taxi-driver, the five little kids who sang songs for us in Quechua and many others who had one message: "Welcome!"[17]

In these terms, Peace Corps Volunteers judged their contribution to human development in the Third World. "Maybe five years from now, one of my pupils will say, 'Oh teacher Fred taught us that,' " said a Volunteer in Liberia. Another hoped for no more than that "When I leave, somebody will go out and dig a latrine."[18] Some of the long-term effects of the Peace Corps went beyond such modest hopes. In several instances, former Volunteers returned to their host communities to find that the locals had adopted the techniques shown them years before. One

Volunteer, who had done some poultry-breeding in India, finished his term of Peace Corps service feeling he had accomplished little. Yet, when he went back ten years later (in his capacity as an AID official), he was astounded to discover tens of thousands of chickens in the area where he had worked. The villagers welcomed him, took him to their homes, and recalled the names of his fellow Volunteers and what each had done.[19]

THE SECOND GOAL: UNDERSTANDING AMERICANS

Jack Vaughn, Shriver's successor as Peace Corps Director, liked to point out that, in twenty-eight languages of the world, the word for "stranger" is the same as the word for "enemy."[20] To communicate that although Americans were different from Third World peoples, they were not their "enemies," was the Peace Corps' second goal.

In 1960, Third World people had seen few Americans who were not missionaries, GIs, businessmen, or affluent tourists. Peace Corps Volunteers penetrated further into the developing countries than ever before and showed them a different kind of American. "They came to live with our people not in hotels, not in sumptuous houses," exclaimed Thanat Khoman, foreign minister of Thailand in the 1960s, "but in our farmer's huts, sharing their food and the roof."[21] Senator Robert Kennedy suggested that this dynamic was perhaps the Peace Corps' most enduring contribution. "It shows what we stand for," he told a group of Volunteers in 1966, "not a selfish society but a society that's interested in other people."[22]

This seemingly new breed of Americans—who spoke the language, lived under local conditions, and were not afraid to get their hands dirty—had a tremendous impact on Third World peoples. In Asmara, Ethiopia, where (thanks to the GI influence) the average American was treated to a greeting of "Fuck you, Joe," Volunteers came to be addressed with the more respectful, "Good evening, teacher." Volunteers in Tanzania recalled that they were often complimented by locals telling them, "We like you much better than the British." In India, Volunteers were told by local educators that they were more valuable than

Fulbright professors "because Volunteers are always eager for more work, not less." A tribal chief in Sierra Leone claimed that the Peace Corps showed his people "a world we never knew existed. We had never seen people from the outside who wanted to help us. We had heard of America but now we know what it means."[23]

To President Kennedy, this cross-cultural dynamic was crucial. In the wake of *The Ugly American*, the great need for the United States to win friends and allies overseas had been one of the issues of the 1960 presidential campaign. "The Peace Corps has already erased some sterotyped images of America," Kennedy told Congress in July 1963, "and brought hundreds of thousands of people into contact with the first Americans they have ever known personally."[24] One of the first groups of Volunteers to arrive in Nigeria was greeted by a long line of students accusing them of being spies and chanting ominously in Ibo: "The elephant tramples everything in its way." By the time the Volunteers were ready to depart two years later, their students wrote: "To our Peace Corps friends about to leave us we say: We are indeed sorry to see you go. We shall miss you and your services."[25]

The Peace Corps played an extraordinary role in American contact with the Third World in the post-colonial period. At a critical juncture in the developing countries' history, when they demanded something other than the paternalistic aid programs of the past, the Peace Corps provided them with a new and culturally sensitive form of assistance. Because it sought to learn from the people it presumed to help, the Peace Corps was, in turn, accepted by them as a shoulder, not as a crutch. President Diori Hamani of Niger expressed this best:

> The vastness and difficulty of our development effort requires that all its facets be coordinated closely, and I have always been favorably impressed by the ease with which the Peace Corps has adjusted to our structures . . . To be sure, our cooperation was not without its problems . . . But there is one point I consider particularly important: we have both gained, we have both given and we have both received.[26]

Both received. That is what made the Peace Corps special. The point was underscored by a local official in Sarawak who, along with Sargent Shriver, watched some Volunteers help Indonesian government workers cut a road through the jungle. The official turned and smiled at Shriver. "These are not your people any more," he said, "they're mine."[27]

THE THIRD GOAL: EDUCATING AMERICANS

In May 1961, Shriver and Indian Prime Minister Nehru met to discuss the possibility of a Peace Corps program. After agreeing that there were a number of tasks Volunteers could help with, Nehru concluded, "In matters of the spirit, I am sure young Americans would learn a good deal in this country and it could be an important experience for them."[28] It was a prescient comment on the significance of the Peace Corps' third goal: to help Americans understand more fully the peoples and cultures of the developing nations. Nehru sensed that an Indian villager's need to acquire certain technical skills to build a dam or a school was matched by the need of the people of the United States to acquire a deeper insight into the ways of the Third World.

When Shriver offered the Peace Corps' services to Ghana, President Nkrumah inquired whether the United States would also be prepared to accept a reverse flow of Africans in return.* In later years, President Julius Nyerere of Tanzania was to welcome a Peace Corps group by saying that he would be glad to have Volunteers share in the development challenges facing his country. He told Peace Corps officials that he would be "especially happy to educate your Americans."[29]

In his "Report to the President" in February 1961, Shriver had stressed the Peace Corps' potential for educating Americans in world affairs:

---

*A "reverse Peace Corps" was established in 1966 and over a hundred volunteers from various Third World countries taught in American schools. Because of lack of congressional support and funding, however, the program folded in 1969.

> The Peace Corps can contribute to the education of America—
> the letters home, the talks later given by returning members of
> the Peace Corps, the influence on the lives of those who spend
> two or three years of hard work abroad—all this may combine
> to provide a substantial popular base for responsible American
> policies toward the world.[30]

This aspect of the Peace Corps held particular appeal for Kennedy. Since his days in the Senate, he had expressed concern at the few citizens who could bring a real international perspective to national debates. He looked to the Peace Corps to help improve this situation and sent the first Volunteers overseas under the invocation to "come back and educate us."

Volunteers returned from overseas more internationally-minded, more concerned with the problems of others at home and abroad, and more prepared to take action to solve them than they had been two years previously. A Harris poll showed that 85 percent of returned Volunteers in 1964 saw racial inequality as the United States' glaring domestic weakness. Poverty in general was listed second. In foreign affairs, the immediate priority of most returnees was to persuade the U.S. government to withdraw the troops from Vietnam. In second place, they put the development needs of the Third World and the inadequacies of America's foreign aid methods to meet them. Ninety-six percent of returned Volunteers said they would be willing to "participate" in achieving these ends. The level of this commitment differed with each Volunteer; 68 percent said they would be willing to take part in a demonstration and 47 percent claimed they would, if necessary, participate in civil disobedience.[31] Many former Volunteers committed themselves to the civil rights struggle in the 1960s; the Committee of Returned Volunteers, formed in 1964, was in the vanguard of protest against the American military presence in Vietnam.

The effect of returned Volunteers on American society was not gauged solely in terms of protest movements and visible commitments to causes. Most made their mark in quieter, less perceptible ways. Encouraged by Kennedy's signing of Executive Order 11103 in April 1963, which provided for the non-competitive federal appointment of former Volunteers, some 15 percent of returnees took up positions with government organizations at home and overseas. Thus they realized Kennedy's hope that the Peace Corps would provide a steady flow of experienced personnel to the Foreign Service and AID. (By the 1970s, State Department statistics showed that 10 percent of each year's new Foreign Service officers were former Volunteers; by 1980, 12.5 percent of AID staff were returnees.)[32] These newcomers to the traditional agencies of American foreign policy started out at low levels. As they gained promotion, however, they began to make their own unique contribution to U.S. policy overseas. In later years, Shriver would claim that he was constantly amazed at the number of Peace Corps alumni working in U.S. embassies overseas. When the followers of Ayatollah Khomeini seized the U.S. embassy in Tehran in 1979, one of the few embassy staff members who could speak Farsi was a former Volunteer.[33]

Four percent of 1964 returnees went into local or state government (this had increased to 12 percent by 1980). Using the skills developed overseas in intercultural communication, they proved particularly helpful in dealing with members of America's own "forgotten subcultures": blacks, Hispanics, and native Americans. Many former Volunteers also became active in their local community groups. A 1979 survey found that almost half worked with voluntary organizations. Many of those who had served overseas as "community developers" went on to advise city boards or become elected officials in their home towns.[34] A prominent example was Carol Bellamy, a Volunteer in Guatemala who later became president of the New York city council.

Perhaps the most exciting and profound impact of returned Volunteers was in the field of education. In the 1960s, almost 30 percent of returnees went into school or college teaching at home.[35] Describing two years in the Peace Corps as an experience "as significant as a Rhodes scholarship," Dean John Monro of Harvard saw Volunteers as a national education resource of untold value.[36] These Peace Corps "teachers" had enjoyed an unprecedented exposure to cultural diversity, to the international currents of political change, and to the problems of Third World development. They were able to impart the lessons learned to their students. A study revealed that 75 percent of Volunteers discussed their overseas experience with social, political, and religious groups back home.[37] In 1977, the Aspen Institute for Humanistic Studies reckoned that virtually every American community had some kind of contact with the Peace Corps through having had a friend or a family member serve as a Volunteer.[38]

Returning Volunteers also served as a catalyst for renewed interest in voluntary service on the home front. In 1963, Kennedy proposed a "domestic Peace Corps" called the National Service Corps (later renamed Volunteers in Service to America or VISTA). First suggested by Eunice Shriver, Attorney General Robert Kennedy took a special interest in laying the groundwork for the program. Just as Peace Corps Volunteers had proven that young Americans were willing to serve overseas, Kennedy was convinced that they were "equally willing to take on the toughest jobs in this country, whether in a city slum, an Indian reservation or a mining town."[39] When Lyndon Johnson declared war on poverty in 1964, the domestic Peace Corps was an integral part of the program. He chose Sargent Shriver to lead the war.

While the Peace Corps had a number of other significant effects on the United States—as the country's most innovative language-learning institution, for example—the greatest impact was on the Volunteers themselves. They usually felt they had undergone a dramatic change overseas. As one returnee put it: "Whatever we were before, and none of us can quite remember, that's all gone." This personal transition was impossible to quantify. "Until one has had the experience," wrote Neil Boyer, a Volunteer who later joined the State Department, "one cannot realize how important two years can be in a lifetime."[40] Highlighting this problem, a Peace Corps official sent to Washington the transcript of a question-and-answer session on "personal impact" which he had conducted with a Volunteer in El Salvador:

>Official: "How will you describe your Peace Corps experience?"
>Volunteer: "Well, I won't sell it." (Pause)
>Official: "What will you say?"
>Volunteer: "I'll tell them what it was like." (Pause)
>Official: "Such as?"
>Volunteer: "The best goddam experience a young man can have. Worth four years of college."[41]

Coming home, Volunteers had to face the painful process of readjusting to aspects of their society that they had previously accepted as "American." Many found the old ways exceedingly difficult to accept. The founders of the Peace Corps had expected that Volunteers would gain a useful familiarity with the Third World; they had not anticipated that many would undergo an intense personal experience that would profoundly alter their view of their own society. For many it was a cathartic experience. "The thing about the Peace Corps," said one returnee, "is that it doesn't end after two years; it lasts a lifetime." Newell Flather, a Volunteer in the first teaching program in Ghana, claimed that the Peace Corps opened his and many Americans' minds to the possibility of personal growth and change. "The Peace Corps gets people at a very formative age and gives them new ideas," he said. "For many it is the opening of a new frontier of the psyche." Flather, who admitted going to Ghana as a rather quiet and reserved graduate student, returned to help form the radical Committee of Returned Volunteers and, later, play a leading role in Oxfam America.[42]

The story of Paul Tsongas of Massachusetts was another dramatic example of how Volunteers underwent personal change overseas. Tsongas had never been outside the eastern seaboard when he applied to the Peace Corps in 1961. "I had a very insulated existence," he said later. "I was in the first group that went overseas, and I didn't know what the hell I was getting myself in for." Tsongas spent three years teaching math and science in Ghion, Ethiopia. As he recalled it:

> I ended up in a village in Ethiopia with five other Peace Corps Volunteers, and I didn't go anywhere on vacations, just stayed in the village. I broke away from the others and set up house by myself, with my students. I took the ten best kids in the school and I lived with them, just a total immersion in their culture. And, you know, nothing I've ever done before or since has given me the same feeling.

When he came home from Ethiopia, Tsongas felt completely out of place. Studying at Yale Law School, he described his first year home as "catastrophic." Such was the force of his "reverse culture shock" that he developed a slight speech impediment.

Although it took him some time to readjust to the "American way," the Peace Corps had sparked his political and intellectual interests. He quickly moved up the ladder from Lowell city councillor to Middlesex county commissioner to U.S. Representative. Finally, he won a seat in the Senate in 1978. Tsongas cited the Peace Corps as "the formative experience of my life. And if I have a meeting with someone and I find out he's a former Peace Corps Volunteer, there's an instant sort of attachment."[43] One such attachment was Christopher Dodd of Connecticut, a former Volunteer in the Dominican Republic; he too was elected to the U.S. Senate in 1978.

Many former Volunteers also maintained ties to their Peace Corps host communities. A 1979 survey found that some two-thirds of all returned Volunteers kept up their overseas contacts.[44] On occasion, returnees joined together in the United States to give emergency assistance to countries where they had once lived and worked. In 1968, Volunteers went back to Nigeria as workers with an ad hoc committee for Nigeria/Biafra Relief (jointly established by a group of former Peace Corps Volunteers and American Friends Service Committee volunteers). Several former Volunteer groups also organized refugee committees, raising money and resources for medical and health programs administered by missions and relief agencies in Ethiopia, Somalia, and Afghanistan.

When Joe Walsh returned to Guatemala in 1978, where he had been a Volunteer in the early 1960s, he found that a native couple he had known had died, leaving a young son to fend for himself. Walsh adopted the boy and took him back with him to Massachusetts.[45] Many other Volunteers kept up correspondence or visited their former counterparts. In this respect, the Peace Corps had a continuing impact down the years—for Volunteers and their hosts. "Volunteers are personally concerned with the vital interests of the people of 46 nations with which our country has had little contact—except for a few economic interests or where Communism scared us in," observed returnee Roger Landrum in 1965. "We are sons and daughters of America but we are in a sense also sons and daughters of a thousand towns and villages scattered around the world."[46]

TO LEAVE SOMETHING BEHIND

"Volunteers joined the Peace Corps to shape, teach, influence and help other people," wrote Bill Moyers in 1963. "They joined to leave something behind . . . It is in the nature of man to want to leave some monument, however small, however insignificant, however intangible."[47] Moyers and his colleagues had no illusions about what the Peace Corps might accomplish. Along with Kennedy, they hoped only that "In some small village, Volunteers will lay a seed which will bring a rich harvest for us all in later days."[48]

In terms of national economic development, the Peace Corps' effects were not great. However, by concentrating on human resource development in small communities, its impact belied its size. In the 1980s, the World Bank conceded that "Nothing can make widespread absolute poverty melt away overnight . . . but the most valuable resource any country has is its people, the means and the end of economic advance."[49] The Peace Corps had recognized this point since its inception. Bringing only themselves as resources, Volunteers had an impact on the people they worked with.

Host nationals readily acknowledged that the Peace Corps' strength was the individual working at the personal level with materials that were locally available on projects that would continue after they left. "We have a saying in Tagalog," said Emanuel Pelaez, vice-president of the Philippines, "*Ang bato na matigas ay maaagnas din sa kapupulak ng ulam*" (Even the hardest stone will wear away under constant drops of rain). "Your labors in our fields and barrios," he told a group of Volunteers, "will be like those constant drops of rain slowly but surely eroding the boulders of poverty, ignorance and disease which block the road to greatness and prosperity in this country."[50]

In terms of its cross-cultural goals, there was no doubt that the Peace Corps broke down numerous psychological and physical barriers between the United States and the Third World. In Chile, a Peace Corps Rep reported that "Although I certainly do not want to imply that our project is going to remake Chile in our 21 months here, I do know that we will leave a mark in many parts of the central valley. Volunteers have made literally thousands of friends who now know and appreciate Americans as they never had a chance to do before."[51] Indeed, the Peace Corps had such an effect that by the mid-1960s, Tanzania, Ethiopia, Panama, Bolivia, Pakistan, El Salvador, and Honduras were among many countries which had established their own "domestic Peace Corps" programs.* Shriver wrote to McGeorge Bundy in 1963 that "the imitation of the President's idea by other countries is the sincerest form of flattery."[52]

Such broad effects tended to confirm Shriver's belief that the Peace Corps' "universal" message transcended attempts to quantify the three goals. In his view, the Peace Corps' greatest impact was as a representation of America's highest ideals, of the spirit of altruism and openness noted by observers as far back as Tocqueville. To Shriver, the Peace Corps was America's attempt, after a long absence, to reach out to the world's majority: "the young and the raw, the colored, the hungry and the oppressed."[53]

To most Americans in the early 1960s, such a measurement of accomplishment was a great intangible. To the recipients of the Peace Corps, it was not. "The Peace Corps is a greater service to this country than Britain was in a hundred years with all her epauletted and sword-carrying governors," wrote Nigerian journalist Tai Solarin. "These people [the Volunteers] are giving something they alone can give," an old Turkish peasant told a Peace Corps Volunteer in his village. "They are giving of themselves." The old man paused for a moment before he added: "There's nothing like it in the world."[54]

---

*In October 1962, the Peace Corps organized an International Conference on Human Skills in Puerto Rico. Forty-one of the forty-three countries attending later formed the International Peace Corps Secretariat. Its aim was to foster the Peace Corps idea in other countries. The U.S. Congress allowed the Peace Corps to contribute a small number of staff and Volunteers to the Secretariat, but no money.

Kennedy's Children:
The Real Best and Brightest

> I'd never done anything political, patriotic or unselfish
> because nobody ever asked me to. Kennedy asked.
> — A Peace Corps Volunteer

John F. Kennedy liked to remind young Americans that they lived "at a very special moment in history . . . Latin America, Africa, the Middle East and Asia are caught up in the adventures of asserting their independence and modernizing their old way of life."[1] He saw the United States, with its anti-colonial heritage and tremendous economic power, as the natural sponsor of the emerging nations. Through the Peace Corps, he sought to identify America with the revolution of rising expectations taking place in the world.

Many of the new Third World leaders believed that Kennedy was indeed on their side. They accepted the Peace Corps as a manifestation of his empathy with them. "For the first time we found in the United States a man who felt as we did, who suffered with us," explained Juan Bosch, president of the Dominican Republic. "And the Peace Corps, what is it? Kennedy in action."[2]

Because of the Third World's admiration and affection for Kennedy, his sudden death in November 1963 dealt the Peace Corps a particularly cruel blow. The seven thousand Volunteers then in service witnessed at first hand the unprecedented phenomenon of Kennedy's popularity as a figure of hope among the world's forgotten and destitute. In a letter to Peace Corps headquarters, a Volunteer described the reaction to Kennedy's assassination in a small, isolated village of Borneo:

> Living in a community where the native people live in relative seclusion, and know only smatterings of world affairs, I was surprised to look up and find several local boys standing at my door saying that they had heard on a radio that "my President and dear friend had been shot and they were sorry for me because they knew I would be sad." A mourning party was arranged . . . and the natives living in the Borneo interior were reminded that John F. Kennedy was more than an important President and world leader in some faraway capital; he will be remembered as the man who sent his personal representative to live and teach in their village and who showed them some concrete evidence of the American willingness to improve the universal dignity of man.[3]

Volunteers from all over the globe wrote to Washington expressing their sense of personal loss. "In the recent days of sadness I have been trying to sort out some of the significant things about Mr. Kennedy's presidency," wrote Volunteer Michael Woldenberg. "It was not until Kennedy's administration," he concluded, "that the people of America could feel that, through a government program, they had definite ties with other peoples of the world." To Volunteer Maureen Carroll, the one source of consolation at Kennedy's death was that she had been "in the chorus that answered him . . . I am proud to have been a part of an already-established living memorial to Kennedy: the Peace Corps."[4]

The Peace Corps was never to recapture the vigor and enthusiasm that characterized it in the Kennedy years. It carried on; moreover, by 1966 it had doubled in size and Lyndon Johnson called for twenty thousand Volunteers by 1970. As the 1960s progressed however, Johnson and all Americans, especially young Americans, were torn apart by the war in Vietnam. When the first conference of returned Volunteers was held in 1965, many returnees were outspoken in their criticism of the war; some new Volunteers began to carry their protest overseas with them. On the domestic side, Peace Corps recruiters were challenged to justify how one could help a government work for peace in the

Third World while that same government was engaged in a bloody war in the Third World. As cynicism took hold, many young Americans applied for the Peace Corps only because they hoped it would save them from the draft.

Although the Peace Corps became ensnared by the problems which afflicted America in the later 1960s, there was no doubt that Kennedy had sparked the imagination of a generation and made many of them aware of the potential of personal action. "My three years in the Peace Corps taught me that you can never know when your individual effort will make a difference," said Senator Paul Tsongas in later years. "I have re-learned the lesson many times since then."[5]

Throughout the 1960s there was strong evidence of a desire by the generation of Americans in their 20s and 30s to participate in the great issues of their time—through the war on poverty, the civil rights crusade, or the anti-war protest. Collectively, they added up to a movement among America's young people. While Kennedy personally provided much of the inspiration behind the movement, the Peace Corps was in its vanguard. As journalist Jack Newfield put it: "Kennedy liberated energies bottled up for a decade . . . he held up a vision of social idealism, represented by the Peace Corps."[6]

The idealistic vision offered by the Peace Corps was, of course, only one side of the multi-faceted and ambiguous Kennedy legacy. Another side was the expansion of U.S. military force in the Third World as represented by the build-up of counterinsurgency forces of Green Berets and, most notably, the increased American presence in Vietnam. The latter strategies were devised by the so-called best and brightest on the New Frontier: McGeorge Bundy, Robert McNamara, Walt Rostow, Maxwell Taylor, and the rest. These were the men who, according to David Halberstam, "were going to get America moving again . . . brilliant men, men of force . . . men who acted rather than waited."[7] While this glittering array of talent led America into disastrous war in the Third World, the Peace Corps sent young Americans to develop human resources and build bridges with other cultures.

Shriver, Wofford, Wiggins, Josephson, Moyers, and the other Peace Corps administrators did not have the reputation of their White House contemporaries. Indeed, the power-brokers surrounding Kennedy regarded the Peace Corps' leaders as "boy scouts," and the geopoliticians of the National Security Council viewed them and the Peace Corps as peripheral at best. Yet, this unusual group of dedicated officials initiated a massive overseas program overnight which harnessed the idealism of a generation of Americans and reached out to the Third World at a salient point in history. In that sense, they were the real best and brightest on the New Frontier. Columnist James Reston was one of the few observers of the Kennedy administration to recognise this. "Of all the agencies of the federal government," he wrote in 1963, "only the Peace Corps has surpassed the hopes and claims of the Kennedy administration . . . [It] stands above the rest as the only thing new and vigorous that has managed to avoid the pessimism of intractable problems."[8]

The Peace Corps' leaders recognized what many White House strategists did not: that the movement for independence in the Southern Hemisphere was one of the great historical forces of the twentieth century. In placing thousands of Americans overseas to work with the emerging nations, the Peace Corps attempted to put the United States on the right side of that movement. Events as far apart as the war in Vietnam and the seizure of the American hostages in Iran were to underscore that this was a far more penetrating policy idea than most American politicians realized. As Shriver had stated in his initial Report on the Peace Corps: "What the world most needs from this country is better understanding of the world."

In the 1970s and 1980s, as the world became an increasingly interdependent place, this kind of understanding became all the more vital to America's future. "We [the United States] are no longer masters of our own destiny," observed historian Henry Steele Commager. "Every major problem that confronts us now is global and can be solved only through cooperation with other nations."[9] The Peace Corps was an early, dramatic step in the direction of global cooperation.

As Kennedy presented it in 1960, the Peace Corps did genuinely open up new frontiers for Americans. Such was the force of the idea, that decades after Kennedy's death, his name continues to be the one most commonly associated with the agency.

As the people of the Dominican Republic had said, the Volunteers were "hijos de Kennedy"—Kennedy's children.

Kennedy said that he got particular satisfaction from the Peace Corps because he felt it was "the most immediate response that the country has seen to the whole spirit which I tried to suggest in my inaugural."[10] In the sense that all Volunteers since 1961 have responded to the challenge to "ask not," they are all Kennedy's children.

Notes

PREFACE

1. There were nine hundred U.S. military advisers in South Vietnam in January 1961 as John F. Kennedy assumed the presidency. The Pentagon immediately requested him to dispatch 3,600 combat troops. Kennedy compromised by sending one hundred military advisers and four hundred Green Berets. Arthur M. Schlesinger, Jr., *Robert Kennedy and His Times* (Boston: Houghton, Mifflin, 1978) p. 703.

2. See, for example, the "Vietnam" series in *The Washington Post*, April 14-19, 1985.

3. In 1985, 5,300 Volunteers were working in sixty countries. *Peace Corps News*, April 1985 (Peace Corps, Washington, D.C.)

4. Paul A. Laudicina, *World Poverty and Development: A Survey of American Opinion* (Washington D.C.: Overseas Development Council, 1973).

5. Of the eighty-eight countries in which the Peace Corps has operated, it has asked or been asked to leave forty. The Peace Corps has subsequently re-entered eleven of these countries.

6. Sargent Shriver, Peace Corps Director from 1961-66, was succeeded by Jack Vaughn (1966-68). He was followed by: Joseph Blatchford (1969-71); Kevin O'Donnell (1971-72); Donald Hess (1972-73); Nicholas Craw (1973-74); John Dellenback (1975-77); Carolyn Payton (1977-78); Richard Celeste (1979-80); and Loret Ruppe (1981-).

7. Sargent Shriver was Peace Corps Director 1961-66. Between 1964 and 1968 he was also Director of the Office of Economic Opportunity (more commonly known as the War on Poverty). Shriver was U.S. ambassador to France between 1968 and 1970. In 1972 he ran for the Vice Presidency of the United States on the Democratic ticket with George McGovern. In 1976 he contested, unsuccessfully, a number of primaries as a presidential candidate. He then practiced international law, while remaining politically active.

Harris Wofford was Kennedy's special assistant for Civil Rights, 1961-62. In 1962 he went to Ethiopia as the Peace Corps' country director and special representative for Africa. Wofford was an associate director of the Peace Corps, 1964-66. In later years, he became president of Bryn Mawr college, international lawyer, adviser to presidential candidates and author of a critically acclaimed book on the 1960s, *Of Kennedys and Kings* (1980).

Warren Wiggins was a deputy director of the Peace Corps. On leaving the agency in 1967, he set up a successful, private development assistance agency, Transcentury Inc., based in Washington, D.C.

William Josephson resigned as Peace Corps general counsel in 1966. He later became special counsel to the New York City Board of Education and, in the 1970s, played an important role in helping to resolve the City's fiscal crisis. Since 1969, Josephson has also been a trustee of the Mexican-American Legal Defense and Education Fund. He went on to found and become first president of the Peace Corps Institute in 1980. The Institute, a non-profit organization, supports efforts that promote understanding within the United States of the developing countries. This objective is commonly referred to as the Peace Corps' "third goal."

Bill Moyers was the Peace Corps' associate director for public affairs and, in 1963, a deputy director of the agency. He was an aide to President Johnson from 1964 until 1966 when his opposition to the Vietnam war forced him to leave the White House. Moyers went on to become one of America's foremost political commentators.

8. William O. Douglas, Oral History Interview conducted by the John Fitzgerald Kennedy Memorial Library, Boston (hereafter referred to as JFKML), p. 36.

1. PEACE CORPS PRECEDENTS

1. Toribio Motolina, *History of the Indians of New Spain* (Berkeley, Calif.: Cortes Society, Bancroft Library, 1950), book 3, chap. 4, pp. 193–96.

2. William Kellaway, *The New England Company* (New York: Barnes & Noble, 1961), p. 85.

3. John Maxwell Hamilton, "The American Perspective on Foreign Aid," World Affairs Seminar, Ohio State University, Jan. 25, 1984.

4. Theodore C. Sorensen, *Kennedy* (New York: Harper & Row, 1966), p. 208; and Norman J. Parmer, "Foreword," *The Annals of the American Academy of Political and Social Sciences* (Philadelphia: May 1966). Hereafter referred to as *Annals*.

5. *Congressional Record* (hereafter referred to as *C.R.*), June 5, 1961, 87th Cong., 1st Sess., vol. 107, pt. 6: 16953 (Moss), 16984 (Young).

6. *New York Times* (hereafter referred to as *NYT*), "The Challenge to Our Youth," editorial, Mar. 14, 1961, p. 34.

7. John F. Kennedy, "Remarks to a Group of Peace Corps Volunteers before Their Departure for Ghana and Tanganyika," Aug. 28, 1961, *Public Papers of the President* (hereafter referred to as *Public Papers*), vol. I, p. 570.

8. Sargent Shriver's remarks in letter to Congressman John M. Ashbrook. Reprinted in *C.R.*, Sept. 13, 1961, 87th Cong., 1st Sess., vol. 107, pt. 15: 19251.

9. Merle Curti, *American Philanthropy Abroad* (New Brunswick, N.J.: Rutgers University Press, 1963), pp. 26–38.

10. John F. Kennedy, "Remarks in Bonn at the Signing of a Charter Establishing the German Peace Corps," June 24, 1963, *Public Papers*, vol. III, p. 503.

11. Charles J. Wetzel, "The Peace Corps in Our Past," *Annals*, May 1966, p. 9.

12. John F. Kennedy, "Remarks to Student Volunteers Participating in Crossroads Africa," June 22, 1962, *Public Papers*, vol. II, p. 504.

13. John F. Kennedy, "Staffing a Foreign Policy for Peace," Nov. 2, 1960. U.S. Subcommittee on *Freedom of Communications*, pt. 1, The Speeches of Senator John F. Kennedy, Presidential Campaign, 1960 (Washington, D.C.: U.S. Government Printing Office), pp. 862–85 (hereafter referred to as *Freedom of Communications*).

14. *International Voluntary Services* (pamphlet printed by IVS Inc., Washington, D.C., 1960).

15. Alec Dickson, "Voluntary Service Overseas," *Times Educational Supplement*, Dec. 2, 1960.

16. Charles E. Wingenbach, *The Peace Corps: Who, How and Where* (New York: McGraw Hill, 1963), pp. 34-35).

17. Sargent Shriver, "Report to the President on the Peace Corps," Feb. 1961, President's Office Files (hereafter referred to as POF), box 85, JFKML.

18. William James, *Memories and Studies* (New York: Longmans, Green & Co., 1911), pp. 267–96.

19. Arthur M. Schlesinger, Jr., *A Thousand Days: John F. Kennedy in the White House* (New York: Fawcett Premier Books, 1971), p. 557.

20. Helen B. Shaffer, "Government Youth Corps," *Editorial Research Report*, Jan. 4, 1961.

21. John F. Kennedy quoted in Teresa Hayter, *Aid as Imperialism* (London: Penguin Books, 1974), p. 5.

22. Point Four tooks its name from President Truman's "bold, new plan" for American technical assistance to and private investment in the Third World announced in 1949. This was, literally, the "fourth point" in a program for American foreign policy which included the UN, the Marshall Plan, and NATO. Point Four evolved into the International Cooperation Administration in the 1950s and then into the Agency for International Development in 1961.

23. Henry Reuss, Oral History Interview, conducted by JFKML, p. 70.

24. Wetzel, "The Peace Corps in Our Past."

25. Sargent Shriver, *Point of the Lance* (New York: Harper & Row, 1964), p. 13.

26. See: Henry Reuss, "A Point Four Youth Corps," in *Commonweal*, May 6, 1960, pp. 146–47; and Henry Reuss, Oral History Interview, conducted by JFKML, p. 71. Richard L. Neuberger of Oregon introduced a companion bill to Reuss's in the Senate.

27. Hubert H. Humphrey, *The Education of a Public Man: My Life in Politics* (New York: Doubleday, 1976), p. 229.

28. Ibid., p. 250.

29. *C.R.*, June 15, 1960, 86th Cong., 2d Sess., vol. 106, pt. 10: 12634–38.

30. Humphrey, *Education of a Public Man*, pp. 229–30.

31. U.S. House of Representatives, Committee on Foreign Affairs, "Mutual Security Act of 1960," *Report* (no. 1464), 86th Cong., 2d Sess., pp. 28–29.

32. For further information on the Peace Corps' "founding fathers" see: *C.R.*, Aug. 24, 1961, 87th Cong., 1st Sess., vol. 107, pt. 12: 16982 (on Javits); *NYT*, Nov. 4, 1960 (on Bowie); Samuel P. Hayes, *An International Peace Corps: The Promise and the Problems* (Washington: Public Affairs Institute, 1961), p. 12 (on Rostow); *C.R.*, Mar. 21, 1961, p. 4340 (on Shapp); James Reston, *Sketches in the Sand* (New York: Vintage Books, 1967), p. 18 (on Reston); William O. Douglas, Oral History Interview, conducted by JFKML, p. 23 (on Douglas); *C.R.*, June 20, 1961, p. 10866 (on Bowles). Congressman Barratt O'Hara of Il-

linois claimed to have given material on the Peace Corps to Chester Bowles during the 1960 campaign; Bowles himself had a long-time, general interest in the idea and gave a speech on the subject at the University of Michigan in late October 1960. Schlesinger in *A Thousand Days*, p. 557 and Sorensen in *Kennedy*, p. 208 both partly attribute Kennedy's final proposal of a Peace Corps to General James Gavin's ideas.

33. Henry Reuss, Oral History Interview, conducted by JFKML, p. 71.

2. THE MEETING OF IDEA AND FATE

1. *NYT*, Nov. 3, 1960, p. 1.

2. Personal interview, David F. Powers, Oct. 30, 1978, Boston. This account of JFK's Cow Palace address owes a great deal to Mr. Powers, who was with Kennedy on every stop of the 1960 campaign.

3. Pierre Salinger letter to George Sullivan, Oct. 28, 1963. Central Subject Files (hereafter referred to as CSF), box 126, JFKML.

4. John F. Kennedy, "Staffing a Foreign Policy for Peace," Nov. 2, 1960, in *Freedom of Communications*, pt. 1, pp. 1237–41.

5. Ibid.

6. *NYT*, Nov. 3, 1960, p. 1.

7. *Freedom of Communications*, pt. 1, pp. 898–943; John F. Kennedy speech in Manchester, New Hampshire, Nov. 7, 1960; speech in Chicago, Nov. 4, 1960.

8. Richard M. Nixon, "Statement by the Vice-President of the United States, Peace Corps," Nov. 6, 1960, in *Freedom of Communications*, pt. 2, p. 1060.

9. *Freedom of Communications*, pt. 1, p. 898; John F. Kennedy, speech in Chicago, Nov. 4, 1960.

10. Richard M. Nixon, quoted in *NYT*, Nov. 7, 1960, p. 3.

11. Ibid.

12. Sorensen, *Kennedy*, p. 239. Kennedy's winning margin in the electoral college was 303 to 219.

13. Arthur M. Schlesinger, Jr., *Kennedy or Nixon: Does It Make Any Difference?* (New York: Macmillan, 1960).

14. Paul B. Fay, *The Pleasure of His Company* (New York: Harper & Row, 1967), p. 59.

15. Gavin quoted by William Safire, *Safire's Political Dictionary* (New York: Ballantine Books, 1978), pp. 520–21. Also, personal interviews, Frederick Dutton, Dec. 15, 1978, Washington, D.C.; J. William Fulbright, Dec. 19, 1978, Washington, D.C.; Ralph Dungan, Dec. 12, 1978, Washington, D.C.; David F. Powers, Oct. 30, 1978, Boston.

16. Pierre Salinger letter to George Sullivan, Oct. 28, 1963, CSF, box 126, JFKML.

17. College News Conference, Feb. 21, 1960, New York City.

18. Richard Goodwin letter to Archibald Cox, Mar. 12, 1960, Staff Files of Theodore C. Sorensen, box 24, JFKML.

19. Humphrey, *The Education of a Public Man*, p. 229.

20. Paul A. Smith, ed., *Official Report of the Proceedings of the Democratic National Convention and Committee* (Washington, D.C.: National Document Publishers, 1964).

21. Solis Horwitz, Oral History Interview, conducted by JFKML, p. 5.

22. Samuel P. Hayes, "Proposal for an International Youth Service," Sept. 30, 1960, Pre-Presidential Files, box 993, JFKML.

23. Lyndon B. Johnson, "Address to the University of Nebraska Student Convocation," Sept. 22, 1960, Lincoln, Nebraska, in Pre-Presidential Daily Diary, Jan. 1959–Mar. 1961, The Lyndon B. Johnson Memorial Library, Austin, Texas.

24. *New Republic*, Dec. 21, 1963.

25. John F. Kennedy, "Message to Nation's New Voters," Oct. 5, 1960, in *Freedom of Communications*, pt. 1, pp., 1083–84.

26. Personal interview, David F. Powers, Oct. 30, 1978, Boston. This account of events at Michigan in the early hours of Oct. 14, 1960 owes much to Mr. Powers.

27. Ibid. Kennedy's remarks at the University of Michigan are reprinted in the *Volunteer* magazine, Dec. 1963, p. 4.

28. Shriver, *Point of the Lance*, p. 10.

29. Harris Wofford, *Of Kennedys and Kings: Making Sense of the Sixties* (New York: Farrar, Straus & Giroux, 1980), p. 247.

30. Ibid., p. 249.

31. *NYT*, Oct. 15, 1960.

32. John F. Kennedy, "Speech to American Legion," Oct. 18, 1960, Miami, Florida, in *Freedom of Communications*, pt. 1, p. 1158.

33. John F. Kennedy, "Speech at Smallenburg Shopping Center," Oct. 29, 1960, Willow Grove, Pennsylvania, in *Freedom of Communications*, pt. 1.

34. Theodore C. Sorensen, "The Election 1960," in *The History of American Presidential Elections* by Arthur M. Schlesinger, Jr., Fred L. Israel, and William P. Hansen (New York: McGraw-Hill, 1971), vol. 4, pp. 34–64.

35. Personal interview, Theodore C. Sorensen, Dec. 8, 1978, New York City.

36. John F. Kennedy, quoted in Schlesinger, *A Thousand Days*, p. 488. Kennedy's great-grandfather, Patrick Kennedy, emigrated to Boston from Ireland in the 1840s.

37. John F. Kennedy quoted in ibid., p. 511.

38. John F. Kennedy, *The Strategy of Peace* (New York: Harper & Row, 1960). "Speech on the Independence of Algeria," July 2, 1957. This speech caused a furor at home and abroad and moved Dean Acheson, assistant secretary of state, to describe Kennedy as "that unformed young man."

39. John F. Kennedy, quoted in Richard D. Mahoney, *JFK: Ordeal in Africa* (New York: Oxford University Press, 1983), p. 29.

40. Ibid., p. 28 (on the African Educational Development Fund); *Congressional Quarterly Almanac*, vol. 16, 1960, pp. 838–39 (on Point Four); John Galloway, ed., *The Kennedys and Vietnam* (New York: Facts on File Inc., 1971), p. 13 (on Friends of Vietnam); and *Freedom of Communications*, pt. 1, p. 1275, "Background Memorandum Prepared by Senator Kennedy's Office – The Facts on Grants to African Students Airlift, Aug. 1960.

41. "Remarks of President Kennedy and President Abboud of the Republic of Sudan," Oct. 4, 1961, in *Public Papers*, vol. I, p. 644.

42. Harris Wofford, Oral History Interview, conducted by JFKML, p. 2.

43. John F. Kennedy, speech entitled "A New Approach on Foreign Policy," June 14, 1960. Reprinted in *The Strategy of Peace*, p. v.

44. John F. Kennedy, "Address to the American Society of African Culture," June 28, 1959. Reprinted in *The Strategy of Peace*, p. 163.

45. John F. Kennedy, "Address at a Democratic Dinner," Dec. 15, 1958. Reprinted in *The Strategy of Peace*, p. 173.

46. John F. Kennedy, "The Situation in Indochina," June 3, 1954, in *A Compilation of Statements and Speeches made during his service in the U.S. Senate and House of Representatives*, (Washington, D.C.: Legislative Reference Service, Library of Congress), p. 1004.

47. Schlesinger, *A Thousand Days*, p. 557.

48. Schlesinger, *Robert Kennedy and His Times*, p. 417.

49. Ibid.

50. John F. Kennedy, speeches at Lorain Stadium, Ohio, Sept. 27, 1960, and Paducah, Kentucky, airport, Oct. 8, 1960, in *Freedom of Communications*, pt. 1, pp. 369 and 529.

51. John F. Kennedy, "Staffing a Foreign Policy for Peace," Nov. 2, 1960, San Francisco, California, in *Freedom of Communications*, pt. 1, p. 1240.

52. The President's Commission on National Goals, *Goals for Americans* (New York: The American Assembly, Columbia University, 1960), p. 1.; Jay H. Cerf and Walter Pozen, eds., *Strategy for the Sixties* (New York: Foreign Policy Clearing House, Praeger Press, 1960), p. 74.; and Walter Lippmann, *The National Purpose* (New York: Holt, Rinehart & Winston, 1960).

53. Nathan M. Pusey quoted in Henry Fairlie, *The Kennedy Promise* (New York: Dell Publishing Co., 1973), p. 22.

54. Arthur M. Schlesinger, Jr., "The Shape of National Politics to Come," Pre-Presidential Papers, JFKML.

55. John F. Kennedy, "Acceptance Speech at the Democratic National Convention," July 14, 1960, in Paul Smith, ed., *Official Report of the Proceedings of the Democratic National Convention*.

56. John F. Kennedy, "The Years the Locusts Have Eaten," Nov. 13, 1959. Speech reprinted in *The Strategy of Peace*, p. 235.

57. Schlesinger, *Robert Kennedy and His Times*, p. 455.

58. Roger Hilsman, *To Move a Nation; The Politics of Foreign Policy in the Administration of John F. Kennedy* (New York: Dell Publishing Co., 1967), p. 86.

59. *Freedom of Communications*, pt. 1, pp. 315, 744, 1239, and 1618.

60. Sorensen, *Kennedy*, p. 229.

61. Eugene Burdick and William J. Lederer, *The Ugly American* (New York: Norton & Co. 1958). Quotations from the cover of the paperback edition (1960). See also, John Kenneth Galbraith, *The Affluent Society* (Boston, 1958); David Riesman, *The Lonely Crowd* (New Haven, 1950); Daniel Bell, *The End Of Ideology: On the Exhaustion of Political Ideas in the Fifties* (Glencoe, Ill., 1960); Thomas Loeber, *Foreign Aid: Our Tragic Experiment* (New York, 1961).

62. Burdick and Lederer, *The Ugly American*, pp. 236–39.

63. John F. Kennedy, "Staffing a Foreign Policy for Peace," Nov. 2, 1960, San Francisco, California, in *Freedom of Communications*, pt. 1, p. 1238.

64. Quoted in Arthur M. Schlesinger, Jr., *The Crisis of Confidence* (New York: Houghton-Mifflin, 1969), p. 153.

65. Hayden quoted in Paul Cowan, *The Making of an Un-American* (New York: Viking Press, 1970), p. 81. Cowan, a Volunteer in the mid-sixties, recalled Hayden talking about Kennedy's speech at Michigan in a "genuine, deeply nostalgic" tone. Hayden was one of the Chicago Seven and was in the

vanguard of protest against the Vietnam War in the late 1960s.

66. David Gelman and Patricia McDermott, Evaluation Report on Recruiting, May 1965, Peace Corps Library (hereafter PCL), Washington, D.C.

3. LAUNCHING THE PEACE CORPS

1. Walt Rostow letter to Fred Holborn (office of Senator Kennedy), Nov. 15, 1960, POF, box 64, JFKML.
2. John F. Kennedy letter to Walt Rostow, Nov. 16, 1960, Personal Papers of Max Millikan, box 1, JFKML.
3. *Washington Post*, Nov. 20, 1960.
4. *NYT*, Nov. 7, 1960, p. 35.
5. Figure given by Senator Hubert Humphrey in *C.R.*, June 1, 1961, 87th Cong., 1st Sess., vol. 107, pt. 6: 9287.
6. Alan C. Elms, "New Frontier: The Peace Corps," *Nation*, Dec. 3, 1960.
7. *NYT*, Dec. 18, 1960, section IV, p. 7.
8. See, for example, Americans Committed to World Responsibility, *Working Papers for the National Conference on Youth Service Abroad* (Ann Arbor: University of Michigan, 1961); Reverend Theodore M. Hesburgh, *A Plan For A Peace Corps in Conjunction with American Universities and Colleges* (Notre Dame, Ind: University of Notre Dame, 1960); United States National Student Association, *Point Four Youth Corps* (Philadelphia: National Student Association, 1960); Victor G. Reuther, *Goals for United States Peace Corps* (Washington, D.C.: United Auto Workers, 1960); Industrial Union Development, *The Kennedy Plan* (University of Utah, 1960); American Friends Service Committee, *Observations Relevant to the Proposed Point Four Youth Corps Program* (Philadelphia, 1960); Committee on Educational Interchange Policy, *A Proposal for the Establishment of an International Youth Service* (New York: Institute of International Education, 1960).
9. See: AFL-CIO Executive Council on the Peace Corps, "Statement," June 29, 1961 (Unity House, Penn.); and International Voluntary Services, "Statement Regarding Its Overseas Experience with Point Four Youth Corps-Type of Personnel," Dec. 19, 1960.
10. Max Millikan memorandum to President-elect Kennedy, Dec. 30, 1960; Personal Papers of Max Millikan, box 1, JFKML.
11. John F. Kennedy, "An International Youth Service" (New York City: Press Office of John F. Kennedy), Jan. 9, 1961, Personal Papers of Gerald Bush (hereafter referred to as Bush Papers), JFKML.
12. *NYT*, Jan. 13, 1961, p. 28; Gallup poll results in *C.R.*, Feb. 2, 1961, 87th Cong., 1st Sess., vol. 107, pt. 2: 1662.
13. John F. Kennedy, "Inaugural Address," Jan. 20, 1961, *Public Papers*, Vol. I, p. 3.
14. Shriver, *Point of the Lance*, p. 12.
15. David Halberstam, *The Best and the Brightest* (New York: Random House, 1969), p. 221.
16. Personal interview, Sargent Shriver, Oct. 3 and 10, 1978, Washington, D.C. For further information on Sargent Shriver's background, see Robert A. Liston, *Sargent Shriver: A Candid Portrait* (New York: Farrar, Straus & Co., 1964).
17. Harris Wofford, Oral History Interview, conducted by JFKML. Also, Wofford, *Of Kennedys and Kings*, p. 253.
18. Harris Wofford, Oral History Interview, conducted by JFKML, p. 100.

19. Personal interview, Sargent Shriver, Oct. 3, 1978, Washington, D.C.

20. The International Cooperation Administration, *The National Peace Corps* (Washington, D.C., Feb. 1961); Hayes, *An International Peace Corps*; Maurice Albertson, Pauline Birky, and Andrew Rice, *A Youth Corps for Service Abroad: Preliminary Report* (Colorado State University Research Foundation, Jan. 1961). Among the academic institutions which sent in reports were Harvard, Princeton, University of California, Yale, New York University, Swarthmore College, American University, University of Utah, Monmouth College, and Grinnell College. Among the foundations and institutions were: Rockefeller, Brookings, the Foreign Policy Clearing House, the National Council of Churches, and the Stanford Research Unit. As well as these, the Kennedy Library and Peace Corps Archives have hundreds of reports from various groups and individuals.

21. Alec Dickson letter to Harris Wofford, Personal Papers of Harris Wofford, box 6, JFKML

22. Reuss quoted in *NYT*, Jan. 29, 1961, p. 45; see also *NYT*, Feb. 26, 1961, section VI, p. 4 (letters to the editor).

23. *NYT*, Jan. 30, 1961, p. 22 (letters to the editor).

24. *NYT*, Feb. 5, 1961, section VI, p. 26.

25. John F. Kennedy, "Annual Message to the Congress on the State of the Union," Jan. 30, 1961, *Public Papers*, Vol. I, p. 19.

26. Names listed in rough draft of article by Sargent Shriver, "Two Years of the Peace Corps," in POF, box 85, JFKML. The final version of the article appeared in *Foreign Affairs* in July 1963.

27. Shriver quoted in "Sargent Shriver Comes Back for a Day," *Peace Corps Times*, Dec. 1978/Jan. 1979, vol. 1, no. 4, p. 11 (Washington, D.C.: U.S. ACTION).

28. Information on Warren Wiggins in *Who's Who in Peace Corps Washington* (Washington, D.C.: U.S Peace Corps, 1962), p. 29.

29. Warren Wiggins, "The Broader Bridge: A New Frontier for Education," address to California Teacher's Association, Mar. 1, 1963, in "Speeches of Warren Wiggins," PCL.

30. William Josephson, Oral History Interview, conducted by JFKML; and personal interview, William Josephson, Dec. 6, 1978, New York City.

31. Warren Wiggins, *The Towering Task* (Washington, D.C.: U.S. Peace Corps, 1961).

32. Personal interview, Warren Wiggins, Oct. 12, 1978, Washington, D.C.

33. Harris Wofford, Oral History Interview, conducted by JFKML, p. 100.

34. Shriver quoted in *Who's Who in Peace Corps Washington*, p. 29.

35. Wiggins, *The Towering Task*.

36. Ibid.

37. Ibid.

38. Sargent Shriver, "Two Years of the Peace Corps," *Foreign Affairs*, July 1963, p. 695; and William Josephson, Oral History Interview, conducted by JFKML, pp. 7–12, 49.

39. William Josephson memorandum to Sargent Shriver, Feb. 27, 1961, Bush Papers, box 2, JFKML.

40. William Josephson memorandum to Sargent Shriver, Feb. 13, 1961, in Personal Papers of William Josephson (hereafter referred to as Josephson Papers), JFKML.

41. Harris Wofford, Oral History Interview, conducted by JFKML, p. 106.
42. Shriver, "Two Years of the Peace Corps," p. 695.
43. John F. Kennedy, "Remarks to the Delegates for the Youth Fitness Conference," Feb. 21, 1961, *Public Papers*, vol. I, p. 113; Shriver recalled Kennedy's phone calls in "Sargent Shriver Comes Back for a Day," *Peace Corps Times*.
44. Sargent Shriver quoted in *Who's Who in Peace Corps Washington*, p. 7.
45. William Josephson, Oral History Interview, conducted by JFKML, p. 8.
46. Sargent Shriver, "Report to the President on the Peace Corps," in POF, box 85, JFKML.
47. Sargent Shriver memorandum to John F. Kennedy, Feb. 24, 1961, POF, box 85, JFKML.
48. Ibid.
49. For further reference to this and other points concerning the "Report," see Sargent Shriver, "Report to the President on the Peace Corps," POF, box 85, JFKML.
50. Ibid.
51. Sargent Shriver memorandum to John F. Kennedy, Feb. 24, 1961, POF, box 85, JFKML.
52. Personal interview, Sargent Shriver, Oct. 3, 1978, Washington, D.C.
53. William Josephson memoranda to Sargent Shriver of Feb. 19, 1961, and Mar. 20, 1961, Josephson Papers, JFKML.
54. Personal interview, Lawrence F. O'Brien, Oct. 12, 1978, New York City.
55. Schlesinger, *A Thousand Days*, p. 627.
56. John F. Kennedy, "Statement by the President upon Signing Order Establishing the Peace Corps," Mar. 1, 1961, *Public Papers* vol. I, p. 35.
57. John F. Kennedy, "Special Message to the Congress on the Peace Corps," Mar. 1, 1961, *Public Papers*, vol. I, p. 144.
58. *NYT*, Mar. 2, 1961, p. 1.
59. Sargent Shriver, "Report to the President on the Peace Corps," p. 20, POF, box 85, JFKML.

4. A SPECIAL IDENTITY

1. Sargent Shriver memorandum to John F. Kennedy, attached to "Report to the President on the Peace Corps," Feb. 24, 1961, box 86, JFKML.
2. Personal interview, Sargent Shriver, Oct. 3, 1978, Washington, D.C.
3. Ibid.
4. Sargent Shriver letter to John F. Kennedy (undated), POF, box 85, JFKML.
5. Sargent Shriver memorandum to all Peace Corps working group members, Feb. 27, 1961, Bush Papers, box 1, JFKML.
6. Al Sims memorandum to Sargent Shriver, Mar. 7, 1961, Bush Papers, box 1, JFKML.
7. Edwin Bayley, Oral History Interview, conducted by JFKML, p. 35.
8. John D. Young memorandum to Sargent Shriver, Mar. 8, 1961, staff files of C. Bellino, box 1642, JFKML.
9. Ibid.
10. Nicholas Hobbs quoted in *Who's Who in Peace Corps Washington*, p. 6.

11. Thomas Quimby, Oral History Interview, conducted by JFKML, p. 36.

12. Charles Peters, Oral History Interview, conducted by JFKML, pp. 27–28.

13. O'Donnell quoted in Harris Wofford, Oral History Interview, conducted by JFKML, p. 102.

14. Johnson quoted in a letter from Bill D. Moyers to Chairman Clement Zablocki (International Relations Committee, U.S. Congress). "Moyers's Views in Support of the Peace Corps Reform Act," June 27, 1978, Appendix 6, p. 86.

15. Shriver, "Two Years of the Peace Corps," p. 694.

16. Sargent Shriver, "Five Years with the Peace Corps," in *Peace Corps Reader* (Washington, D.C.: U.S. Peace Corps, 1967), p. 21.

17. Shriver, "Two Years of the Peace Corps," p. 694.

18. John D. Young memorandum to Sargent Shriver, Mar. 20, 1961, Bush Papers, box 1, JFKML.

19. Shriver, "Five Years with the Peace Corps," p. 24.

20. William Josephson memorandum to Sargent Shriver, Aug. 22, 1961, Josephson Papers, JFKML.

21. William Josephson, Oral History Interview, conducted by JFKML, p. 15.

22. Ibid., p. 49.

23. Ibid., pp. 48–49.

24. C. Payne Lucas, "Looking Back" in *Peace Corps Times* (Washington, D.C.: U.S. ACTION), vol. 1, no. 2, Aug. 1978.

25. Shriver quoted in William Haddad, "Handshaker with a Vision," *Harper's*, Dec. 1965; also, personal interview, Genoa Godbey, Oct. 13, 1978, Washington, D.C.

26. Wofford, *Of Kennedys and Kings*, p. 281.

27. Lucas, "Looking Back."

28. Chester Bowles memorandum to John F. Kennedy, Mar. 6, 1961, Chester Bowles Papers, Yale University.

29. Sargent Shriver, "Report to the President on the Peace Corps, POF, box 86, JFKML.

30. Transcript of tape recorded message from Sargent Shriver to Dean Rusk, May 26, 1961, Bush Papers, box 3, JFKML.

31. William Josephson memorandum to Sargent Shriver, Feb. 19, 1961, Josephson Papers, JFKML.

32. Bill D. Moyers letter to Chairman Clement Zablocki, p. 86.

33. Personal interview, Henry Labouisse, Dec. 7, 1978, New York City.

34. Wofford, *Of Kennedys and Kings*, p. 274; and Bill Moyers memorandum to Sargent Shriver, Feb. 27, 1961, Bush Papers, box 2, JFKML.

35. Chester Bowles memorandum to John F. Kennedy, Mar. 6, 1961, Chester Bowles Papers, Yale University; Dean Rusk quoted by Sargent Shriver in a letter to Chester Bowles, Feb. 28, 1961, Bush Papers, box 2, JFKML.

36. Bill D. Moyers letter to Chairman Clement Zablocki, p. 86.

37. Wofford, *Of Kennedys and Kings*, p. 262. This reconstruction of these events owes a great deal to William Josephson's Oral History Interview, conducted by JFKML, p. 16.

38. John F. Kennedy, "Special Message to the Congress on Foreign Aid," Mar. 22, 1961, Public Papers, vol. I, pp. 207–8.

39. Sargent Shriver memorandum to Richard Goodwin, Mar. 24, 1961, "Memos" file, Peace Corps Archives (hereafter PCA), Washington, D.C.

40. John F. Kennedy memorandum to Sargent Shriver, Mar. 30, 1961, CSF, box 126, JFKML.

41. Sargent Shriver memorandum to Henry Labouisse (undated), Records of Government Agencies, The Peace Corps, Roll 9, JFKML.

42. Ibid.

43. William Josephson, "Memorandum of Conversation, April 26, 1961, White House Meeting to Consider Relationship of Peace Corps to Foreign Aid Program," Records of Government Agencies, The Peace Corps, Roll 9, JFKML.

44. Warren Wiggins cable to Sargent Shriver, April 26, 1961, Records of Government Agencies, The Peace Corps, Roll 9, JFKML.

45. Sargent Shriver quoted in Liston, *Sargent Shriver: A Candid Portrait.*

46. William Josephson memorandum to Warren Wiggins, May 28, 1962, Josephson Papers, JFKML.

47. William Josephson memorandum to John F. Kennedy, May 1, 1961, Josephson Papers, JFKML.

48. Lyndon Johnson quoted in Bill D. Moyers letter to Chairman Clement Zablocki, p. 86.

49. Ibid.

50. William Josephson, Oral History Interview, conducted by JFKML, p. 26.

51. Ibid. This story is corroborated by other Oral Histories in the JFKML. See, Harris Wofford, p. 104 and Bradley Patterson, p. 23.

52. Ralph Dungan memorandum to Dean Rusk, May 2, 1961, CSF, box 126, JFKML.

53. *NYT*, May 4, 1961, p. 1.

54. Harris Wofford, Oral History Interview, conducted by JFKML, p. 100.

55. William Josephson, Oral History Interview, conducted by JFKML, p. 26. In a personal interview, Ralph Dungan confirmed that he had been much displeased with Wiggins and Josephson (December 1978, Washington, D.C.)

56. Shriver, *Point of the Lance*, p. 15.

57. Bill D. Moyers letter to Chairman Clement Zablocki, p. 87.

58. Harris Wofford memorandum to John F. Kennedy, May 25, 1961, POF, box 86, JFKML.

59. *Life*, "Peace Corps Catches Fire in Colleges", Mar. 17, 1961, pp. 34–35.

60. *C.R.*, April 12, 1961, vol. 107, pt. 5, 87th Cong., 1st Sess., p. 5636 (for poll results); and *NYT*, April 2, 1961, p. 61 (for survey by American Council on Education).

61. Ralph Dungan memorandum to Harris Wofford, Mar. 7, 1961, CSF, box 670, JFKML.

62. *Guardsman*, March 22, 1961.

63. *NYT*, Mar. 5, 1961, p. 86 (on Organization of American States); June 25, 1961, p. 23 (on educational establishments); Mar. 18, 1961, p. 11 (on students at New York University); and Mar. 5, 1961, p. 46 (on Fairleigh Dickinson University).

64. *C.R.*, 87th Cong., 1st Sess., p. 3333 (Humphrey); p. A2722 (Keating); p. 5926 (Goldwater); and p. 4352 (Bible).

65. *Newsweek*, Feb. 5, 1961 (on Macmillan); *NYT*, Mar. 4, 1961, p. 2 (on Parliament); *NYT*, Mar. 7, 1961, p. 29 (on Brandt); *NYT*, Mar. 3, 1961, p. 3

(on embassies); and Sargent Shriver, "Transcript of Background of Press and Radio Briefing," Mar. 6, 1961, POF, box 85, JFKML (on "interest").

66. Lou Harris, Confidential Poll to President Kennedy, "Public Reaction to President Kennedy During First Sixty Days of Administration," POF, box 63, JFKML.

67. NYT, Feb. 26, 1961, Section 6, p. 4 (editorial); NYT, Mar. 24, 1961, p. 25 (on Young Republicans); NYT, April 19, 1961, p. 25 (on Daughters of the American Revolution); and New Republic, Mar. 13, 1961.

68. Memoranda from Carroll Wilson to Sargent Shriver, June 11, 1961; Morris Abram to Sargent Shriver, May 18, 1961, Bush Papers, box 3, JFKML.

69. Val Burati memorandum to Arthur Schlesinger, Jr., May 4, 1961, Personal Papers of Arthur Schlesinger, Jr., JFKML; NYT, Mar. 29, 1961, p. 7 (on Harriman); and NYT, Jan. 20, 1961, p. 3 (on Keita).

70. New York Herald Tribune, Mar. 27, 1961.

71. Times of India comment quoted in Sargent Shriver, "Two Years of the Peace Corps," p. 695.

72. Sargent Shriver, "The Job was Tough," address to the Seventeenth National Congress on Higher Education, Chicago, April 6, 1962, in "Speeches of Sargent Shriver," PCL. Kennedy's comment is from the "Presidential News Conference," Mar. 8, 1961, in Public Papers, vol. I, p. 159.

73. Personal interview, Sargent Shriver, Oct. 10, 1978, Washington, D.C.

74. Wofford, Of Kennedys and Kings, p. 269.

75. Ibid.

76. Ibid.

77. Shriver, Point of the Lance, p. 42.

78. John Kenneth Galbraith, Ambassador's Journal (New York: Houghton Mifflin, 1969), p. 103.

79. Harris Wofford memorandum to President Kennedy, May 25, 1961, POF, box 85, JFKML.

80. John F. Kennedy, "Remarks to the National Advisory Council for the Peace Corps," May 25, 1961, Public Papers, vol. I, p. 391.

5. ASSAULT ON THE HILL

1. Mike Mansfield, Oral History Interview, conducted by JFKML, p. 5.

2. Hubert Humphrey in introduction to The Peace Corps Experience by Roy Hoopes (New York: Crown Publishers, 1968).

3. John F. Kennedy, "Special Message to the Congress on the Peace Corps," Mar. 1, 1961, Public Papers, vol. I, p. 143.

4. New Republic, Mar. 13, 1961, p. 4.

5. C.R., Mar. 2, 1961, 87th Cong., 1st Sess., vol. 107, pt. 3, p. 3104.

6. William Josephson, Oral History Interview, conducted by JFKML, p. 11.

7. Roger S. Kuhn memorandum to Sargent Shriver, Aug. 6, 1961, Josephson Papers, JFKML.

8. William Josephson, Oral History Interview, conducted by JFKML, p. 27.

9. Humphrey, The Education of a Public Man, p. 250.

10. Sargent Shriver letter to Sam Rayburn, Mar. 5, 1961, Bush Papers, box 2, JFKML.

11. Director's Staff Meeting, March 22, 1961, Records of Government Agencies, The Peace Corps, Roll 1, JFKML.

12. Quotations from *C.R.*, March-April, 1961, 87th Cong., 1st Sess., pp. 5282 (Libonati), 4759 (McGee), 3790 (Muskie), 5361 (Hart), 4284 (Young), 5926 (Goldwater), 6833 (Wiley); Bolton quoted in *NYT*, Mar. 9, 1961, p. 18 and Rhodes quoted in *NYT*, Mar. 24, 1961, p. 17.

13. William Josephson, Oral History Interview, conducted by JFKML.

14. Ibid.

15. Warren Wiggins memorandum to Dean Rusk, May 11, 1961, Josephson Papers, JFKML.

16. Sargent Shriver memorandum to President Kennedy, March 14, 1961, POF, box 85, JFKML.

17. William Josephson memorandum to Charles Nelson, Feb. 2, 1962, Josephson Papers, JFKML.

18. Personal interview, Sargent Shriver, Oct. 3, 1978, Washington, D.C.

19. Ibid.

20. Sargent Shriver memorandum to President Kennedy, Sept. 6, 1961, POF, box 710, JFKML.

21. Personal interview, Sargent Shriver, Oct. 10, 1978, Washington, D.C.

22. Haddad, "Handshaker with a Vision," p. 45.

23. Sargent Shriver memorandum to Wiggins, Josephson, and Moyers, June 5, 1961, Josephson Papers, JFKML.

24. Sargent Shriver letter to Hubert Humphrey, Sept. 1, 1961, "Peace Corps Congressional Liaison Files," PCA, Washington, D.C.

25. U.S. Senate, Committee on Foreign Relations, Hearings on S. 2935: "Peace Corps Act Amendments, 87th Cong., 2nd Sess., vol. 5, p. 21.

26. U.S. House of Representatives, Committee on Foreign Affairs, Hearings on H.R. 7500: "The Peace Corps Act," 87th Cong., 1st Sess., vol. 4, Aug. 11, 1961.

27. Dean Rusk letter to author, Dec. 8, 1978.

28. Bill Moyers memorandum to William Josephson, May 25, 1961, Josephson Papers, JFKML.

29. *C.R.*, Aug. 24, 1961, 87th Cong., 1st Sess., vol. 107, pt. 12, p. 16917.

30. Personal interview, Donald Romine, Oct. 6, 1978, Washington, D.C.

31. *C.R.*, June 1, 1961, 87th Cong., 1st Sess., vol. 107, pt. 6, p. 9287.

32. H. R. Gross quoted in *C.R.*, Sept. 14, 1961, 87th Cong., 1st Sess., vol. 107, pt. 15, p. 19502. Until he retired (in 1974), Gross was a consistent opponent of government spending, especially foreign aid. In 1949 he voted against the Marshall Plan. He was variously described as "a pillar of parsimony," "the antidote to boondoggling," "a reactionary nitpicker," and "the abominable no-man." His final statement on foreign aid was: "I leave Congress with an unblemished record of opposition to foreign aid. If I could have but one epitaph on my grave it would be a simple one—foreign aid was always cheaper by the Gross." His statements were usually entertaining—after a cantankerous fashion—but his attitude was deadly serious and indeed, was shared by many southern and midwestern Republicans. See *The Congressional Quarterly Weekly Report* (Nov. 9, 1974), p. 3093.

33. George Aiken, Oral History Interview, conducted by JFKML, p. 32.

34. Personal interview, J. William Fulbright, Dec. 19, 1978, Washington,

D.C. Former Senator Fulbright was a candid interviewee. He also expressed himself in numerous letters to, and about, the Peace Corps between 1961 and 1963. On January 23, 1962, for example, he wrote a long letter to Secretary of State Dean Rusk criticizing the Peace Corps and complaining that Volunteer subsistence levels were too high in Colombia when compared to the Fulbright grantees there. See, Records of Government Agencies, The Peace Corps, Roll 3, JFKML.

35. *NYT*, Aug. 3, 1961, p. 3.

36. Sargent Shriver memorandum to President Kennedy, Aug. 2, 1961, CSF, box 710, JFKML.

37. John F. Kennedy, "Presidential News Conference," Aug. 10, 1961, *Public Papers*, vol. I, p. 554.

38. *C.R.*, Aug. 24, 1961, 87th Cong., 1st Sess., vol. 107, pt. 6, p. 16980.

39. *Congressional Quarterly Almanac*, 1961, vol. 17, p. 327.

40. *C.R.*, Aug. 25, 1961, 87th Cong., 1st Sess., vol. 107, pt. 6. Although considered a liberal in foreign affairs, Fulbright's domestic constituency was notably conservative (Arkansas) and, at times, his voting record reflected this. His negative stance on civil rights, for instance, probably prevented Kennedy from choosing him as Secretary of State in 1961.

41. *C.R.*, Aug. 25, 1961, 87th Cong., 1st Sess., vol. 107, pt. 6, pp. 16972–79.

42. Sargent Shriver letter to Congressman William Harsha, Aug. 10, 1961, Josephson Papers, JFKML.

43. Anonymous Congressman quoted in *Newsweek*, Sept. 4, 1961.

44. William Josephson memorandum to Larry Dennis, Sept. 1, 1961, Josephson Papers, JFKML. Josephson went on record as saying he definitely did not consider Kamen a "security risk."

45. John F. Kennedy's "Presidential News Conference," Aug. 30, 1961, *Public Papers*, vol. I, p. 575.

46. *Newsweek*, Sept. 4, 1961.

47. Edwin Bayley, Oral History Interview, conducted by JFKML, p. 90.

48. *NYT*, editorial, "Badly Timed Applause," Aug. 21, 1961, p. 22.

49. *C.R.*, Nov. 13, 1963, 88th Cong., 1st Sess., vol. 109, pt. 16, p. 21640.

50. Bill Moyers memorandum to Sargent Shriver, Oct. 25, 1961, Bush Papers, box 2, JFKML.

51. The Peace Corps Act (Public Law 87-293), sec. 2.

52. U.S. Senate, Committee on Appropriations, Hearings, Sept. 14, 1961.

53. Mark Evans, *Metromedia* interview with Sargent Shriver, Mar. 8, 1962: "Mr. Shriver, your association with Congress has become almost a love affair. Would you care to tell us how?" Transcript in POF, box 85, JFKML.

54. *Washington Daily News*, editorial, "Praise for the Peace Corps," Nov. 8, 1963. *Congress and the Nation, 1954–64* said that: "Over a twenty-year period . . . no single policy came under so frequent and so critical scrutiny by Congress as did foreign aid" (Congressional Quarterly publication, Washington, D.C.), p. 161.

55. Sargent Shriver memoranda to President Kennedy, Feb. 12, 1962, Mar. 8, 1962, and Mar. 27, 1962, POF, box 85, JFKML.

56. John F. Kennedy, "Remarks upon Signing the Peace Corps Bill," Sept. 22, 1961, *Public Papers*, vol. I, p. 615.

6. AN ANTIBUREAUCRATIC BUREAUCRACY

1. Shriver quoted in Wofford, *Of Kennedys and Kings*, p. 267, and Sargent Shriver memorandum to Dean Rusk, May 26, 1961, Bush Papers, box 3, JFKML.

2. John D. Young letter to author, Mar. 27, 1979.

3. Young's memorandum of Mar. 8, 1961 on "Basic Concepts for Peace Corps Interim Organization," is referred to in Ch. 4.

4. William Josephson memorandum to Sargent Shriver, Aug. 6, 1961, Josephson Papers, JFKML.

5. For a first-hand observation on the National Advisory Council, see William O. Douglas, Oral History Interview, conducted by JFKML, p. 36.

6. Sargent Shriver memorandum to Peace Corps staff, Mar. 28, 1961; Josephson Papers, JFKML (on written materials being sent through Shriver's office); and Bradley Patterson, Oral History Interview, conducted by JFKML, p. 36.

7. Bradley Patterson, Oral History Interview, conducted by JFKML, p. 27; personal interview, Newell Flather, May 8, 1978, Boston.

8. Bradley Patterson, Oral History Interview, conducted by JFKML, pp. 13–14.

9. Ibid.

10. Sargent Shriver memorandum to John F. Kennedy, Dec. 15, 1961, POF, box 86, JFKML. According to Lewis H. Butler, "The Overseas Staff" in *Annals*, May 1966, p. 90, Peace Corps Reps came from the following occupations: 12 percent from the legal profession; 12 percent from universities; 9 percent from secondary education; 8 percent from government agencies; 7 percent from private business; 7 percent from international organizations; 18 percent from public health, social work, local administration, etc.

11. Personal interview, William Josephson, Dec. 6, 1978, New York City.

12. William Josephson, Oral History Interview, conducted by JFKML, p. 73.

13. Sargent Shriver letter to George L. Noue, Aug. 25, 1964, Bush Papers, box 2, JFKML. See also, Richard E. Neustadt, *Presidential Power: The Politics of Leadership* (New York: John Wiley, 1960).

14. Robert B. Textor, ed., *Cultural Frontiers of the Peace Corps* (Cambridge, Mass.: MIT Press, 1966), pp. 6–7.

15. Harris Wofford, Oral History Interview, conducted by JFKML, p. 15.

16. Bradley Patterson, Oral History Interview, conducted by JFKML, p. 45.

17. Phrase used by Harris Wofford in a speech to Swarthmore College, Nov. 22, 1965; in "Speeches of Harris Wofford," PCL.

18. Anonymous staff member quoted in Liston, *Sargent Shriver: A Candid Portrait*, p. 151.

19. Shriver's handwritten question to Vaughn is in the margin of an Evaluation Report on Guatemala, 1963; Richard Ottinger's memorandum to Charles Peters is attached to an Evaluation Report on Peru, 1963.

20. Personal interview, Robert Gale, Dec. 21, 1978, Washington, D.C.

21. William Josephson memorandum to Sargent Shriver, Sept. 15, 1961, Records of Government Agencies, The Peace Corps, JFKML.

22. Personal interviews, Don Romine, Oct. 6, 1978, Washington, D.C.; and Thomas Quimby, Dec. 15, 1978, Washington, D.C.

23. Warren Wiggins, *The Ambitious Task: New Approaches to the Peace Corps and Private and Voluntary Organization Efforts to Promote Third World Development* (Washington, D.C.: U.S. Peace Corps, 1977), p. 14.

24. Sargent Shriver, "Report to the President on the Peace Corps", Feb. 1961; POF, box 86, JFKML.

25. William Josephson quoted in Hearings before the House Committee on Foreign Affairs, "Executive Session," Feb. 5, 1964: "A Bill to Amend Further the Peace Corps Act." Transcript in PCL.

26. Memoranda from Gordon Boyce to Sargent Shriver, Mar. 8, 1961, and Carroll Wilson to Sargent Shriver, June 11, 1961, Bush Papers, boxes 1–3, JFKML.

27. John F. Kennedy, "Special Message to the Congress on the Peace Corps," Mar. 1, 1961, *Public Papers*, vol. I, p. 145.

28. U.S. Senate, Hearings, "Nomination of Robert Sargent Shriver to be Director of the Peace Corps," Mar. 21, 1961, 87th Cong., 1st Sess., vol. 4, p. 2.

29. Sargent Shriver quoted in Director's Staff Meeting, Mar. 30, 1961, Records of Government Agencies, The Peace Corps, Roll 1, JFKML.

30. Harris Wofford, Oral History Interview, conducted by JFKML, p. 109. Wofford's view was reinforced by personal interviews with Wiggins, Kelly, and Josephson.

31. Sargent Shriver memorandum to senior staff, September 1961; in "Beginnings" folder, PCL.

32. The attitude of the professional administrators in the Peace Corps (Wiggins and Kelly) toward the private sector is drawn from personal interviews with Warren Wiggins, Oct. 12, 1978, Washington, D.C. and William Kelly, Dec. 16, 1978, Washington, D.C. Reinforcement of these views can be found in the oral history interviews of William Josephson and Harris Wofford conducted by JFKML.

33. Harris Wofford, Oral History Interview, conducted by JFKML, p. 105.

34. Thomas D. Scott, "The Peace Corps and the Private Sector: The Failure of a Partnership", *Annals*, May 1966, pp. 97–98.

35. For these and other statistics on the Peace Corps' participation with the private sector, see: *Peace Corps Congressional Presentation*, Fiscal Year 1964, vol. 3, pp. 56–57. (Washington, D.C.: U.S. Peace Corps, 1963).

36. U.S. Peace Corps, *Second Annual Report* (Washington, D.C., 1964), p. 40.

37. Statistics from U.S. Peace Corps, *Past Failures and Future Hopes for a Deep Involvement of Universities, Private Organizations and Other Groups in the Peace Corps*. A Report prepared for the National Advisory Council Meeting, Jan. 27, 1965, PCL.

38. Sargent Shriver memorandum to John F. Kennedy, July 24, 1962, Records of Government Agencies, The Peace Corps, Roll 3, JFKML.

39. Sargent Shriver letter to George La Noue, Aug. 25, 1964, Bush Papers, box 2, JFKML.

40. Gerald Bush, "The Peace Corps, 1961–65: A Study in Open Organization." Unpublished Ph.D. dissertation (Northern Illinois University: Department of Political Science, 1966).

41. Personal interview, William Kelly, Dec. 16, 1978, Washington, D.C.

42. William Josephson, Oral History Interview, conducted by JFKML, pp. 37–38.

43. Ibid.

44. Sargent Shriver memorandum to Peace Corps staff, Dec. 1961, POF, box 86, JFKML.

45. Sargent Shriver quoted in Lewis H. Butler, "The Overseas Staff," *Annals*, May 1966, p. 84.

46. William Josephson letter to Charles Houston, Sept. 18, 1963, Josephson Papers, JFKML.

47. Harris Wofford, "The Future of the Peace Corps," *Annals*, May 1966, p. 131.

48. Warren Wiggins memorandum to Regional Directors, June 19, 1964, Bush Papers, box 1, JFKML.

49. Galbraith, *Ambassador's Journal*, p. 137.

50. William Haddad memorandum to Sargent Shriver, May 17, 1961, Bush Papers, box 2, JFKML.

51. Sargent Shriver memorandum to the Peace Corps staff, Dec. 1961, POF, box 86, JFKML.

52. Warren Wiggins memorandum to Dean Rusk, May 3, 1961, Josephson Papers, JFKML.

53. Bill D. Moyers memorandum to Sargent Shriver, Mar. 5, 1964, Bush Papers, box 1, JFKML.

54. Warren Wiggins, "The Broader Bridge," address to the California Teacher's Association, Mar. 1, 1963. In "Speeches of Warren Wiggins," PCL.

55. Bradley Patterson, Oral History Interview, conducted by JFKML, p. 42.

56. Warren Wiggins, "Some Questions," address to the World Congress on Engineering Education, Chicago, June 25, 1965; in "Speeches of Warren Wiggins," PCL.

57. Bush, "The Peace Corps, 1961–65", p. 155.

58. Sargent Shriver memorandum to Peace Corps staff, Dec. 1961, POF, box 86, JFKML.

59. Personal interview, Charles Peters, Dec. 18, 1978, Washington, D.C.

60. Personal interview, Sargent Shriver, Oct. 10, 1978, Washington, D.C.

61. Charles Peters memorandum to Sargent Shriver (attached to Evaluation Report on Brazil, 1963), PCL.

62. Information on evaluation from personal interview, Charles Peters, Dec. 18, 1978; and Thomas Quimby, Oral History Interview, conducted by JFKML, p. 54.

63. Joseph Kauffman memorandum to Bill D. Moyers, Sept. 27, 1962, Bush Papers, box 3, JFKML.

64. Sargent Shriver quoted in Meridan Bennett, "Evaluation and the Question of Change," *Annals*, May 1966, p. 122.

65. William Haddad memorandum to Sargent Shriver, Jan. 16, 1963 (attached to Evaluation Report on Ivory Coast, 1963), PCL.

66. Charles Peters, Evaluation Report on Afghanistan, 1964, PCL.

67. Phrase used to describe Peters by two of his former colleagues, C. Payne Lucas and Kevin Lowther in *Keeping Kennedy's Promise: The Peace Corps, Unmet Hope of the New Frontier* (Boulder, Colo: Westview Press, 1978), p. 5.

68. Andrew Kopkind, "The Peace Corps' Daring New Look," *New Republic*, February 5, 1966, p. 15.

69. William Haddad memorandum to Peace Corps Senior Staff, July 23, 1962, Bush Papers, box 2, JFKML.

70. Statistics quoted in Textor, *Cultural Frontiers of the Peace Corps*, pp. 323–24.

71. William Josephson, Oral History Interview, conducted by JFKML, p. 39.

72. Franklin Williams memorandum to Peace Corps Staff, Mar. 6, 1963, Bush Papers, box 1, JFKML.

73. William Haddad memorandum to Sargent Shriver, April 8, 1963, Bush Papers, box 1, JFKML.

74. Sargent Shriver memorandum to Kermit Gordon (Bureau of the Budget), May 21, 1963, Josephson Papers, JFKML.

75. Bill D. Moyers memorandum to Myer Feldman, Aug. 12, 1963, Staff Files of Myer Feldman, box 1544, JFKML.

76. Sargent Shriver, record of conversation with George Ball, April 29, 1963, Personal Papers of George Ball.

77. John W. Macy memorandum to Sargent Shriver, June 12, 1963, Staff Files of Myer Feldman, box 1544, JFKML.

78. Textor, *Cultural Frontiers of the Peace Corps*, p. 323. In later years, Charles Peters pointed out that the Peace Corps' "five-year rule" had its negative, as well as positive side: "When I worked at the Peace Corps in the 1960s, there was a five-year limit on employment. The result was a steady, stimulating infusion of new blood and a much more adventurous group of employees than are attracted by the security of tenure. There was, however, a lack of continuity, and by the time I left, staff meetings had begun to seem like broken records. I heard problems discussed again and again as if they were brand new and the agency had no experience that would suggest their solutions." Charles Peters, *How Washington Really Works* (Addison-Wesley Publishing Company, 1980), pp. 49–50.

7. PRINCIPLES, POLICIES AND THE PRESIDENT

1. Sargent Shriver memorandum to the President, Dec. 15, 1961, POF, box 86, JFKML.

2. Memoranda from William Delano to Melvin Schuweiler, May 4, 1962, and William Josephson to Melvin Schuweiler, May 29, 1962, Josephson Papers, JFKML.

3. William Delano memorandum to Melvin Schuweiler, May 4, 1962, Josephson Papers, JFKML.

4. Sargent Shriver memorandum to all Peace Corps Reps, July 6, 1962, Director's Chronological File, PCA.

5. William Josephson, Oral History Interview, conducted by JFKML, p. 50 (on FBI); and memoranda from Morris Abram to Warren Wiggins, Mar. 22, 1961 (on diplomatic privileges); William Josephson to Sally Bowles, May 27, 1963 (on "Santa Clauses"); and Sargent Shriver to all Peace Corps Reps, Aug. 6, 1962 (on guns). Josephson Papers, JFKML.

6. Sargent Shriver memorandum to all Peace Corps Reps, Aug. 8, 1963, "Beginnings" folder, PCL.

7. Sargent Shriver memorandum to all Peace Corps Reps, Dec. 15, 1961, POF, box 86, JFKML.

8. Sargent Shriver letter to all Peace Corps Reps, May 22, 1963, Josephson Papers, JFKML.

9. Sargent Shriver memorandum to President Kennedy, Dec. 15, 1961, POF, box 86, JFKML.

10. Bill Moyers memorandum to Sargent Shriver, July 13, 1961, Records of Government Agencies, The Peace Corps, Roll 9, JFKML.

11. Sorensen, *Kennedy*, p. 244.

12. *NYT*, July 13, 1961. The reference in the last part of this editorial is to Kennedy's bill proposing federal aid to all schools, including Catholic ones. This was a highly controversial and unsuccessful proposal. Federal aid to religious schools had to wait for President Johnson.

13. Thomas D. Scott, "The Peace Corps and the Private Sector: The Failure of a Partnership," p. 96.

14. William Josephson, Oral History Interview, conducted by JFKML, p. 42.

15. William Josephson mentions Shriver's meeting with Kennedy in a memorandum to Theodore Sorensen, June 30, 1961. Josephson Papers, JFKML.

16. William Josephson memorandum on Church-State issue, June 21, 1961, Josephson Papers, JFKML.

17. Sargent Shriver telegram to U.S. embassy, Lagos, Nigeria, July 14, 1961, Records of Government Agencies, The Peace Corps, Roll 9, JFKML.

18. The "Religious Policies of the Peace Corps" in Staff Files of Theodore Sorensen, box 68, JFKML; and William Josephson memorandum to Sargent Shriver, Oct. 13, 1961, Josephson Papers, JFKML.

19. Sargent Shriver address to Private Voluntary Agencies Conference, Dec. 15, 1961, "Speeches of Sargent Shriver," PCL.

20. Bishop Swanstrom quoted at Private Voluntary Agencies Conference, Dec. 15, 1961, New York City.

21. Bradley Patterson, Oral History Interview, conducted by JFKML, p. 53. By 1963, religious organizations had seen the valuable work done by the Peace Corps overseas and toned down their criticism. In early 1964, Shriver even persuaded Bishop Swanstrom to act as a supportive witness for Peace Corps legislation in Congress.

22. Sargent Shriver memorandum to President Kennedy, Jan. 8, 1962, POF, box 85, JFKML.

23. Sargent Shriver address to the National Conference on Religion and Race, Jan. 15, 1963 (Chicago, Ill.), "Speeches of Sargent Shriver," PCL.

24. Derek Singer memorandum to Warren Wiggins, Feb. 24, 1961; Charles Nelson memorandum to Sargent Shriver, Aug. 13, 1961; Paul Geren and Franklin Williams memorandum to Harris Wofford, Nov. 10, 1961. In Records of Government Agencies, JFKML.

25. Sargent Shriver, "Weekly Report to the President," July 13, 1962, Bush Papers, JFKML.

26. *NYT*, June 23, 1961, p. 10.

27. William Josephson, Oral History Interview, conducted by JFKML, p. 59.

28. *NYT*, June 28, 1962, p. 28 (on universities), and *NYT*, July 13, 1962, p. 10 (on the inn in Maryland).

29. Statistics given by Brent K. Ashabranner (one of the first black Peace Corps administrators) in his book, *A Moment in History: The First Ten Years of*

the Peace Corps (New York: Doubleday, 1971), p. 258.

30. Lucas, "Looking Back," *Peace Corps Times.*

31. Figures on race given by Sargent Shriver, "Two Years of the Peace Corps," p. 499.

32. Kevin Delany and David Gelman, Evaluation Report on Liberia, 1963, PCL.

33. See, Director's Staff Meeting, Mar. 7, 1961 (in Records of Government Agencies, JFKML); Sargent Shriver, quoted during first meeting of Peace Corps National Advisory Council, May 22, 1961 (transcript in PCL); Sargent Shriver address "On Women in the Peace Corps," YWCA, Oct. 18, 1961 (in "Speeches of Sargent Shriver," PCL).

34. Sargent Shriver, Senate Committee on Foreign Relations, Hearings, "Amendment to the Peace Corps Act," Feb. 24, 1964, 88th Cong., 2nd Sess.

35. Sargent Shriver address "On Women" to the General Federation of Women's Clubs, June 26, 1962, "Speeches of Sargent Shriver," PCL.

36. Personal interview, Warren Wiggins, Oct. 12, 1978, Washington, D.C.

37. Harris Wofford, Oral History Interview, conducted by JFKML, p. 108.

38. William Josephson memoranda to Sargent Shriver on "Interagency Relationships," May 17 and May 18, 1961, Josephson Papers, JFKML.

39. Dean Rusk, letter to author, Dec. 8, 1978.

40. Ibid.

41. William J. Crockett memorandum to the Peace Corps, June 6, 1961, box 13, PCA.

42. William Josephson memorandum to Sargent Shriver, July 13, 1961, Josephson Papers, JFKML.

43. Chester Bowles, Oral History Interview, conducted by JFKML, p. 77.

44. Sargent Shriver letter to Chester Bowles, Mar. 14, 1961, Bush Papers, JFKML.

45. William Haddad memorandum to Sargent Shriver, July 16, 1962, PCA.

46. William Josephson memorandum to Sargent Shriver, July 12, 1962, Josephson Papers, JFKML.

47. Sargent Shriver letter to Peace Corps staff, Dec., 1961, POF, box 86, JFKML.

48. Philip II. Coombs letter to author, Mar. 9, 1979.

49. See, Charles Baldwin, Oral History Interview, conducted by JFKML, p. 60; William Stevenson, Oral History Interview, conducted by JFKML, pp. 109–11; Charles Cole, Oral History Interview, conducted by JFKML, p. 11; and William Mahoney quoted in Evaluation Report on Ghana, 1964, PCL.

50. Bill Moyers memorandum to Sargent Shriver, July 17, 1961, Josephson Papers, JFKML.

51. See, Evaluation Reports on India, 1963, p. 6 (on Ty Wood); Bolivia, 1963, p. 8 (on "ill-will" toward the Peace Corps). Also, Lawrence H. Fuchs, *Those Peculiar Americans* (New York: Meredith Press, 1967), p. 22.

52. Robert G. Carey, *The Peace Corps* (New York: Praeger Press, 1970), p. 182.

53. *NYT*, March 16, 1961, p. 5.

54. David Wise and Thomas B. Ross, *The Invisible Government* (New York: Vintage Books, 1974), pp. 277–78.

55. Ibid.

56. William Josephson, Oral History Interview, conducted by JFKML, p. 52.; and personal interview, Dec. 6, 1978, New York City. The CIA also agreed that should it enlist a former Volunteer, it would never send him to the country in which he had served with the Peace Corps.

57. Stanley J. Grogan memorandum to Pierre Salinger, Feb. 28, 1962, CSF, box 126, JFKML.

58. Dean Rusk airgram to all Third World U.S. embassies, Mar. 25, 1963, National Security Files, boxes 284–90, JFKML.

59. John Griffin, Evaluation Report on Thailand, 1963, p. 6., PCL. Very few documents are available on the CIA-Peace Corps relationship. The information in this chapter owes a good deal to personal interviews with: Charles Peters, Dec. 18, 1978, Washington, D.C.; Thomas Quimby, Dec. 15, 1978, Washington, D.C.; and to the oral history interviews of William Josephson and Bradley Patterson conducted by JFKML. For the information on the AID-CIA relationship, see Herbert S. Parmet, *JFK: The Presidency of John F. Kennedy* (New York: The Dial Press, 1983), p. 213.

60. Bradley Patterson, Oral History Interview, conducted by JFKML.

61. William Josephson memorandum to Sargent Shriver, Sept. 6, 1961, Records of Government Agencies, The Peace Corps, Roll 9, JFKML. The Directive is quoted by Josephson.

62. Personal interview, William Delano, Dec. 5, 1978, New York City. Ed Bayley quoted in Parmet, *JFK: The Presidency of John F. Kennedy*, p. 213.

63. Senator Dodd quoted in U.S. Congress, Senate Committee on Foreign Relations, "The Organization of Federal Volunteer Programs in ACTION," 96th Cong., 1st Sess., 1979, p. 19. William Josephson is quoted from an Oral History Interview conducted by JFKML, pp. 54–55.

64. Personal interview, Sargent Shriver, Oct. 10, 1978, Washington, D.C.

65. See, Sargent Shriver memoranda to John F. Kennedy, Jan. 5, 1962 (India), POF, box 85; Dec. 12, 1962 (on North Borneo-Sarawak), NSF Boxes 284–90; June 19, 1961 (on Harvard), POF, box 85, JFKML.

66. Sargent Shriver, handwritten letter to President Kennedy, Oct. 27, 1961, POF, box 85, JFKML.

67. Weekly Report to the President, Feb. 5, 1963, Records of Government Agencies, The Peace Corps, Roll 3, JFKML.

68. Evelyn Lincoln (JFK's private secretary) memorandum to Sargent Shriver, Dec. 28, 1961, POF, box 86, JFKML.

69. Harris Wofford memorandum to John F. Kennedy, Jan. 20, 1962 (staff files of Theodore Sorensen, box 68, JFKML); personal interviews with Frederick Dutton, Dec. 15, 1978, Washington, D.C.; David Powers, Oct. 30, 1978, Boston; and John Kenneth Galbraith, Mar. 16, 1979, Boston. Also, Charles Baldwin, Oral History Interview, conducted by JFKML, p. 60.

70. Harris Wofford, Oral History Interview, conducted by JFKML, p. 108.

71. Personal interviews with Harris Wofford, June 8, 1979, Bryn Mawr, Pa.; Ralph Dungan, Dec. 12, 1978, Washington, D.C.; Fred Dutton, Dec. 15, 1978, Washington, D.C.; McGeorge Bundy letter to author, Nov. 27, 1978.

72. Bradley Patterson quoted from Oral History Interview, conducted by JFKML, pp. 18–20; William Kelly expressed his view during a personal interview, Dec. 16, 1978, Washington, D.C.

73. Shriver quoted by Bradley Patterson, Oral History Interview, con-

ducted by JFKML, pp. 18–20. Shriver's remark on "easier to fire a relative than a friend," was made in his article "Two Years of the Peace Corps."

74. Harris Wofford, Oral History Interview, conducted by JFKML, p. 97.

75. Personal interview with Frederick Dutton, Dec. 15, 1978, Washington, D.C.

76. Bill Moyers quoted in Scott, "The Peace Corps and the Private Sector," p. 95.

77. Halberstam, *The Best and the Brightest*, p. 383 (on Shriver as "family Communist") and p. 4 on JFK. Also, Harris Wofford, Oral History Interview, conducted by JFKML, p. 16.

78. Shriver quoted in Liston, *Sargent Shriver: A Candid Portrait*, p. 177.

79. Personal interview with Sargent Shriver, Oct. 3, 1978, Washington, D.C.

80. Handwritten remarks of Jacqueline Kennedy Onassis. The photograph referred to hangs in Sargent Shriver's office at the Watergate in Washington, D.C. Kennedy's comment came during his "Remarks to Peace Corps Headquarters Staff," June 16, 1962; *Public Papers*, vol. II, p. 482.

81. John F. Kennedy, "Remarks to a Group of Peace Corps Trainees," Aug. 9, 1962, *Public Papers*, vol. II, p. 608.

82. John D. Young letter to author, Mar. 27, 1979.

83. See, Evaluation Reports on Tanganyika, 1963 (for "Wakina Kennedy") and Togo, 1963 (for "Kennedy in Bassari"); for "los hijos de Kennedy," see Wofford, "The Future of the Peace Corps," p. 130.

84. Letter from anonymous Volunteer, 1964, to Peace Corps/Washington, Records of Government Agencies, The Peace Corps, Roll 5, JFKML.

8. VOLUNTEERS FOR PEACE

1. Lyndon B. Johnson to Sargent Shriver. Story recalled by Warren Wiggins in "A One Act Fantasy Dialogue: A Memorial Service for Alex Firfer." (The Trans Century Pink Bag Luncheon, July 2, 1978). Paper given to author by Warren Wiggins.

2. Personal interview, Sargent Shriver, Oct. 10, 1978, Washington, D.C.

3. Sargent Shriver memorandum to President Kennedy, Aug. 1, 1961, Bush Papers, box 3, JFKML.

4. Sargent Shriver, Director's Staff Meeting, Feb. 19, 1962, personal papers of Harris Wofford, box 6, JFKML.

5. Nicholas Hobbs, Oral History Interview, conducted by JFKML, p. 5.

6. Gerald Bush, Robert Iverson, and Lowell E. Kelly, *Peace Corps: Selection and Training* (Policy Paper published by U.S. Peace Corps, 1964), p. 6.

7. Warren Wiggins telegram to Sargent Shriver, May 1, 1961, Records of Government Agencies, Peace Corps, Roll 9, JFKML.

8. *NYT*, May 7, 1961. It might be noted that a second Placement Test on June 5, 1961 took the number up to 5,210. By the end of 1961 nearly 12,000 tests had been taken.

9. *NYT*, June 1, 1961, indicates Shriver's public statement. But in a personal interview with the author, Shriver recalled that he was "in a sweat" about the low number of applications.

10. *NYT*, June 19, 1962; and Sargent Shriver letter to Nathan Pusey, April 20, 1963, Shriver Chronological File, box 11, PCA.

11. Personal interview, Robert Gale, Dec. 21, 1978, Washington, D.C.

12. David Gelman and Patricia MacDermott, Evaluation Report on Recruiting, May, 1965, p. 8, PCL.

13. Robert Gale reported in minutes of a small staff meeting, Jan. 12, 1964, Records of Government Agencies, JFKML.

14. Sargent Shriver, "Meet the Press," Dec. 15, 1963.

15. David Gelman and Patricia MacDermott, Evaluation Report on Recruiting, May 1965, p. 4, PCL.

16. A Volunteer speaking to David Gelman in Sierra Leone, Evaluation Report on Sierra Leone, 1962, p. 65, PCL.

17. Gale quoted by David Gelman and Patricia MacDermott in Evaluation Report on Recruiting, May 1965, p. 32, PCL.

18. Timothy Adams, Evaluation Report on Bangladesh, 1963, p. 103, PCL. See also, Jim Fisher (Volunteer in Nepal), Letter to Peace Corps Washington, June 1, 1962, Records of Government Agencies, JFKML; the Volunteer in Venezuela was talking to evaluators Kevin Delany and Dee Jacobs in Evaluation Report on Venezuela, 1963, p. 59. PCL.

19. Roger Landrum reported at a Peace Corps Staff meeting, May 19, 1964, Bush Papers, box 1, JFKML.

20. Bill Moyers memorandum to Sargent Shriver, Dec. 18, 1961, Bush Papers, box 3, JFKML.

21. The figures for Volunteer recruitment are drawn from the Peace Corps' own *Quarterly Statistical Summaries*. In 1961, there were 12,644 applications; in 1962, 20,048; in 1963, 33,762; and in 1964, 45,653.

22. Dr. Virgil M. Hancher letter to Senators Hickenlooper, Miller, and Mansfield. Quoted in Sargent Shriver's "Weekly Report to the President," April 9, 1963, Records of Government Agencies, Peace Corps, Roll 3, JFKML.

23. Joseph Kauffman, "Preparation for Effective Job-Functioning in a Cross-Cultural Setting," a paper written for the Peace and Behavioral Sciences Conference, March 4–5, 1963. See also, *Peace Corps Training Program: A Guide to Its Basic Components* (Washington, D.C.: Peace Corps), 1963.

24. David Hapgood and Meridan Bennett, *Agents of Change: A Close Look at the Peace Corps* (Boston, 1968) pp. 162–63.

25. The British Outward Bound Schools began during World War II and were later used by British industry as a technique for training potential leaders. The schools stressed the ideals of community and service. Two members of the Outward Bound Trust, Sir Spencer Summers and Captain Frederick Fuller, helped the Peace Corps establish its first outdoors camp in Puerto Rico in 1961.

26. William Sloane Coffin quoted in *Who's Who in the Peace Corps*.

27. Bush, "The Peace Corps, 1961–66," p. 117.

28. Ian Sclanders, "The Peace Corps: Nursery for Diplomats," *Nation*, July 27, 1964, pp. 31–33.

29. Textor, *Cultural Frontiers of the Peace Corps*, p. 305.

30. Paul Jacobs, Evaluation Report on the Philippines, Feb. 1962, p. 61, PCL.

31. David Gelman, Evaluation Report on Sierra Leone, 1962, p. 6, PCL.

32. Volunteer quoted in Evaluation Report on Sierra Leone by David Gelman, 1962, p. 39, PCL.

33. See Evaluation reports by Richard Elwell, Malawi, 1964, p. 35; Kenneth Love, Morocco, 1963, p. 133; and Herb Wegner and Paul Underwood, Brazil, 1963, pp. 65–68, PCL.

34. Paul Jacobs, Eugene Burdick, and William Lederer, Evaluation Report on the Philippines, Jan. 1963, p. 8, PCL.

35. Shriver's comments on Afghanistan were handwritten in the margin of an Evaluation Report by Thorburn Reid in 1963, p. 14. The information on the letter sent out to all Peace Corps missions comes from a memorandum from Charles Peters to Shriver, Jan. 15, 1963, attached to an evaluation report on the Ivory Coast.

36. Charles Peters memorandum to Sargent Shriver, Sept. 17, 1963 (attached to Evaluation Report on Morocco by Kenneth Love, 1963, PCL).

37. Allan M. Kulakow, *To Speak As Equals: Language Training in the Peace Corps, 1961–68*, Peace Corps Faculty Paper, no. 1 (U.S. Peace Corps, 1968).

38. From Evaluation Report on Uruguay by Dee Jacobs, 1964, p. 17; End-Of-Term Conference on Sierra Leone, 1963, p. 64; and Evaluation Report on Iran by Charles Caldwell, 1964, p. 5, PCL.

39. From Evaluation Reports on Afghanistan by Charles Peters, 1964, p. 15; and on the Dominican Republic by Dee Jacobs and Philip Hardberger, 1964, pp. 59–62, PCL.

40. Section 8(c) of the Peace Corps Act prescribed the anti-Communist component for Peace Corps training.

41. From Evaluation Reports by Herb Wegner, Peru, 1963, p. 25; David Gelman, Tanganyika, 1963, p. 88; Richard Richter, Ghana, 1964, p. 68, PCL.

42. Personal interview, Joe Walsh, May 1, 1979, Boston.

43. Sargent Shriver's handwritten comment in the margin of Evaluation Report on Guatemala by Dee Jacobs, 1962, p. 20, PCL.

44. Barbara Wilder letter from Malawi to Peace Corps Washington, May 29, 1963, Records of Government Agencies, Peace Corps, Roll 5, JFKML; and Neil Boyer (Ethiopia), "Volunteers in the Field: Great Expectations" in *Annals*, May 1966, p. 58.

45. Personal interview, William Hutchinson, Nov. 28, 1978, Cambridge, Mass.

46. Richard Richter, Evaluation Report on Ghana, 1964, pp. 32–37, 76, PCL.

47. Edwin R. Henry, "Selection of Volunteers," *Annals*, May 1966, p. 28.

48. Ibid., p. 26.

49. William Josephson memorandum to Harry Van Cleve, Aug. 8, 1961, Josephson Papers, JFKML.

50. Joseph Colmen reported in Director's Staff Meeting, Sept. 7, 1962, Records of Government Agencies, Peace Corps, Roll 1, JFKML.

51. Sargent Shriver memorandum to Peace Corps Senior Staff, Aug. 1, 1962, Bush Papers, box 3, JFKML.

52. William Josephson memorandum to Bill Moyers, May 11, 1962, "Senate Foreign Relations Committee Action on Janie F. Fletcher," Josephson Papers, JFKML.

53. Sargent Shriver memorandum to Peace Corps Senior Staff, Aug. 1, 1962, Bush Papers, box 3, JFKML.

54. Volunteer quoted in Evaluation Report on Morocco by Kenneth Love, 1963, p. 139, PCL.

55. Volunteer quoted in Evaluation Report on Sierra Leone by David Gelman, 1962, p. 65, PCL.

56. Volunteers quoted in Evaluation Report on Ethiopia by Richard Elwell, 1963, p. 3; and in Evaluation Report on Sri Lanka by Arthur Dudden,

1962, p. 13, PCL.

57. Evaluation Reports on the Dominican Republic by Dee Jacobs and Philip Hardberger, 1964, pp. 53–55; Pakistan by Timothy Adams, 1964; and Guatemala by Dee Jacobs, 1963, p. 12, PCL.

58. Evaluation Reports on Uruguay by Dee Jacobs, 1964, p. 15; Bangladesh by Timothy Adams, 1963 (Peters memorandum to Shriver, dated July 19, 1963 is attached); Costa Rica by Dee Jacobs, 1963, p. 22; and Malawi by Richard Elwell, 1963, p. 27, PCL.

59. Timothy Adams memorandum to Sargent Shriver and Shriver's handwritten reply in the margin, October 15, 1963. Attached to Evaluation Report on Guatemala by Dee Jacobs, 1963, PCL.

60. Ibid.

61. Evaluation Report on Venezuela by Kevin Delany and Dee Jacobs, 1963, p. 28; and Evaluation Report on Jamaica, 1963, p. 42, PCL.

62. Evaluation Report on St. Lucia by Richard Elwell, 1963, p. 17; and Evaluation Report on Iran by Charles Caldwell, 1963, p. 19, PCL.

63. Evaluation Report on British Honduras (Belize) by Richard Elwell, 1963, p. 44; and Evaluation Report on Somalia by Richard Richter, 1963, PCL.

64. Paul Jacobs, Eugene Burdick, and William Lederer, Evaluation Report on the Philippines, 1963, pp. 33–34, PCL.

65. Nicholas Hobbs, Oral History Interview, conducted by JFKML, p. 6.

66. Paul Jacobs, Eugene Burdick, and William Lederer, Evaluation Report on the Philippines, 1963, p. 36, PCL.

67. Kopkind, "The Peace Corps' Daring New Look," p. 19.

68. Figures quoted in a Harris Wofford memorandum to President Kennedy, Jan. 20, 1962, Personal Papers of Harris Wofford, JFKML.

69. "Peace Corps Avoids South: Negro, White Colleges Alike" by Victor Wilson, New York Herald Tribune, June 29, 1962.

70. Suzanne N. Gordon and Nancy K. Sizer, Why People Join the Peace Corps (Washington, D.C.: Institute for International Services, 1963). Findings reported in Annals, May 1966, p. 14.

71. Paul Jacobs, Eugene Burdick, and William Lederer, Evaluation Report on the Philippines, 1963, p. 35, PCL.

72. Wofford, Of Kennedys and Kings, p. 275.

73. Duncan Yaggy quoted in The Volunteer, Dec. 1963 (Washington, D.C.: U.S. Peace Corps); Paul Tsongas described his motivation in a personal interview, May 9, 1979, Boston.

74. Ashabranner, A Moment in History, p. 97.

75. Wofford, Of Kennedys and Kings, p. 282.

76. Lyndon B. Johnson, quoted in Annals, May 1966, p. 20.

9. PROGRAMMING FOR PEACE

1. Leopold Sedar Senghor quoted in Time, Jan. 16, 1984.

2. The World Bank, Accelerated Development in Sub-Saharan Africa: An Agenda For Action (Washington, D.C.: The World Bank, 1981).

3. Personal interview, Frank Mankiewicz, Dec. 19 and 20, 1978, Washington D. C. Mankiewicz was the driving force behind the Peace Corps' com-

munity development programs. He told the author of this early meeting.

4. Personal interview, Sargent Shriver, Oct. 10, 1978, Washington, D.C.

5. John F. Kennedy, "Special Message to the Congress on the Peace Corps," Mar. 1, 1961, *Public Papers*, vol. I, p. 143.

6. William Josephson, Oral History Interview, conducted by JFKML, p. 45. Lee St. Lawrence also programmed the first Peace Corps projects in Tunisia and Indonesia.

7. John F. Kennedy, Presidential News Conference, April 21, 1961, *Public Papers*, vol. I, p. 307.

8. Shriver, *Point of the Lance*, p. 50.

9. Warren Wiggins, "Peace Corps Programming Guidelines for 1962," PCL.

10. George Carter, "The Beginnings of Peace Corps Programming," *Annals*, May 1966, p. 45.

11. Warren Wiggins quoted in David Gelman, Evaluation Report on Tanganyika, 1963, p. 46, PCL.

12. Brent K. Ashabranner quoted in the *Washington Monthly*, Sept. 1978, "Sam Brown: All Talk, No ACTION," by Joseph Nocera, p. 38.

13. Personal interview, Thomas Quimby, Dec. 15, 1978, Washington, D.C.

14. David Gelman, Evaluation Report on Tanganyika, 1963, p. 2, PCL.

15. Dan Chamberlain, Evaluation Report on Colombia, 1962, p. 21, PCL.

16. Roger L. Landrum, *The Role of the Peace Corps in Education in Developing Countries: A Sector Study*, (Washington, D.C.: U.S. Peace Corps, 1981).

17. Esther Ruth Ferington, "Politics and the Peace Corps: The Conflict between Long-term and Short-term Goals," pp. 65–66. Unpublished B.A. diss., Princeton, New Jersey, 1984.

18. Landrum, *Role of Peace Corps in Education*, p. 6.

19. Barbara Ward Jackson, "Foreign Aid: Strategy or Stop-Gap," *Foreign Affairs*, October 1962.

20. Richard Elwell, Evaluation Report on Ethiopia, 1963. Also, George Sullivan, *The Story of the Peace Corps* (New York: Fleet Publishing Corporation, 1964), p. 114.

21. Landrum, *Role of Peace Corps in Education*, p. 14.

22. Ibid.

23. In the 1980s major development institutions such as the World Bank and AID underscored the importance of basic education to social and economic progress. "In the difficult economic conditions of the past six years," stated the World Bank's 1980 *World Development Report*, "as in earlier years, most of the fastest-growing developing countries without oil have had well-educated populations . . . more education can help the poorest people climb out of their poverty."

24. Ferington, "Politics and the Peace Corps,'" p. 71.

25. Landrum, *Role of Peace Corps in Education*, p. 93.

26. Ibrahim quoted in the Peace Corps' *Congressional Presentation*, fiscal year 1965.

27. Frank Mankiewicz, *The Peace Corps: A Revolutionary Force* (Washington, D.C.: U.S. Peace Corps), pp. 4–11.

28. Ibid.

29. Roy Hoopes, *The Complete Peace Corps Guide* (New York: The Dial Press, 1966), pp. 102–3.

30. Neil Boyer, "Volunteers in the Field: Great Expectations," *Annals*, May 1966, p. 57.

31. Quotes from Ashabranner, *A Moment in History*, p. 157.

32. Thorburn Reid, Evaluation Report on Panama, 1963, pp. 2–3, PCL.

33. Kevin Delany and Dee Jacobs, Evaluation Report on Venezuela, 1963, pp. 24–26; Thorburn Reid, Evaluation Report on El Salvador, 1963, p. 27, PCL.

34. Personal interviews, Charles Peters, Dec. 18, 1978, Washington, D.C.; Frank Mankiewicz, Dec. 19 and 20, 1978, Washington, D.C.

35. Lowther and Lucas, *Keeping Kennedy's Promise*, pp. 63 and 81.

36. Ashabranner, *A Moment in History*, p. 156.

37. Herb Wegner, Evaluation Report on Peru, 1963, PCL.

38. Meridan Bennett, Evaluation Report on Colombia, 1964, pp. 10 and 53, PCL.

39. Charles Peters, Evaluation Report on the Dominican Republic, 1962, p. 2; Thorburn Reid, Evaluation Report on Chile, 1963, p. 2, PCL.

40. Jack Vaughn quoted in Kirby Jones, "The Peace Corps Volunteer in the Field: Community Development," *Annals*, May 1966, p. 64.

41. Sullivan, *The Story of the Peace Corps*, p. 102.

42. Ashabranner, *A Moment in History*, p. 135.

43. Sargent Shriver memorandum to senior staff, Sept. 1961, "Beginnings" folder, PCL.

44. Lawrence Fuchs, Oral History Interview, conducted by JFKML, p. 49.

45. Kevin Delany and David Gelman, Evaluation Report on Liberia, 1963, p. 3, PCL.

46. From Evaluation Report on West Pakistan by Timothy Adams, 1963, p. 35; and extract from an Evaluation Report on Ecuador quoted in Lowther and Lucas, *Keeping Kennedy's Promise*, p. 25.

47. Charles Peters memorandum to Sargent Shriver, July 31, 1963, memo attached to Evaluation Report on Brazil, 1963, by Herb Wegner and Paul Vanderwood, PCL.

48. Perfirio Gomez quoted in Evaluation Report on Panama, 1964, by Dee Jacobs and Philip Hardberger, p. 24; Volunteer in Pakistan quoted in Evaluation Report on West Pakistan, 1963, by Timothy Adams, p. 3., PCL.

49. Kevin Delany and David Gelman, Evaluation Report on Liberia, 1963, PCL.

50. Sargent Shriver memorandum to President Kennedy, June 7, 1962, POF, box 86, JFKML. Shriver quotes Kennedy as having said this.

51. Sargent Shriver, "Two Years of the Peace Corps," p. 699.

52. Lowther and Lucas, *Keeping Kennedy's Promise*, p. 54.

53. Dee Jacobs, Evaluation Report on the Dominican Republic, 1964, pp. 4–26, PCL.

54. Timothy Adams, Evaluation Report on East Pakistan, 1963, pp. 27–33; Charles Peters's memorandum to Sargent Shriver dated July 19, 1963 is attached to this Evaluation Report.

55. John Griffin, Evaluation Report on Thailand, 1963, PCL.

56. Philip Cook, Evaluation Report on Gabon, 1963, pp. 1–5, PCL.

57. Thorburn Reid, Evaluation Report on Afghanistan, 1963, p. 1, PCL.

58. Evaluation Reports by Dee Jacobs, Uruguay, 1964, p. 2.; Richard Elwell, British Honduras, 1963, p. 3.; Dee Jacobs, Costa Rica, 1963, PCL.

59. Paul Jacobs, Eugene Burdick, and William Lederer, Evaluation Report on the Philippines, 1963, pp. 58–59, PCL.

60. Shriver quoted in *Peace Corps Handbook* (Washington, D.C.: U.S. Peace Corps, 1961), p. 9.

61. Volunteer quoted by Dan Chamberlain, Evaluation Report on Colombia, 1962, p.1, PCL.

62. Sargent Shriver quoted in Lowther and Lucas, *Keeping Kennedy's Promise*, p. 45.

63. Mankiewicz, *The Peace Corps: A Revolutionary Force*, pp. 4–11.

64. Roger Landrum quoted in minutes of large staff meeting, May 19, 1964, Bush Papers, box 1, JFKML.

65. Bill Moyers memorandum to Warren Wiggins, Aug. 17, 1963, Bush Papers, box 3, JFKML.

66. Edward Seaga, Address to the Second National Returned Peace Corps Volunteer Conference, June 28, 1981, Washington, D.C.

67. Personal interview, Sargent Shriver, Oct. 10, 1978, Washington, D.C.

10. A SPECIAL GROUP OF AMERICANS

1. Shriver, *Point of the Lance*, "Acknowledgements."

2. Sargent Shriver quoted in Sullivan, *The Story of the Peace Corps*, p. 71.

3. John F. Kennedy, "Remarks in the Rose Garden to the First Group of Volunteers before their Departure to Tanganyika and Ghana," August 28, 1961.

4. Shriver, "Five Years with the Peace Corps," p. 20.

5. Shriver, "Two Years of the Peace Corps," p. 700.

6. U.S. Peace Corps, *Quarterly Statistical Summary*, Mar. 31, 1969. The attrition rate for 1961–63 was 9.9. percent.

7. Volunteer quoted in Fuchs, *Those Peculiar Americans*, pp. 109–10. Fuchs was Peace Corps Rep in the Philippines.

8. Boyer, "Volunteers in the Field," p. 56.

9. Volunteer quoted in Fuchs, *Those Peculiar Americans*, p. 110.

10. Ibid.

11. Tom Carter letter to Peace Corps/Washington, Dec. 6, 1963, Records of Government Agencies, The Peace Corps, Roll 5, JFKML.

12. Patricia MacDermott quoted in *The Peace Corps Reader*, p. 115.

13. David Roseborough quoted in *The Peace Corps Reader*, p. 115.

14. Paul Theroux speaking on "The Dick Cavett Show," PBS Television, July 3, 1978.

15. Volunteer quoted in Luce, *Letters from the Peace Corps*, p. 128.

16. Mary Seberger letter to Peace Corps/Washington, Sept. 6, 1962; Carol Langford letter to Peace Corps/Washington, Jan. 10, 1963, Records of Government Agencies, The Peace Corps, Roll 5, JFKML.

17. Boyer, "Volunteers in the Field," p. 59.

18. Volunteer quoted in Fuchs, *Those Peculiar Americans*, p. 113.

19. Volunteer quoted in Lowther and Lucas, *Keeping Kennedy's Promise*, p. 17.

20. Volunteer quoted in Kenneth Love, Evaluation Report on Morocco, 1963, p. 104, PCL.

21. Volunteer quoted in Luce, *Letters from the Peace Corps*, pp. 124-25.

22. Eugene Burdick and William Lederer, Evaluation Report on the Philippines, 1963, PCL.

23. Anonymous Volunteer letter to Peace Corps/Washington, summer 1963, Records of Government Agencies, The Peace Corps, Roll 5, JFKML.

24. Anonymous Volunteer letter to Peace Corps/Washington, undated, Records of Government Agencies, The Peace Corps, Roll 5, JFKML.

25. Volunteers quoted in Dan Chamberlain, Evaluation Report on Colombia, 1962, p. 1, PCL.

26. Kenneth Love, Evaluation Report on Morocco, 1963, p. 104, PCL.

27. Volunteer quoted in Fuchs, *Those Peculiar Americans*, p. 111.

28. Mike O'Donnell letter to Peace Corps/Washington, Jan. 10, 1962, Records of Government Agencies, The Peace Corps, Roll 5, JFKML.

29. David Schickele quoted by Wofford, *Of Kennedys and Kings*, pp. 282–83.

30. William Stevenson, Oral History Interview, conducted by JFKML, p. 112.

31. David Gelman, Evaluation Report on Tanganyika, 1963, p. 25, PCL.

32. Evaluation Report by Dee Jacobs, Uruguay, 1964, p. 9; Richard Elwell, British Honduras, 1963, p. 35; John Griffin, Thailand, 1963, p. 34; David Hapgood, Senegal, 1964, p. 35; Dan Chamberlain, Sierra Leone, 1962, p. 8. PCL.

33. David Espey letter to Peace Corps/Washington, April 18, 1963; and anonymous letter from Volunteer in Togo to Peace Corps/Washington, summer of 1963, Records of Government Agencies, The Peace Corps, Roll 5, JFKML.

34. Evaluation Reports by Charles Caldwell, Iran, 1964, p.17; Richard Richter, Ethiopia, 1964, p. 64, PCL.

35. Evaluation Reports by Thomas Dugan, Turkey, 1963, p. 24; Dee Jacobs and Philip Hardberger, the Dominican Republic, 1964, p. 14; and Charles Peters, Afghanistan, 1964, p. 27, PCL.

36. Volunteer quoted in the *Volunteer* magazine, tenth anniversary issue (1971), p. 55.

37. David Szanton, "Cultural Confrontation in the Philippines," in Textor, *Cultural Frontiers of the Peace Corps*, pp. 51–52.

38. Nicholas Hobbs memorandum to Sargent Shriver, July 23, 1962, Bush Papers, box 3, JFKML.

39. Kevin Delany, Evaluation Report on India, 1963, p. 12, PCL.

40. Evaluation Reports by Herb Wegner, Peru, 1963, pp. 3 and 61; Dee Jacobs, Panama, 1964, p. 50; and Thorburn Reid, Chile, 1963, PCL.

41. Tom Carter letter to Peace Corps/Washington, Dec. 6, 1963, Records of Government Agencies, The Peace Corps, Roll 5, JFKML.

42. Volunteer (at Kilimanjaro) quoted in Boyer, "Volunteers in the Field," p. 59; and David Gelman, Evaluation Report on Tanganyika, 1963, p. 6, PCL.

43. Volunteer quoted in Luce, *Letters from the Peace Corps*, p. 128.

44. Ibid, pp. 126–27.

45. Evaluation Reports by Kevin Delany and David Gelman, Liberia, 1963, p. 12; and Richard Elwell, Nyasaland, 1963, p. 10, PCL.

46. David Gelman, Evaluation Report on Sierra Leone, 1962, p. 11, PCL; and Arnold Deutchman, "Volunteers in the Field: Teaching," *Annals*, May 1966, p. 78.

47. Volunteer quoted in Timothy Adams, Evaluation Report on East Pakistan, 1963, p. 63, PCL.

48. Peace Corps End-of-Term Conference on Nigeria, June 17–19, 1963, p. 9, PCL.

49. Volunteer quoted in David Gelman, Evaluation Report on Tanganyika, 1963, p. 19, PCL.

50. On the rumors spread by British teachers about Peace Corps women, see Barbara Wilder letter to Peace Corps/Washington, May 29, 1963, Records of Government Agencies, The Peace Corps, Roll 5, JFKML; on British doctors and Peace Corps nurses, see David Gelman, Evaluation Report on Tanganyika, 1963, PCL.

51. On the response of the British government to the Peace Corps see Sargent Shriver's "Weekly Report to the President," July 3, 1962, Records of Government Agencies, The Peace Corps, Roll 3, JFKML. At this stage, the British overseas effort depended upon 13 private voluntary organizations. In 1962, the British government doubled its contribution to those agencies from 17,000 to 35,000 pounds. In the same year, the U.S. Congress appropriated $59 million to the Peace Corps.

52. The "crusty old expat" is quoted in David Gelman, Evaluation Report on Tanganyika, 1963, p. 32, PCL.

53. William Stevenson, Oral History Interview, conducted by JFKML, pp. 109–11.

54. Embassy staff quoted in Kenneth Love, Evaluation Report on Morocco, 1963, p. 95, PCL.

55. Handwritten comments by Shriver in margin of Evaluation Report on Afghanistan, by Thorburn Reid, 1963, PCL.

56. Evaluation Reports by Philip Cook, Guinea, 1964, p. 54; and Kenneth Love, Morocco, 1963, p. 95, PCL.

57. Dan Chamberlain, Evaluation Report on Colombia, 1962, p. 14, PCL.

58. William Haddad memorandum to Sargent Shriver, Jan. 16, 1963, attached to Evaluation Report on Ivory Coast, 1963, by L. Gray Cowan, PCL.

59. Evaluation Report by Herb Wegner, Peru, 1963, p. 67; Dee Jacobs, Guatemala, 1963; Richard Elwell, Ecuador, 1962, p. 24; Philip Cook and Thorburn Reid, Bolivia, 1963, p. 56, PCL.

60. Evaluation Report by David Hapgood, Senegal, 1964, p. 15, PCL.

61. Evaluation Reports by Kevin Delany and David Gelman, Liberia, 1963, p. 16; Thorburn Reid, El Salvador, 1962, p. 2, PCL.

62. Evaluation Reports by Wilson McCarthy, Cameroons, 1962, p. 8; David Gelman, Sierra Leone, 1962, p. 11, PCL.

63. Richard Elwell, Evaluation Report on Ecuador, 1963, p. 3, PCL.

64. NYT, November 19, 1963.

65. Jim Crandel letter to Peace Corps/Washington, June 24, 1963, Records of Government Agencies, The Peace Corps, Roll 5, JFKML.

66. Jerry Parsons quoted in Sullivan, The Story of the Peace Corps, p. 145.

67. Evaluation Report by Kevin Delany and David Gelman, Liberia, 1963, p. 63; and Peace Corps End-of-Term Conference on Nigeria, June 17–19, 1963, PCL.

68. Barman quoted by Richard Elwell, Evaluation Report on British Honduras, 1963, p. 36, PCL.

69. Chuck Guminer (Volunteer in Senegal) letter to Peace Corps/Washington, March 20, 1963, Records of Government Agencies, The Peace Corps, Roll 5, JFKML.

70. David Gelman, Evaluation Report on Sierra Leone, 1962, p. 4, PCL.

71. Sargent Shriver, handwritten comments in the margin of Evaluation Report on Colombia, by Dan Chamberlain, 1962, p. 1, PCL.

72. Paul Jacobs, Eugene Burdick, and William Lederer, Evaluation Report on the Philippines, 1963, pp. 51–52, PCL.

73. Philip Cook, Evaluation Report on Niger, 1963, p. 9, PCL.

74. Eugene Burdick and William Lederer, Evaluation Report on the Philippines, 1962, p. 5, PCL.

75. Peace Corps End-of-Term Conference on Colombia, June 14–18, 1963, PCL.

76. Volunteer quoted in David Gelman, Evaluation Report on Sierra Leone, 1962, p. 45, PCL.

77. Volunteers quoted by Timothy Adams, Evaluation Report on East Pakistan, 1963, p. 115; and by Kenneth Love, Evaluation Report on Morocco, 1963, PCL.

78. Volunteer quoted by Timothy Adams, Evaluation Report on East Pakistan, 1963, p. 54, PCL.

79. Herb Wegner and Paul Vanderwood, Evaluation Report, Brazil, 1963, p. 18, PCL.

80. Roderick E. Buller quoted by Kevin Delany and Dee Jacobs, Evaluation Report on Venezuela, 1963, p. 12, PCL.

81. Evaluation Reports by Herb Wegner, Peru, 1963, p. 28; Dee Jacobs, Costa Rica, 1963, p. 26, PCL.

82. Evaluation Reports by Thorburn Reid, Afghanistan, 1963, p. 5; Philip Cook, Togo, 1964, p. 6, PCL.

83. Sargent Shriver quoted in *Who's Who in the Peace Corps*, p. 4.

84. Evaluation Reports by David Gelman, Sierra Leone, 1962, pp. 3–5; Kenneth Love, Morocco, 1963, p. 119; L. Gray Cowan, Ivory Coast, 1963, p. 1; and Herb Wegner and Paul Vanderwood, Brazil, 1963, p. 11, PCL.

85. Kevin Delany and Dee Jacobs, Evaluation Report on Venezuela, 1963, p. 37, PCL.

86. Charles Peters, Evaluation Report on Afghanistan, 1964, p. 28, PCL.

87. Philip Cook and Thorburn Reid, Evaluation Report on Bolivia, 1963, p. 33, PCL.

88. Dee Jacobs and Philip Hardberger, Evaluation Report on the Dominican Republic, 1964, p. 47, PCL.

89. Kevin Delany and Dee Jacobs, Evaluation Report on Venezuela, 1963, p. 37, PCL.

90. Charles Peters memorandum to Sargent Shriver, Sept. 17, 1963, attached to Evaluation Report on Morocco by Kenneth Love, 1963, PCL.

91. This Volunteer is mentioned in Herb Wegner and Paul Vanderwood, Evaluation Report on Brazil, 1963, p. 82, PCL.

92. Kevin Delany and David Gelman, Evaluation Report on Liberia, 1963, p. 34, PCL.

93. Sargent Shriver, "Two Years of the Peace Corps," p. 274.

94. Evaluation Reports by Dee Jacobs, Panama, 1964, p. 58; Kevin Delany and David Gelman, Liberia, 1963, pp. 88–90; Timothy Adams, West Pakistan, 1963, p. 10; Herb Wegner, Peru, 1963, p. 61; and Richard Richter, Ethiopia, 1964, p. 44, PCL.

95. Evaluation Reports by Philip Cook, Niger, 1963, p. 11; Richard Elwell, Ethiopia, 1963, p. 49; John Griffin, Indonesia, 1963, p. 69; Kenneth Love, Morocco, 1963, p. 64, PCL.

96. Herb Wegner and Paul Vanderwood, Evaluation Report on Brazil, 1963, p. 75, PCL.

97. Timothy Adams, Evaluation Report on East Pakistan, 1963, p. 47, PCL.

98. Charles Peters memorandum to Sargent Shriver, July 3, 1963, attached to Evaluation Report on Togo by Philip Cook, 1963, p. 29, PCL.

99. Kevin Delany and Dee Jacobs, Evaluation Report on Venezuela, 1963, p. 41, PCL.

100. Timothy Adams, Evaluation Report on Pakistan, 1964, pp. 48–49, PCL. Shriver's handwritten comments are in the margin.

101. Evaluation Reports by Dee Jacobs, Guatemala, 1963; Kevin Delany and David Gelman, Liberia, 1963, p. 8, PCL.

102. The story of the young Volunteer being sent home "sick"after marrying a Colombian grandmother is from *Time* magazine, July 5, 1963.

103. John Griffin, Evaluation Report on Thailand, 1963, PCL.

104. John Griffin, Evaluation Report on Indonesia, 1963, p. 59, PCL.

105. Arthur Dudden, Evaluation Report on Ceylon, 1963, p. 12, PCL.

106. Evaluation Reports by Thomas Dugan, Turkey, 1963, p. 31; Richard Elwell, Ecuador, 1962, p. 12; and Peace Corps End-of-Term Conference on the Philippines, 1963, p. 12, PCL.

107. John Griffin, Evaluation Report on Thailand, 1963, p. 33, PCL.

108. Evaluation Reports by Philip Cook, Gabon, 1963, pp. 4–14; Richard Elwell, British Honduras, 1963, p. 12; and Herb Wegner, Peru, 1963, p. 14, PCL.

109. Dee Jacobs and Philip Hardberger, Evaluation Report on the Dominican Republic, 1964, p. 14, PCL.

110. Lowther and Lucas, *Keeping Kennedy's Promise*, pp. x, 99, and 139.

111. Charles Peters quoted in the *Volunteer* magazine, Dec. 1964.

112. Volunteers quoted in Luce, *Letters from the Peace Corps*, p. 129.

113. Volunteer Bertha Evosevich quoted by Sullivan, *The Story of the Peace Corps*, p. 292.

114. Timothy Adams, Evaluation Report on East Pakistan, 1963, p. 61, PCL.

115. Tom Carter letter to Peace Corps/Washington (from Peru), Dec. 6, 1963; Ross Burckhardt letter to Peace Corps/Washington (from Tunisia), 1963, Records of Government Agencies, The Peace Corps, Roll 5, JFKML

116. Volunteer Carol Fineran in Venezuela quoted in *The Peace Corps Reader*, p. 83; Volunteer in Sub-Saharan Africa quoted by Luce, *Letters from the Peace Corps*, p. 7; Volunteer in the Philippines quoted in the *Volunteer* magazine, tenth anniversary issue (1971); Volunteer in Sierra Leone quoted by Luce, *Letters from the Peace Corps*, p. 130.

117. Figures quoted by Ashabranner, *A Moment in History*, p. 208.

118. Rep in Chile quoted by Luce, *Letters from the Peace Corps*, p. 133.

119. Mike O'Donnell letter to Peace Corps/Washington, Jan. 10, 1962, Records of Government Agencies, The Peace Corps, Roll 5, JFKML

120. Quoted by Shriver, *The Point of the Lance*, p. 38.

11. THE IMAGE

1. Quoted by Sullivan, *The Story of the Peace Corps*, p. 54.

2. Sargent Shriver, "Two Years of the Peace Corps," p. 694.

3. *NYT*, Mar. 4, 1961.

4. *Nation*, "Peace Corps," Mar. 18, 1961.

5. See, *Time*, Mar. 10, April 7, Aug. 11 and Sept. 8, 1961; *Newsweek*, Mar. 13, April 17, 1961; *Journal of Home Economics*, April 1961.

6. Quoted by Hoopes, *The Complete Peace Corps Guide*, pp. 26–27.

7. See, *New Yorker*, "Letter from Washington," Mar. 16, 1961, and *New Republic*, Mar. 20, 1961, for a summary of Buchwald's satire.

8. *New Republic*, "The Peace Corps at Home," Mar. 20, 1961.

9. *Time*, "She Had No Idea," Oct. 27, 1961. Postcard reprinted.

10. Quoted by Wofford, *Of Kennedys and Kings*, p. 276.

11. Margery Michelmore letter to President Kennedy, Oct. 30, 1961, POF, box 85, JFKML.

12. *Time*, Oct. 27, 1961; *U.S. News and World Report*, Oct. 30, 1961.

13. *San Francisco Chronicle*, Oct. 26, 1961.

14. *Commonweal*, Nov. 3, 1961.

15. James Wechsler, *New York Post*, Oct. 18, 1961.

16. Ibid.

17. Charles Peters memorandum to Sargent Shriver, Sept. 17, 1963, attached to Evaluation Report on Morocco, 1963, by Kenneth Love, PCL.

18. President Kennedy letter to Margery Michelmore, Oct. 18, 1961, POF, box 85, JFKML. The President instructed that the letter should be handed to Miss Michelmore on arrival in London en route from Nigeria.

19. Quoted by Wofford, *Of Kennedys and Kings*, p. 284.

20. *Time*, July 5, 1963; *Vogue*, Feb. 1, 1963; *Parade*, Nov. 17, 1961; *U.S. News and World Report*, Dec. 4, 1961; ABC Telecast, Jan. 20, 1963 (Howard K. Smith); *Newsweek*, July 10, 1961.

21. *Time*, Nov. 17, 1961; *Good Housekeeping*, April 1963 (on "apple pie").

22. *Baltimore Sun*, May 18, 1962.

23. *Time*, Dec. 29, 1961 and July 13, 1963. See also *Washington Post*, Feb. 10, 1962.

24. Story told by Boyer, "Volunteers in the Field," pp. 61–62.

25. *Time*, July 5, 1963; *Newsweek*, Dec. 25, 1961; *U.S. News and World Report*, Mar. 25, 1963; *Washington Star*, Dec. 25, 1962.

26. *New York Herald Tribune*, July 8, 1963; *Los Angeles Times*, July 2, 1963; *Washington Post*, Feb. 28, 1962; *NYT*, Mar. 4, 1963. The *Guardian* quote is from "Press Reaction to the Peace Corps," April 1961, Research Note, 10/61, PCA.

27. *Manchester Guardian*, Jan. 29, 1962.

28. Sargent Shriver memorandum to President Kennedy, Dec. 18, 1961, POF, box 85, JFKML.

29. Sargent Shriver, "Weekly Report to the President," Aug. 14, 1962, Records of Government Agencies, The Peace Corps, JFKML.

30. Ed Bayley memorandum to Richard McGuire, Aug. 4, 1961, Personal Papers of Ed Bayley, box 1, JFKML.

31. Sargent Shriver, "Weekly Report to the President," Aug. 14, 1962, Records of Government Agencies, The Peace Corps, JFKML.

32. President Kennedy to Stephen C. Riddleberger, April 13, 1962, CSF, box 670, JFKML.

33. Ed Bayley memorandum to Richard McGuire, Aug. 4, 1961, Personal Papers of Ed Bayley, box 1, JFKML. See also *NYT*, May 3, 1961 and *NYT*, June 25, 1962.

34. Ed Bayley memorandum to Richard McGuire, Aug. 4, 1961, Personal Papers of Ed Bayley, box 1, JFKML.

35. William Josephson memorandum to William Haddad (undated),

1963, Josephson Papers, JFKML.

36. Doug Kiker memorandum to Public Information Staff, Feb. 8, 1963, Public Information, box 6, PCA.

37. *NYT*, Dec. 17, 1961; *Look*, Nov. 7, 1961.

38. Sargent Shriver memorandum to Ed Bayley, Mar. 23, 1961, Personal Papers of Ed Bayley, box 1, JFKML.

39. Ed Bayley, Oral History Interview, conducted by JFKML, p. 93.

40. Sargent Shriver memorandum to all Peace Corps Reps, Sept. 9, 1963, Publicity, box 3, PCA.

41. Sargent Shriver handwritten letter to President Kennedy (undated), 1961, POF, box 85, JFKML.

42. Sargent Shriver memorandum to President Kennedy, Oct. 26, 1962, POF, box 86, JFKML.

43. Bradley Patterson, Oral History Interview, conducted by JFKML, p. 44.

44. "Meet the Press," Dec. 15, 1963; *National Geographic*, Sept. 1964.

45. Volunteer quoted by Thorburn Reid, Evaluation Report on Chile, 1963, p. 17, PCL.

46. Roger Landrum quoted in minutes of large staff meeting, May 19, 1964, Bush Papers, box 1, JFKML.

47. Volunteer quoted by Herb Wegner and Paul Vanderwood, Evaluation Report on Brazil, 1963, p. 35, PCL.

48. Volunteer quoted by David Gelman, Evaluation Report on Tanganyika, 1963, p. 45, PCL.

49. Evaluation Reports on the Dominican Republic, 1962, by Charles Peters; and on East Pakistan, 1963, by Timothy Adams, PCL.

50. David Gelman, Evaluation Report on Tanganyika, 1963, pp. 48–59, PCL.

51. Harris poll published in the *Washington Post*, Aug. 19, 1963.

52. "JFK's Legacy: The Peace Corps," by Ira Mothner in *Look*, June 14, 1966.

53. Timothy Adams, Evaluation Report on East Pakistan, 1963, p. 102, PCL.

54. Personal interview, Sargent Shriver, Oct. 3, 1978, Washington, D.C.

55. Sargent Shriver, "Weekly Report to the President," Dec. 3, 1963, Records of Government Agencies, The Peace Corps, JFKML.

56. Personal interview, Sargent Shriver, Oct. 3, 1978, Washington, D.C.

57. Wofford, "The Future of the Peace Corps," p. 130.

12. POLITICS AND IDEALS

1. Kennedy and Khrushchev quoted in Bruce Miroff, *Pragmatic Illusions* (New York: David McKay Co., 1976), p. 47. In later years, David Halberstam argued that Kennedy's interpretation of Khruschchev's speech had been mistaken. Halberstam claimed that Khrushchev had been warning the Chinese against incursions into the Third World. It was some years before American strategists realized that the Sino-Soviet split had taken place around 1960.

2. John F. Kennedy, "Annual Message to the Congress on the State of the Union," Jan. 30, 1961, *Public Papers*, 1961, vol. I, pp. 19–27.

3. Lowther and Lucas, *Keeping Kennedy's Promise*, p. 23; and Wetzel, "The Peace Corps in our Past," p. 1.

4. *C.R.*, 86th Cong., 2d Sess., vol. 106, pts. 8 and 10, May 12, 1960, p. 10175 (Mutual Security Act); June 15, 1960, p. 12635 (Humphrey).

5. John F. Kennedy, "Staffing a Foreign Policy for Peace," Nov. 2, 1960, *Freedom of Communications*, part 1, pp. 1238–40.

6. *Newsweek*, July 10, 1961; *Reporter*, April 18, 1961; and Halberstam, *The Best and The Brightest*, p. 100.

7. Sargent Shriver, Commencement Address at University of Notre Dame, Indiana, June 4, 1961, in the "Speeches of Sargent Shriver," PCL.

8. Sargent Shriver memorandum to Peace Corps Senior Staff, "The Shape of the Peace Corps Program," Sept. 1961, in "Beginnings" folder, PCL.

9. Sargent Shriver, "Report to the President on the Peace Corps," Feb. 1961, POF, box 85, JFKML.

10. Sargent Shriver, Director's Staff Meeting, Dec. 6, 1961, Records of Government Agencies, Peace Corps, Roll 7, JFKML.

11. Sargent Shriver, "Meet the Press," Dec. 15, 1963.

12. "Record of conversation between Sargent Shriver and Sekou Touré," June 14, 1961, POF, box 85, JFKML.

13. Interim Policy Directive, 2.1, Subsec. 2, "Policies and Criteria for Selection of Peace Corps Projects," July 19, 1962, PCA.

14. Sargent Shriver memorandum to Peace Corps Senior Staff, "The Shape of the Peace Corps Program," Sept. 1961, "Beginnings" folder, PCL.

15. Warren Wiggins memorandum to Sargent Shriver, Sept. 15, 1961, "Beginnings" folder, PCL.

16. Ibid.

17. Arthur Dudden, Evaluation Report on Ceylon, 1962, p. 1, PCL.

18. John Griffin, Evaluation Report on Indonesia, 1963, p. 43, PCL.

19. Dee Jacobs, Evaluation Report on Uruguay, 1964, p. 2, PCL.

20. Philip Cook, Evaluation Report on Guinea, 1964, p. 4; and Evaluation Report on Ghana, 1964, p. 4, PCL.

21. Richard Richter, Evaluation Report on Ghana, 1964, p. 4, PCL.

22. Ibid., p. 35.

23. Ibid., pp. 32–37.

24. Sargent Shriver memorandum to John F. Kennedy, June 20, 1961, National Security Files, boxes 284–90, JFKML.

25. Ibid.

26. Sargent Shriver handwritten letter to John F. Kennedy (undated), POF, box 85, JFKML.

27. Sargent Shriver, "Weekly Report to the President," Mar. 19, 1963, Records of Government Agencies, Peace Corps, Roll 3, JFKML.

28. Sargent Shriver handwritten letter to Eunice Kennedy Shriver (undated), POF, box 85, JFKML.

29. Dee Jacobs, Evaluation Report on Uruguay, 1964, PCL.

30. Sargent Shriver memorandum to John F. Kennedy, Jan. 8, 1962, POF, box 85, JFKML.

31. *NYT*, Nov. 13, 1963, p. 15.

32. Shriver, *Point of the Lance*, p. 25.

33. Dean Rusk, airgram to all United States Overseas Missions, Mar. 25, 1963, National Security Files, boxes 284–90, JFKML.

34. Dean Rusk letter to author, Dec. 8, 1978.

35. Personal interviews with McGeorge Bundy, Dec. 5, 1978, New York; Harris Wofford, Mar. 31, 1979, Bryn Mawr, Pennsylvania.

36. Harold Saunders memorandum to McGeorge Bundy, Jan. 18, 1963, National Security Files, boxes 284–90, JFKML.

37. McGeorge Bundy memorandum to Sargent Shriver, Jan. 19, 1963, National Security Files, boxes 284–90, JFKML.

38. Sargent Shriver memorandum to G. Mennen Williams, April 13, 1963, Director's File, box 66A, PCA.

39. Personal interview, Sargent Shriver, Oct. 10, 1978, Washington, D.C.

40. John F. Kennedy, "Statement by the President on Foreign Aid," Sept. 19, 1962, *Public Papers*, vol. II, 1962.

41. John F. Kennedy, "Remarks in New Orleans at a Civic Reception," May 4, 1962, *Public Papers*, vol. II, 1962.

42. Personal interview, Sargent Shriver, Oct. 10, 1978, Washington, D.C.

43. Schlesinger, *Robert Kennedy and His Times*, p. 440.

44. John F. Kennedy, "Remarks to the National Advisory Council to the Peace Corps," May 22, 1961, *Public Papers*, vol. I, 1961, p. 392.

45. John F. Kennedy note to Sargent Shriver, Aug. 29, 1962, POF, box 86; and Sargent Shriver memorandum to John F. Kennedy, June 21, 1961, POF, box 85, JFKML.

46. John F. Kennedy, "Remarks to the Delegates to the Youth Fitness Conference," Feb. 21, 1961, *Public Papers*, vol. I, 1961, p. 113; and John F. Kennedy, "Remarks to Peace Corps Headquarters' Staff," June 14, 1962, *Public Papers*, vol. II, 1962, p. 482.

47. John F. Kennedy, "Remarks to Peace Corps Headquarters' Staff," June 14, 1962, *Public Papers*, vol. II, 1962, p. 482; Schlesinger, *A Thousand Days*, p. 558.

48. Marshall Windmiller, *The Peace Corps and Pax Americana* (Washington, D.C.: Public Affairs Press, 1970).

49. Personal interview, Sargent Shriver, Oct. 10, 1978, Washington, D.C.

50. Fairlie, *The Kennedy Promise*, pp. 229–30; and Windmiller, *The Peace Corps and Pax Americana*.

51. Fuchs, *Those Peculiar Americans*, pp. 40–41.

52. Sargent Shriver, "Report to the President on the Peace Corps," Feb. 1961, POF, box 85, JFKML; and Sargent Shriver, "Outlook For Corpsmen: Army Could Be Better," *Life*, Mar. 17, 1961.

53. Volunteer quoted in Evaluation Report on East Pakistan by Timothy Adams, 1963, p. 81, PCL.

54. Charles Peters, "The Relevance of the Peace Corps," *New York Daily Herald Tribune*, Oct. 27, 1965.

55. Windmiller, *The Peace Corps and Pax Americana*, p. vi; Soviet comment reported in the Director's Staff Meeting, Aug. 22, 1961, Records of Government Agencies, Peace Corps, Roll 3, JFKML.

56. Sargent Shriver memorandum to Walt Rostow, June 16, 1961, National Security Files, box 284–90, JFKML.

57. Ambassador Joseph Greene telegram to Dean Rusk, July 21, 1961, National Security Files, box 284–90, JFKML.

58. "Record of Conversation between Sargent Shriver and Sekou Touré," June 14, 1961, POF, box 85, JFKML.

59. Mankiewicz, "The Peace Corps: A Revolutionary Force."

60. Ibid.

61. Sargent Shriver, Commencement Address at The Agricultural and Technical College, North Carolina, June 1, 1963, "Speeches of Sargent Shriver," PCL. Also, Evaluation Report on Ethiopia, 1964, p. 20, and Evaluation Report on Ecuador, 1962, p. 25, PCL.

62. Arthur Dudden, Evaluation Report on Ceylon, 1962, p. 10, PCL.

63. Richard Elwell, Evaluation Report on Nyasaland, 1963, p. 2, PCL.

64. John Griffin, Evaluation Report on Indonesia, 1963, p. 10; Richard Richter, Evaluation Report on Tanganyika, 1964, p. 6, PCL.

65. Thorburn Reid, Evaluation Report on Afghanistan, 1963, PCL.

66. Timothy Adams, Evaluation Report on Pakistan, 1964, PCL.

67. Richard Richter, Evaluation Report on Ghana, 1964, PCL. Mahoney quoted by Richter.

68. David Scott Palmer, "Expulsion from a Peruvian University," in Textor, *Cultural Frontiers of the Peace Corps*, p. 251.

69. Volunteer quoted by Gelman in Evaluation Report on Tanganyika, 1963, p. 34, PCL.

70. Volunteer quoted in Charles Caldwell, Evaluation Report on Iran, 1964, p. 40, PCL.

71. William Friedland, "Nurses in Tanganyika," in Textor, *Cultural Frontiers of the Peace Corps*, p. 53.

72. Eugene Burdick and William Lederer, Evaluation Report on the Philippines, 1963, p. 8; Richard Elwell, Evaluation Report on Ethiopia, 1963, p. 80, PCL. For the "romantic involvement" incident, see "Peace Corps Exit Interviews" file, box 16, PCA.

73. Richard Richter, Evaluation Report on Ghana, 1964, p. 10; Philip Cook, Evaluation Report on Togo, p. 31; and Philip Cook, Evaluation Report on Guinea, 1964, p. 7, PCL.

74. Shriver, *The Point of the Lance*, p. 7.

75. John F. Kennedy, "Presidential News Conference," Dec. 12, 1962, *Public Papers*, vol. II, 1962, p. 872.

76. Harris Wofford memorandum to John F. Kennedy, Jan. 20, 1962, Staff Files of Theodore Sorensen, box 68, JFKML.

77. Harris Wofford memorandum to John F. Kennedy, May 25, 1961, POF, box 85; and Harris Wofford memorandum to John F. Kennedy, July 17, 1961, Staff Files of Chester Bowles, box 28, JFKML.

78. Remark reported during the Director's Staff Meeting, Nov. 20, 1961, Records of Government Agencies, Peace Corps, Roll 3, JFKML.

79. Dee Jacobs and Philip Hardberger, Evaluation Report on the Dominican Republic, 1964, p. 41; Philip Cook, Evaluation Report on Gabon, 1963, pp. 28–29, PCL.

80. Dee Jacobs, Evaluation Report on Panama, 1964, p. 5, PCL.

81. Thanat Khoman quoted in Schlesinger, *A Thousand Days*, p. 560

82. John Kenneth Galbraith letter to Sargent Shriver, reprinted in *C.R.*, Aug. 23, 1961, 87th Cong., 1st Sess., vol. 107, pt. 12, p. 1680.

83. Anonymous Volunteer letter to Peace Corps/Washington, Dec. 1962, Records of Government Agencies, Peace Corps, Roll 4, JFKML.

84. *NYT*, editorial, "Idealism at Work," Nov. 21, 1963. Sargent Shriver asked his question in an address before the American Foreign Policy Association, Dec. 11, 1963.

13. THE THREE GOALS

1. Shriver, "Two Years of the Peace Corps," p. 707.
2. Humphrey, *The Education of a Public Man*, p. 250.
3. Eric Sevareid quoted by Sargent Shriver, "Two Years of the Peace Corps."
4. Lowther and Lucas, *Keeping Kennedy's Promise*, p. 54.
5. Sargent Shriver, "I Have the Best Job in Washington," *New York Times* magazine, June 9, 1963.
6. Warren Wiggins quoted in Kopkind, "The Peace Corps' Daring New Look."
7. Frank Lynch, Thomas Maretzki, Alfred B. Bennett, Jr., Susan M. Bennett, Linda D. Nelson, *The Philippines Peace Corps Survey: Final Report* (Hawaii: Social Research Institute, University of Hawaii, 1966), p. 258.
8. Henry F. Dobyns, Paul L. Doughty, and Alan R. Holmberg, *Peace Corps Program Impact in the Peruvian Andes*, (Ithaca, N.Y.: Department of Anthropology, Cornell University, 1964).
9. Volunteer quoted by David Hapgood, Evaluation Report on Senegal, 1964, p. 34, PCL.
10. Shriver, "Two Years of the Peace Corps," p. 704.
11. Shriver quoted these statistics in Hearings before the House Subcommittee on Appropriations, May 26, 1964.
12. The World Bank, *World Development Report*, 1980 (Washington, D.C.: The World Bank, 1980), p. 1.
13. Shriver, "Two Years of the Peace Corps"; and Robert McGuire, Evaluation Report on Sierra Leone, 1964, p. 48, PCL.
14. Herb Wegner, Evaluation Report on Peru, 1963, PCL.
15. Dobyns, Doughty, and Holmberg, *Peace Corps Program Impact in the Peruvian Andes*.
16. Jack Vaughn quoted in *Saturday Review*, Jan. 6, 1968, p. 21.
17. Volunteers quoted in Evaluation Reports by Kevin Delany and David Gelman, Liberia, 1963, p. 30; Dan Chamberlain, Sierra Leone, 1962, p. 52; Timothy Adams, East Pakistan, 1964, p. 66; and Herb Wegner, Evaluation Report on Peru, 1963, p. 7, PCL.
18. Kevin Delany and David Gelman, Evaluation Report on Liberia, 1963, p. 30, PCL.
19. Statement of Carolyn R. Payton, Director of the Peace Corps, before the Committee on International Relations Subcommittee on International Development, Feb. 14, 1978.
20. Jack Vaughn quoted during testimony before the House Subcommitte on International Development, Sept. 8, 20, and 29, 1977, *Peace Corps: Purpose and Perspective*, House Hearings, p. 33.
21. Thanat Khoman, Oral History Interview, conducted by JFKML, p. 5.
22. Robert F. Kennedy quoted in *Volunteer* magazine, Nov. 1966.
23. Evaluation Reports by Richard Richter, Ethiopia, 1964, p. 5; David Gelman, Tanganyika, 1963, p. 83; Kevin Delany, India, 1963. Tribal chief quoted in Shriver, "I Have the Best Job in Washington."
24. John F. Kennedy, "Letter to the Congress on a Bill to Strengthen the Peace Corps," July 4, 1963, *Public Papers*, vol. 111, p. 555.
25. Wofford, *Of Kennedys and Kings*, p. 277.
26. Diori Hamani quoted in *Volunteer* magazine, tenth anniversary issue

(1971), p. 14.

27. Shriver, *The Point of the Lance*, p. 38.

28. Nehru quoted in Wofford, *Of Kennedys and Kings*, p. 272.

29. The Shriver-Nkrumah meeting is described in Wofford, *Of Kennedys and Kings*, p. 270; Julius Nyerere quoted in *ACTION Update*, (Washington, D.C.: U.S. ACTION, February 14, 1979).

30. Sargent Shriver, "Report to the President on the Peace Corps," POF, box 85, JFKML.

31. Louis Harris and Associates, *A Survey of Returned Peace Corps Volunteers*, (New York, 1969).

32. The figures on the number of former Volunteers working with government organizations is from the Peace Corps' own *Survey of Former Peace Corps Volunteers and VISTA Volunteers*, 1979; the number of former Volunteers in the State Department is from *INTERACTION* magazine (Washington, D.C.: U.S. ACTION), Sept. 1976; the AID figures are from *Front Lines* magazine (Washington, D.C.: U.S. AID), May 22, 1980.

33. "Peace Corps in Malaysia Works Its Way Out of a Job," *Chicago Tribune*, April 24, 1984.

34. Statistics from the Peace Corps' *Survey of Former Peace Corps Volunteers and VISTA Volunteers*, 1979.

35. Harris and Associates, *A Survey of Returned Peace Corps Volunteers*.

36. John Monro quoted in *Volunteer* magazine, Feb. 1963.

37. *Survey of Former Peace Corps Volunteers and VISTA Volunteers*, 1979.

38. Harlan Cleveland, *The Future of the Peace Corps* (Aspen Institute for Humanistic Studies, 1977), p. 3.

39. For a brief account of the establishment of VISTA, see Wofford, *Of Kennedys and Kings*, p. 289.

40. Boyer, "Volunteers in the Field."

41. Thorburn Reid, Evaluation Report on El Salvador, 1963, p. 24, PCL.

42. Personal interview, Newell Flather, May 8, 1979, Boston.

43. David S. Broder, *The Changing of the Guard* (New York: Simon and Schuster, 1980), pp. 60–61.

44. *Survey of Former Peace Corps Volunteers and VISTA Volunteers*, 1979.

45. Personal interview, Joe Walsh, May 1, 1979, Boston.

46. For Roger Landrum's views and the views of other returned Volunteers in the 1960s, see *Citizen in a Time of Change: The Peace Corps Volunteer* (Report of The First National Returned Volunteer Conference, March 5–7, 1965), edited by Ernest Fox, George Nicolau, and Harris Wofford.

47. Bill Moyers memorandum to Warren Wiggins, Aug. 17, 1963, Bush Papers, JFKML.

48. John F. Kennedy, "Remarks in Bonn at the Signing of a Charter Establishing the German Peace Corps," June 24, 1963, *Public Papers*, vol. 111, p. 503.

49. The World Bank, *World Development Report, 1980* (Washington, D.C.: The World Bank) p. 98.

50. Emanuel Palaez quoted in *Volunteer* magazine, Oct. 1962.

51. Peace Corps Rep quoted in Luce, *Letters from the Peace Corps*.

52. Sargent Shriver memorandum to McGeorge Bundy, Feb. 12, 1963, National Security Files, boxes 284–90, JFKML.

53. Sargent Shriver, "Two Years of the Peace Corps," p. 707.

54. Turkish peasant quoted in a letter from anonymous Volunteer to Peace Corps/Washington (undated), Records of Government Agencies, The Peace Corps, Roll 5, JFKML. Tai Solarin quoted by Ashabranner, *A Moment in History*, p. 112.

EPILOGUE: KENNEDY'S CHILDREN

1. John F. Kennedy, "Special Message to the Congress on Foreign Aid," Mar. 22, 1961.
2. Juan Bosch, Oral History Interview, conducted by JFKML, p. 21.
3. John English letter to Peace Corps/Washington, Jan. 13, 1964, Records of Government Agencies, The Peace Corps, Roll 5, JFKML.
4. Michael Woldenberg and Maureen Carroll quoted in *Volunteer* magazine, Dec. 1963.
5. Paul E. Tsongas, Commencement Address to Bradford College, May 19, 1979.
6. Jack Newfield, *A Prophetic Minority* (New York, 1967), p. 27–28.
7. Halberstam, *The Best and the Brightest*, p. 38.
8. *NYT*, Mar. 6, 1963.
9. Henry Steele Commager spoke before the House Subcommittee on International Development, Sept. 8, 20, and 29, 1977. Reprinted in *Peace Corps: Purpose and Perspective* (U.S. Government Printing Office, 1977).
10. John F. Kennedy, "Remarks to the First Group of Volunteers before their Departure for Ghana and Tanganyika," Aug. 28, 1961.

Index

DATE DUE